Cybersecurity Culture

The culture of cybersecurity is a complex subject. We can look at cybersecurity culture from different perspectives. We can look at it from the organizational point of view or from within the culture. Each organization has a culture. Attitudes toward security have different manifestations in each organizational culture. We also see how the cybersecurity phenomenon unfolds in other cultures is complicated. Each culture reacts differently to this phenomenon. This book will emphasize both aspects of cybersecurity. From the organizational point of view, this book will emphasize the importance of the culture of cybersecurity in organizations, what it is, and how it can be achieved. This includes the human aspects of security, approach and awareness, and how we can design systems that promote the culture of security. It is also important to emphasize the psychological aspects briefly because it is a big part of the human approach.

From a cultural point of view, this book will emphasize how different cultures approach the culture of cybersecurity. The cultural complexity of cybersecurity will be noted by giving examples from different cultures. How leadership in different cultures approach security and how different cultures approach change. Case studies from each culture will be presented to demonstrate different approaches to implementing security and training practices. Overall, the textbook will be a good resource for cybersecurity students who want to understand how cultures and organizations within those cultures approach security. It will also provide a good resource for instructors who would like to develop courses on cybersecurity culture.

Finally, this book will be an introductory resource for anyone interested in cybersecurity's organizational or cultural aspects.

Cybersecurity Culture

Gulsebnem Bishop

CRC Press
Taylor & Francis Group
Boca Raton London New York

CRC Press is an imprint of the
Taylor & Francis Group, an **informa** business

Designed cover image: The Golden Gate of Kyiv. 11th Century Fortification, Main Gate. Photo by Dr. Yucel Tanyeri.

First edition published 2025
by CRC Press
2385 NW Executive Center Drive, Suite 320, Boca Raton FL 33431

and by CRC Press
4 Park Square, Milton Park, Abingdon, Oxon, OX14 4RN

CRC Press is an imprint of Taylor & Francis Group, LLC

ISBN: 9781032437019 (hbk)
ISBN: 9781032437026 (pbk)
ISBN: 9781003368496 (ebk)

DOI: 10.1201/9781003368496

Typeset in Sabon
by KnowledgeWorks Global Ltd.

To my parents

Companies spend millions of dollars on firewalls and secure access devices, and it's money wasted because none of these measures address the weakest link in the security chain: the people who use, administer and operate computer systems

Kevin Mitnick

Contents

List of figures

List of tables

Preface

This book came out of necessity while I was teaching cybersecurity culture classes without a comprehensive textbook. As instructors, when assigned a class, the first task is often to find a textbook that covers the fundamental areas of the course. It's even better when the selected book comes with supplementary materials such as PowerPoints, test banks, and case studies. However, I found that no such book existed for a course on cybersecurity culture.

Cybersecurity culture is a multifaceted subject that presents unique challenges when taught without a structured resource. While there are many publications that cover aspects of cybersecurity, very few books focus specifically on the culture that shapes and influences cybersecurity practices in organizations. I wrote this book to fill that gap—not only to provide comprehensive material for teaching this course but also to offer students and professionals a foundational reference that they can use as a guide.

This book is designed to support instructors by offering chapter-by-chapter resources, making the complex subject of cybersecurity culture easier to teach and understand. Students can rely on this single text throughout the course to gain a thorough understanding of the topic without having to sift through multiple sources. It can also serve as a training guide for organizations looking to develop or strengthen their internal cybersecurity culture. Written in a straightforward style, this book ensures that even readers new to cybersecurity will come away with a solid grasp of the key principles.

The book is divided into 14 chapters, each covering various dimensions of cybersecurity culture, from leadership to emerging threats, to keep the content digestible and well organized.

Chapter 1 introduces the core concepts of cybersecurity and cybersecurity culture, explaining the critical difference between them. It highlights the importance of a strong cybersecurity culture in preventing cyber threats, noting that leadership, communication, and awareness are key to fostering such a culture. The chapter also emphasizes the global nature of cybersecurity, in which collaboration, shared standards, and public-private partnerships play vital roles. Understanding these elements sets the stage for the rest of the book, which explores how organizations can build resilient cybersecurity cultures to protect against evolving threats.

Chapter 2 provides an understanding of the key components that shape and influence an organization's cybersecurity culture. It emphasizes the significant role that leadership plays in setting the tone for security practices, highlights the importance of strong policies, procedures, and communication, and discusses how an organization's size, industry, location, and technological adaptability contribute to its unique security needs. Furthermore, it examines the critical role of education, training, and awareness in developing a security-conscious workforce. The chapter concludes by stressing the importance of continuous improvement and recognition systems in sustaining and strengthening an organization's cybersecurity culture, ensuring that everyone remains engaged, accountable, and motivated to protect against evolving threats.

Chapter 3 explores the evolving cybersecurity threat landscape and the different types of threats, risks, and vulnerabilities that organizations face daily. It introduces various attack vectors, such as social engineering, malware, ransomware, insider threats, zero-day exploits, and supply chain attacks, explaining how they work and how they can compromise organizational security. One of the core concepts discussed is the significance of cultural responses to these threats, which involve regular training, open communication, and a proactive mindset in dealing with potential security risks. The chapter also highlights the need for continuous adaptation as cyber threats evolve.

Chapter 4 explores the concept of attack surfaces and vulnerabilities in cybersecurity, highlighting the critical role they play in an organization's overall security posture, breaking down attack surfaces into three primary categories—network, software, and human—and emphasizing the importance of understanding and addressing these vulnerabilities to protect sensitive data and maintain system integrity. By presenting real-world examples, the chapter illustrates how unpatched software, weak passwords, outdated systems, and poor security practices can lead to significant security breaches. It also underscores the importance of a strong cybersecurity culture, where continuous education, proactive behavior, and leadership support are essential for mitigating risks.

Chapter 5 explores the diverse landscape of cyber threat actors, categorized into 12 distinct groups, including cybercriminals, nation-states, hacktivists, and more. These actors vary widely in their intentions, from financial gain to political or ideological agendas, and target a range of entities, from individuals and small businesses to governments and critical infrastructure. Understanding who these actors are and how they operate is essential for organizations to develop effective defense strategies. By analyzing case studies and real-world examples, the chapter illustrates how these actors exploit vulnerabilities and emphasize the importance of building a resilient cybersecurity culture. It also examines the roles of ethical hackers (white hats), unethical hackers (black hats), and those who operate in the gray area (gray hats), highlighting the complexities of the cybersecurity landscape. The chapter concludes by stressing the importance of continuous learning, vigilance, and proactive security measures to stay ahead of evolving threats and safeguard organizational assets effectively.

Chapter 6 focuses on the essential role of education, training, and awareness (ETA) in fostering a strong cybersecurity culture. It begins by explaining the role of formal education, certifications, and continuous learning in developing skilled cybersecurity professionals before highlighting the importance of various types of training programs, including hands-on training and simulations, to equip employees with practical skills for responding to real-world cybersecurity incidents. The chapter also addresses common challenges in implementing ETA initiatives and offers case studies and best practices to overcome these obstacles. Finally, it explores future trends in ETA, such as the impact of emerging technologies like AI, the evolution of cyber threats, and the importance of global perspectives, all of which are critical for staying ahead in the dynamic field of cybersecurity.

Chapter 7 examines the psychological aspects of cybersecurity culture, focusing on how human behavior and psychology significantly influence an organization's security and emphasizing the importance of understanding human motivations, cognitive biases, and the impact of stress on cybersecurity practices. The chapter begins by exploring the basics of human behavior and how it shapes cybersecurity practices. It covers key areas such as cyberpsychology, which looks at the cognitive, emotional, and social dynamics that influence cyber behavior. Additionally, the chapter examines common human factors such as fear of authority, boredom, and gullibility, offering strategies to mitigate these risks. It also explores how cognitive biases, such as overconfidence or confirmation bias, can impact decision-making and lead to security vulnerabilities, offering ways to mitigate these biases.

Finally, the chapter underscores the importance of understanding the human element in cybersecurity.

Chapter 8 looks at the pivotal role of leadership in establishing and maintaining a strong cybersecurity culture within organizations. It emphasizes that leadership is essential for setting strategic direction, fostering accountability, and creating an environment where cybersecurity practices are fully integrated into daily operations. The chapter highlights the roles and responsibilities of leaders at different levels—executive, IT, and middle management—and how their actions collectively contribute to a strong cybersecurity culture. Critical leadership traits, including vision, strategic thinking, communication skills, and much more, are explored in detail. The chapter also discusses common challenges faced by cybersecurity leaders, such as balancing security with business objectives and building trust within the organization, and offers practical solutions, including risk-based approaches, continuous learning, collaboration, and the use of advanced technologies.

Chapter 9 emphasizes the critical role of policies, procedures, and compliance in establishing a resilient cybersecurity culture within organizations. It outlines the essential components of developing effective policies and procedures, ensuring compliance with various cybersecurity regulations, and maintaining a secure organizational environment. By examining real-world frameworks and compliance requirements such as PCI DSS and HIPAA, the chapter provides an in-depth look into the regulations that help organizations manage and protect sensitive information. The chapter also highlights the benefits of compliance, including enhanced security, operational efficiency, risk management, and improved relationships with stakeholders. Finally, it identifies common challenges in achieving compliance, such as keeping up with evolving regulations, managing resource constraints, and balancing security with usability, and provides practical solutions to address these issues, ensuring that organizations can effectively meet compliance requirements and maintain a strong cybersecurity culture.

Chapter 10 focuses on measuring the success of a cybersecurity culture within an organization. It emphasizes the importance of using various metrics to assess the effectiveness of cybersecurity initiatives, such as incident response times, employee engagement, policy compliance, and the financial impact of security measures, and explores how these metrics help identify areas for improvement, guide resource allocation, and support continuous adaptation to evolving threats. The chapter also discusses tools and techniques for gathering and analyzing data, such as audits, surveys, and incident analysis, as well as best practices for setting clear objectives, regularly reviewing strategies, and involving employees in the measurement process. Ultimately, it demonstrates how continuous measurement fosters a resilient, adaptive cybersecurity culture that aligns with broader organizational goals.

Chapter 11 explores the role of national cybersecurity initiatives in protecting the digital infrastructure of the United States, highlighting key government agencies, such as NIST, CISA, DHS, and the FBI, and their efforts to develop policies, frameworks, and programs that strengthen cybersecurity across public and private sectors. It also examines collaborative efforts between government and private organizations to promote resilience against cyber threats and discusses the role of cybersecurity education and workforce development initiatives in building a skilled workforce to meet the growing challenges they present. The chapter concludes by stressing the importance of a coordinated national cybersecurity strategy and underscoring that, as cyber threats evolve, collaboration and adherence to established standards are critical for maintaining a resilient and secure digital environment.

Chapter 12 examines the global landscape of cybersecurity, emphasizing the need for international collaboration to address the borderless nature of cyber threats. It highlights the roles of key international organizations and initiatives such as the European Union Agency for Cybersecurity and discusses important international treaties such as the

Budapest Convention on Cybercrime that help establish legal frameworks and standards for cybersecurity across nations. Additionally, it explores the challenges of aligning cybersecurity efforts due to differences in legal systems, priorities, and technological capabilities among countries. The chapter concludes by stressing the importance of continued global cooperation in building a secure digital environment, setting the stage for the next chapter's exploration of diverse cybersecurity cultures around the world.

Chapter 13 covers diverse cybersecurity cultures and initiatives worldwide. It examines how different countries approach the challenge of securing their digital environments, highlighting key nations such as Canada, the United Kingdom, Germany, and Japan, each with its unique blend of government initiatives, policies, and organizational practices. The chapter also underscores the importance of tailoring cybersecurity measures to specific regional needs and promotes the idea of fostering a global cybersecurity culture built on cooperation and shared learning.

Chapter 14 gives us a glimpse into the future of cybersecurity culture by analyzing emerging trends, ethical challenges, and new threats. It highlights how technological advancements, such as AI, IoT, and quantum computing, present new challenges and emphasize the need for organizations to adopt innovative defense strategies to stay ahead of cyber threats. The chapter also explores the shifting dynamics of the cybersecurity workforce, emphasizing continuous education and evolving leadership roles, such as the CISO, which now require a balance between technical knowledge and strategic business alignment. The ethical implications of cybersecurity, such as the balance between privacy and security, data use, and human rights in the digital age, are increasingly critical, while emerging threats, including AI-driven attacks, deepfakes, and IoT vulnerabilities, underline the need for proactive measures. Finally, the chapter discusses the role of cybersecurity in sustainable development and how regulations, policies, and global cooperation will drive future strategies.

In writing this book, my intention was not to cover every topic in cybersecurity culture in exhaustive detail—such a task would be impossible given the breadth and complexity of the field. Instead, my goal is to provide a comprehensive yet concise guide that will serve as a foundational resource for instructors, students, and professionals alike.

I hope this book offers valuable insights, whether you're using it as a course textbook, as a reference for training, or simply to deepen your understanding of cybersecurity culture. If you have any feedback or suggestions, I encourage you to reach out. I look forward to hearing from you.

Wishing all instructors, students, cybersecurity enthusiasts, and professionals the best as you embark on this rewarding and dynamic journey. I hope you find this book as enriching to read as it was to write.

Sincerely,
Dr. Gulsebnem Bishop

Acknowledgments

This journey has been one of the most rewarding experiences of my life. While it came with its challenges, the encouragement and support I received along the way made it truly fulfilling. I am deeply grateful to the many family members, friends, and colleagues who made this book possible. It represents not only my efforts but also the collective support, guidance, and encouragement of everyone mentioned here. Thank you all for being part of this journey.

First and foremost, I would like to thank my dear friend and colleague, Dr. Miriam O'Callaghan, for encouraging me to embark on this journey of writing and publishing. Without your encouragement, this book would not have been written.

A special thank you to Dr. Amir Afzal for his invaluable feedback and suggestions. Your insights greatly enhanced the quality of this work.

I owe immense thanks to the many who supported me throughout this process. To my Cape Vincent family, thank you for your unwavering support and sense of humor—now you all know what passwords not to use!

My deepest gratitude goes to my uncle, Dr. Yucel Tanyeri, for providing the beautiful cover photo from his incredible collection. Your talent as a photographer is truly inspiring, and your constant support means the world to me.

To my mother, Dr. Esra Findik, who has always been my greatest inspiration and role model, thank you for your unwavering belief in me. Your guidance and support have shaped not only this book but also so much of who I am today.

Lastly, to my husband, John E. Rae—your patience, feedback, and sense of humor helped carry me through this journey. From edits to encouragement, you were always there to help, and for that, I am endlessly grateful.

About the author

Dr. Gulsebnem Bishop is an accomplished academic and professional with a strong foundation in computer science, information systems, and cybersecurity. Holding multiple advanced degrees, including a doctorate in Computer Science and Information Systems from Pace University and several master's degrees including Cybersecurity and Business Administration, Dr. Bishop has a unique blend of expertise spanning both technical and academic disciplines. In addition to these credentials, Dr. Bishop is a certified PMP and has specialized certifications in Big Data Analytics and Database Administration, reinforcing her ability to contribute effectively to academic and industry settings alike.

As an Assistant Professor of Computer Information Systems and Computer Science at Campbellsville University since 2018, Dr. Bishop has demonstrated a strong commitment to education and curriculum development. She has designed and taught graduate-level courses in Advanced Database Systems, Disaster Recovery, and Current and Emerging Technologies, among other subjects. She also held faculty and leadership roles at multiple institutions, such as the University of Maryland, Washington State University, Stratford University, and South University where she taught various courses including emerging technologies, database systems, and cybersecurity.

Dr. Bishop has been a prolific speaker and contributor at international conferences on technology in education, particularly in Virtual Reality (VR) applications in classroom settings. Her research has been published in prestigious journals, and she has presented at numerous conferences, focusing on VR's role in transforming online learning.

Dr. Bishop's extensive professional experience also spans senior roles in database systems and IT leadership across several prestigious organizations, including The American Museum of National History, the NAACP Legal Defense Fund, the United Nations Foundation, and the Human Rights Campaign. In these roles, she led initiatives to streamline data systems, and enhance IT infrastructure, consistently ensuring data security and compliance with best practices.

Chapter 1

Cybersecurity and cybersecurity culture

An overview

This chapter delves into the global understanding of cybersecurity culture, placing a strong emphasis on shared responsibilities, the importance of consistent standards and regulations, cultural differences, education and awareness, public-private partnerships, cross-cultural collaboration, and global research and development. The goal is to lay the groundwork for comprehending the significance and distinctiveness of cybersecurity culture on a global scale.

Security is a vital component of today's technology and online communication. The widespread use of digital devices and the internet significantly heightens the risk of cyberattacks and data breaches; therefore, it's imperative to have a comprehensive understanding of cybersecurity and how it safeguards systems, networks, devices, and sensitive information from unauthorized access. Various sources have provided descriptions of cybersecurity, highlighted its significance, and underscored the urgent need for robust security practices that protect against cyber threats. This amplifies the importance of your role in implementing effective cybersecurity measures.

Cybersecurity culture is also a crucial element in today's organizations. It encompasses an organization's collective attitudes, beliefs, values, and behaviors toward safeguarding its digital assets and data from cyber threats; moreover, it includes practices, policies, and procedures that are specifically designed to cultivate a robust security culture within an organization, hence building customer trust and confidence.

Cybersecurity and cybersecurity culture are two different terms that are sometimes used interchangeably. It is important to realize that cybersecurity covers a vast area that includes all aspects of the security world. It protects computer systems, networks, and sensitive data from unauthorized access, theft, or damage. Cybersecurity culture, on the other hand, refers to the shared values, attitudes, and behaviors within an organization that influence the approach to cybersecurity. As shown in Figure 1.1, the former is the overarching term, and the latter is an important aspect within the larger concept and related to a specific organization (Figure 1.1).

This chapter will be dedicated to examine various descriptions of cybersecurity and then describe cybersecurity culture. It will concentrate on cybersecurity culture's importance and global understanding of beliefs, assumptions, and values. Finally, the chapter will close by discussing how these concepts impact an organization's cybersecurity culture.

1.1 WHAT IS CYBERSECURITY?

Since cybersecurity has been a widely discussed topic, numerous descriptions exist. Although only a few descriptions are presented in this chapter, they provide a comprehensive

DOI: 10.1201/9781003368496-1

Figure 1.1 Cybersecurity vs. cybersecurity culture.

understanding of cybersecurity. It is essential to define cybersecurity before entering the subject of cybersecurity culture, a subcategory of cybersecurity.

One of the best descriptions of cybersecurity comes from Zhang, who emphasizes cybersecurity as "Cyber Security is the practice of securing networks, devices, and data against unauthorized access or illegal usage, as well as the art of maintaining information confidentiality, integrity, and availability"[1] Lindemulder and Kosinski similarly describes cybersecurity as "Cybersecurity refers to any technologies, practices and policies for preventing cyberattacks or mitigating their impact. Cybersecurity aims to protect computer systems, applications, devices, data, financial assets and people against ransomware and other malware, phishing scams, data theft and other cyberthreats.. "[2] The National Institute of Standards and Technology (NIST) glossary adds the specific cyber threats into the mix and describe cybersecurity as "the practices, technologies, and policies used to protect computer systems, networks, and sensitive information from cyber threats such as malware, phishing, and other forms of cyberattacks."[3] Finally, the US Department of Homeland Security describes cybersecurity as "Cybersecurity is the art of protecting networks, devices, and data from unauthorized access or criminal use and the practice of ensuring confidentiality, integrity, and availability of information."[4]

When searched, you will find many worthy descriptions of cybersecurity similar to the ones above. In almost all cases, the sources describe cybersecurity as protecting devices, networks, and data from unauthorized access, modification, and theft by using technologies, processes, and policies. It involves protecting data by preventing and responding to cyber threats and attacks. All cybersecurity practices focus on the same goals: securing networks, systems, and applications from unauthorized access, cyberattacks, and data breaches. Cyber threats that cybersecurity protects against are many. The vast list includes malware, phishing, and other forms of cyberattacks, all of which will be covered in Chapter 3.

1.2 WHAT IS CYBERSECURITY CULTURE?

Cybersecurity culture refers to the shared values, attitudes, and behaviors within an organization that influence its approach to cybersecurity. A strong cybersecurity culture can have a significant impact on an organization's overall performance, as it can reduce the risk of security incidents and improve the organization's resilience to cyber threats. It develops within the organization, just like the other elements of organizational culture, such as communication, teamwork, or leadership. It highlights the importance of developing a strong partnership within the organization. These partnerships can involve educating employees, creating awareness, promoting good security practices, or aligning cybersecurity culture with an organization's overall goals and values.

Cybersecurity culture is defined in many resources. This section will examine different descriptions and understand cybersecurity culture and its role in preventing security incidents.

One of the best descriptions of cybersecurity culture comes from Roer, describing it as follows, "Security culture is a part of your organization's culture that focuses on security, to help people into the state of being free from threat or danger."[5] Everard, a cyberculture expert, describes cybersecurity culture as follows, "The concept of cyber security culture refers to the attitudes, knowledge, assumptions, norms and values of the workforce of an organisation with respect to cyber security. These are shaped by the goals, structure, policies, processes, and leadership of the organisation."[6] Spitzner describes cybersecurity culture as such and compares it to an iceberg: "Culture is defined as people's shared attitudes, perceptions and beliefs. A common metaphor is comparing culture to an iceberg. Like an iceberg, culture is hard to see as most of it is hidden. Like an iceberg, culture is also hard to move"[7] (Figure 1.2). In general, like the other descriptions, he refers to cybersecurity culture as the "workforce's

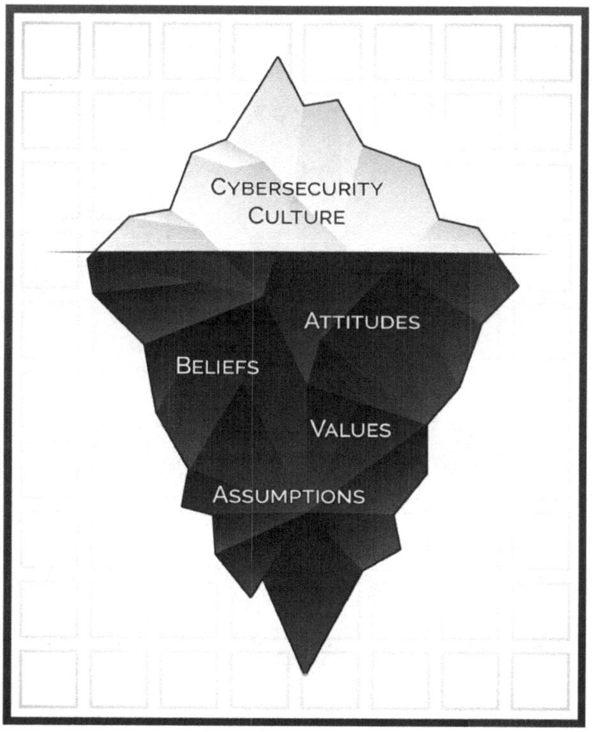

Figure 1.2 Cybersecurity culture iceberg metaphor.

shared attitudes, perceptions and beliefs towards cybersecurity."[8] One last description is from Perry Carpenter, chief evangelist and strategy officer for KnowBe4 Inc. and a Forbes council member, "It is the ideas, customs and social behaviors of an organization that influences its security. It is the most important element in an organization's security strategy."[9]

As we can see, the common elements among these definitions are the organizational values, norms, assumptions, attitudes, and knowledge that shape the organizational goals, policies, and procedures. An organization's culture dictates everything. To understand cybersecurity culture better, it is imperative to understand organizational culture. Since they are closely related, it will be helpful to briefly introduce organizational culture before delving into cybersecurity culture; hence, the comparison between the two will be clearer.

1.3 ORGANIZATIONAL CULTURE VS. CYBERSECURITY CULTURE

Organizational culture is a more holistic approach to an organization's values and attitudes. Cote refers to it as "the collection of values, beliefs, assumptions, and norms that guide activity and mindset in an organization."[10] According to her, culture influences every aspect of an organization. This can range from how employees talk to each other or their understanding of work-life balance to how employees feel about their work and how the teams collaborate. The organizational culture affects everything from achieving organizational goals to the retention of employees. It can determine whether an organization succeeds or fails.

The organizational culture is under the influence of the leaders; only they can change an organization's culture from the top. It is not an option to eliminate organizational culture, but it is an option to shape it. According to Cote, there are many ways to shape organizational culture, as shown in Figure 1.3.

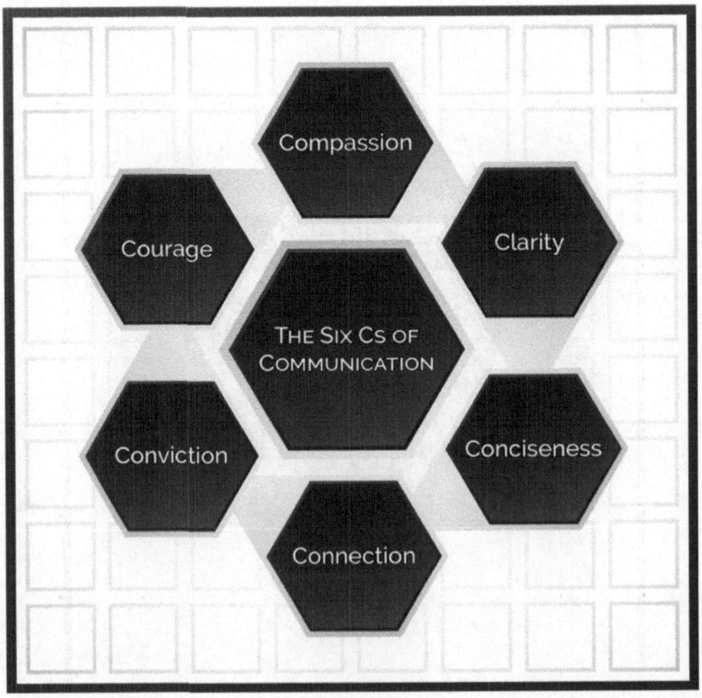

Figure 1.3 Six Cs of communication.

First, we must ensure everyone is aligned with the organization's values, mission, and purpose. Purpose is a great motivator for employees to do their work. According to a Salesforce report, free snacks or game rooms do not motivate employees but a sense of purpose and teamwork does.[11]

Second, inspiring confidence from a leader in times of challenges can impact the shape of the organizational culture. When the organization is going through rough times, the leaders should step up and confidently lead the employees. Convincing the employees that they are safe and secure during challenging times can significantly impact the culture.

Third, learning from mistakes and owning up to them can significantly impact the culture. If the employees are punished for their mistakes, this will stifle their creativity in all areas of their work.

Finally, communication is another crucial aspect of the culture. Information can be communicated in different ways. These can take the form of memos, emails, meetings, newsletters, etc. as internal communication. Externally, it can be media releases, client communication, and stakeholder meetings. The six Cs of communication—compassion, clarity, conciseness, connection, conviction, and courage—play a crucial role in organizational interactions.[12]

An effective leader can shape an organization's culture with crucial elements, such as communication. These elements are also directly related to the effective implementation and reshaping of a cybersecurity culture within an organization.

First, if organizational culture can predict cybersecurity success, it can also predict the implementation of a thriving cybersecurity culture. If a company's organizational culture can be changed by aligning the employees with the organization's values, mission, and purpose, this can also apply to the cybersecurity culture. The processes and procedures can be implemented more efficiently when the purpose becomes clear.

Second, inspiration from leadership in rough times can also apply to a cybersecurity culture. Leadership should inspire employees to take charge of their own IT security.

Third, mistakes are inevitable. An employee might accidentally open a harmful file. This is a common occurrence; however, turning such incidents into learning experiences can foster a significant cultural shift.

Finally, communication is a fundamental element of any culture, whether organizational or related to cybersecurity. Without clearly explaining the goals and purposes of processes, the culture needed to ensure proper security cannot be created.

1.4 IMPORTANCE OF CYBERSECURITY CULTURE

According to Stackpole, given that eighty-five percent of cyberattacks or data breaches involve human error, and according to a 2024 IBM Report, the average cost of a breach in 2024 was $4.88 million, the importance of a strong cybersecurity culture becomes evident.[13]

First and most importantly, without a strong cybersecurity culture the organizational data will be in jeopardy. The stronger the culture, the stronger your organization and your workforce. The more reliance that is placed upon technology, the greater the need to secure all digital assets and connections. As Carpenter indicated, "The security culture of an organization is foundational to its ability to protect information, data, and employee and customer privacy."[14] Second, cyberattacks are constantly evolving and becoming more robust. A strong cybersecurity culture will raise awareness and encourage employees to take precautions. Third, since humans are the weakest link due to insufficient training and a lack of awareness, a strong cybersecurity culture promotes training and education at all levels and reduces breaches caused by human error. Fourth, most industries have strong regulations

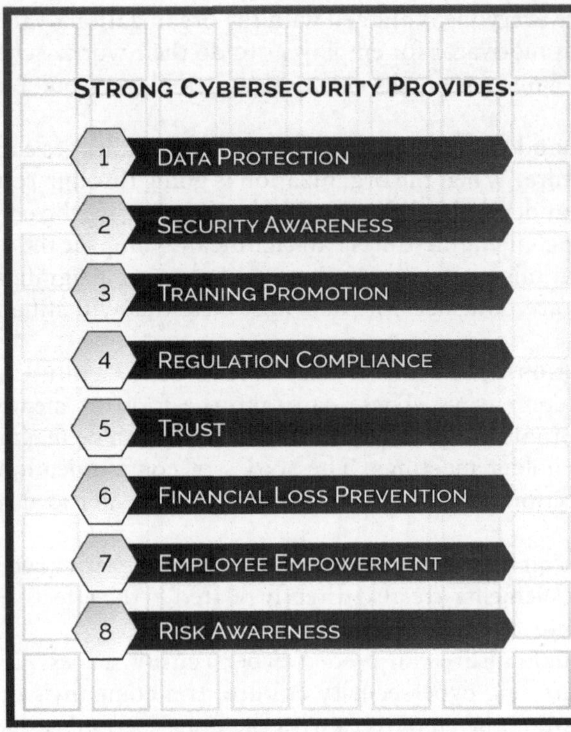

Figure 1.4 Key benefits of cybersecurity culture.

such as HIPAA (Health Insurance Portability and Accountability Act) or PCI DSS (Payment Card Industry Data Security Standard). A robust cybersecurity culture will help organizations comply with these regulations. Fifth, a strong cybersecurity culture will promote trust not only among the employees but also build and maintain trust with the customers who, as well as employees, need to know that their personal data is always protected.

Sixth, a robust cybersecurity culture helps prevent financial losses. Cyberattacks can be expensive for an organization, leading to business disruption, financial setbacks, and damage to infrastructure. Seventh, a strong cybersecurity culture empowers employees. It instills in them the knowledge that they must protect the system and take responsibility for creating a more secure environment. Finally, a strong cybersecurity culture heightens employees' awareness of the risks and their potential consequences.

In summary, as shown in Figure 1.4, a strong cybersecurity culture is crucial because it helps protect organizations and individuals from cyber threats, ensures compliance with regulations, builds trust, and prevents financial losses by empowering employees to take responsibility for their actions.

1.5 GLOBAL UNDERSTANDING AND EFFECTS OF CYBERSECURITY CULTURE

Global understanding of cybersecurity culture refers to the widespread awareness, shared beliefs, and collective commitment to cybersecurity best practices across organizations, industries, and nations. This worldwide perspective acknowledges the borderless nature of

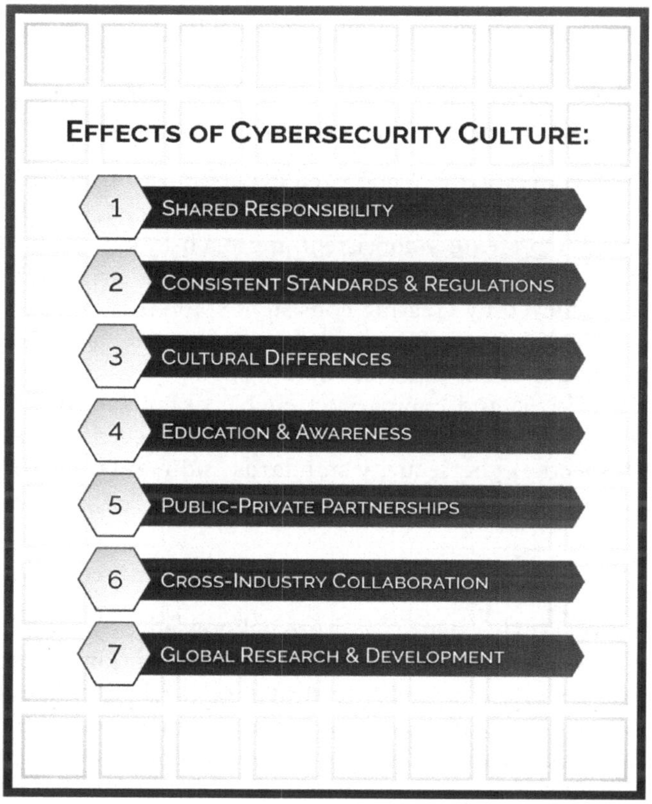

Figure 1.5 Effects of cybersecurity culture.

cyber threats and the need for global cooperation to protect digital assets effectively. Several shared beliefs contribute to the global understanding of cybersecurity culture. In this section, as Figure 1.5 summarizes, seven of these beliefs will be covered as follows.

1.5.1 Shared responsibility

Individuals, organizations, and governments all have a role to play in protecting digital infrastructure and information. The collective effort and responsibility to build a secure digital environment is paramount. Individuals must be aware of their personal information, devices, and online accounts. This includes but is not limited to using strong, unique passwords, enabling multifactor authentication, avoiding phishing scams, and keeping software up-to-date. Employees of an organization should understand their roles in organizational security. This includes adhering to security policies, reporting suspicious activities, and following best practices for protecting sensitive data and systems. Organizations must prioritize cybersecurity and implement appropriate measures to protect their digital assets, which amounts to adopting robust security policies, conducting regular risk assessments, providing employee training, and ensuring timely responses to cyber incidents. Governments must enforce regulations, invest in cybersecurity infrastructure, foster public-private partnerships, and support education and awareness initiatives. Cross-industry collaboration allows organizations to share best practices, threat intelligence, and resources, helping to create a more secure environment for all. When it comes to cyber threats, international collaboration is a must and is best accomplished by sharing threat intelligence, developing joint defense strategies, and providing support during cyber incidents.

1.5.2 Consistent standards and regulations

Developing and adhering to globally recognized cybersecurity standards and frameworks, such as NIST (National Institute of Standards and Technology) or GDPR (General Data Protection Regulation), help create a consistent approach to cybersecurity across borders. This uniformity helps foster trust and cooperation among organizations and cultures. Collaboration can be achieved by creating consistent standards and regulations, including common language and terminology. This can help communicate and understand cybersecurity concepts and risk management processes more effectively. Establishing baseline security requirements, benchmarking, and comparison enable organizations to identify areas for improvement and track progress over time. Compliance and certification require organizations to comply with specific cybersecurity standards and regulations. The details of these standards and regulations will be addressed in Chapter 5.

1.5.3 Cultural differences

A global understanding of cybersecurity culture acknowledges that cultural and regional factors may influence cybersecurity practices and risk perceptions. Respecting and incorporating these differences into cybersecurity strategies can help create more effective and inclusive security policies. For example, risk perception and attitudes can differ among cultures. Some cultures may prioritize security and privacy more than others, leading to varying levels of investment in cybersecurity measures. Other critical differences among cultures can be communication styles. This will directly affect how cybersecurity policies, incidents, and awareness campaigns are communicated within the organization. Understanding these factors can help tailor messaging and training materials more effectively.

Trust in technology, governments, and other institutions can also vary among cultures, influencing the adoption of cybersecurity practices and the willingness to cooperate in security initiatives. Building trust and understanding the cultural context is crucial for successful cybersecurity efforts. Countries have their own legal and regulatory frameworks that can be influenced by cultural values and norms, leading to variations in the level of protection, enforcement, and compliance requirements.

Cultures will also have their own unique privacy guidelines, which can influence expectations, attitudes toward data collection, sharing, and security measures. Understanding and respecting these differences can help organizations balance the need for data protection with the privacy requirements of their users and customers.

Language barriers can present challenges in cybersecurity, hindering communication, understanding, and adoption of security best practices. Providing multilingual resources and training materials can help address this issue and ensure that cybersecurity guidance is accessible to a broader audience.

Social norms and behavior related to technology use and online activities will also be culturally specific. Awareness can help organizations develop more culturally sensitive security policies and educational initiatives.

Collaboration and knowledge sharing could also vary between cultures. These differences can impact the willingness and ability of organizations and nations to collaborate and share knowledge about cybersecurity threats and best practices. Encouraging cross-cultural dialogue and cooperation can help build trust and foster a more inclusive global cybersecurity community.

1.5.4 Education and awareness

Promoting cybersecurity education and awareness at a global level is crucial for cultivating a security culture. This involves training IT professionals and empowering nontechnical users with the knowledge and skills necessary to protect themselves and their organizations.

Educational awareness refers to the process of informing and training individuals, organizations, and the public about the importance of cybersecurity. This way, they learn potential risks and best practices for protecting digital assets and information in their personal lives as well as their organizations. Effective educational awareness programs can help create a security culture and empower people to take responsibility for cybersecurity.

To do this effectively, it is important to carefully consider the target audience and tailor the approach accordingly. Some target audiences may include employees, IT professionals, executives, and policymakers. Each group has different needs and levels of understanding, so the content and approach should differ for each group.

When considering educational awareness, a multifaceted approach should be adopted. Cybersecurity is a multidisciplinary field that involves not only technical knowledge but also an understanding of human behavior, risk management, and legal and regulatory frameworks. Educational awareness programs should encompass all of these aspects in order to provide a comprehensive understanding.

Ongoing training is a crucial component of educational awareness. Since cyber threats and technologies are continuously evolving, educational awareness programs must be constantly updated. This ensures that individuals and organizations stay informed about best practices and are well-equipped to handle the latest threats and vulnerabilities.

Educational awareness programs should be engaging and interactive to capture the target audience's attention and facilitate learning. Assessing the effectiveness of educational awareness programs is crucial for continuous improvement. This can involve tracking participation, conducting surveys, and monitoring changes in behavior, knowledge, and attitudes toward cybersecurity.

1.5.5 Public-private partnerships

Collaboration between governments and private sector organizations is essential to address the complexity of the global threat landscape. Public-private partnerships can facilitate information sharing, resource allocation, and the development of innovative solutions to cybersecurity challenges. Sharing threat intelligence, vulnerabilities, and best practices between government agencies and private sector organizations can be a vital source of identifying the root causes of the threats. This collaboration helps both parties stay informed about emerging threats and develop more effective defense strategies.

Public-private partnerships can pool resources from both the public and private sectors, enabling more efficient and effective use of funding, technology, and expertise. This collaboration can lead to greater investment in cybersecurity infrastructure, research and development, and training programs. Collaborating on cybersecurity initiatives can drive innovation by bringing together the unique strengths and capabilities of both public and private sector organizations.

A coordinated response to cyber incidents can be an effective way of dealing with current and future threats. In the event of a cyberattack or data breach, public-private partnerships can enable government agencies and private sector organizations to work together to mitigate the impact, share information, and provide support to affected parties.

This partnership can also affect cybersecurity policies and regulations by bringing together the perspectives and expertise of both government and industry stakeholders.

This collaboration can lead to more balanced and effective policy frameworks that consider the needs and concerns of all parties involved. Extending beyond national borders, enabling cooperation and collaboration with international partners, this global approach to cybersecurity can facilitate the sharing of threat intelligence and best practices, as well as the development of joint strategies to address cross-border cyber threats.

1.5.6 Cross-industry collaboration

Cybersecurity issues often affect multiple industries, making cross-industry collaboration an important aspect of a global cybersecurity culture. Communicating experiences and lessons learned can help organizations across different sectors strengthen their cybersecurity posture. Establishing a shared understanding of cybersecurity concepts, threats, and best practices is essential for effective cross-industry collaboration. This common ground can help build trust, facilitate communication, and ensure that everyone can work toward achieving the same goals.

Cross-cultural collaboration can enable a coordinated international response in the event of a cyberattack or data breach. It allows governments and organizations to work together to mitigate the impact, share information, and support affected parties.

1.5.7 Global research and development

Investing in global research and development efforts can drive innovation and lead to more advanced and effective cybersecurity solutions. This collaboration fosters a shared understanding of emerging technologies, vulnerabilities, and potential countermeasures. The global nature of cyber threats requires international cooperation to drive innovation and develop effective and practical solutions.

Researchers from different countries and cultures can collaborate on joint projects, pooling their expertise, resources, and perspectives to address cybersecurity challenges. Such collaborations can lead to breakthroughs and novel solutions that would be difficult to achieve independently.

The global understanding of cybersecurity culture emphasizes the need for shared responsibility, international cooperation, and collaborative efforts to address the complex and ever-evolving cyber threat landscape. Recognizing and respecting cultural and regional differences and fostering education, awareness, and cross-industry collaboration can contribute to building a more secure digital world.

1.6 CONCLUSION

It should now be evident that the importance of cybersecurity culture cannot be overstated. As the world increasingly relies on digital technologies, the risks and threats associated with cyberattacks continue to grow. A robust cybersecurity culture is essential for individuals, organizations, and governments to protect their digital assets effectively. This can only be done by fostering a strong cybersecurity culture; organizations can create a proactive, resilient, and security-aware environment by changing their cultures. This is not an easy task. It involves promoting shared responsibility, consistent standards and regulations, educational awareness, cross-cultural collaboration, and leveraging public-private partnerships and global research and development efforts.

A strong cybersecurity culture empowers individuals to take responsibility for their own digital safety, encourages organizations to adopt best practices, and supports governments in creating policies and regulations that protect citizens and critical infrastructure. It ensures the security, privacy, and trust necessary for societies to thrive in the digital age.

DISCUSSION QUESTIONS

1. Why is cybersecurity important in today's interconnected world, and what are some potential consequences of not implementing effective cybersecurity practices?
2. Describe cybersecurity in your own words. What would you add that is not in the descriptions mentioned in this chapter?
3. According to the provided cybersecurity descriptions, what are the key objectives of cybersecurity, and why are these objectives important in today's technology and online communication?
4. The descriptions emphasize the need for effective cybersecurity practices to safeguard against cyber threats. What are some examples of these practices, and how can individuals and organizations implement them?
5. How can individuals and organizations stay up-to-date on the latest cybersecurity trends and best practices, and what are some resources available to help them do so?
6. How are organizational culture and cybersecurity culture related? Give examples.
7. How do human behaviors and attitudes impact the effectiveness of cybersecurity measures in an organization? What strategies can be employed to positively influence these behaviors?
8. What are the common challenges organizations face when trying to build and maintain a robust cybersecurity culture? How can these challenges be overcome?
9. Can you think of any real-world case studies where a strong cybersecurity culture either prevented or mitigated a cyber-attack? What lessons can be learned from these examples?
10. How can cybersecurity practices be integrated into the daily operations of an organization? What steps can be taken to ensure that employees view cybersecurity as a part of their routine responsibilities?

NOTES

1. Zhang, Y., et al. (2022). Explainable Artificial Intelligence Applications in Cyber Security: State-of-the-Art in Research *IEEE Access, 10*, 93104–93139. https://ieeexplore.ieee.org/stamp/stamp.jsp?arnumber=9875264
2. Lindemulder, G., & Kosinski, M. (2024). What is cybersecurity? https://www.ibm.com/think/topics/cybersecurity.
3. National Institute of Standards and Technology. (n.d.). *Glossary: Cybersecurity terms.* U.S. Department of Commerce. https://csrc.nist.gov/glossary/term/cybersecurity?utm_source=chatgpt.com
4. Cybersecurity and Infrastructure Security Agency. (n.d.). *What is cybersecurity?* U.S. Department of Homeland Security. https://www.cisa.gov/news-events/news/what-cybersecurity
5. Roer, K. (2015). *Build a security culture.* IT Governance Publishing.
6. Everard, T. (n.d.). What is cyber security culture and why does it matter for your organisation? https://www.paconsulting.com/insights/what-is-cyber-security-culture-and-why-does-it-matter-for-your-organisation/
7. Spitzner, L. (2021). Why a strong security culture? SANS Blog. https://www.sans.org/blog/why-strong-security-culture/
8. IBM.com. (2024). Cost of Data Breach Report. https://www.ibm.com/reports/data-breach
9. Carpenter, P. (2021, May 27). The importance of a strong security culture and how to build one. https://www.forbes.com/sites/forbesbusinesscouncil/2021/05/27/the-importance-of-a-strong-security-culture-and-how-to-build-one/?sh=7050ed4f6d49.

10. Cote, C. (2023, March 2). How does leadership influence organizational culture? https://online.hbs.edu/blog/post/organizational-culture-and-leadership.
11. Salesforce. (2022, September 15). Reveals top drivers of exceptional employee experience. Spoiler alert: It's not free snacks. https://www.salesforce.com/news/stories/how-to-engage-employees-2022/
12. Cote, C. (2023, March 2). How does leadership influence organizational culture? https://online.hbs.edu/blog/post/organizational-culture-and-leadership.
13. Stackpole, B. (2022, March 15). How to build a culture of cybersecurity. https://mitsloan.mit.edu/ideas-made-to-matter/how-to-build-a-culture-cybersecurity.
14. Carpenter, P. (2021, May 27). The Importance of a strong security culture and how to build one. https://www.forbes.com/sites/forbesbusinesscouncil/2021/05/27/the-importance-of-a-strong-security-culture-and-how-to-build-one/?sh=7050ed4f6d49.

BIBLIOGRAPHY

Aksoy, C. (2024). Building a cyber security culture for resilient organizations against cyber attacks. *İşletme Ekonomi Ve Yönetim Araştırmaları Dergisi*, 7(1), 96–110. https://doi.org/10.33416/baybem.1374001

Carpenter, P., & Roer, K. (2022). *The security culture playbook: An executive guide to reducing risk and developing your human defense layer* (1st ed.). KnowBe4.

Carre, A. (2019). *The cybersecurity playbook: How every leader and employee can contribute to a culture of security*. Wiley.

Corradini, I. (2020) Building a cybersecurity culture. In *Building a cybersecurity culture in organizations*. Springer International Publishing, 63–83.

Dornheim, P., & Zarnekow, R. (2024). Determining cybersecurity culture maturity and deriving verifiable improvement measures. *Information and Computer Security*, 32(2), 179–196. https://doi.org/10.1108/ICS-07-2023-0116

Georgiadou, A., Mouzakitis, S., Bounas, K., & Askounis, D. (2020). A cyber-security culture framework for assessing organization readiness. *Journal of Computer Information Systems*, 62(3), 452–462. https://doi.org/10.1080/08874417.2020.1845583

Hayden, L. (2015). *People-centric security: Transforming your enterprise security culture*. McGraw-Hill Education.

King, N. (2023). *The cybersecurity mindset: Cultivating a culture of vigilance*. Aude Publishing.

Marotta, A., & Pearlson, K. (2019) A culture of cybersecurity at Banca Popolare di Sondrio. *25th Americas Conference on Information Systems (AMCIS 2019)*, 1–10.

Ogden, S. E. (2021). Cybersecurity: Creating a cybersecurity culture [Master's thesis)]. California State University, San Bernardino.

Roy, M. (n.d.). *5 tips for building a cybersecurity culture at your company*. TechTarget. https://www.techtarget.com/searchsecurity/tip/5-tips-for-building-a-cybersecurity-culture-at-your-company.

Reegård, K., Blackett, C., & Katta, V. (2019). The concept of cybersecurity culture. *Proceedings of the 29th European Safety and Reliability Conference (ESREL)*. Institute for Energy Technology, Norway. https://doi.org/10.3850/978-981-11-2724-3_0761-cd.

Uchendu, B., Nurse, J. R. C., Bada, M., & Furnell, S. (2021). Developing a cyber security culture: Current practices and future needs. *Computers & Security*, *109*, 102387. https://doi.org/10.1016/j.cose.2021.102387

Upton, D., & Trim, P. R. J. (2016). *Cyber security culture: Counteracting cyber threats through organizational learning and training*. Routledge.

Van't Wout, C. (2019, February). Develop and maintain a cybersecurity organisational culture. *ICCWS 2019 14th International Conference on Cyber Warfare and Security: ICCWS* (Vol. 457). https://www.researchgate.net/profile/Carien-Van-t-Wout/publication/334052953_Develop_and_Maintain_a_Cybersecurity_Organisational_Culture/links/5d14bafaa6fdcc2462a96854/Develop-and-Maintain-a-Cybersecurity-Organisational-Culture.pdf

Walton, H. (2024). *Security culture: A how-to guide for improving security culture and dealing with people risk in your organisation*. Routledge.

Wiley, A., McCormac, A., & Calic, D. (2020). More than the individual: Examining the relationship between culture and information security awareness. *Computers & Security*, *88*, 101640. https://doi.org/10.1016/j.cose.2019.101640

Chapter 2

Organizational aspects of cybersecurity culture

Each organization's cybersecurity culture is a unique tapestry woven with its own approach to security. In turn, this approach is heavily influenced by the industry in which it operates. For instance, an organization in the IT field has distinct security needs, such as network security or user access control, compared to one in the marketing field, which can be client data protection or social media security. The industry not only shapes these needs but also determines the regulations and compliance to which they need to adhere, and these rules determine how they approach cybersecurity priorities and practices.

Cybersecurity culture is additionally affected by the size of the organization and its resources. There is a positive correlation between organization size and cybersecurity resource allocation. The smaller the organization, the fewer resources are allocated to security; likewise, the larger the organization, the bigger the budget available for cybersecurity purposes.

Smaller organizations generally have limited budgets and staff available to allocate. This can mean the difference between reactive and proactive approaches to security. The individual approach can also vary; it can be more informal, an approach that can create security problems. Since larger organizations have greater resources available for cybersecurity, they have the budget and staff on hand. This allows more proactive measures, which heightens security. The formalization of roles also can have a positive impact on how larger organizations approach security. The security procedures and policies are more defined, and they also have large teams that can be dedicated to security and taking proactive measures.

The organization's location can be an important factor that determines the legal and regulatory requirements. These can differ from state to state and country to country and will determine how security should be handled.

The organization's past experiences also contribute to the unique nature of the culture. If an organization has had previous incidents, its approach to security would be very different from that of others which have not had similar experiences. Because of this, some organizations take a more rigid approach to security than others.

Another contributing factor to this uniqueness is how tech-savvy an organization is or how it approaches adopting new technologies. Early adopters might have cutting-edge technology to prevent incidents. A tech-savvy culture might better understand how security can be affected and play a significant role in promoting policies and procedures.

The final contributor to the uniqueness of cybersecurity culture is leadership. In general, an organization's culture is determined by its leadership, which is also true for cybersecurity culture. If the leadership emphasizes the importance of security and deems it crucial, the organizational attitude will change dramatically. Leadership that promotes a strong security culture will bring awareness throughout the organization.

Each element mentioned above contributes to the composition and forms the bedrock of the cybersecurity culture, shaping an organization's values, beliefs, attitudes, behaviors, and

DOI: 10.1201/9781003368496-2

practices. This foundation must be robust for the organization to safeguard its assets and valuable data from cyber threats.

Going forward, this chapter explores the crucial elements of cybersecurity culture in detail. These include leadership, policies and procedures, education, training and awareness, attributes and behaviors, communication, compliance, risk assessment, incident response, continuous improvement, and recognition.

2.1 ELEMENTS OF CYBERSECURITY CULTURE

Understanding the critical elements of cybersecurity culture is not just an academic exercise. It is a vital step toward building a robust security culture that requires active participation and commitment from all levels of the organization. Each of these fundamental elements discussed in this chapter, as shown in Figure 2.1 and summarized in Table 2.1, must be carefully considered to establish a secure environment. The stakes are high. If any of these elements are out of sync or omitted, the security could eventually fail.

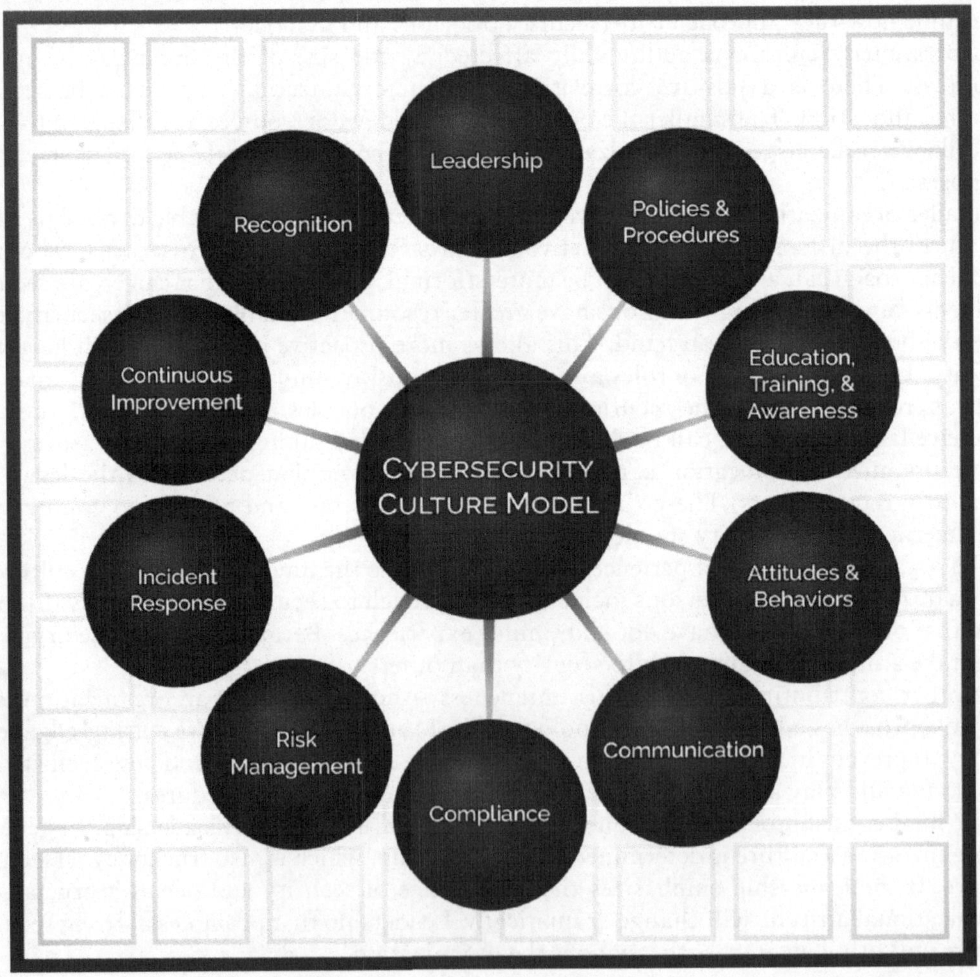

Figure 2.1 Cybersecurity culture model.

Table 2.1 Summary of fundamental elements of cybersecurity culture

Aspect	Description	Impact on Security
Leadership	Leadership's commitment to cybersecurity, setting the tone for organizational security.	Sets organizational priorities, allocates resources, and drives a culture of security.
Policies	Development and enforcement of security policies and procedures.	Ensures that all members follow established security protocols, reducing vulnerabilities.
Education, Training, & Awareness	Comprehensive education programs, regular training sessions, and awareness campaigns to build cybersecurity knowledge and skills.	Equips employees with the knowledge to recognize and respond to threats, reducing human error and enhancing overall security awareness.
Attitudes & Behavior	Employees' perceptions, attitudes, and behaviors towards cybersecurity practices and policies.	Shapes the overall security culture by influencing how seriously employees take security measures and respond to threats.
Communication	Effective communication of security policies, incidents, and expectations.	Keeps all employees informed, ensuring a cohesive approach to security.
Compliance	Adherence to industry standards and regulations.	Maintains legal compliance and minimizes risks of regulatory penalties.
Risk Management	Processes for identifying, assessing, and mitigating security risks.	Helps the organization anticipate and mitigate potential threats.
Incident Reponse	Preparedness and structured response to security incidents.	Limits damage during incidents and ensures swift recovery.
Continuous Improvement	Ongoing efforts to improve security practices and adapt to new threats.	Promotes adaptability and resilience against evolving cyber threats.
Recognition	Acknowledging and rewarding employees for their adherence to security protocols and contributions to cybersecurity.	Encourages a proactive security culture and motivates employees to remain vigilant against potential threats.

2.1.1 Leadership

Leadership commitment to cybersecurity culture is an important element of success. To establish and maintain a strong culture, leadership must be on board. When there is a genuine commitment by the leadership, there will be a genuine commitment by the staff. Setting the tone is everything, and success starts here.

The leaders should set priorities and establish the importance of security in the organization's mission and values. They should also allocate time and resources to cybersecurity initiatives, such as personnel, budget, and technology.

Leadership should lead by example and follow the cybersecurity protocols themselves. If the organization's leader keeps his or her passwords under the keyboard, so will the staff. The leadership should be instrumental in developing, implementing, and enforcing the policies. They should communicate the importance of cybersecurity rules and regulations. They should inform the staff of new threats and where the organization stands regarding them. They should discuss security breaches openly, take responsibility for and prepare to lead during incidents, and promote collaboration between departments to eliminate threats at all levels. Transparency can benefit everyone. Leaders should encourage continuous improvement so that threats are caught early and do not become a continuous source of vulnerability or risk to the organization.

Leadership has a significant role in promoting an organization's cybersecurity culture; like any aspect, it is no different from promoting a genuine organizational culture. Leaders must play an active role in keeping organizational assets safe and secure. This can be done through training, raising awareness, or creating incident response plans. When leaders are committed, there is a big chance that everyone else will be. Their response to any breach or threat is crucial and can significantly impact the amount of damage and recuperation.

Leadership should integrate cybersecurity into the organization's culture, making it a natural part of everyday operations, decision-making, and, most importantly, the organization's business strategy.

When leadership gets involved in fostering an integrated culture that understands, values, and implements cybersecurity measures, the leaders not only protect their organizations from potential threats but also build a foundation of trust with customers and stakeholders.

2.1.2 Policies and procedures

Policies and procedures are essential aspects of organizational culture and constitute the rules and regulations that must be followed. They reflect the organization's practices, values, and culture and provide a framework for decision-making. The term "policies" is all-inclusive and ranges from IT to human resources. Policies are necessary to make the employees aware of the expectations and requirements. They also dictate legal compliance and accountability. By making them transparent and using them as a communication tool, the organization can minimize risk and optimize efficiency in decision-making. Overall, policies provide a framework for decision-making that considers risk mitigation and legal compliance. Accountability, efficiency, communication, transparency, and culture building are also benefits that policies provide.

Procedures are step-by-step guidelines on how the policies are implemented. They can be technical or behavior related. For example, your organization will have a password policy to eliminate unauthorized access to your computer. The procedure outlines what must be done to create that password. Procedures will provide staff members with the steps to perform a policy. As you can see, procedures and policies work together. They create a secure environment and protect sensitive organizational information from getting into the wrong hands. They are vital because they provide consistency. Since they are adhered to throughout the organization, this eliminates errors and inconsistencies. All employees abide by the same policies and procedures, creating a more secure environment. Having the policies and regulations outlined can eliminate legal complications and consequences. They provide a common language to communicate security measures across the organization. By regularly updating them, there exists a culture of continuous improvement of security, and during crises, the documented policies and procedures can provide guidance and efficient response.

Cybersecurity policies and procedures are formal frameworks that establish how security is handled within a business environment. Many organizations operate under regulatory requirements, and the policies and procedures ensure compliance. As with any policies and procedures, they are subject to regular audits and updates as the organization changes its requirements.

2.1.3 Education, training, and awareness

Education, training, and awareness are frequently mentioned as three important aspects to fend off cyber threats. First, it is necessary to distinguish between the three. Education provides a broad understanding of the topic in the context of cybersecurity. It tends to be more formal and theoretical. Cybersecurity education aims to build a deep understanding and knowledge of the field and critical thinking to solve cybersecurity challenges.

Some examples of cybersecurity education would be learning about cybersecurity culture and different types of cyberattacks or studying how cyberattacks impact global business operations.

Training, on the other hand, is a focused and more practical approach to organizational security. It aims to arm employees with the knowledge to perform tasks responding to specific situations, such as implementing security procedures or customizing. When training is involved, there is usually a targeted role and a targeted skill, and the information is transferred through a workshop, simulation, or hands-on practice.

Employees must be trained regularly on the most recent cyber threats and how to recognize them. For example, ongoing phishing training and practice that include phishing emails from the IT department can teach employees to recognize such threats and take immediate action. Since the human link is the weakest, the training sessions are of great importance. Almost 85% of all breaches happen because of human error. To eliminate these breaches, we must train the employees regardless of their title, department, and level of IT knowledge. In these training sessions, we need to ensure that the employees are aware of the most recent threats, how to recognize them, and how to respond to them. Most importantly, they must know what to do if they are involved in an incident.

The most important areas in which to train employees include phishing, password creation and management, handling sensitive data, doing research safely on the internet, security updates and patches, and social engineering. It is imperative to implement simulated exercises to test their knowledge, skills, and awareness. These simulated exercises could be simple phishing emails created by the IT department to test the employees' responses. The training should be done regularly to keep the employees vigilant and proactive.

In cybersecurity, awareness means being conscious of risks and their consequences. It involves awareness of malware, phishing, and social engineering risks and how they can impact the organization. Awareness also involves recognizing threats, understanding cybersecurity policies, and acknowledging that they are a shared responsibility of everyone in the organization. Promoting awareness is the key to a strong cybersecurity culture.

Creating awareness is the most challenging of the three. Education and training can be provided to all members of an organization; however, awareness is highly dependent on the individual. Although education and training are provided, this does not guarantee individuals will have awareness. Security awareness training is one way to involve individuals; however, there are more effective ways. Simulation campaigns, as well as recognition and rewards, are effective ways to create security awareness as well.

As you can see, all three approaches have their purposes in creating a secure environment. All employees should be aware of risks, their outcomes, and how they can damage an organization. Our best defense against threats is our employees. If they have the necessary tools, education, training, and, most importantly, awareness, we have a chance to secure our most important organizational assets.

2.1.4 Attitudes and behaviors

Two critical factors that shape an organization's cybersecurity culture are employee attitudes and behaviors. They have much to do with influencing the cybersecurity culture, and they drive how individuals interact with each other. Understanding this interaction can shed light on several problems regarding individuals' productivity and their organizational commitment, both of which directly impact security. Regarding cybersecurity, attitudes and behaviors play an important role, especially in the areas discussed in this chapter.

Employee attitudes toward cybersecurity can be telling in the areas of education, training, and awareness. These attitudes can reflect their proactivity in engaging in education and training. They also reflect how seriously they take risks, as well as their understanding of the consequences of those risks. Employee attitudes toward reporting security incidents can be the difference between a security breach and catching it on time. The attitude toward open communication can promote teamwork, and sharing information can protect the organization from threats. As a result, a positive attitude and behavior will result in a successful organizational security culture, therefore protecting the organization from cyber threats. Positive attitudes, such as reporting suspicious emails and security incidents, using strong passwords, completing updates on time, and attending training, will significantly reduce the risk of any threats and breaches. On the other hand, negative attributes and behaviors, such as ignoring security policies, resistance to change, lack of communication, and complacency, will create a vulnerable environment. The best thing an organization can do to avoid this is to focus on awareness training, leadership commitment, positive reinforcement, and transparent communication.

Employee behaviors, such as following policies and procedures, will reduce the risk of security incidents. They will become evident in how they use security measures in their work environment.

2.1.5 Communication

As in an organization, communication is the backbone of a cybersecurity culture. It connects everything discussed previously. Communication should be open, transparent, and honest. Only in this way can organizational information be shared and possible threats avoided. Effective and timely communication is needed in an organization. Communication should raise awareness and empower individuals to make informed decisions. It should be a shared responsibility and not just the job of the IT department.

Cyber threats should be openly communicated to the staff, the consequences dealt with immediately, and policies and procedures clearly reflect the measures taken. Various communication channels, such as emails, reports, and meetings, should be utilized to disseminate information. Regular updates and changes in policies and procedures should be communicated immediately.

Trust and transparency are two critical aspects of communication. Trust is the belief that staff has confidence in each other, the leadership, and any protocol to keep organizational assets safe. The individuals will believe that others will follow the processes and procedures as well. They will have faith in the leadership and that they are making the right decisions. The individuals believe that the organization has taken appropriate security measures, such as access controls, user rights, firewalls, etc., to keep the organizational assets safe. Trust is essential in cybersecurity culture because it creates a collaborative environment, ensures compliance with security policies, and increases morale and engagement.

Transparency, on the other hand, is open communication about security threats, risks, and incidents. Organizations should inform their staff about any incident that occurs and the damage it has caused. Clear communication of what is being done to mitigate the incident is paramount. Transparency is also needed in communicating policies and procedures so that everyone knows their roles. Regular updates should be a part of communication, and the staff's concerns should be acknowledged openly.

A lack of transparent communication can be disastrous for an organization. It will lead to a lack of trust in the leadership, decreased morale, and increased risk of insider threats. To avoid these consequences, it is necessary to open clear communication channels, communicate frequently, be transparent about incidents, and encourage feedback.

2.1.6 Compliance

Compliance has a complex relationship with cybersecurity culture. It adheres to industry standards, regulations, and laws; however, cybersecurity culture encompasses the attitudes, beliefs, and behaviors of individuals in an organization. There are many regulations that an organization needs to comply with. Compliance with regulations helps organizations protect their assets and data. For example, HIPAA (Health Insurance Portability and Accountability Act) governs healthcare information. An organization that deals with healthcare must abide by HIPAA regulations. PCI DSS (Payment Card Industry Data Security Standard) governs the credit card industry. If a company is using credit cards, it needs to abide by the PCI DSS regulations. This way, credit card records and healthcare records are safe. When an organization has a strong cybersecurity culture, compliance with any regulation becomes significantly easier because the culture knows the significance of compliance. The education, training, and awareness make them aware of the consequences of noncompliance. Since the employees are aware of the consequences, everyone will strive to improve.

Compliance with regulations establishes a baseline for organizations, including cybersecurity. Once that baseline is established, the organization can create security policies and procedures. It will also initiate education and training for the staff, which can raise awareness of its importance. Compliance regulations also encourage continuous improvement. Organizations must regularly monitor and improve security by adopting new policies, processes, and technologies.

Compliance alone has limitations, such as providing minimum standards. It can be seen as a checklist assignment, and its restrictive nature can create resistance; however, compliance and fostering a solid cybersecurity culture are the keys to a robust cybersecurity posture.

2.1.7 Risk management

Just like compliance, risk management is closely associated with cybersecurity culture. It involves identifying, assessing, mitigating, monitoring, and communicating any risk, including cyber risks, that an organization can face. Risk management can involve internal and external risks, human errors, or natural disasters. Assessing the risk determines its likelihood of happening, and it also helps with prioritizing the risks. Mitigating the risk involves implementing strategies to reduce its impact and likelihood of occurring. Continuously monitoring the risk helps us identify new threats, and communicating the risk involves all parties understanding the risk and their roles.

The stronger an organization's culture, the greater the possibility of identifying these risks. An organization with adequate risk management can easily identify and mitigate cyber risks. This will result in asset protection, crisis preparedness, and, hence, stakeholder confidence.

Risk management is vital for cybersecurity culture because it prompts organizations to take proactive steps. When the risks are known, it is easier to plan for them. Resource optimization becomes more efficient and much easier. The resources that the risk will deplete will not be a surprise. An organization can prepare in advance, budget wise and staff wise. By planning for it, the impacts can be greatly reduced.

Hopefully, you can see that there is a close relationship between risk management and cybersecurity culture. Organizations navigate a challenging cybersecurity landscape, of which risk management is an integral part. Aligned with risk management, a strong cybersecurity culture will help an organization to effectively identify, assess, mitigate, and respond to cyber risks.

2.1.8 Incident response

Incident response is how effectively an organization responds to threats. It is a structured and organized approach to cyber threats that needs to be dealt with immediately. It is a

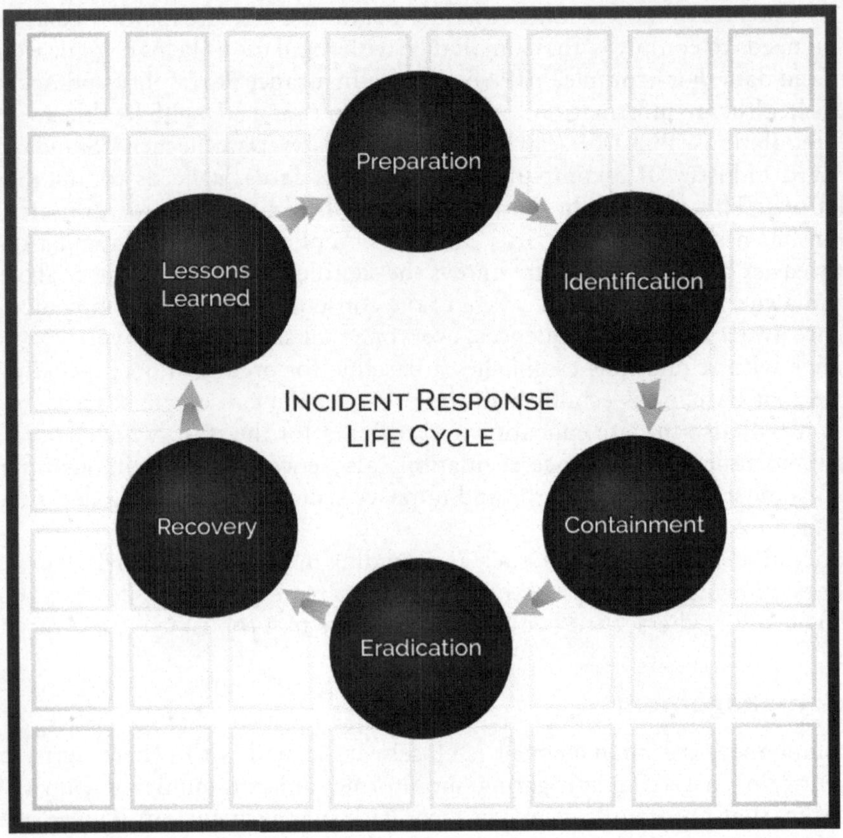

Figure 2.2 Incident response life cycle.

unified approach to effectively identifying, assessing, mitigating, and responding to cyber risks. The main goal of incident response is to minimize the effect of the cyber incident. The event needs to be contained as quickly as possible to prevent further damage. As soon as the event is contained, it's crucial to restore normal operations, thoroughly analyze the situation, and incorporate lessons learned to prevent future occurrences.

The incident response process has six stages, as illustrated in Figure 2.2:

1. Preparation: This phase takes place before the event occurs. It is the planning stage where the necessary steps to take in the event of a threat are determined. From that information, a plan is created, communication channels established, and preparedness ensured by way of training and drills.
2. Identification: This phase involves detecting and verifying the incident. It can be done using various methods, such as antivirus alerts, user reports, and Intrusion Detection System (IDS) alerts. After verifying the attack, its scope and severity are determined.
3. Containment: After the incident has been confirmed, the focus should be on containing the event to prevent its further spread. Some actions you can take are separating the affected network or systems, enabling external access, quarantining suspicious files, and changing passwords.
4. Eradication: In this phase, it is necessary to find the root cause of the event and remove it. This can be done in various ways, such as through antivirus scans, antimalware

scans, identifying and patching vulnerabilities, restoring data from backups, and performing a root cause analysis to get further details.

5. Recovery: In this phase, the system and the data are restored to their pre-event phase. This can be done by restoring the system and data from backup, reimaging or rebuilding systems, and restoring network services. Additional recovery measures, such as testing, validation, and documentation, could also be implemented.
6. Lessons Learned: In this last phase, it is important to analyze what happened in detail and improve the incident response process after the event occurred. This can be done by updating the incident response plan, providing additional staff training, or implementing new security measures.

An organization with a positive culture will identify, report, and manage an incident much better. Incident response is not just about responding to an event; it is a proactive approach whereby the organization identifies, contains, eradicates, and recovers from an incident. A solid incident plan will eliminate the impact of an event and will make the organization resilient to other occurrences. Accountability will help identify the incident rapidly, and a culture that embraces accountability will learn from its mistakes and find ways to eliminate them.

2.1.9 Continuous improvement

Continuous improvement is how an organization enhances its ongoing processes and performance. It is crucial for an organization to work on improvements regularly, and this should not be taken lightly. It is an incremental process where the goal is to make changes to the existing procedures to see a difference over time. Since the cybersecurity threat landscape constantly changes, continuous improvement must also do so. Continuous improvement indicates that the organization is keeping up with the trends, and this way, it minimizes risks.

Continuous improvement can also help organizations identify weaknesses and strengthen the incident response process. By identifying weaknesses and gaps, you can build more robust incident responses. It involves employees from all levels of the organization actively participating in cybersecurity practices and measures. These collective efforts make the organization stronger and foster resiliency. Identifying issues, sharing knowledge, and contributing to finding solutions bind the organization together. Ownership and engagement help employees build a stronger cybersecurity culture and create an open environment where their feedback and opinions are valued.

Continuous improvement should be data driven and embrace a problem-solving environment. Leadership should always promote continuous improvement for sustained success. Many continuous improvement methodologies, including Kaizen and Six Sigma, serve different organizations. For example, Kaizen focuses on small incremental changes, which can lead to significant improvements. This methodology is suitable for awareness training, employee feedback, and process improvements. Alternatively, Six Sigma aims to reduce defects and enhance quality and efficiency. It is data driven and puts emphasis on root cause analysis and standardized processes.

An organization must consider several factors to implement continuous improvement, as shown in Figure 2.3. First, a feedback loop must be established. Employees should be encouraged to give feedback without fear of retaliation, and there should be several channels through which they could do so. These can be public, such as meetings, or private, such as anonymous reporting tools. The most important thing here is for the employee to feel comfortable.

Figure 2.3 Implementing continuous improvement.

Second, cybersecurity processes, policies, and technologies should be assessed regularly. The areas that need improvement should be identified early, and action plans should be developed immediately. According to the action plans, the process could be renewed, new technologies could be implemented, and additional training could be set up.

Third, the importance of training should be emphasized. Ongoing training is a crucial part of continuous improvement. It gives employees confidence and empowers them to make informed decisions and protect sensitive information.

Fourth, a culture that celebrates and recognizes successes and learns from failures must be created. Employees who have identified and warned necessary staff should be recognized and publicly acknowledged. Conducting a Root Cause Analysis (RCA) and learning from the experience is a helpful tool when an incident occurs. For example, if an employee opens a suspicious email attachment, trying to investigate the reason he or she opened the questionable email is the preferred approach. Learning from these incidents helps us eliminate the problem going forward.

Finally, in cybersecurity culture, it is important to encourage collaboration and open communication. Without the two, you will not be successful in the efforts to save your organization from cyberattacks.

Organizations can create a proactive, resilient cybersecurity culture that evolves with emerging threats and technological advancements. They can become dynamic and adaptable to any incident by embracing continuous improvement. They will be prepared to face any challenge and changes in the digital landscape.

2.1.10 Recognition

Creating, fostering, and sustaining a cybersecurity culture is not an easy task. Since employee commitment to cybersecurity culture is of paramount importance, it is necessary to ensure that this commitment is recognized and rewarded. This will only reinforce the culture and make it sustainable. By doing so, you should encourage good action, acknowledge it when it occurs, and provide positive reinforcement. The employees will be engaged in secure behavior, which will be the best defense against cyber threats.

Personal leadership acknowledgment has been shown to be very effective. Recognition can be verbal, written, or through certifications, gifts, and awards. Considering the severity of cybersecurity breaches and how dearly the organization will pay for them, this approach is acknowledged as a way to create and maintain a sustainable cybersecurity culture.

Reporting incidents should never be penalized or frowned upon; on the contrary, it should be encouraged and rewarded. This will reinforce positive behavior. When individuals are rewarded for reporting suspicious activity or a breach, they will continue this behavior. Rewards are motivators and will create the desired positive outcome. Every time you reward positive behavior, it reinforces the message that cybersecurity is a shared responsibility and the strongest way your organization's digital environment can truly be safe. Rewards and recognition also positively affect peers and promote a healthy culture of continuous learning and improvement.

While there are several ways to recognize employees, public recognition, where the employees are acknowledged through companywide announcements, newsletters, or social media posts, can be highly effective. Monetary incentives, such as bonuses, gift cards, or other financial rewards, can also be a compelling incentive for exceptional cybersecurity performance. Career advancement opportunities have shown to be another factor in employee motivation. Incorporating gamification elements, such as leaderboards and badges, to make cybersecurity training and awareness activities more engaging and rewarding, are additional ways to motivate employees.

Recognition plays a crucial role in a thriving cybersecurity culture. Reinforcing positive behavior, employee motivation, and morale ultimately reinforces the cybersecurity culture. When recognition is incorporated into the cybersecurity culture, it creates a positive feedback loop that reinforces desired behaviors, strengthens security practices, and empowers employees to actively safeguard the organization's digital assets.

2.2 CONCLUSION

Creating a robust cybersecurity culture is challenging and requires a comprehensive approach that integrates policies, education, technology, and continuous improvement. Top-down leadership commitment, endorsing and supporting cybersecurity initiatives, and demonstrating their importance to the organization are necessary. They must also ensure that adequate budget, staff, and resources are allocated to cybersecurity efforts. Only then can a robust cybersecurity culture be created.

Clear policies and procedures must outline expected behaviors, access controls, incident response protocols, and data protection. Unless the employees across the organization are aware of these policies, there can be no reliable cybersecurity culture. The policies and procedures must also be revised and updated regularly to keep up with the changing cybersecurity landscape.

Ongoing training in employee engagement and accountability must be part of this landscape. Training for different levels of employees and awareness programs should be made available to the staff on a regular basis. Publicly or anonymously, through different methodologies, employees should be able to report incidents freely and without fear of retaliation in these meetings. The accountability of the employees should be stated clearly.

The organization should use state-of-the-art cybersecurity tools for threat detection, prevention, and response, including firewalls, antivirus software, intrusion detection systems, and endpoint protection. All systems should be regularly monitored and updated.

Collaboration between all departments (IT, HR, etc.) should be encouraged throughout the organization to ensure a cohesive approach to cybersecurity. Collaboration with external resources, such as partners, industry experts, and government bodies, should be encouraged when necessary. Open communication and trust between all parties must be the foundation of the organizational cybersecurity culture. This holistic approach, combined with leadership support and transparent policies and communication, will be the root of a strong cybersecurity culture.

With a solid understanding of the elements that constitute a robust cybersecurity culture, the following chapters will delve into the evolving threat landscape that organizations face. Beginning with the next chapter, the various types of cyber threats, their origins, and the tactics employed by cybercriminals will be explored. By examining the threat landscape in detail, you can better understand the risks and develop strategies to protect your digital assets effectively. This knowledge is crucial for building a proactive defense and ensuring the resilience of a cybersecurity culture.

DISCUSSION QUESTIONS

1. What role does leadership play in shaping an organization's cybersecurity culture, and how can leaders effectively promote security awareness among employees?
2. How do organizational size, industry, and location influence the development of a cybersecurity culture?
3. What are the key differences between education, training, and awareness in the context of cybersecurity, and why are all three necessary?
4. How can organizations ensure that their cybersecurity policies and procedures remain relevant and effective over time?
5. Discuss the importance of incident reporting and response in maintaining a resilient cybersecurity culture. How can organizations improve their incident response processes?
6. What are the benefits and challenges of integrating continuous improvement into cybersecurity practices? Provide examples.
7. How does communication within an organization impact its cybersecurity culture, and what strategies can be used to improve communication?
8. Why is compliance important in cybersecurity, and how does it interact with an organization's overall security culture?
9. How can positive reinforcement and recognition influence employee behavior and contribute to a stronger cybersecurity culture?
10. In what ways can organizations foster a proactive rather than reactive approach to cybersecurity?

BIBLIOGRAPHY

Abrahams, T. O., Farayola, O. A., Kaggwa, S., Uwaoma, P. U., Hassan, A. O., & Dawodu, S. O. (2024). Cybersecurity awareness and education programs: A review of employee engagement and accountability. *Computer Science & IT Research Journal*, *5*(1), 100–119. https://doi.org/10.51594/csitrj.v5i1.708

Andronache, A. (2021). Increasing security awareness through lenses of cybersecurity culture. *Journal of Information Systems & Operations Management*, *15*(1), 7. JISOM-SU21-A01.pdf (researchgate.net)
Azeus Convene. (n.d.). Cybersecurity risk management: Why it is needed and how to proceed [White paper]. https://www.azeusconvene.com/whitepaper/cybersecurity-risk-management
Clarke, N., & Furnell, S. (Eds.). (2022). *Human aspects of information security and assurance: Proceedings of the 16th IFIP WG 11.12 International Symposium on Human Aspects of Information Security and Assurance (HAISA 2022)*, Mytilene, Lesbos, Greece, July 6–8, 2022.
Edemekong, P. F., Annamaraju, P., & Haydel, M. J. (2024, February 12). Health Insurance Portability and Accountability Act. *StatPearls*. StatPearls Publishing. https://www.ncbi.nlm.nih.gov/books/NBK500019/
Ertan, A., Crossland, G., Heath, C., Denny, D., & Jensen, R. (2020). Cyber security behaviour in organisations. https://doi.org/10.48550/arXiv.2004.11768
Florackis, C., Louca, C., Michaely, R., & Weber, M. (2023). Cybersecurity risk. *The Review of Financial Studies*, *36*(1), 351–407. https://doi.org/10.1093/rfs/hhac024
Georgiadou, A., Mouzakitis, S., & Askounis, D. (2021). Detecting insider threat via a cyber-security culture framework. *Journal of Computer Information Systems*, *62*(4), 706–716. https://doi.org/10.1080/08874417.2021.1903367
Georgiadou, A., Mouzakitis, S., Bounas, K., & Askounis, D. (2020). A cyber-security culture framework for assessing organization readiness. *Journal of Computer Information Systems*, *62*(3), 452–462. https://doi.org/10.1080/08874417.2020.1845583
Hussain, A., Mohamed, A., & Razali, S. (2020). A review on cybersecurity: Challenges & emerging threats. In *Proceedings of the 3rd International Conference on Networking, Information Systems & Security* (NISS '20) (Article No. 28, pp. 1–7). https://doi.org/10.1145/3386723.3387847
Keyton, J. (2017). Communication in organizations. *Annual Review of Organizational Psychology and Organizational Behavior*, *4*(1), 501–526. https://doi.org/10.1146/annurev-orgpsych-032516-113341
Maheu, M. (2018, October 4). Cybersecurity and HIPAA compliance go hand in hand: Here's why. https://telehealth.org/cybersecurity-and-hipaa-compliance/?utm_medium=adwords&utm_campaign=&utm_source=&gad_source=1&gclid=CjwKCAjwhvi0BhA4EiwAX25uj-OPgCgTlC3bYEFfimsY6rX9k9gHLhw4_hMtT8XE_YoyfgiS1sZXsRoCkocQAvD_BwE
National Institute of Standards and Technology (NIST). (n.d.). NIST Cybersecurity Framework. https://www.nist.gov/cyberframework
Northouse, P. G. (2021). *Leadership: Theory and practice* (9th ed.). Sage Publishing.
Parenty, T. J., & Domet, J. J. (2019). *A leader's guide to cybersecurity: Why boards need to lead—and how to do it.* Harvard Business Review Press.
Poehlmann, N., Caramancion, K. M., Tatar, I., Li, Y., Barati, M., & Merz, T. (2021). The organizational cybersecurity success factors: An exhaustive literature review. In: Daimi, K., Arabnia, H.R., Deligiannidis, L., Hwang, MS., Tinetti, F.G. (Eds.), *Advances in security, networks, and internet of things. Transactions on computational science and computational intelligence.* Springer. https://doi.org/10.1007/978-3-030-71017-0_27
Seaman, J. (2020). *PCI DSS: An integrated data security standard guide* (1st ed.). Apress.
Todd, F. (2019). *CISO COMPASS: Navigating cybersecurity leadership challenges with insights from pioneers.* (1st ed.). Auerbach Publications.
Triplett, W. J. (2022). Addressing human factors in cybersecurity leadership. *Journal of Cybersecurity and Privacy*, *2*(3), 573–586. https://doi.org/10.3390/jcp2030029
U.S. Department of Health and Human Services. (2022, October 19). Summary of the HIPAA Security Rule. https://www.hhs.gov/hipaa/for-professionals/security/laws-regulations/index.html
Wirkuttis, N., & Klein, H. (2017). Artificial intelligence in cybersecurity. *Cyber, Intelligence, and Security*, *1*(1), 103–119. https://www.academia.edu/36264684/Artificial_Intelligence_in_Cybersecurity
World Economic Forum. (2023). *Global cybersecurity outlook 2023: Insight report.* Retrieved from https://www3.weforum.org/docs/WEF_Global_Security_Outlook_Report_2023.pdf

Chapter 3

Threat landscape and cybersecurity culture

Understanding the threat landscape is not a one-time task but an ongoing process. Navigating this landscape and understanding each threat and what it entails is of utmost importance. Comprehending the different categories of threats can help organizations prioritize their security efforts, allocate resources effectively, and develop an all-inclusive cybersecurity strategy; however, it's equally important to recognize that the threat landscape is constantly evolving. This understanding should instill a sense of responsibility and vigilance in organizations, prompting them to continuously adapt their defenses accordingly.

Although this chapter represents a simplified version of the threat landscape, it is important to remember that it is much more complex. You will be introduced to attack vectors, what they are, how they work, and the appropriate cultural responses.

As shown in Figure 3.1, the attack vectors that will be explored are as follows:

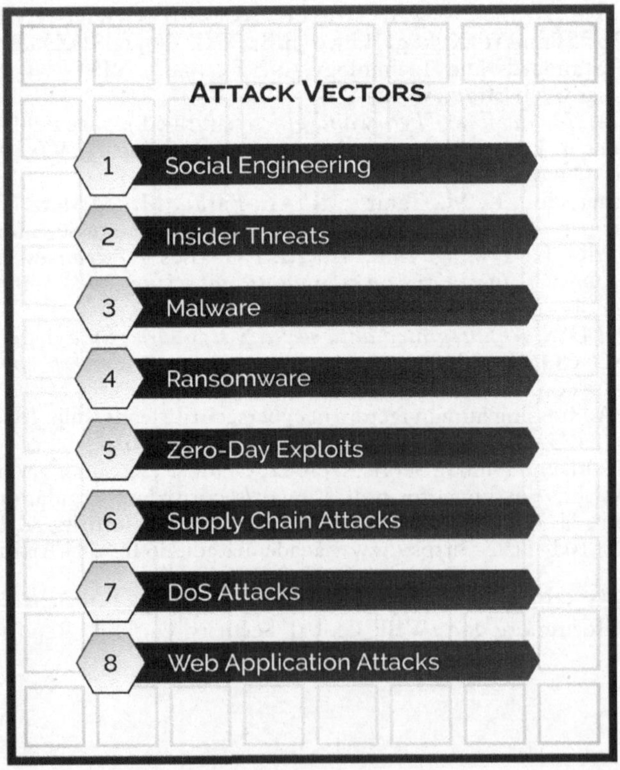

Figure 3.1 Attack vectors.

DOI: 10.1201/9781003368496-3

ATTACK VECTORS

An attack or threat vector is a method or passageway hackers use to access a network, a system, or a device. Understanding these methods is valuable for an organization not only to protect itself against them but also to develop strategies and build resilient cybersecurity frameworks, creating proactive defense measures. With effective incident response, organizations can swiftly mitigate potential damages and maintain operational continuity. They can maintain trust and security by complying with regulations and making continuous improvements. By staying informed about attack vectors, organizations can better protect their digital assets and ensure long-term security.

3.1 SOCIAL ENGINEERING

Social engineering is a manipulation technique that exploits human psychology rather than technical vulnerabilities. It aims to trick individuals into revealing confidential information or performing actions that compromise security by researching them and their vulnerabilities. It preys on humans' natural tendencies, such as trust, fear, and curiosity, to bypass security measures. Understanding what social engineering is and how it works helps in developing effective ways to implement solutions that would protect organizational assets. As shown in Figure 3.2, some common types of social engineering used by attackers are as follows.

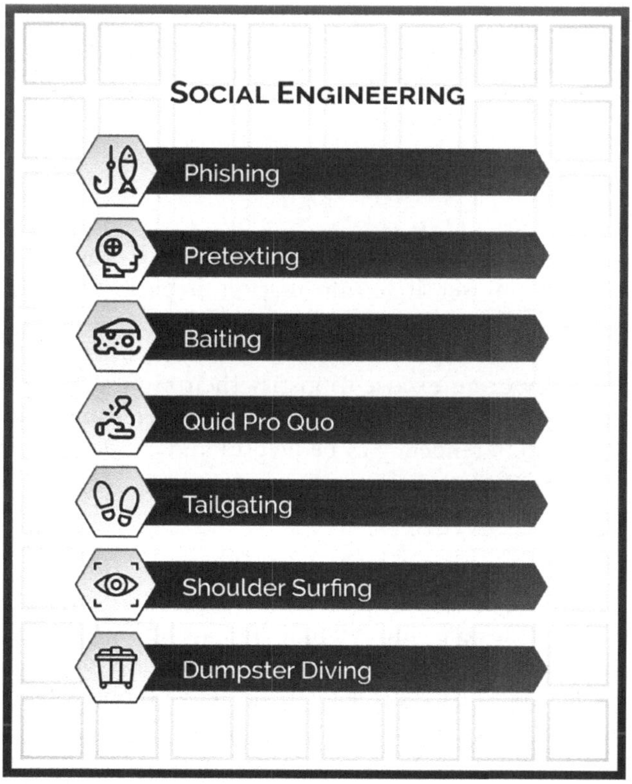

Figure 3.2 Common types of social engineering.

3.1.1 Phishing

This is the most common social engineering method that attackers use to obtain sensitive information from individuals or install malware on devices. Phishing is the act of sending deceptive emails or messages to trick people. There are many types of phishing, but email phishing is the most common type. Deceptive emails mimic legitimate companies or individuals to lure victims into clicking malicious links or attachments. Spear phishing is a more targeted form where attackers tailor their emails to specific individuals or groups. They often use personal information to make the message seem more convincing. Whaling is a high-profile type of spear phishing that targets executives or other high-ranking individuals within an organization.

When phishing attacks are conducted through SMS (Short Message Service) messages, it is called smishing. The messages often contain urgent or enticing content to trick victims into clicking on malicious links. Another type of phishing is vishing, in which attacks use phone calls or voice messages to manipulate victims into exposing personal information or performing actions that benefit the attacker. Angler phishing attacks occur on social media platforms, where attackers impersonate customer service representatives or offer fake deals to lure victims. Pharming is a more sophisticated attack that redirects users to fraudulent websites even when they type the correct address into their browser.

Phishing attacks are typically delivered through emails, text messages (smishing), or phone calls (vishing). The attacker crafts a message that appears to be from a legitimate source, such as a bank, social media platform, or government agency. This is the lure, where they get the attention of the target. The message urges the victim to take immediate action, such as clicking on a link or opening an attachment, to provide personal information. After this call to action, the payload (malicious code that performs the action) is delivered by clicking on the link or opening the attachment, often leading to a fake website designed to collect sensitive information or download malware onto the victim's device.

3.1.2 Pretexting

The act of pretexting is where an attacker creates a pretense or fabricated scenario to manipulate their target into exposing sensitive information or performing actions that compromise security. This deceptive strategy involves the attacker assuming a fake identity, often posing as someone in authority or a trusted individual, such as a service provider. They may invent a plausible story or an excuse to justify their request for information or access by exploiting the victim's trust and willingness to help. Pretexting can be highly effective because it leverages the human tendency to be helpful and cooperative, making individuals more vulnerable to manipulation.

3.1.3 Baiting

The act of baiting is a tactic used to lure victims into a trap by promising them something desirable. This could be a free gift or software download; the bait appeals to the victim's curiosity, greed, or other emotions. This leads them to click on a malicious link or open a compromised attachment, disclosing sensitive information.

Baiting can be used in online and offline scenarios, such as leaving infected USB drives in public places or sending phishing emails with enticing subject lines. The goal is to bypass security measures by exploiting the victim's eagerness to obtain the promised reward.

3.1.4 Quid pro quo

A Latin phrase meaning "something for something," quid pro quo is a social engineering tactic where an attacker offers a favor, service, or valuable information in exchange for something they desire. What they seek is often sensitive data or unauthorized access. Attackers create a sense of obligation in the victim, making them more likely to comply with their request. The exchange can be explicit or implicit, but the underlying principle is the same: The attacker leverages the victim's desire for reciprocity to manipulate him or her into compromising security.

3.1.5 Tailgating

Also known as piggybacking, tailgating is a social engineering technique where an unauthorized individual gains access to a restricted area by closely following an authorized person through a door, security checkpoint, or other controlled entry point. This can be done without the authorized person's knowledge or consent. The attacker may use a variety of tactics, such as pretending to be lost or distracted, holding a large package, or simply blending in with a group of people. Once inside the restricted area, the attacker can access sensitive information, systems, or physical assets.

3.1.6 Shoulder surfing

Another social engineering technique used to steal sensitive information like passwords, PINs, or credit card numbers by an attacker who secretly observes someone's screen or keypad, shoulder surfing can happen in public places like cafes, airports, or even offices, where people may be less vigilant about protecting their information. Attackers can simply glance over the victim's shoulder or use more sophisticated methods like hidden cameras or binoculars to capture the data. Shoulder surfing is a low-tech but effective way to steal information, relying on the victim's unawareness rather than technical vulnerabilities.

3.1.7 Dumpster diving

This deceptive act is when attackers rummage through an organization's or individual's trash to find discarded documents or materials containing sensitive information. This could include anything from financial records and customer data to passwords and network diagrams. By sifting through the garbage, attackers can piece together valuable information that can be used to launch further attacks, such as phishing scams, identity theft, or network intrusions. Dumpster diving is often overlooked as a low-tech threat, but it can be surprisingly effective in gaining unauthorized access to sensitive data.

3.1.8 How does social engineering work?

Attackers who use social engineering first research and gather information about their target, which could be as simple as their job title, interests, or social media activity. As depicted in Figure 3.3, using this information, they build trust and establish rapport with the target, impersonating a trusted authority figure or colleague. Using psychological tactics, the attacker manipulates the target's behavior, such as appealing to their emotions or creating a sense of urgency. The last step is exploitation, where the attacker convinces the target to reveal confidential information, click on a malicious link, or perform another action compromising security.

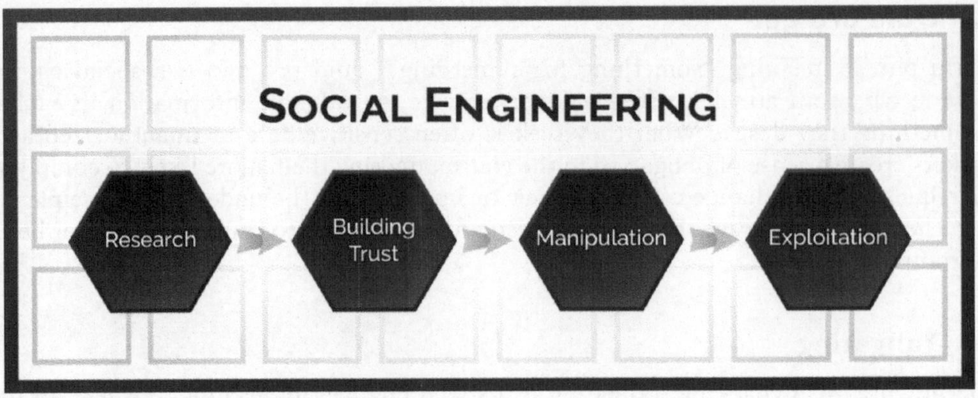

Figure 3.3 Technique of social engineering.

3.1.9 Cultural response to social engineering

A cultural response to social engineering within an organization involves fostering a security-conscious environment that can be achieved by employees being aware of potential social engineering threats and feeling responsible for maintaining security. This begins with regular training and awareness programs where the employees will be educated on recognizing and responding to various social engineering tactics. Knowing different types of social engineering tactics will make the employees more aware of the situation.

Encouraging open communication and transparent reporting mechanisms for suspicious activities empowers employees to act swiftly when they encounter potential threats. Implementing strict verification processes for sensitive information requests and emphasizing the importance of skepticism toward unsolicited communications further strengthens this culture. By promoting a sense of collective vigilance and accountability, organizations can build a resilient defense against the manipulative tactics of social engineering.

As employees acquire more knowledge, they will be more skeptical and will not trust unsolicited requests for personal information or urgent actions. They will need to verify the identity of anyone requesting sensitive information, even if they seem legitimate. They will be cautious of unsolicited offers and sharing data online and through social media. Trusting our instincts and saying no when we feel uncomfortable is the key to not falling into these traps. Reporting suspicious activity to the appropriate authorities must be encouraged.

3.2 INSIDER THREATS

An insider threat refers to a security risk that originates from within an organization. It involves a current or former employee, contractor, or business partner who misuses his or her legitimate access to harm the organization's systems, data, or reputation. Insider threats can be intentional (malicious) or unintentional (negligent), but the consequences can be equally devastating.

There are two types of insider threats; they can be both harmful, intentionally, and unintentionally.

3.2.1 Malicious insiders

These individuals intentionally abuse their access for personal gain, revenge, or ideological reasons. They might steal sensitive data, sabotage systems, or leak confidential information.

Some common motivations for malicious insiders are for financial gain. Selling stolen data, intellectual property, or trade secrets can bring large amounts of cash. Revenge can also be a motivating factor. This can be done by sabotaging systems or leaking information to harm the organization or specific individuals. Ideology can also be a factor. Exposing wrongdoing or promoting a political agenda can be a motivation. Espionage or providing sensitive information to a competitor or foreign government can also be a goal for a malicious insider.

3.2.2 Negligent insiders

These are individuals who unintentionally expose the organization to risk. This is usually due to carelessness, lack of awareness, or poor security practices. Negligent insider threats manifest in various scenarios. For instance, an employee might fall for a phishing scam, clicking on a link in an email that appears to be from the IT department, and providing their credentials on a fraudulent website. This can allow attackers to gain access to sensitive information, leading to data breaches or financial loss. Another example is when an employee misplaces sensitive documents, such as leaving confidential client files in a public area like a coffee shop or on public transportation, risking unauthorized access to critical information.

3.2.3 How do insider threats work?

Malicious or negligent, some telltale signs of activity are as follows. As depicted in Figure 3.4, first, there might be unusual or unauthorized access to sensitive data or systems. Second, there might be downloads or transfers of large amounts of data without a valid reason. Third, individuals working odd hours or accessing systems outside of regular business hours can be worrying. Fourth, exhibiting disgruntled behavior or making threats against the organization should not be taken lightly. Finally, financial difficulties or sudden lifestyle changes should be taken into consideration.

3.2.4 Cultural response to insider threats

Insider threats can be challenging to detect and prevent; however, a multilayered approach that combines technical controls, employee education, and vigilance can significantly reduce the risk.

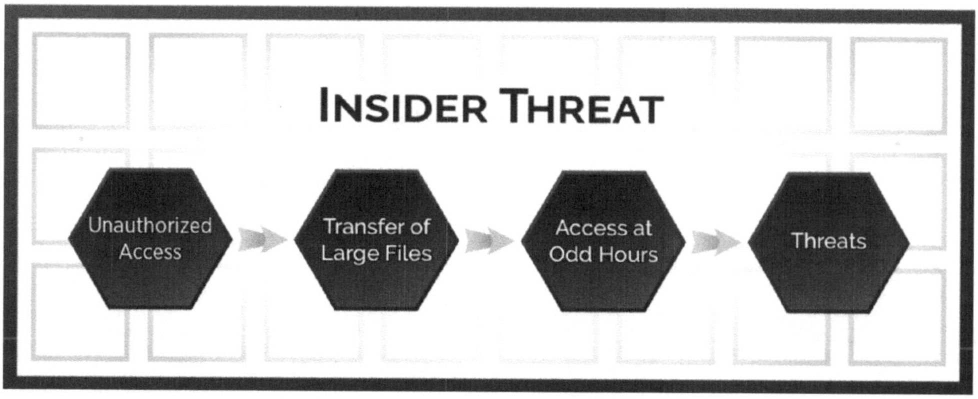

Figure 3.4 How insider threat works.

The following measures can help identify insider threats. Implementing strong access controls based on the principle of least privilege and granting employees only the access necessary to perform their job duties could be the first line of defense. Monitoring and logging user activity for suspicious behavior and maintaining detailed logs of system access and data transfers can identify when and where these activities occur. Regular security awareness training will help employees identify and report potential insider threats. Implementing Data Loss Prevention (DLP) solutions will detect and prevent unauthorized data exfiltration. Conducting thorough background checks on employees and contractors before granting them access to sensitive information would minimize the risk. Developing a comprehensive incident response plan to address insider threats quickly and effectively will help the organization have an immediate action plan.

3.3 MALWARE

Malware is short for "malicious software." It encompasses a wide range of harmful programs designed to infiltrate and disrupt computer systems, networks, or devices. It's a broad term that covers viruses, worms, Trojans, spyware, adware, and ransomware.

3.3.1 How does malware work?

Similar to phishing, as depicted in Figure 3.5, Malware infiltrates a system by clicking on malicious links, opening infected attachments, or exploiting software vulnerabilities. After the infection takes place, and once inside the system, the malware executes its malicious code. Depending on the type and purpose of this code, the malware becomes active in the system. The malware's payload is the action it performs once it has infected the system. This can include stealing sensitive data, encrypting files, disrupting operations, displaying unwanted ads, or installing additional malware. Some malware can also spread to other systems or devices. This can happen either by self-replication or by exploiting vulnerabilities in network connections.

3.3.2 Cultural response to malware

It is easy to take precautions against malware. The organizational policy on software updates should mandate regular updates of your operating system, browser, and antivirus

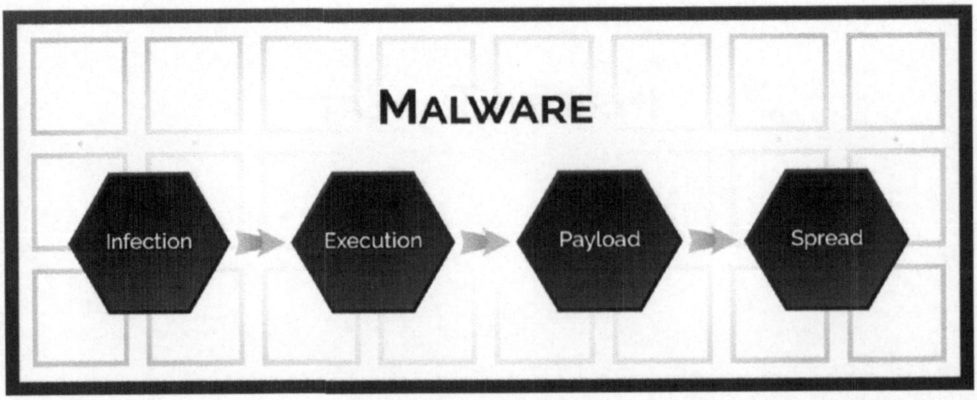

Figure 3.5 How malware works.

software to patch security vulnerabilities. Installing reputable antivirus and anti-malware software and keeping it updated should eliminate the problem. Employees should be warned and trained to be cautious about downloads and links. Consistently remind personnel to avoid clicking on suspicious links or opening attachments from unknown sources. Systems should be backed up regularly. Important files should be backed up and stored offline or in a secure cloud location. Employees should be educated about the latest malware threats and trained on how to recognize and avoid them.

3.4 RANSOMWARE

Ransomware is a specific type of malware that encrypts a victim's files or locks them out of their entire system, demanding a ransom payment to restore access. It has become a significant threat to individuals, businesses, and organizations worldwide.

3.4.1 How does ransomware work?

Ransomware often spreads through phishing emails, malicious attachments, or drive-by downloads from compromised websites. After the suspicious file has been opened, and once the ransomware is installed, the ransomware encrypts the victim's files, making them inaccessible as shown in the beginning of Figure 3.6. The attacker displays a message demanding payment, usually in cryptocurrency, to decrypt the files. Attackers often use scare tactics and time pressure to coerce victims into paying the ransom. If the victim pays the ransom, the attacker may (or may not) provide a decryption key to unlock the files.

3.4.2 Cultural response to ransomware

The same responses as in malware apply to this type of threat. Regular software updates for the operating systems, browsers, and antivirus software to patch security vulnerabilities should be regularly performed. Employees should be warned and trained to be cautious about downloads and links, as well as consistently reminded to avoid clicking on suspicious links or opening attachments from unknown sources. Again, systems should be backed up regularly, and important files should be backed up and stored offline or in a secure cloud location. Employees should be educated about the latest malware threats and trained on

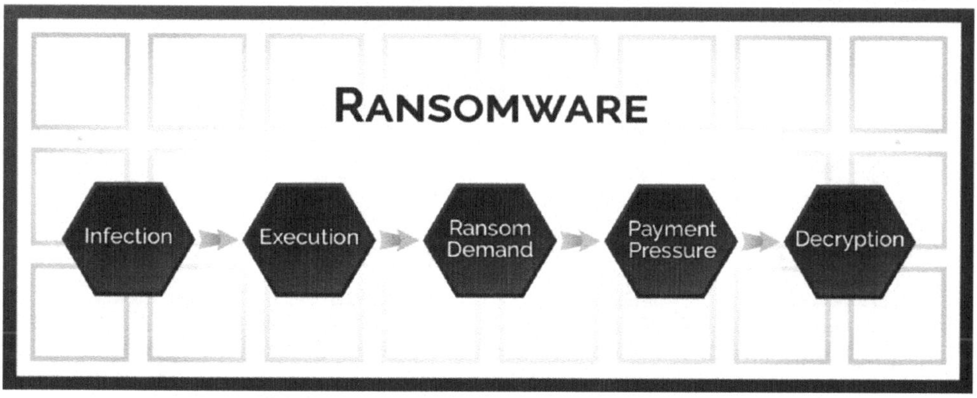

Figure 3.6 How ransomware works.

how to recognize and avoid them. One additional concern with ransomware is that paying ransom does not guarantee that the files will be decrypted. Paying the ransom may encourage further attacks.

3.5 ZERO-DAY EXPLOITS

A zero-day exploit is a cyberattack that targets a software vulnerability unknown to the software vendor or security researchers. The term "zero-day" refers to the fact that the developers have zero days to patch the vulnerability since it's already being exploited by attackers. There are three characteristics of zero-day exploits. First, these are unknown vulnerabilities. The vendor is unaware of this vulnerability, so there is no patch. Second, they are high-impact attacks with devastating effects because there is no fix. These attacks can be in the form of data breaches, system takeovers, and widespread malware distribution. Finally, they are stealthy. They are often used in highly targeted attacks, making them difficult to detect. Zero-day exploits represent a significant challenge to any organization due to their unknown nature and lack of immediate remedies.

3.5.1 How do zero-day exploits work?

Once a threat actor discovers a software vulnerability, as depicted in Figure 3.7, they create code (an exploit) to exploit it. They use this exploit to gain unauthorized access to systems, steal data, or disrupt operations. When the vulnerability is publicly disclosed, the software vendor rushes to develop a patch to fix it; however, until the patch is released and applied, systems remain vulnerable.

3.5.2 Cultural response to zero-day exploits

Since threat actors exploit a vulnerability unknown to the vendor, it is one of the most difficult problems to fix; however, a couple of effective ways exist to deal with it. One way to minimize the risk is patch management. Applying security patches promptly to close known vulnerabilities might reduce the vulnerability. Deploying emergency patches quickly when zero-day vulnerabilities are discovered will help remedy the situation. Intrusion Detection

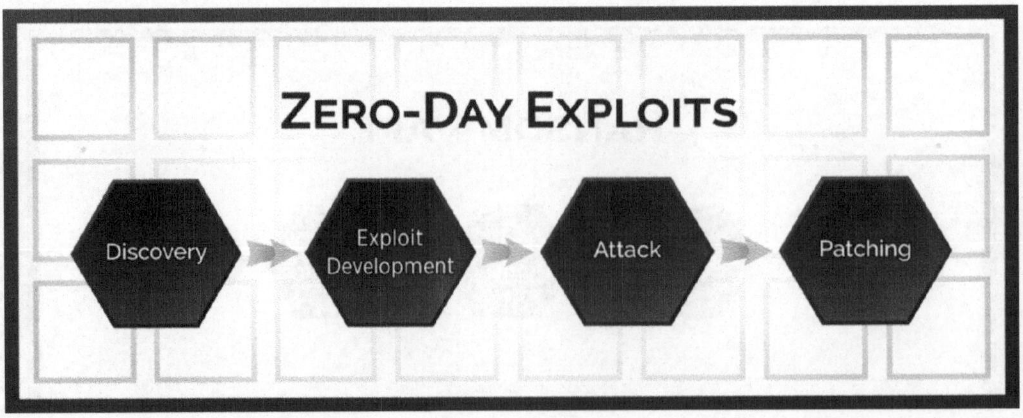

Figure 3.7 How zero-day exploit works.

and Prevention Systems (IDPS) to detect and block suspicious activity can be helpful, even if it doesn't match known attack patterns. Security Information and Event Management (SIEM) systems can help collect and analyze security logs for early signs of compromise. Threat intelligence can help us stay informed about emerging threats and vulnerabilities through feeds and security advisories. Implementing multiple layers of security to create a defense-in-depth strategy, including firewalls, antivirus software, intrusion detection, and employee training, can be another way to minimize the problem.

3.6 SUPPLY CHAIN ATTACKS

A supply chain attack is a cyberattack that targets an organization indirectly by compromising elements within its supply chain. This can involve targeting suppliers, vendors, or other third-party partners who provide the organization with software, hardware, or services. This is a growing concern in the threat landscape because they exploit organizations' trust in their suppliers and partners. It is also important because their impact is widespread and can affect several organizations that use the products. The supply chain attacks can remain dormant for extended periods, making them hard to identify and remove.

There are three types of supply chain attacks:

1. **Software Supply Chain Attacks** are where the malware is inserted into software updates or installations, infecting the target organization's systems.
2. **Hardware Supply Chain Attacks** are where malicious components are embedded in hardware during manufacturing, compromising the target organization's devices.
3. **Third-Party Vendor Attacks** represent a compromise for third-party vendors to gain access to the target organizations' systems or data.

3.6.1 How do supply chain attacks work?

These attacks, often involve inserting malicious code or malware into legitimate software or hardware during the manufacturing or distribution process. The compromised product, as the process is depicted in Figure 3.8, is then delivered to the target organization, where it can wreak havoc once installed or activated.

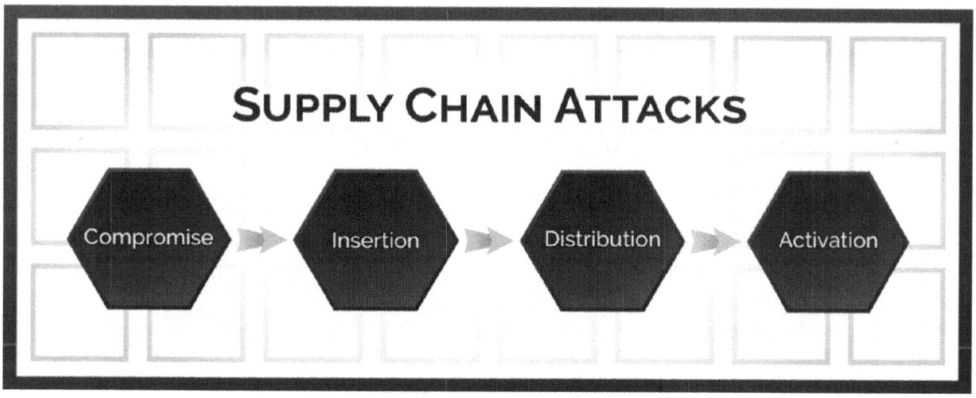

Figure 3.8 How supply chain attack works.

3.6.2 Cultural response to supply chain attacks

Organizations can take action against supply chain attacks in a couple of ways. One way is to have a vendor risk management plan. It is of utmost importance to carefully assess and monitor the security practices of your suppliers and vendors. Implementing secure software development practices will help enforce robust code and encourage regular software and hardware security reviews. Organizations can stay informed about the latest supply chain threats and vulnerabilities by practicing threat intelligence. IDPS can help monitor for suspicious activity and block potential attacks. Creating Incident Response Plans can help address supply chain attacks quickly and effectively.

3.7 DENIAL OF SERVICE (DoS)

A Denial of Service (DoS) attack is a malicious attempt to make a machine or network resource unavailable to its intended users by temporarily or indefinitely disrupting its services. It achieves this by flooding the target with an overwhelming amount of traffic or requests, exceeding its capacity to handle them. When multiple systems are used to launch a coordinated DoS attack, it becomes a Distributed Denial of Service (DDoS) attack. These attacks can be highly disruptive, causing significant downtime, financial losses, and reputational damage.

Depending on the targets, there are several types of DoS attacks. Volumetric attacks flood the target with a large volume of traffic, consuming bandwidth and overwhelming resources. Protocol attacks exploit vulnerabilities in network protocols to disrupt communication or consume resources. The third type, application layer attacks, targets specific applications or services running on the target system, such as web servers or databases.

3.7.1 How does DoS work?

DoS attacks start with the selection of the target. This can be a website, server, or network. As the technique is described in Figure 3.9, the attackers then send a massive amount of traffic to the target from a single source. This traffic can be in the form of requests for data, connection attempts, or malformed packets designed to consume resources. The targeted system becomes overwhelmed and unable to process legitimate user requests, resulting in service denial. This can manifest as slow performance, errors, or complete unavailability.

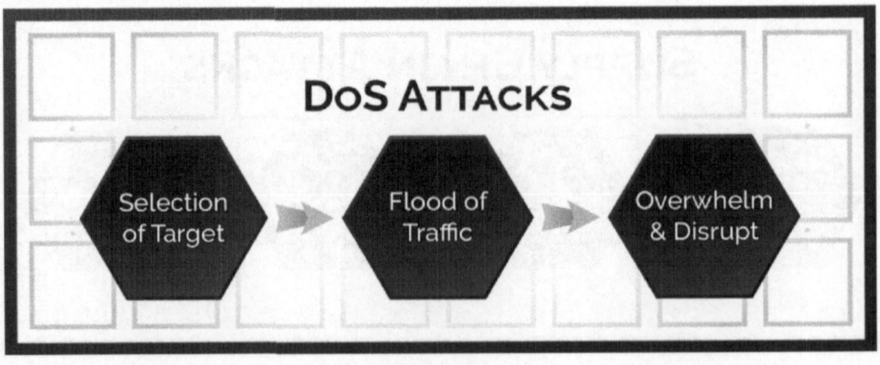

Figure 3.9 How DoS attack works.

3.7.2 Cultural response to DoS

Organizations can take several steps to prevent DoS attacks. The first line of defense is filtering traffic, which can be done by implementing firewalls and intrusion prevention systems (IPS) to detect malicious activity and block attacks. Rate limiting can also be applied, which limits incoming traffic so that a single source will not overwhelm the system. Load balancing can distribute traffic across multiple servers to prevent any single server from overloading. Cloud-based DDoS protection can absorb and filter large volumes of traffic before it reaches your network. A solid Incident Response Plan in place can help tremendously to quickly detect and respond to DoS and DDoS attacks.

3.8 WEB APPLICATION ATTACKS

Web application attacks exploit vulnerabilities in web applications, software that runs on web servers and is accessible through a web browser. These attacks can lead to data breaches, unauthorized access, system compromise, and financial losses. Web applications like online banking portals, e-commerce sites, and social media platforms are essential for businesses. The attackers gain unauthorized access, steal sensitive data, or disrupt operations. These types of attacks pose a significant risk to organizations of all sizes, making it crucial to understand the different types of attacks and implement adequate security measures.

There are many types of web application attacks. Understanding each type can provide the knowledge needed to prevent them. For example, in injection attacks, such as SQL injection, malicious code is injected into input fields or parameters, allowing it to manipulate the application's behavior or access sensitive data. In broken authentication, attackers can exploit weak passwords, session management flaws, or insecure login processes to gain unauthorized access to user accounts.

3.8.1 How do web application attacks work?

The attacker's first goal is to identify a potential web application as a target, as depicted in Figure 3.10. He or she can use automated tools to scan for vulnerabilities or manually explore the application's features to find weaknesses. Once the vulnerability is discovered, the attacker investigates further to confirm its existence and understand its potential impact. Once the existence is confirmed and the potential impact is determined, the attacker

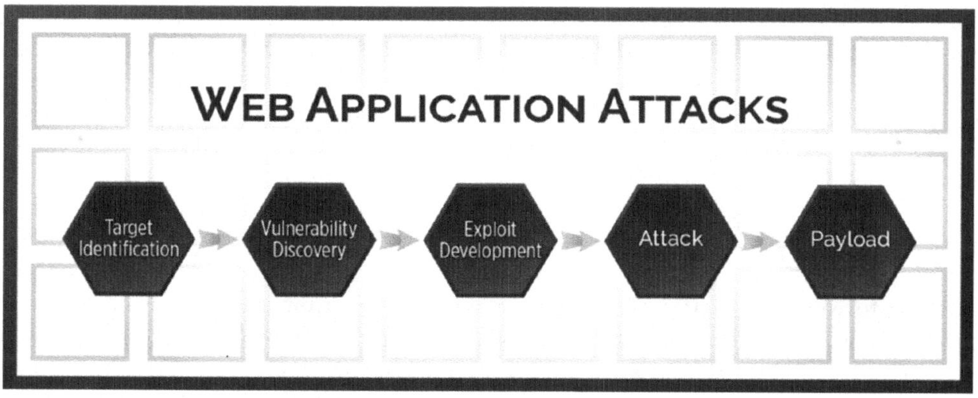

Figure 3.10 How web application attacks work.

develops the type of exploit to be used. This can be a code or a sequence of actions that leverage the vulnerability to achieve the attacker's goal. Once the attack is executed, the exploit against the web application is launched. This could involve sending malicious input to the application, manipulating parameters in requests, or injecting malicious code into the application's data. If the exploit is successful, the attacker's payload is delivered. The payload is the malicious code that carries out the attacker's intended actions, such as stealing data, modifying content, or disrupting the application. The impact of the attack depends on the nature of the vulnerability and the attacker's goals. It could range from minor data leakage to a complete system compromise.

3.8.2 Cultural response to web application attacks

Web application attacks trigger a range of cultural responses within an organization and in society at large. The responses can be categorized under five domains.

First is the awareness and education domain. At the company level, it is imperative to invest more in cybersecurity awareness training for employees, educating them about the risks of web application attacks and how to identify and report suspicious activity. At the public level, there is a growing awareness among individuals about the importance of online security. Users are aware of the need to be cautious when interacting with websites and online services; however, there is an increased demand for information and resources on how to protect oneself from cyber threats. The organizational response should be providing adequate education and training, not only at the organizational level but also at the public level for their clients.

The second domain is the shift in organizational culture. As mentioned in the first chapter, the concept of organizational culture must change. A "security first" mindset, where security considerations are integrated into every stage of web application development and deployment, should be emphasized at all levels of the organization.

The third domain is technological advancements. The organization should be up-to-date on what current technologies are available. For example, web application firewalls (WAFs) can filter and monitor web traffic to protect against attacks and have become more widespread. Organizations widely use automated security testing. These automated tools scan web applications for vulnerabilities and identify potential attack vectors. Threat intelligence sharing is a growing trend. Threat intelligence is shared between organizations and security communities to stay ahead of emerging threats and vulnerabilities, which can work for all to eliminate attacks.

The fourth domain is the regulatory and legal framework. Data protection guidelines set by governments expose stricter data protection regulations, which require organizations to implement strong security measures to protect personal data. Cybersecurity insurance has grown, incentivizing organizations to adopt more robust security practices to qualify for coverage. Organizations can face consequences if they fail to adequately protect their web applications from attacks, resulting in legal action and financial penalties.

Finally, the fifth domain is public discourse and media attention. Increased media coverage of web application attacks often raises public awareness and puts pressure on organizations to improve their security practices. Cybersecurity advocacy is growing, and organizations are pushing for stronger security standards and better consumer protection.

In conclusion, the cultural response to web application attacks is evolving toward a more proactive and comprehensive approach to cybersecurity. Organizations recognize the importance of building a strong security culture, investing in technology and training, and collaborating to combat the ever-changing threat landscape.

3.9 CONCLUSION

This chapter discussed the multifaceted nature of the cybersecurity threat landscape. Understanding this landscape is paramount for fostering a robust cybersecurity culture within organizations. Anticipating, preparing for, and mitigating potential security risks ultimately reduces the likelihood and impact of security incidents.

A key takeaway is the dynamic nature of cyber threats. This necessitates continuous vigilance and adaptation. Organizations must prioritize their security efforts, allocate resources effectively, and develop comprehensive cybersecurity strategies. Their efforts must include continuous education, firm policies, advanced technological defenses, and a proactive mindset.

By categorizing and understanding different types of threats, from phishing and social engineering to insider threats and ransomware, organizations can better respond to challenges; moreover, the cultural response to these threats is critical. Building a security-conscious environment through regular training, fostering a sense of responsibility, and encouraging vigilance can significantly enhance an organization's resilience against cyber threats. As the threat landscape continues to evolve, organizations must remain agile, informed, and proactive in their cybersecurity efforts, ensuring the protection of their digital assets.

In conclusion, navigating the cybersecurity threat landscape requires a holistic and dynamic approach. Organizations can better protect themselves in an increasingly hostile digital world by understanding the threat landscape and fostering a strong cybersecurity culture.

DISCUSSION QUESTIONS

1. What are the key characteristics that distinguish social engineering attacks from other types of cyber threats?
2. How can an organization foster a culture that effectively mitigates insider threats?
3. Discuss the impact of ransomware attacks on both small and large organizations. How should the cultural response differ in these cases?
4. Why are zero-day exploits particularly challenging for organizations to defend against, and how can they prepare for these types of threats?
5. In what ways can organizations ensure the security of their supply chains, especially when dealing with third-party vendors?
6. Explain how Denial of Service (DoS) attacks can affect an organization's operations and reputation. What steps can be taken to prevent and mitigate such attacks?
7. What are the most common vulnerabilities exploited in web application attacks, and how can organizations better protect against them?
8. How can continuous education and awareness programs contribute to a stronger cybersecurity culture within an organization?
9. Discuss the role of leadership in creating and maintaining a cybersecurity culture that is responsive to the evolving threat landscape.
10. How do technological advancements, such as AI and machine learning, influence the way organizations detect and respond to cyber threats?

BIBLIOGRAPHY

Afolabi, J. (2022, July 16). What is baiting in cybersecurity? Techniques, examples, protection. *EasyDMARC*. https://easydmarc.com/blog/what-is-baiting-in-cybersecurity-techniques-examples-protection/

Alabdan, R. (2020). Phishing attacks survey: Types, vectors, and technical approaches. *Future Internet*, *12*(10), 168. https://doi.org/10.3390/fi12100168

Baki, S., & Verma, R. M. (2023). Sixteen years of phishing user studies: What have we learned? *IEEE Transactions on Dependable and Secure Computing*, *20*(2), 1200–1212. https://doi.org/10.1109/TDSC.2022.3151103

Biju, J. M., Gopal, N., & Prakash, A. J. (2019). Cyber attacks and its different types. *International Research Journal of Engineering and Technology*, *6*(3), 4849–4852.

Cybersecurity and Infrastructure Security Agency. (2020, November). Insider threat mitigation guide. https://www.cisa.gov/sites/default/files/2022-11/Insider%20Threat%20Mitigation%20Guide_Final_508.pdf

Cybersecurity and Infrastructure Security Agency. (2021, February 1). *Understanding denial-of-service attacks*. CISA. https://www.cisa.gov/news-events/news/understanding-denial-service-attacks

Diogenes, Y., & Ozkaya, E. (2018). *Cybersecurity – Attack and defense strategies*. Packt Publishing.

Guembe, B., Azeta, A., Misra, S., Osamor, V. C., Fernandez-Sanz, L., & Pospelova, V. (2022). The emerging threat of AI-driven cyber attacks: A review. *Applied Artificial Intelligence*, *36*(1), 1–34. https://doi.org/10.1080/08839514.2022.2037254

Gururaj, H. L., Janhavi, V., & Ambika, V. (Eds.). (2024). *Social engineering in cybersecurity: Threats and defenses* (1st ed.). CRC Press. https://doi.org/10.1201/9781003406716

Hama Saeed, M. A. (2020). Malware in computer systems: Problems and solutions. *IJID (International Journal on Informatics for Development)*, *9*(1), 1–8. https://doi.org/10.14421/ijid.2020.09101

Hermans, K. (2023). *Cyber Security for Beginners A comprehensive guide to learn the basics of cyber security and prepare for a career in cybersecurity*. Cybellium Ltd.

Hon, K. W. (2024). Attack vectors. In *Technology and security for lawyers and other professionals* (pp. 158–180). Edward Elgar Publishing. https://doi.org/10.4337/9781803923918.00018

Khachunts, H. (2022, July 10). What is a quid pro quo attack? *EasyDMARC*. https://easydmarc.com/blog/what-is-quid-pro-quo/

Martínez, J., & Durán, J. M. (2021). Software supply chain attacks, a threat to global cybersecurity: SolarWinds' case study. *International Journal of Safety and Security Engineering*, *11*(5), 537–545. https://doi.org/10.18280/ijsse.110505

Shahbaznezhad, H., Kolini, F., & Rashidirad, M. (2020). Employees' behavior in phishing attacks: What individual, organizational, and technological factors matter? *Journal of Computer Information Systems*, *61*(6), 539–550. https://doi.org/10.1080/08874417.2020.1812134

Sonowal, G. (2022). *Phishing and communication channels: A guide to identifying and mitigating phishing attacks*. Apress.

Subbalakshmi, C., Pareek, P. K., & Sayal, R. (2022). A study on social engineering attacks in cybersecurity. In H. S. Saini, R. Sayal, A. Govardhan, R. Buyya (Eds.), *Innovations in computer science and engineering. Lecture notes in networks and systems*, vol 385. Springer. https://doi.org/10.1007/978-981-16-8987-1_7

Unic, V. (2023, May 10). 8 types of web application attacks and protecting your organization. Bright. https://brightsec.com/blog/8-types-of-web-application-attacks-and-protecting-your-organization/

Wang, Z., Sun, L., & Zhu, H. (2020). Defining social engineering in cybersecurity. *IEEE Access*, *8*, 85094–85115. https://doi.org/10.1109/ACCESS.2020.2992112

Chapter 4

Attack surfaces and vulnerabilities

Learning about these attack surfaces shown in Figure 4.1 and vulnerabilities provides insights into how these weaknesses can be exploited and can lead to valuable measures to mitigate them. It's important to remember that understanding attack surfaces and vulnerabilities is not just a technical necessity but also a crucial component of fostering a healthy cybersecurity culture within organizations. A cybersecurity culture is formed by the shared attitudes, beliefs, and practices that safeguard an organization's digital assets. Understanding how vulnerabilities and attack surfaces influence this culture is crucial for fostering awareness and encouraging proactive behavior and continuous improvement—all vital components of a strong cybersecurity posture.

To mitigate risks effectively, it's crucial to investigate specific vulnerabilities that can significantly impact an organization's security. This chapter will delve deeper into these vulnerabilities and examine real-world examples, their causes, the risks they pose to organizations, and how organizational culture should respond to them. Figure 4.2 displays the attack surfaces discussed in this chapter.

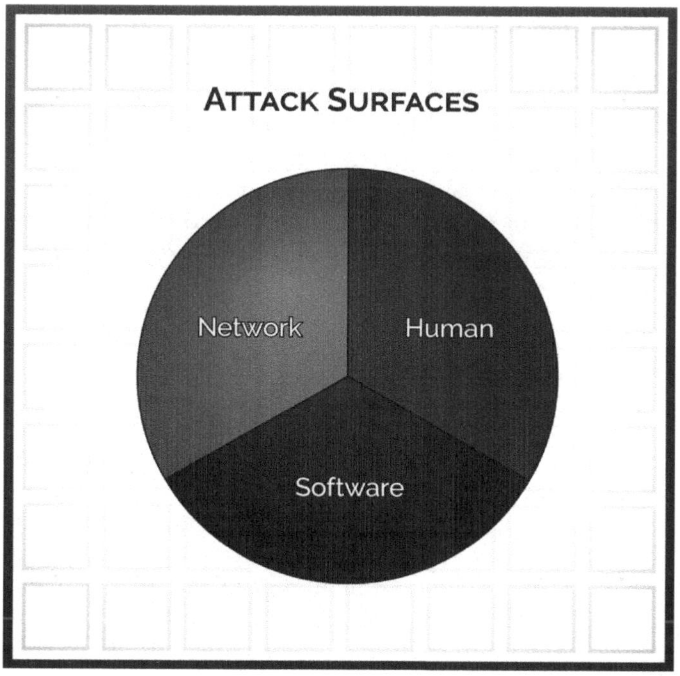

Figure 4.1 Three main types of attack surfaces.

DOI: 10.1201/9781003368496-4

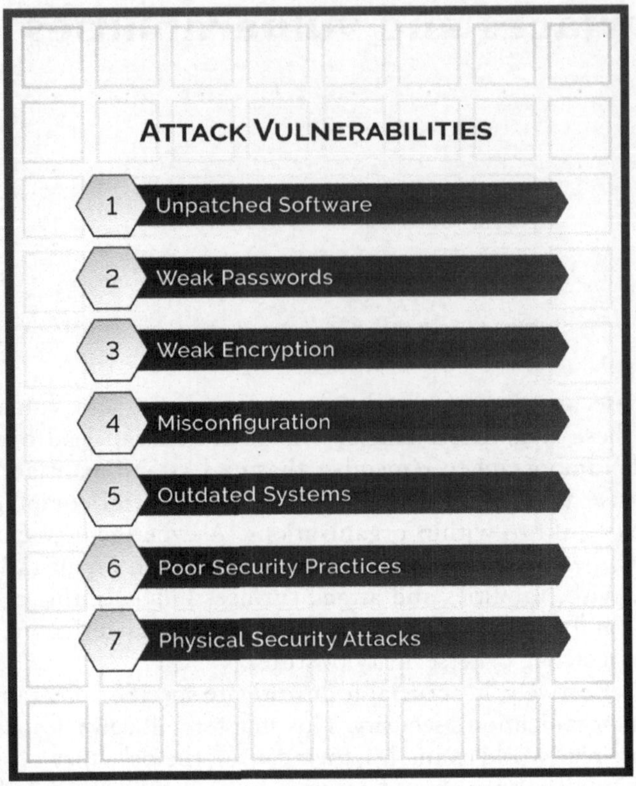

Figure 4.2 Attack vulnerabilities.

4.1 UNPATCHED SOFTWARE

Unpatched software is one of the most dangerous vulnerabilities organizations face. Even though there are significant advancements in technology and increasing awareness of cyber threats, many organizations still struggle with maintaining up-to-date software. Unpatched software refers to applications or systems that have not been updated with the latest security patches provided by the software vendor. The vendor releases these patches to correct security flaws, fix bugs, and enhance functionality. When software remains unpatched, systems are vulnerable to exploits that could compromise data integrity, confidentiality, and availability.

4.1.1 Real-world examples

There are two significant examples of this type of attack: the Equifax Data Breach (2017) and the WannaCry Ransomware Attack (2017). There are also many recent ones, but these two are the best examples of their kind.

The Equifax Data Breach of 2017 was one of the best examples of the dangers of unpatched software. Equifax is one of the largest credit reporting agencies in the United States. It suffered a massive breach due to a known vulnerability in the Apache Struts web application framework. Despite the availability of a patch, Equifax failed to apply it. This resulted in the compromise of the personal information of approximately 147 million individuals. The breach led to significant financial losses, legal consequences, and a severe blow to the company's reputation.

The WannaCry Ransomware Attack in 2017 exploited a vulnerability in Microsoft Windows systems. The ransomware spread rapidly across the globe, affecting hundreds of thousands of computers in over 150 countries. Organizations such as the UK's National Health Service (NHS) were severely impacted. Microsoft had patched the vulnerability months before the attack, but many organizations had not applied the update.

4.1.2 Causes of unpatched software

There are numerous reasons for unpatched software. Many organizations, especially small- to medium-sized businesses, may lack the necessary resources to consistently update their software. They might lack time, money, or skilled personnel. They might not have dedicated IT staff to manage updates, leading to delayed or missed patches. Testing and applying patches can be challenging and time-consuming in larger organizations with complex IT environments and numerous interconnected systems and applications. Compatibility concerns can be a third cause. Organizations may hesitate to apply patches due to fears that updates could disrupt critical business operations. Some patches might cause compatibility issues with other software or custom applications, leading to operational disruptions. Finally, lack of awareness can be a fatal cause. Some organizations simply might not be aware of the available patches and the severity of the vulnerabilities they address. This lack of awareness can stem from inadequate communication channels within the organization or insufficient cybersecurity training.

4.1.3 Risks posed by unpatched software

There are many risks associated with unpatched software. These can be categorized under increased attack surfaces, data breaches, financial losses, and operational disruptions.

Unpatched software creates entry points for attackers to exploit known vulnerabilities, creating increased attack surfaces. Cybercriminals actively scan for systems with known vulnerabilities, and unpatched software is an easy target. Once the unpatched software is exploited, it can lead to significant data breaches. These breaches expose sensitive information such as personal data, financial records, and intellectual property as we saw in the Equifax breach in 2017.

Cyberattacks resulting from unpatched software can lead to substantial financial losses. These can include costs related to incident response, legal fees, regulatory fines, and lost business due to reputational damage. Attacks like ransomware can cripple an organization's operations by encrypting critical data and systems, demanding a ransom for their release. The WannaCry attack, which exploited a vulnerability in Windows systems, disrupted services in over 150 countries, including critical sectors like healthcare.

4.1.4 Cultural response

Unpatched software represents a significant risk and reflects a broader issue within cybersecurity culture: the importance of vigilance and responsibility. When organizations neglect to apply software patches, they disregard proactive security measures. A culture that prioritizes regular patch management and recognizes the critical role of updates in protecting systems demonstrates a commitment to cybersecurity. This proactive stance can be instilled through continuous education and clear communication about the potential consequences of leaving vulnerabilities unaddressed.

Implementing robust policies and procedures for patch management is critical. This includes establishing a regular schedule for applying patches, prioritizing updates based on the severity of vulnerabilities, and ensuring that all systems, including those not directly managed by IT, are included in the patch management process. Automated patch management solutions can streamline the process, ensuring that patches are applied promptly and consistently. Automated systems can also help monitor and report on the status of updates, which will show compliance with patch management policies. Recognizing and rewarding proactive behavior reinforces the importance of vigilance.

Regular cybersecurity drills and simulations can help prepare employees for real-world scenarios and reinforce the importance of staying updated with patches. When top management actively supports and participates in cybersecurity initiatives, it sends a strong message about the organization's commitment to security. Implementing incentive programs for departments or individuals who consistently comply with cybersecurity best practices, including patch management, can motivate adherence.

By fostering a culture that emphasizes the critical nature of patch management, organizations can significantly reduce their risk of cyberattacks. They will ensure their data and systems' integrity, confidentiality, and availability.

4.2 WEAK PASSWORDS

Passwords serve as the first line of defense against unauthorized access to personal and organizational data. They remain a significant vulnerability in cybersecurity. Despite the increasing sophistication of cyber threats, many users continue to use simple, easily guessable passwords, putting themselves and their organizations at risk.

Weak passwords are easily exploitable vulnerabilities in cybersecurity. Many users opt for simple passwords that are easy to remember, such as "123456" or "password," which attackers can quickly guess. Additionally, reusing passwords across multiple accounts intensifies the risk, as a breach of one account can lead to compromised credentials for others. To strengthen password security, organizations should enforce policies that require the use of complex passwords combining letters, numbers, and special characters. Implementing multifactor authentication (MFA) adds an additional layer of security, requiring users to verify their identity through multiple means before gaining access to sensitive information.

As an alternative to traditional passwords, biometrics offer a more secure and user-friendly approach to authentication. Biometrics are unique physical characteristics that can be used to verify an individual's identity, such as a fingerprint or facial recognition. They provide an additional layer of security that is not easily compromised, making them a powerful tool in the fight against weak password practices.

4.2.1 Real-world examples

There are many incidents related to and caused by weak password practices. The two important ones we will cover are the Zoom Credential Stuffing Attack of 2020 and the Colonial Pipeline Ransomware Attack of 2021.

In early 2020, Zoom experienced a significant user surge due to the COVID-19 pandemic, as remote work and virtual meetings became the norm; however, the platform faced a credential stuffing attack, which exploited weak password practices among its users. Credential stuffing is a type of cyberattack where attackers use automated tools to input large volumes of username-password pairs, often obtained from previous data breaches, into a target website's login page. Many Zoom users reused passwords that had already been compromised in other breaches. Because of this, attackers could easily access Zoom accounts by inputting these known credentials. Users' reliance on simple and reused passwords made them vulnerable to this attack.

The impact of the attack was significant. It resulted in unauthorized access to Zoom accounts and potentially exposing private meetings, recorded sessions, and personal information. This raised privacy concerns as sensitive meetings, including corporate discussions and private communications, were at risk of being accessed by unauthorized individuals. Additionally, the attack led to a loss of trust in Zoom's security measures, prompting widespread concern among users about the safety of their information.

In May 2021, Colonial Pipeline, one of the largest fuel pipelines in the United States, was targeted by a ransomware attack. This forced the company to shut down its operations and led to significant fuel shortages and disruptions across the eastern United States. The attack was attributed to the DarkSide ransomware group. The attackers gained access to Colonial Pipeline's network through a compromised Virtual Private Network (VPN) account. This account used a weak password and did not employ multifactor authentication, making it an easy target for cybercriminals. Once inside the network, the attackers deployed ransomware that encrypted critical data and demanded a ransom payment to restore access. The impact of the attack was severe, causing operational disruption, financial loss, and regulatory scrutiny. The pipeline shutdown led to widespread fuel shortages, affecting transportation and causing economic disruption. Colonial Pipeline paid the attackers a ransom of approximately $4.4 million in Bitcoin to regain access to their data, although not all data was fully restored. The attack also drew attention from federal regulators, leading to increased scrutiny of cybersecurity practices within critical infrastructure sectors.

4.2.2 Causes of weak passwords

There are several causes of weak passwords. First and most important is the lack of awareness and education. Many users are not educated about the importance of strong passwords. They often resort to easy-to-remember passwords, which are easily guessable and can be a reason for vulnerability.

Second, convenience causes weak passwords. Simple, easy-to-remember passwords are convenient for users to remember and use. When we select a simple password, such as "123456," there will be no effort on the user's end to remember it. These guessable passwords can easily give attackers unauthorized access.

Third, reusing passwords causes weak passwords. This also stems from convenience. Every three months, the user does not have to change his or her password or use a very similar one to the one previously used. However, this can lead to vulnerabilities.

Fourth, a lack of policy enforcement can stem from the organization's emphasis on security. Without policies that require the user to select complex passwords, regularly change passwords, and prevent reusing them, the user will fall back on weaker passwords.

Finally, not changing the weak default password causes weak passwords. Most software and devices come with default passwords such as "Admin" or "password." If these passwords are not changed, attackers can easily access the system.

If the causes of weak password practices are not addressed, the organization will be exposed to the risks covered in the next section.

4.2.3 Risks posed by weak passwords

Weak passwords have consequences for both individuals and organizations. Figure 4.3 shows eight significant risks that weak passwords could expose organizations and individuals to. These are unauthorized access, data breaches, financial loss, reputational damage,

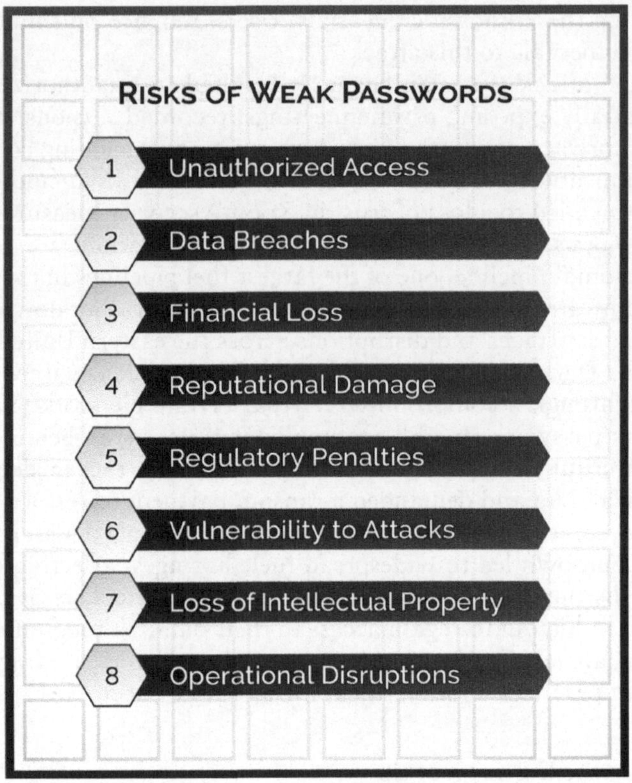

Figure 4.3 Eight risks of weak passwords.

regulatory penalties, increased vulnerability to further attacks, loss of intellectual property, and operational disruption.

For example, weak passwords can be easily guessed using social engineering techniques, and once the attacker gains access, he or she can access sensitive information. This can be sold on the dark web or used for identity theft. Data breaches can result in losing proprietary information, customer data, and trade secrets. Unauthorized access can also result in unauthorized transactions, purchases, or bank transfers. For businesses, the financial implications can be even more severe, including theft of funds, disruption of operations, and costly legal fees. These financial implications can lead to reputational damage. Customers' and partners' loss of trust can have devastating results on a business, not to mention negative media coverage.

As mentioned earlier, addressing the risks of weak passwords requires a multifaceted approach that includes user education, strong password policy implementation, and advanced security measures such as multifactor authentication. By recognizing and mitigating these risks, organizations can enhance their overall security posture and protect against potential threats.

4.2.4 Cultural response

Weak password use is a direct result of the inefficiency of the cybersecurity culture within an organization. If employees consistently use simple or reused passwords, it suggests a lack of awareness and training regarding the importance of strong authentication practices.

Cultivating a cybersecurity culture that emphasizes the creation and use of strong, unique passwords requires regular training sessions and the implementation of password policies. Multifactor authentication (MFA) should be promoted not just as a policy but as a norm within the organization. By doing so, employees will understand their critical role in safeguarding sensitive information.

4.3 WEAK ENCRYPTION

Encryption protects sensitive information by converting it into an unreadable format that can only be deciphered with the appropriate decryption key; however, not all encryption methods provide the same level of security. Weak encryption refers to methods that are easily breakable or outdated. This leaves data vulnerable to interception and unauthorized access. Understanding what constitutes weak encryption and its associated risks is essential for maintaining robust data security. Outdated algorithms, short key lengths, poor implementation, and a lack of complexity are the primary culprits behind this weakness. Algorithms that were once considered secure are now easily bypassed due to advancements in computing power. Similarly, short key lengths offer minimal protection as modern computers can quickly brute force them. Poor implementation of even strong cryptographic systems can introduce vulnerabilities that attackers can exploit. Finally, a lack of complexity in a system makes it a simpler target for attackers, as there are fewer obstacles to overcome. Additionally, organizations must ensure that encryption keys are securely managed and regularly updated to prevent unauthorized decryption.

4.3.1 Real-world examples

There are many examples of weak encryption causing data breaches. Two notable ones are the Marine Corps data breach (2018) and the Accellion data breach (2020–2021).

In 2018, the US Marine Corps suffered a data breach that exposed the personal information of over 20,000 people, including current and former Marines and their family members. The breach occurred due to the use of unencrypted email to send sensitive personal information, including social security numbers, dates of birth, and contact information. This incident highlighted the critical need for strong encryption protocols in email communications to protect sensitive data from unauthorized access.

The aftermath of the breach led to significant scrutiny of the Marine Corps' data handling practices and prompted an urgent review of their cybersecurity measures. In response, the Marine Corps implemented stricter encryption protocols and conducted comprehensive training programs to ensure personnel understood the importance of securing sensitive information. Additionally, the breach emphasized the need for continuous improvement in cybersecurity practices, leading to the adoption of more advanced encryption technologies and the establishment of stricter data protection policies. This incident serves as a stark reminder of the potential consequences of weak encryption and the necessity of strong cybersecurity measures to safeguard personal and sensitive information.

In late 2020 and early 2021, Accellion, a well-known provider of secure file transfer services, faced a series of data breaches due to multiple vulnerabilities in its File Transfer Appliance (FTA) software. Attackers exploited these vulnerabilities, including zero-day exploits and weak encryption practices, to gain unauthorized access to sensitive data from various organizations that utilized Accellion's services. This widespread breach impacted numerous high-profile organizations across various sectors, including healthcare providers, universities, government agencies, and major corporations.

The breach was partly facilitated using outdated and inadequate encryption algorithms in the FTA software. These weak encryption practices made it easier for attackers to decrypt and access sensitive information, including personally identifiable information (PII), protected health information (PHI), financial data, and confidential documents. The attackers leveraged these vulnerabilities to exfiltrate large amounts of data, which they then used for extortion, threatening to publish the stolen data unless a ransom was paid. The Accellion data breach resulted in significant financial losses and reputational damage to numerous organizations, triggering regulatory investigations and lawsuits. It also exposed millions of individuals to potential identity theft and fraud due to the leaked sensitive data.

4.3.2 Causes of weak encryption

Weak encryption is often a result of outdated cryptographic algorithms and insufficient key lengths. Cryptographic algorithms like MD5 and SHA-1, once considered secure, have been proven vulnerable to various attacks. These include collision attacks, where an attacker finds two different inputs that produce the same output, and brute-force attacks, which involve systematically trying every possible combination of characters until the correct one is found. Despite their known vulnerabilities, these algorithms are still in use in many legacy systems due to the costs associated with updating to more secure algorithms like SHA-2 or SHA-3. Additionally, shorter encryption keys, which were once sufficient, can now be easily cracked with modern computational power. For example, a 56-bit DES key can be brute-forced in a relatively short amount of time with today's technology, necessitating the transition to keys of 128 bits or longer to ensure security.

Another cause of weak encryption is the improper implementation of even secure algorithms. This can occur due to poor programming practices, a lack of understanding of fundamental cryptographic principles, or insufficient security testing. Such errors can introduce vulnerabilities that undermine the strength of the encryption, allowing attackers to potentially bypass it. For instance, using hardcoded encryption keys within application code makes it easier for attackers to reverse engineer the software and retrieve the keys. Similarly, improper management of encryption keys, such as storing them in plain text or easily accessible locations, can severely undermine the security provided by encryption. Weak encryption can also stem from the use of flawed random number generators, which can produce predictable keys or initialization vectors, making encrypted data easier to decrypt. To mitigate these vulnerabilities, organizations must prioritize the adoption of cutting-edge cryptographic standards. Implementing strong key management practices, such as regular key rotation (periodically replacing encryption keys to limit the potential damage of a compromised key) and secure storage (protecting encryption keys from unauthorized access using methods like hardware security modules), is essential. Additionally, rigorous testing and validation procedures should be established to identify and rectify implementation flaws before systems are deployed.

4.3.3 Risks posed by weak encryption

Weak encryption poses significant risks that can have severe consequences on organizations and individuals. One of the primary risks, just like any other weakness, is unauthorized access to sensitive data. When encryption is weak, attackers can easily decrypt confidential information, such as personal identification details, financial data, and intellectual property. This can lead to data breaches, identity theft, financial loss, and damage to an organization's reputation. For example, if an organization uses weak encryption to protect customer data, a breach can result in the exposure of customers' personal information, leading to loss of customer trust and potential legal liabilities.

Another risk associated with weak encryption is the increased vulnerability to man-in-the-middle (MITM) attacks. In such attacks, an adversary can intercept and potentially alter the communication between two parties without their knowledge. Weak encryption makes it easier for attackers to decrypt intercepted messages, inject malicious content, or eavesdrop on confidential communications. This can compromise the integrity and confidentiality of data transmissions, leading to further security incidents. Additionally, regulatory noncompliance is a significant risk, as many industries have strict data protection requirements that mandate strong encryption standards. Failure to comply with these regulations can result in hefty fines and sanctions, further exacerbating an organization's financial and reputational damage.

4.3.4 Cultural response

Weak encryption practices often stem from a lack of understanding about the importance of data protection. In a strong cybersecurity culture, there is a shared responsibility to ensure that all data, both in transit and at rest, is adequately protected. This requires ongoing education and training about the latest encryption standards and the risks associated with weak encryption. Organizations should emphasize the value of data security in their communications and ensure that employees are equipped with the knowledge and tools to implement strong encryption. Regular audits and updates to encryption protocols should be a standard practice, reflecting the organization's commitment to data security.

4.4 MISCONFIGURATION

Misconfiguration is the improper setup or management of security settings within systems, applications, or networks. This vulnerability often arises from human error, lack of knowledge, or oversight and can lead to significant security breaches. Misconfigurations are among the most common and critical security issues. By creating entry points, attackers can exploit them to gain unauthorized access, steal data, or disrupt operations. Understanding the nature of misconfiguration and its implications is essential for maintaining effective cybersecurity defenses. Leaving default settings unchanged, unnecessary open ports, granting users or applications excessive permissions, failing to implement proper access controls, and not securing configurations of web servers, databases, or other critical components can be disastrous.

4.4.1 Real-world examples

Misconfiguration breaches are common and often preventable security incidents. Two notable ones are the Capital One data breach (2019) and the Facebook data breach (2019).

Capital One's data breach was a misconfiguration catastrophe, even though it wasn't a sophisticated hack. A misconfigured web application firewall in Capital One's cloud environment allowed a hacker to gain access to sensitive customer data, including names, addresses, and social security numbers. This breach affected over 100 million people in the United States and six million in Canada. Three factors played an important role in this hack: misconfigured web application firewall (WAF), inadequate cloud security controls, and delayed detection. The Capital One breach resulted in significant financial and reputational damage to the company. They faced regulatory fines, lawsuits, and a decline in customer trust.

Facebook has had data breaches before, but this was the most notable one, affecting over 540 million users. The 2019 breach happened primarily because of a vulnerability in Facebook's "Add Friend" feature, and the misconfigured third-party servers amplified the impact. Two Amazon cloud servers owned by companies using Facebook data for marketing and analytics were not properly secured, and this misconfiguration allowed anyone with internet access to view and potentially download the data.

4.4.2 Causes of misconfiguration

The causes of misconfiguration are straightforward. Human error is the number one factor. Administrators or developers might lack the necessary knowledge or experience to configure systems securely. Even experienced staff can make mistakes because of the complexity of the systems and pressure. Inadequate training in system configuration and best practices can cause vulnerabilities.

System complexity is also another critical factor. Numerous configuration options make it challenging to select the appropriate settings. Interdependencies also cause vulnerabilities because different system components can interact in unexpected ways and create security gaps. Lacking proper documentation can make it difficult for administrators to figure out how to implement the configuration securely.

The last two causes of misconfiguration are rapid technological changes and organizational factors. Technology changes so quickly that updates are released continuously. Keeping up with these changes and securing systems can be challenging. When we add legacy systems with outdated security features to this mix, configurations are no longer adequate to protect the system. On the organizational side, a lack of prioritization of security, resource and budget constraints, and poor communication can tremendously contribute to inconsistencies in configuration practices.

4.4.3 Risks posed by misconfiguration

Misconfigurations within IT systems are a significant cybersecurity concern and can result in devastating consequences. They cause many risks, such as unauthorized access, data leaks, Denial of Service (DoS) attacks, and regulatory noncompliance, to name a few. When systems are not properly configured, they can grant unauthorized access to critical data and infrastructure. This vulnerability can be exploited to steal confidential information, resulting in severe financial losses, legal repercussions, and irreparable damage to an organization's reputation.

Misconfigurations of databases and cloud services can expose sensitive data to the public internet, enabling malicious actors to engage in identity theft, corporate espionage or launch further cyberattacks; moreover, misconfigured network devices and services become easy targets for Denial of Service (DoS) attacks, disrupting operations and causing significant downtime.

Misconfigurations can also create a breeding ground for malware and ransomware infections. Exploitable vulnerabilities in web servers or endpoints can allow malware to spread rapidly through a network, encrypting data and crippling essential functions. Such incidents often lead to regulatory noncompliance, as strict data protection laws mandate rigorous security measures. Failure to adhere to these regulations can result in fines, legal battles, and a loss of credibility.

Ultimately, the erosion of customer trust and the damage to an organization's reputation due to security breaches stemming from misconfigurations can have a lasting negative impact on business operations and brand image; therefore, prioritizing proper configuration management is not merely a technical necessity but a strategic imperative for any organization that values its data, customers, and future.

4.4.4 Cultural response

Misconfiguration issues highlight the need for meticulous attention to detail and adherence to best practices within a cybersecurity culture. Organizations must foster a culture where thoroughness and precision are valued and where employees are trained to configure systems securely from the start. Regular configuration audits and the use of automated tools to detect misconfigurations can help reinforce this culture. Organizations should prioritize continuous learning through regular, up-to-date training on security protocols and common configuration pitfalls. This training should empower all employees to understand their roles in identifying and reporting potential issues, promoting a sense of shared responsibility for security. Additionally, robust policies and procedures should be implemented to enforce configuration best practices, ensuring swift identification and remediation of errors.

Employing automated tools to detect anomalies can further enhance these efforts. Organizations should create a culture of transparency where mistakes are viewed as learning opportunities rather than punishable offenses. Establishing clear lines of accountability for addressing misconfigurations fosters a proactive approach to security. This will ultimately build trust among stakeholders and boost the organization's overall security posture.

4.5 OUTDATED SYSTEMS

Outdated systems are defined as hardware, software, or network infrastructures no longer supported by their vendors or having not been updated to meet current technology standards. These systems pose significant security risks, operational inefficiencies, and compliance challenges for organizations. Most importantly, they are easily exploited. Understanding the implications of using outdated systems and strategies to mitigate these risks is essential for maintaining robust cybersecurity and operational effectiveness. For instance, the continued use of Windows 8, an operating system that reached its end of support in January 2023, poses a significant risk. While Windows 8 users could upgrade to Windows 8.1, which also extended support until January 2023, both versions no longer receive security updates from Microsoft. To mitigate the vulnerabilities associated with these outdated systems, organizations should proactively review their IT assets, decommission unsupported systems, and prioritize migration to currently supported platforms like Windows 10 or 11. Additionally, employing virtualization or segmentation can help isolate outdated systems, reducing their exposure to potential attacks.

4.5.1 Real-world examples

Two examples of outdated systems causing data breaches are the Target data breach (2013) and the Maersk data breach (2017). Both had devastating consequences. Even though they were not directly related to outdated systems, outdated systems played a big role in both breaches.

The Target data breach (2013) compromised 40 million credit and debit card accounts and was facilitated by a vulnerability in an outdated third-party vendor's software used within Target's network. While not directly caused by Target's own systems, this incident demonstrates the interconnectedness of supply chain security. The attackers exploited the weakness to gain access and subsequently installed malware on Target's point-of-sale systems. This resulted in the theft of massive amounts of customer data. This breach underscores the importance of comprehensive security measures, extending beyond an organization's internal systems to include the entire supply chain.

Similarly, the 2017 Maersk breach, caused by the NotPetya ransomware, was exacerbated by outdated infrastructure. While the ransomware exploited a known vulnerability in Microsoft Windows, the abundance of outdated patches on Maersk's systems facilitated the rapid spread of the malware, causing significant operational disruption and financial losses. These cases underscore the importance of maintaining up-to-date systems and software as part of a strong cybersecurity strategy. Outdated systems not only increase the likelihood of a breach but also compound the damage, making them a significant liability for organizations.

4.5.2 Causes of outdated systems

Multiple factors contribute to potential vulnerabilities caused by outdated systems. As shown in Figure 4.4, these can be grouped into five causes: budget constraints, legacy dependencies, lack of awareness, fear of change, and vendor-related issues.

Maintaining and upgrading IT infrastructure requires significant investment, for which many organizations may not prioritize or allocate sufficient funds. This causes organizations to rely on legacy systems that may have been custom-built or extensively modified over the

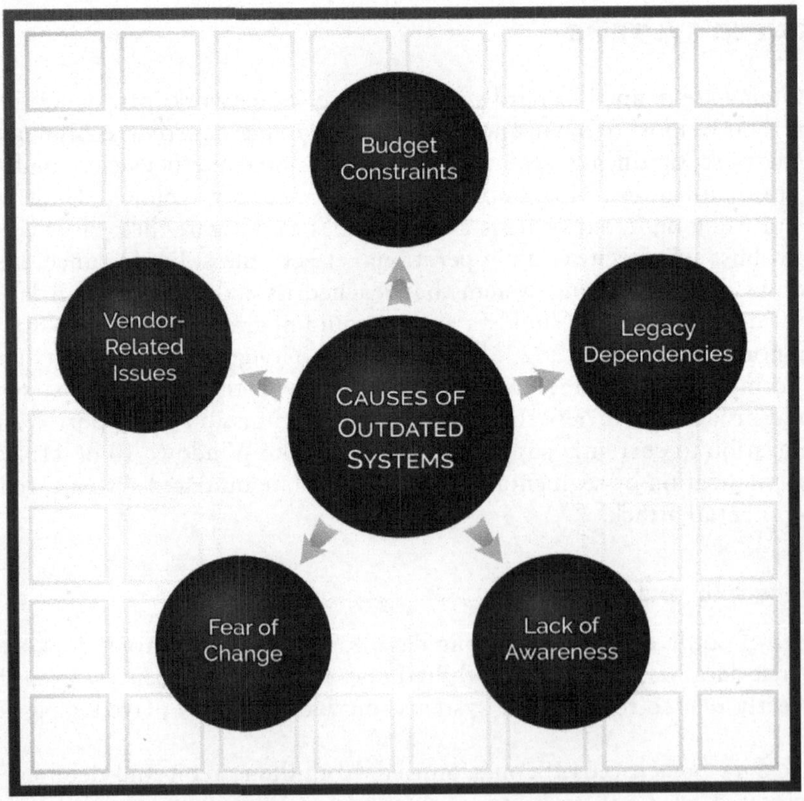

Figure 4.4 Causes of outdated systems.

years, making it difficult to replace them without disrupting business processes. This might also stem from IT staff and management not being fully aware of the risks associated with outdated systems or underestimating the importance of regular updates and patches. This lack of awareness can result from inadequate training or insufficient communication between departments responsible for IT and those overseeing the organization's broader strategy.

Resistance to change can also be a contributing factor. Employees may resist change due to familiarity and comfort with existing systems and processes. Adopting new technology, fearing disruption, a steep learning curve, or a temporary decline in productivity during the transition period might hold organizations back. Finally, organizations lacking incentives to upgrade may continue using software or hardware even after vendors have discontinued support or maintenance. Additionally, reliance on specific third-party applications that lack compatibility with newer systems can discourage organizations from upgrading their technology, even when it is advisable for security or efficiency.

4.5.3 Risks posed by outdated systems

Outdated systems pose significant risks to organizations and individuals due to several factors. These can be increased vulnerability to attacks, limited or no security support, compatibility issues, decreased functionality and performance, compliance risks, reputational damage, and increased cost.

As technology advances, older software and hardware accumulate known security flaws that remain unpatched due to discontinued support from vendors. This exposes organizations to a wide range of threats, including malware infections, data breaches, and ransomware attacks. Furthermore, compatibility issues with newer technologies and security solutions make maintaining a secure IT environment challenging, increasing the risk of misconfigurations and security gaps.

Beyond cybersecurity risks, outdated systems hinder operational efficiency. Their decreased functionality and performance can lead to slowdowns, crashes, and disruptions, impacting productivity and potentially creating opportunities for attackers to exploit weaknesses. Additionally, older systems may not comply with current data security and privacy regulations, thereby exposing organizations to legal liabilities and financial penalties. Over time, the mounting costs of maintaining and securing outdated infrastructure, coupled with the potential reputational damage from security breaches, can severely impact an organization's bottom line and long-term viability.

4.5.4 Cultural response

If we look at it from the cybersecurity culture perspective, continued use of outdated systems within an organization can be an indication of the undervalued importance of staying current with technology. A proactive cybersecurity culture encourages regularly reviewing and upgrading systems to ensure they meet current security standards. This involves not only technical updates but also educating employees about the risks associated with using unsupported systems. Organizations should promote a mindset that views technology updates as critical to overall security and operational efficiency, fostering a culture prioritizing modernization and resilience. Organizations should maintain an up-to-date inventory of IT assets, implement robust patch management processes, adopt virtualization and network segmentation, enhance security measures, and educate employees on best practices. By proactively addressing the challenges posed by outdated systems, organizations can improve their cybersecurity posture, ensure operational efficiency, and maintain compliance with regulatory standards.

4.6 POOR SECURITY PRACTICES

Human behavior and practices play a critical role in maintaining an organization's systems and data security. Poor security practices are actions, habits, or policies that increase the risk of security breaches and vulnerabilities. These practices can stem from a lack of awareness, inadequate training, or complacency, and undermine even the most advanced technical defenses.

Poor security practices can result in data breaches, financial losses, operational disruptions, and reputational damage for organizations. Understanding common poor security practices and their impact is essential for fostering a strong cybersecurity culture within organizations.

These practices include using unsecured public Wi-Fi to access sensitive information, failing to log out of accounts, clicking on phishing links, lacking multifactor authentication (MFA), and neglecting to use security tools like VPNs. Social engineering attacks, where attackers manipulate individuals into revealing confidential information, are particularly effective against organizations with weak security awareness.

4.6.1 Real-world examples

There are many examples of poor security practices, and studying them gives us valuable insight into the risks organizations face when they neglect essential cybersecurity measures. The two cases we will look at are the Yahoo data breach (2013–2014) and the Uber data breach (2016).

In 2013 and 2014, Yahoo suffered two massive data breaches. The 2013 breach collectively exposed the personal information of all 3 billion user accounts. The 2014 breach affected around 500 million accounts. The breaches, which were not publicly disclosed until 2016, resulted in the theft of names, email addresses, phone numbers, dates of birth, hashed passwords, and security questions and answers. The attackers exploited vulnerabilities in Yahoo's systems, including outdated encryption and a lack of two-factor authentication, to gain unauthorized access to user data. Inadequate monitoring to detect the breaches promptly resulted in a second wave. The Yahoo data breach is a cautionary tale for all organizations, emphasizing the importance of strong security practices, proactive threat detection, and timely incident response.

In 2016, Uber experienced a significant data breach that exposed the personal information of 57 million users. The breach occurred due to a combination of poor security practices, including the exposure of login credentials on a public GitHub repository and inadequate access controls on Uber's cloud storage. Instead of disclosing the breach, Uber paid the hackers $100,000 to delete the stolen data and keep the incident quiet, a decision that was later revealed and heavily criticized. The incident resulted in significant financial penalties for Uber. It underscored the importance of strong security measures, including secure coding, vigorous access controls, continuous monitoring, and transparent disclosure in the event of a data breach.

4.6.2 Causes of poor security practices

Poor security practices can stem from several factors and can collectively undermine an organization's cybersecurity posture. One of the primary causes is the lack of awareness and training among employees. This leaves them vulnerable to phishing scams, weak passwords, and mishandling of sensitive information. Employees can become a significant security risk without continuous education on potential threats and the importance of following security protocols. Additionally, insufficient resources and budget allocations for cybersecurity lead to outdated software, inadequate security tools, and an understaffed IT department. This lack of investment makes it difficult for organizations to implement and maintain their security measures, increasing their vulnerability to attacks.

Complacency and overconfidence in existing security measures can also contribute to poor security practices. Organizations that have not experienced significant cyber incidents may neglect essential security protocols, such as software updates and regular security audits. Poor governance and policy enforcement further exacerbate the issue and lead to inconsistently applied or ignored security measures. Rapid technological changes and complex IT environments add to the challenge, making it difficult for organizations to adapt their security practices effectively. Finally, human error, such as misconfigurations and negligence, remains a significant cause of security breaches. Implementing checks and balances and automated monitoring can help mitigate the impact of these errors. Understanding these causes is crucial for developing strategies to enhance security practices and protect organizational assets from cyber threats.

4.6.3 Risks posed by poor security practices

Poor security practices pose significant risks to organizations. These can range from data breaches and financial losses to reputational damage and legal consequences. When security practices are inadequate, organizations become prime targets for cybercriminals who exploit vulnerabilities to gain unauthorized access to sensitive information. This can lead to data breaches. Data breaches lead to personal, financial, and proprietary data being stolen, resulting in severe financial implications for organizations and individuals. These costs can be related to direct theft or the costs associated with responding to the breach, such as incident response, remediation, and potential fines for regulatory noncompliance.

Furthermore, poor security practices can result in operational disruptions. Cyberattacks, such as ransomware, can cripple an organization's operations by locking critical systems and data until a ransom is paid. Even without ransomware, other attacks like Distributed Denial of Service (DDoS) can render systems unavailable, causing downtime and loss of productivity. Additionally, weak security practices can erode customer trust and tarnish an organization's reputation. Customers are increasingly aware of data privacy issues, and a single breach can lead to loss of business, negative media coverage, and long-term damage to brand credibility. Effective security measures are essential not just for protecting data but also for maintaining operational integrity and customer confidence.

4.6.4 Cultural response

A strong cultural response to poor security practices involves fostering an organizational environment that prioritizes cybersecurity awareness, accountability, and continuous improvement. The first step is to cultivate a mindset that recognizes cybersecurity as a shared responsibility. This involves comprehensive training programs that educate employees at all levels about the importance of security protocols, recognizing phishing attempts, using strong passwords, and understanding the risks associated with poor security practices. Regular simulations and drills can reinforce these lessons and ensure employees are prepared to respond effectively to potential threats.

As stated in a previous chapter, leadership plays a critical role in shaping this culture. Executives and managers should lead by example, demonstrating a commitment to cybersecurity through their actions and decisions. Establishing clear policies and procedures that outline security expectations, as well as regular audits and reviews of security practices, can help maintain high standards. Encouraging open communication and providing channels for employees to report security concerns without fear of reprisal is also crucial. By creating a culture that values vigilance, accountability, and proactive measures, organizations can significantly reduce the risks posed by poor security practices and build a resilient defense against cyber threats.

4.7 PHYSICAL SECURITY ATTACKS

Physical security attacks target the hardware and physical infrastructure of an organization. Some examples are theft of devices, tampering with hardware, and gaining unauthorized physical access to secure areas. Physical security is often overlooked in cybersecurity strategies, yet it is crucial for protecting sensitive information. To mitigate physical security risks, organizations should implement strict access controls, such as biometric authentication and surveillance systems, and ensure that all sensitive hardware is stored in secure, restricted-access areas. Additionally, policies should be put in place to secure hardware disposal and prevent data retrieval from discarded devices.

4.7.1 Real-world examples

Several physical security attacks have occurred in the last decade. Two noteworthy ones are Tesla's (2018) and Sony Pictures' breaches (2014).

In 2018, Tesla's Gigafactory in Nevada experienced a physical security breach. A disgruntled former employee used his insider knowledge and access to infiltrate the facility. He intentionally sabotaged manufacturing equipment and stole sensitive data, including trade secrets and production information, which he leaked to the media. This incident caused significant operational disruptions and financial losses for Tesla. This incident emphasized the importance of robust physical security measures alongside cybersecurity protocols.

The 2014 Sony Pictures breach involved both cyber and physical security breaches. Hackers, believed to be backed by North Korea, not only stole and leaked sensitive data but also physically damaged Sony's computer systems, causing widespread disruption and financial losses. This attack demonstrated how physical and cyber threats can converge, amplifying the impact and complicating recovery efforts.

Both examples underscore the necessity of a holistic security approach that addresses digital and physical vulnerabilities. Integrating physical security measures with cybersecurity strategies creates a comprehensive security approach that protects both digital and physical assets.

4.7.2 Causes of physical security attacks

Physical security attacks are often the result of several critical factors. The primary reason is usually inadequate access controls, which allow unauthorized individuals to enter the secure areas through poorly managed entry points or insufficient security checkpoints. Lack of employee training further exacerbates this issue. Untrained staff may fail to recognize social engineering tactics or other suspicious behaviors and unintentionally aid attackers. Insufficient surveillance and monitoring systems, such as CCTV cameras and alarm systems, leave facilities vulnerable by failing to detect and deter intruders effectively. Poor physical infrastructure, including weak fences and unprotected entry points, makes it easier for attackers to penetrate secure areas. Additionally, insider threats, whether malicious or accidental, pose significant risks as individuals with legitimate access can exploit their positions or assist external attackers.

Addressing these causes requires a multifaceted approach to physical security. Implementing robust access controls, continuous employee training, advanced surveillance systems, and strong physical infrastructure are essential measures. Vigilant monitoring for insider threats is also crucial to mitigate internal risks. By understanding and mitigating these factors, organizations can significantly enhance their physical security posture and protect against unauthorized access, ensuring the safety and integrity of their operations.

4.7.3 Risks posed by physical security attacks

Poor physical security poses several significant risks that can impact an organization's operations. First, it increases the likelihood of unauthorized access to sensitive areas, resulting in theft, vandalism, or sabotage. For instance, if an attacker gains entry to a data center, they could steal or damage critical equipment, leading to data breaches and operational disruptions. The lack of proper access controls, such as secure locks and monitoring systems, facilitates such breaches, compromising both physical assets and the data they contain.

Another significant risk is the potential for insider threats. Poor physical security can make it easier for disgruntled employees or contractors to exploit their access privileges to cause harm. This could involve stealing sensitive information, introducing malware, or physically damaging infrastructure. In addition, inadequate surveillance and monitoring systems mean that any suspicious activity or breaches may go undetected. This leads to financial losses and can damage an organization's reputation and erode trust with customers and stakeholders. Robust physical security measures are essential to prevent these risks and protect tangible and intangible assets.

4.7.4 Cultural response

The cultural response to physical security attacks should emphasize the importance of vigilance, proactive measures, continuous education, and appropriate budgeting within an organization. Establishing a strong security culture begins with leadership setting the tone, demonstrating the importance of physical security, and prioritizing it alongside cybersecurity measures. This includes regular training sessions for all employees on the importance of physical security protocols. This training will enable employees to recognize potential threats and the correct procedures to follow in case of an incident. Employees should feel empowered and responsible for reporting suspicious activities without fear of repercussion. Regular simulations can help ensure that everyone knows their role in maintaining security and can act swiftly and appropriately in response to a threat.

In addition to training and empowerment, organizations should foster an environment where security is an integral part of daily operations. This can be achieved by implementing robust access control measures, such as biometric systems, secure ID cards, and surveillance cameras, and by maintaining strict protocols for visitors and contractors. Secure disposal of hardware should also be an important consideration when acquiring new hardware. Adequate budgeting is crucial for these initiatives, as it allows for procuring and maintaining advanced security technologies. Security should be a shared responsibility, with clear communication channels for reporting issues and ongoing evaluations to identify and address potential vulnerabilities. A culture of continuous improvement and awareness should be encouraged. The security measures should evolve with emerging threats and enhance the overall resilience of the organization against physical security attacks. This comprehensive approach underscores the need for sufficient funding to support vital security measures.

4.8 CONCLUSION

In conclusion, understanding and addressing cybersecurity attack surfaces and vulnerabilities are critical for protecting organizational assets and maintaining the integrity of information systems. By focusing on all the above-mentioned attack surfaces and vulnerabilities, as summarized in Table 4.1, organizations can significantly reduce their risk of attacks. Continuous education, regular audits, and the implementation of best practices are essential components of an effective cybersecurity strategy. As cyber threats continue to evolve, staying informed and proactive in addressing these vulnerabilities will be crucial for maintaining a secure digital environment. Understanding and addressing attack surfaces and vulnerabilities are integral to fostering a strong cybersecurity culture. By promoting awareness, proactive behavior, and continuous improvement, organizations can create an environment where security is a shared responsibility and a fundamental aspect of daily operations. Regular education, clear communication, and the implementation of best practices are essential for cultivating a culture that prioritizes cybersecurity. Maintaining a vigilant and informed cybersecurity culture will be crucial for protecting organizational assets and ensuring long-term security as cyber threats continue to evolve.

DISCUSSION QUESTIONS

1. What are the key differences between network, software, and human attack surfaces, and why is it important to address all three in a cybersecurity strategy?
2. Discuss the impact of unpatched software on an organization's security posture. How can organizations ensure timely patch management?
3. Why do weak passwords remain a common vulnerability despite widespread awareness of their risks? What strategies can organizations implement to improve password security?
4. Explain the significance of strong encryption in protecting sensitive data. What are the potential consequences of relying on weak or outdated encryption methods?

Table 4.1 Overview of attack surfaces and vulnerabilities

OVERVIEW OF ATTACK SURFACES AND VULNERABILITIES

ATTACK SURFACE	EXAMPLES OF VULNERABILITIES	CAUSES OF VULNERABILITIES	RISKS POSED	CULTURAL RESPONSE
Network	Open ports, unsecured Wi-Fi, outdated firewall rules	Misconfigurations, lack of regular updates	Unauthorized access, data breaches, DDoS attacks	Regular network audits, employee training, automated monitoring tools
Software	Unpatched applications, weak encryption, improper configurations	Delayed updates, inadequate patch management	Malware infections, ransomware attacks, data loss	Patch management policies, software inventory, regular updates
Human	Phishing, weak passwords, social engineering	Lack of awareness, poor security practices	Data breaches, unauthorized access, insider threats	Continuous security awareness training, implementing MFA, promoting a strong security culture

5. How can misconfigurations lead to security breaches? Discuss ways to prevent and detect misconfigurations in an organization's IT infrastructure.
6. Why is it challenging for organizations to update or replace outdated systems? What steps can be taken to mitigate the risks posed by these systems?
7. In what ways can poor security practices among employees undermine an organization's cybersecurity efforts? How can a strong cybersecurity culture address these issues?
8. How do physical security attacks differ from digital attacks, and why is it important for organizations to integrate physical security into their overall cybersecurity strategy?
9. Discuss the role of leadership in fostering a cybersecurity culture that prioritizes continuous improvement. How can leaders ensure that their organization stays ahead of emerging threats?
10. Why is it important to regularly review and update security practices, policies, and procedures? How can organizations create a culture of continuous improvement in cybersecurity?

BIBLIOGRAPHY

Avery, D. (2022, September 30). Capital One $190 million data breach settlement: Today is the last day to claim money. *CNET.* https://www.cnet.com/personal-finance/capital-one-190-million-data-breach-settlement-today-is-deadline-to-file-claim/

Canadian Centre for Cyber Security. (2024, February). Secure your accounts and devices with multi-factor authentication (ITSAP.30.030). https://www.cyber.gc.ca/en/guidance/secure-your-accounts-and-devices-multi-factor-authentication-itsap30030

CISA (Cybersecurity and Infrastructure Security Agency). (2021). Exploitation of Accellion file transfer appliance. https://www.cisa.gov/news-events/cybersecurity-advisories/aa21-055a

Cluley, G. (2018, June 19). Tesla saboteur caused extensive damage and leaked highly sensitive data, claims Elon Musk. *Bitdefender.* https://www.bitdefender.com/blog/hotforsecurity/tesla-saboteur-caused-extensive-damage-and-leaked-highly-sensitive-data-claims-elon-musk/

CQR. (2023, March 2). Weak encryption algorithms. CQR. https://cqr.company/blog/weak-encryption-algorithms

Daswani, N., & Elbayadi, M. (2021). The Yahoo Breaches of 2013 and 2014. In *Big breaches*. Apress. https://doi.org/10.1007/978-1-4842-6655-7_7

Easterly, J., & Fanning, T. (2023, May 7). The attack on Colonial Pipeline: What we've learned & what we've done over the past two years. *Cybersecurity and Infrastructure Security Agency (CISA).* https://www.cisa.gov/news-events/news/attack-colonial-pipeline-what-weve-learned-what-weve-done-over-past-two-years

Fruhlinger, J. (2020, February 12). Equifax data breach FAQ: What happened, who was affected, what was the impact? CSO. Equifax data breach FAQ: What happened, who was affected, what was the impact? | CSO Online

Fruhlinger, J. (2022, August 24). WannaCry explained: A perfect ransomware storm. *CSO.* https://www.csoonline.com/article/563017/wannacry-explained-a-perfect-ransomware-storm.html

Greenberg, A. (2018, August 22). The untold story of NotPetya, the most devastating cyberattack in history. *Wired.* https://www.wired.com/story/notpetya-cyberattack-ukraine-russia-code-crashed-the-world/

Gregory, J. (2021, September 1). What has changed since the 2017 WannaCry ransomware attack? Security Intelligence. https://securityintelligence.com/articles/what-has-changed-since-wannacry-ransomware-attack/

Ikeda, S. (2020, April 27). Half a million Zoom accounts compromised by credential stuffing, sold on dark web. CPO Magazine. https://www.cpomagazine.com/cyber-security/half-a-million-zoom-accounts-compromised-by-credential-stuffing-sold-on-dark-web/

Irwin, L. (2023, April 11). What is a MITM attack? Definition, prevention & examples. *IT Governance.* https://www.itgovernance.eu/blog/en/how-to-defend-against-man-in-the-middle-attacks

Jennings, C., Johnson, E., & Yépez, D. (2020, September 1). Executive responsibilities and consequences: A case study of Uber's data breaches. Corporate Compliance Insights. https://www.corporatecomplianceinsights.com/responsibilities-consequences-uber-data-breaches/

Kerner, S. M. (2022, April 26). Colonial Pipeline hack explained: Everything you need to know. *TechTarget*. https://www.techtarget.com/whatis/feature/Colonial-Pipeline-hack-explained-Everything-you-need-to-know

Lee, M. (2022, March 31). On the radar: Is 2022 the year encryption is doomed? Cisco Talos. https://blog.talosintelligence.com/on-radar-is-2022-year-encryption-is/

Lyskoit, V. (July 16, 2024). A timeline of Facebook data breaches. NordVPN.com. https://nordvpn.com/blog/facebook-data-breach/#:~:text=In%20a%20public%20statement%2C%20the,to%20scrape%20public%20profile%20data.

National Institute of Standards and Technology (NIST). (2019). *NIST special publication 800-131A Revision 2: Transitions: Recommendation for transitioning the use of cryptographic algorithms and key*. https://nvlpubs.nist.gov/nistpubs/SpecialPublications/NIST.SP.800-131Ar2.pdf

Novaes Neto, N., Madnick, S., Moraes, G., de Paula, A., & Borges, N. M.. (2020, March 30-April 1). A case study of the Capital One data breach. Cybersecurity at MIT Sloan, MIT Sloan School of Management, Massachusetts Institute of Technology. Information Institute Conferences, Las Vegas, NV. https://cams.mit.edu/wp-content/uploads/capitalonedatapaper.pdf

Opinnate.com. (2023). Guarding the gate: Security breaches caused by Firewall misconfigurations. https://opinnate.com/guarding-the-gate-security-breaches-caused-by-firewall-misconfigurations/

Owaida, A. (2020, April 16). Half a million Zoom accounts for sale on the dark web. *WeLiveSecurity*. https://www.welivesecurity.com/2020/04/16/half-million-zoom-accounts-sale-dark-web/

Plachkinova, M., & Maurer, C. (2018). Teaching case security breach at target. *Journal of Information Systems Education*, *29*(1). https://www.researchgate.net/publication/324454307_Teaching_Case_Security_Breach_at_Target

Prevalent. (2021). Accellion Data Breach: Four strategies for third-party risk response. https://www.prevalent.net/blog/accellion-data-breach-four-strategies-for-third-party-risk-response/

Snow, S. (2018, February 28). Major data breach at Marine Forces Reserve impacts thousands. Marine Corps Times. https://www.marinecorpstimes.com/news/your-marine-corps/2018/02/28/major-data-breach-at-marine-forces-reserve-impacts-thousands/

Srinivasan, S., Pitcher, Q., & Goldberg, J. S. (2017). Data breach at Equifax (Revised April 2019). Harvard Business School Case Collection. Data Breach at Equifax - Case - Faculty & Research - Harvard Business School (hbs.edu)

Steinberg, S., Stepan, A., & Neary, K. (2021). The hacking of Sony Pictures: A Columbia University case study. Picker Center Digital Education Group at Columbia's School of International and Public Affairs (SIPA). *SIPA-21-0023.1*. https://www.sipa.columbia.edu/sites/default/files/2022-11/Sony%20-%20Written%20Case.pdf

Vinberg, S., & Overson, J., with contributions by Woods, D., Ghosemajumder, S., Boddy, S., Pompon, R., & Koritz, A. (2021, February 9). *2021 credential stuffing report*. F5 Labs. https://www.f5.com/labs/articles/threat-intelligence/2021-credential-stuffing-report

Chapter 5

Threat actors, targets, and motivation

In the complex and ever-evolving landscape of cybersecurity, understanding the various threat actors, their targets, and their motivations is paramount for developing defense strategies. Threat actors encompass a broad spectrum as shown in Figure 5.1: from cybercriminals driven by financial gain to nation-states engaging in espionage, from hacktivists

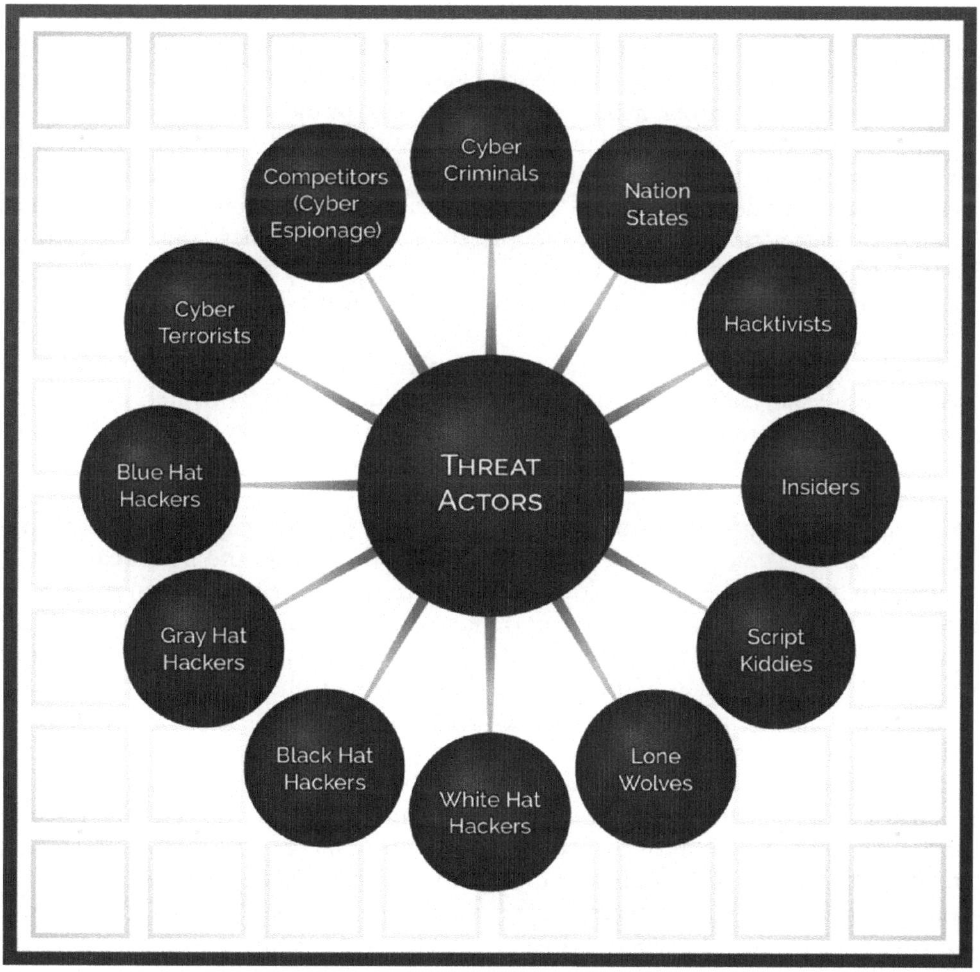

Figure 5.1 Threat actors.

DOI: 10.1201/9781003368496-5

promoting ideological causes to insiders exploiting their access. Each type presents unique challenges. As the threat landscape evolves, so must the understanding of these actors and their tactics. Identifying who these actors are, what they seek to achieve, and how they operate provides invaluable insights for organizations aiming to protect their assets and maintain security.

Analyzing the targets of these threat actors is equally important. Different actors focus on various targets, ranging from individuals and small businesses to large corporations, governments, and critical infrastructure. While financial gain remains a significant driver, motivations can vary widely, encompassing political goals, ideological beliefs, or personal grievances. Understanding these dynamics allows organizations to prioritize their security measures effectively, recognizing that the impact of attacks can extend beyond financial losses to affect national security, critical infrastructure, and societal well-being. By studying the actors, their targets, and their motivations, organizations can better anticipate potential threats, allocate resources wisely, and implement tailored security measures to mitigate risks.

THREAT ACTORS

It is important to frequently emphasize how understanding the landscape of cyber threats is crucial for safeguarding information systems and data. One of the most important elements of this landscape is threat actors, defined as groups or individuals who exploit vulnerabilities to access, disrupt, or damage information systems and data. They have different motivations and attack methods. These actors range from cybercriminals and nation-states to hacktivists and insiders. They pose significant risks to individuals, organizations, and governments. Their actions can lead to financial loss, data breaches, and even disruptions in critical infrastructure.

Studying threat actors is crucial for effective cybersecurity measures for several reasons as summarized in Figure 5.2.

First, understanding who they are, their motivations, and their tactics allow us to develop tailored defense strategies. For example, combating financially motivated cybercriminals requires different approaches other than defending against state-sponsored espionage. Financially motivated cybercriminals primarily seek monetary gain. Their tactics often revolve around speed, efficiency, and maximizing profit. They may use ransomware, phishing, or credit card fraud. State-sponsored espionage is driven by political, economic, or military objectives. These actors are often highly skilled, patient, and persistent, aiming to steal intellectual property, disrupt critical infrastructure, or gather intelligence.

Second, by analyzing past behavior and trends, one can anticipate the most likely attack vectors for specific threat actors. Armed with that knowledge, it is important to prioritize resources and focus on vulnerabilities that are most likely to be exploited. For instance, if a threat group has historically targeted financial institutions using phishing emails, it is crucial to enforce email security measures and employee training. Similarly, if a nation-state actor has been known to exploit zero-day vulnerabilities in industrial control systems, it necessitates a focus on patching those systems and implementing advanced threat detection.

Third, cyber threats constantly evolve, and new actors emerge with new tactics. Studying threat actors allows one to stay ahead of the curve, adapting security measures to counter new and emerging threats. For example, the rapid rise of ransomware attacks has necessitated investments in data backup and recovery solutions, while the increased sophistication of state-sponsored cyber espionage requires advanced threat detection and incident response capabilities.

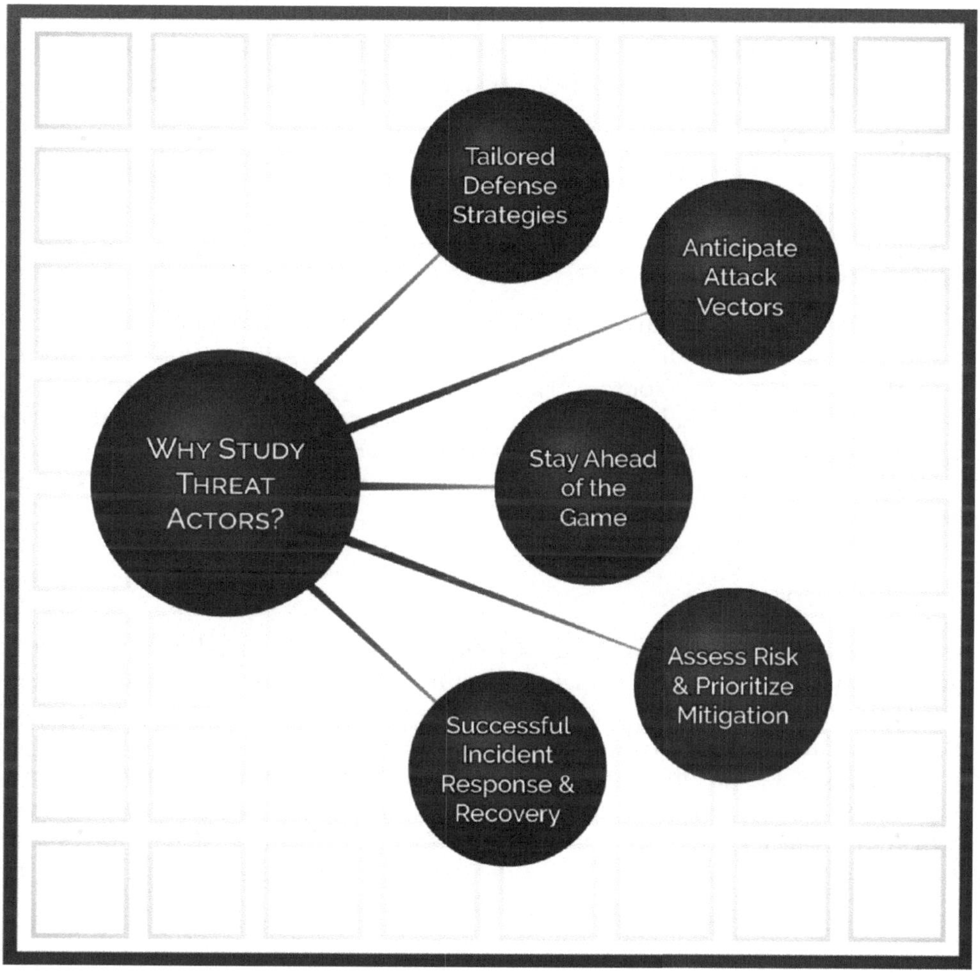

Figure 5.2 Why study threat actors?

Fourth, it is possible to assess the risks and prioritize mitigation efforts by understanding the specific characteristics, tactics, and objectives associated with each type of actor. A good example includes recognizing that financially motivated cybercriminals often target vulnerabilities in email systems with phishing attacks. This would prompt one to invest in robust email security and employee training. Conversely, understanding that state-sponsored espionage groups may focus on intellectual property theft through supply chain attacks necessitates stringent vendor risk management and monitoring of critical infrastructure.

Finally, in the unfortunate event of an attack, knowledge of the threat actor can be a guiding light in successful incident response and recovery efforts. Understanding the attacker's motivations and tactics can significantly aid in determining the scope of the attack, identifying the compromised systems, and restoring operations more effectively. For instance, if a ransomware attack is suspected to be the work of a financially motivated cybercriminal group, the incident response team can prioritize data recovery efforts and focus on negotiating a potential ransom payment while also considering law enforcement involvement.

In essence, studying threat actors provides valuable insights into the who, what, why, and how of cyberattacks. This knowledge is essential for building a robust cybersecurity strategy that can effectively protect against a wide range of threats. This chapter will expose these threat actors.

5.1 CYBERCRIMINALS

5.1.1 Who are they?

Cybercriminals are groups or individuals who use technology to commit illegal acts in cyberspace. They exploit vulnerabilities in computer systems, networks, and digital infrastructure to steal money, data, or resources. They operate independently or as part of organized crime networks. Cybercriminals range from skilled hackers with deep technical knowledge to amateurs known as "script kiddies" who use prewritten software tools to execute attacks. The term *cybercriminal* can also be used as a general term that covers all groups or individuals who execute attacks in cyberspace.

5.1.2 What do they do?

Cybercriminals engage in various illegal activities aimed at financial gain, data theft, or causing disruption. Their activities include hacking, phishing, malware distribution, and identity theft. Hacking involves unauthorized access to computer systems to steal, alter, or destroy data. In contrast, phishing uses deceptive emails or messages to trick individuals into revealing personal information like passwords or credit card numbers. Malware distribution involves creating and spreading malicious software like viruses, ransomware, and spyware to infect systems and steal or encrypt data. Identity theft involves stealing personal information to commit fraud or theft. Chapter 3 has covered attack vectors in detail.

5.1.3 How do they operate?

Cybercriminals use various methods and tools to carry out their attacks. Social engineering is one of the methods they use to manipulate individuals to give up confidential information by posing as trustworthy entities. They also exploit vulnerabilities by identifying software, hardware, or network configuration weaknesses to gain unauthorized access. Brute force attacks use automated tools to guess passwords through trial and error. Botnets are networks of infected computers controlled remotely to conduct large-scale attacks, such as Distributed Denial-of-Service (DDoS) attacks. Cybercriminals use the dark web to buy and sell stolen data, malware, and other illegal services.

5.1.4 Who do they target?

Cybercriminals target a wide range of victims, including individuals, businesses, financial institutions, healthcare providers, government agencies, and critical infrastructure. Individuals are targeted for identity and personal data theft as well as financial fraud; however, their prime targets are businesses, particularly those with valuable intellectual property, customer data, and financial assets. Small businesses often lack necessary security measures, making them attractive targets. Financial institutions are targeted due to the potential for significant financial gain. Healthcare providers hold sensitive patient data, making them targets for ransomware attacks. Government agencies are attacked to yield confidential information and disrupt services. Critical infrastructure, including utilities and transportation systems, is targeted to cause widespread disruption and potential harm. The globalized nature of the digital landscape has made cybercrime a transnational issue, with cybercriminals often operating across borders to evade law enforcement.

5.1.5 What motivates them?

The primary motivations behind cybercriminal activities are a long list. These include financial gain, political or ideological goals, revenge or personal grievances, intellectual challenge, and corporate espionage. Financial gain is the most common motivation, as cybercriminals seek to make money through theft, fraud, and ransomware attacks. Political or ideological goals drive hacktivists and nation-state actors to conduct cyberattacks to promote political agendas, influence elections, or sabotage rival nations. Revenge or personal grievances motivate disgruntled employees or individuals to engage in cybercrime to retaliate against employers, ex-partners, or others. Intellectual challenge drives some hackers to break into secure systems and gain recognition in the hacking community. Corporate espionage involves competitors hiring cybercriminals to steal trade secrets and proprietary information or sabotage rivals. As the cyber landscape evolves, so too do the motivations of cybercriminals, with new incentives emerging.

5.1.6 Effects on cybersecurity culture

Cybercriminals pose a significant threat to any organization's cybersecurity culture. Their relentless pursuit of financial gain, coupled with evolving tactics, necessitates a proactive and adaptable security culture to counter their efforts. A robust cybersecurity culture must be established and nurtured within the organization to effectively combat cybercriminals. This involves creating a security-conscious environment where employees are aware of the risks and understand their roles in safeguarding critical assets. Regular security awareness training, promoting a culture of vigilance and implementing strong security practices, are essential components of this effort. As was mentioned in previous chapters, strong leadership support is crucial in driving a culture of cybersecurity, with executives setting the tone and demonstrating their commitment to security at all levels of the organization.

Cybercriminals have some positive and negative impacts on cybersecurity culture. Positive impacts can be grouped under heightened awareness, technological innovation, strengthening of the culture, and increased collaboration. Relentless attacks have heightened the awareness of security risks, both within organizations and among individuals. This increased awareness has led to greater investment in security measures, employee training, and the adoption of safer online practices. The constant evolution of cybercriminal tactics has also spurred technological innovation in the cybersecurity field, leading to the development of more sophisticated tools for detection, prevention, and response. Additionally, the threat of cybercrime has fostered a stronger sense of community and collaboration among cybersecurity professionals, law enforcement agencies, and industry groups. This has led to improved threat intelligence sharing and coordinated responses to attacks; however, there are some negative impacts as well. These can be grouped under loss of trust, financial losses, reputational damage, psychological impact, and increased secu rity costs. Eroding trust in online systems and institutions is a big cost for cybercriminals. Their malicious activities lead to significant financial losses for both individuals and businesses through fraud, theft, and the expenses incurred in incident response and recovery.

The reputational damage inflicted on organizations that fall victim to cyberattacks can be devastating. This can result in lost customers, decreased market share, and diminished investor confidence. Furthermore, the psychological toll on victims of cybercrime, particularly those who experience identity theft or harassment, is often substantial. As the threat of cybercrime escalates, the need for strong security measures also increases, imposing a financial burden on organizations, especially smaller businesses with limited resources. Additionally, the increasing frequency and severity of cyberattacks have led to a growing body of cybersecurity regulations, which can add complexity and costs to businesses while potentially stifling innovation.

Overall, cybercriminals have a complex and often contradictory impact on cybersecurity culture. While their actions can drive positive change, they also create significant challenges and costs for individuals, businesses, and society as a whole.

Cybercriminals represent a diverse and evolving threat to us all. From individuals to businesses and governments, their methods continually adapt to new technologies and defenses, making cybersecurity a critical and ongoing priority. Understanding who cyber criminals are, how they operate, their targets, and their motivations can help develop effective strategies to mitigate risks and protect digital assets. By staying informed and vigilant, organizations and individuals can better defend against the ever-present threat of cybercrime.

5.2 NATION-STATES

5.2.1 Who are they?

Nation-states represent a highly organized category of threat actors in the cybersecurity landscape. These actors are government-sponsored groups or individuals who operate under the directive of a sovereign state. Unlike other threat actors, nation-states possess vast resources, including financial backing, cutting-edge technology, and skilled personnel. Their operations are often aligned with their country's strategic interests, which can include economic dominance, political influence, and military superiority.

5.2.2 What do they do?

Nation-states engage in a wide array of cyber activities: from espionage and sabotage to misinformation campaigns and intellectual property theft. Their operations aim to gather intelligence, disrupt critical infrastructure, influence political processes, or gain a strategic advantage over other nations. These activities can include stealing classified information, disrupting communication networks, and spreading propaganda. The sophistication and scale of their operations often mean they can conduct prolonged and complex campaigns without detection. Nation-state actors often operate as Persistent Threat Actors (PTAs), maintaining long-term access to target networks to conduct espionage, data theft, and sabotage over extended periods. This level of persistence and sophistication makes them particularly challenging to detect and counter.

5.2.3 How do they operate?

Nation-states employ a diverse set of tactics and techniques to achieve their objectives. They often use Advanced Persistent Threats (APTs), which are prolonged and targeted cyber intrusions aimed at accessing and extracting information without being detected.

These actors utilize sophisticated malware, zero-day exploits, and social engineering techniques to infiltrate systems, which was thoroughly explained in Chapter 3. They also engage in supply chain attacks, compromising a less secure part of the supply chain to eventually breach the primary target. Additionally, nation-states have the capability to conduct coordinated attacks that combine cyber operations with traditional espionage and military activities.

5.2.4 Who do they target?

Nation-states have varying targets, including government agencies, military institutions, critical infrastructure providers, and large corporations. The organizations are especially involved in technology, defense, finance, and energy. Universities and research institutions are also frequent targets because of their involvement in cutting-edge research and development. Additionally, political entities and media organizations are targeted to influence public opinion and political outcomes. In some cases, high-profile individuals, such as government officials, activists, or journalists, may also be targeted for surveillance, harassment, or even physical harm.

5.2.5 What motivates them?

The motivations behind nation-state cyber activities are deeply rooted in the pursuit of national interests. Economic gain is a significant driver, with nation-states aiming to boost their economies by stealing intellectual property and trade secrets. Political and military objectives are also central, as cyber operations can destabilize adversaries, gather intelligence, and prepare the battlefield for potential conflicts. Ideological motivations play a role as well, with nation-states seeking to promote their governance models and undermine opposing ideologies. The desire to project power and influence on the global stage motivates nation-states to engage in high-profile cyber operations. Often, these motivations are intertwined, with cyber operations forming a key component of hybrid warfare strategies that combine military, diplomatic, economic, and informational measures to achieve national objectives.

5.2.6 Effects on cybersecurity culture

Nation-states significantly influence cybersecurity culture by elevating threat awareness and requiring advanced security protocols to be implemented. Since they have sophisticated and well-funded cyber activities, they have made organizations acutely aware of the heightened threat landscape, driving a culture of continuous vigilance and learning. This has led to the adoption of advanced security measures like multifactor authentication, zero-trust architecture, and regular security audits. Additionally, there is a shift toward proactive defense strategies, such as threat hunting and cyber threat intelligence, fostering a culture of anticipation and preparedness.

The threat from nation-state actors has also emphasized the importance of collaboration and information sharing among organizations, industries, and government entities. This collective approach enhances defense capabilities through shared threat intelligence and best practices. Stricter cybersecurity regulations and compliance requirements, driven by government responses to these threats, have instilled a culture of accountability and transparency within organizations. Furthermore, the focus on insider threats has increased, leading to comprehensive insider threat programs that promote a culture of trust and responsibility among employees. Overall, the influence of nation-states has resulted in a more resilient and security-conscious organizational culture.

In conclusion, nation-states are highly organized and resource-rich actors in the realm of cybersecurity. Their sophisticated operations target a broad spectrum of entities driven by economic, political, military, and ideological motivations. Understanding their methods and objectives is crucial for developing strong defenses and mitigating the risks posed by these powerful adversaries.

5.3 HACKTIVISTS

5.3.1 Who are they?

Hacktivists are groups or individuals who use hacking techniques to promote political agendas, social causes, or ideological beliefs. Unlike traditional cybercriminals who seek financial gain, hacktivists aim to draw attention to specific issues or bring about political and social change. They operate at the intersection of activism and hacking, combining technical skills with a passion for advocacy.

5.3.2 What do they do?

Hacktivists engage in various activities to further their causes. They often conduct cyberattacks to disrupt services, deface websites, or steal and leak sensitive information. These actions are intended to embarrass or harm their targets, raise public awareness, and generate media coverage for their causes. Common hacktivist tactics include DDoS attacks, website defacements, data breaches, and information leaks.

5.3.3 How do they operate?

Hacktivists employ a range of hacking techniques to achieve their goals. DDoS attacks are used to overwhelm and shut down websites or online services, preventing legitimate users from accessing them. Website defacement involves altering the content of a website to display messages that support the hacktivists' agenda. Data breaches and information leaks involve infiltrating networks to steal sensitive data, which is then publicly released to expose wrongdoing or unethical behavior. Social engineering and phishing are also common methods to gain access to systems and information.

5.3.4 Who do they target?

Hacktivists target entities they perceive as unethical, corrupt, or oppressive. This includes government agencies, large corporations, financial institutions, law enforcement agencies, and other organizations associated with perceived injustices. Their targets are often chosen based on their involvement in controversial activities, such as censorship, environmental harm, human rights abuses, or corporate greed. By attacking these targets, hacktivists aim to disrupt their operations, expose their activities, and hold them accountable in the public eye.

5.3.5 What motivates them?

The motivation behind hacktivism is driven by a desire for social, political, or ideological change. Hacktivists are often motivated by a sense of justice, a commitment to free speech, or a desire to expose corruption and wrongdoing. They seek to leverage the power of the internet and digital technologies to amplify their messages and mobilize public opinion. Hacktivism is often rooted in a belief that traditional forms of protest and activism are insufficient or ineffective, prompting hacktivists to take more direct and disruptive actions in the digital realm.

5.3.6 Effects on cybersecurity culture

Hacktivists significantly impact cybersecurity culture by highlighting the political and social dimensions of cyber threats. Their activities emphasize the importance of viewing cybersecurity not only through a technical lens but also as a platform for social and political expression. This dual perspective requires organizations to adopt a more holistic approach to security, considering the motivations behind attacks and the potential societal impacts. Consequently, cybersecurity strategies must incorporate elements of public relations and crisis management, preparing for the reputational damage that hacktivist actions can inflict.

Moreover, the presence of hacktivists in the threat landscape drives organizations to enhance their security measures and practices. The high-profile nature of hacktivist attacks, which often target well-known entities and aim for maximum public exposure, raises awareness of the vulnerabilities within organizational systems. This heightened awareness encourages the adoption of better security protocols, continuous monitoring, and regular security audits. Additionally, hacktivist activities underscore the need for greater transparency and ethical behavior, prompting organizations to review and improve their practices to mitigate the risk of becoming targets. This comprehensive response fosters a more resilient cybersecurity culture that is proactive and adaptive to the evolving threat landscape.

In summary, hacktivists are cyber activists who use their technical skills to promote political and social causes. They engage in various cyberattacks to disrupt, deface, or expose their targets, aiming to raise awareness and effect change. Their motivations are rooted in a desire for justice, transparency, and accountability, making them distinct from other cyber threat actors. While they can raise awareness of important issues and promote positive change, their actions can also inadvertently harm innocent individuals and businesses, creating collateral damage and undermining public support for their causes. The challenge is to find a balance between free speech and security, ensuring that hacktivist activities are not used as a pretext for suppressing legitimate activism or stifling public discourse.

5.4 INSIDERS

5.4.1 Who are they?

Insiders are individuals within an organization who have legitimate access to its systems and data. These insiders include employees, contractors, business partners, and anyone else with authorized access to the organization's resources. Insiders can pose a significant threat because they are trusted and often have extensive knowledge of the organization's operations, systems, and security measures. They can exploit their access and knowledge to cause harm, whether intentionally or unintentionally.

5.4.2 What do they do?

Insiders can engage in a variety of harmful activities. They can steal sensitive data, such as intellectual property, customer information, or financial records, to sell to competitors or other malicious actors. They can also sabotage systems by introducing malware, deleting critical files, or disrupting operations. Sometimes, insiders misuse their access for personal gain, such as fraudulently transferring funds or manipulating company records. Their actions can lead to financial loss, reputational damage, and legal consequences for the organization.

5.4.3 How do they operate?

Insiders exploit their legitimate access to perform malicious activities. They might use their credentials to access sensitive areas of the network or systems. Often, they take advantage of weak security controls, such as poorly managed permissions, lack of monitoring, or inadequate separation of duties. Insiders may also use social engineering tactics to manipulate colleagues into providing additional access or information. Because they are familiar with the organization's security protocols and potential vulnerabilities, they can often carry out their actions without raising immediate suspicion.

5.4.4 Who do they target?

Insiders typically target the organization they work for, but their actions can also affect the organization's clients, partners, and suppliers. They can aim at specific departments or systems that house valuable data or critical operations. For instance, they might focus on financial systems to facilitate fraud, human resources databases to steal personal information, or research and development departments to exfiltrate intellectual property. The broader impact of insider threats can extend to customers and third parties whose data is compromised in the breach.

5.4.5 What motivates them?

The motivations of insiders vary widely and can include financial gain, revenge, ideology, or coercion. Some insiders act out of greed, seeking to profit by selling stolen information or committing fraud. Others can be disgruntled employees looking to retaliate against their employer for perceived wrongdoings, such as unfair treatment or dismissal. Ideological insiders may be motivated by a desire to expose unethical practices or support a cause in which they believe. In some cases, insiders might be coerced or blackmailed by external actors to conduct malicious activities on their behalf. Understanding these motivations is crucial for developing effective strategies to mitigate the risks posed by insider threats.

5.4.6 Effects on cybersecurity culture

Insider threats have a profound impact on an organization's cybersecurity culture. One of the most significant effects is the erosion of trust within the workplace. Since insiders are trusted individuals who have legitimate access to sensitive systems and data, their malicious actions can lead to increased suspicion and reduced morale among employees. This mistrust can create a tense work environment where employees feel monitored and scrutinized, which can lead to decreased job satisfaction and productivity. To mitigate this, organizations often implement more stringent access controls and monitoring systems, which can further affect the perceived autonomy and trustworthiness of the workforce.

Another important effect is the increased emphasis on security training and awareness programs. Insider threats highlight the need for comprehensive security education that extends beyond technical staff to include all employees. Organizations are compelled to develop and enforce policies that emphasize the importance of recognizing and reporting suspicious behavior. This cultural shift toward heightened security awareness encourages employees to take an active role in protecting the organization, fostering a collective sense of responsibility; however, balancing this with the need to maintain a positive and trusting work environment is a delicate challenge that requires careful management and communication from leadership.

Insider threats represent a unique and significant challenge to cybersecurity culture. They undermine trust, necessitate more rigorous monitoring, and emphasize the need for comprehensive security education. By fostering a culture of awareness and shared responsibility, organizations can better defend against the risks posed by insiders while striving to maintain a positive and collaborative work environment. Balancing security measures with employee trust remains a critical aspect of effectively managing insider threats.

Insiders, whether malicious or negligent, pose a significant threat. They have the potential to cause considerable damage due to their access to sensitive information and systems. Addressing insider threats requires a multifaceted approach that includes rigorous security policies, continuous monitoring, and fostering a culture of security awareness. By recognizing the unique risks posed by insiders and implementing comprehensive mitigation strategies, organizations can better protect their assets and maintain a secure and trustworthy environment.

5.5 SCRIPT KIDDIES

5.5.1 Who are they?

Script kiddies, also known as skids or skiddies, are individuals who use existing computer scripts or codes to hack into systems, websites, or networks without understanding the underlying technology. They lack the sophisticated knowledge of professional hackers and rely on prewritten programs or scripts that they download from the internet. These individuals are often young, inexperienced, and motivated by the desire to impress peers or create minor disruptions rather than cause significant harm.

5.5.2 What do they do?

Script kiddies typically engage in low-level cyberattacks, such as defacing websites, launching Denial-of-Service (DoS) attacks, or spreading malware. They exploit known vulnerabilities in systems using tools developed by others. Their actions can range from mere nuisances, like altering website content, to more disruptive activities that can temporarily disable online services.

5.5.3 How do they operate?

Script kiddies use automated tools and scripts freely available on the internet. These tools are designed to exploit known vulnerabilities in software, networks, or websites. Since they lack advanced technical skills, script kiddies often rely on trial and error, blindly running scripts until they find one that works. They may also use forums and online communities to share tools, techniques, and advice on how to conduct their attacks.

5.5.4 Who do they target?

Script kiddies usually target low-hanging fruit, which means systems that are poorly secured and easy to exploit. This includes personal websites, small business networks, and individual user accounts. They often choose targets that require minimal effort to breach. They aim for maximum visibility and impact with the least amount of technical complexity.

5.5.5 What motivates them?

The primary motivation for script kiddies is often the thrill of the hack and the recognition from their peers. They seek to build a reputation within online communities and gain a sense of accomplishment from disrupting systems. Unlike professional cybercriminals who are motivated by financial gain or political objectives, script kiddies are generally driven by the desire for attention, entertainment, or proving their capabilities to others.

5.5.6 Effects on cybersecurity culture

The presence and activities of script kiddies significantly influence the broader cybersecurity culture, primarily by highlighting the importance of basic security measures and continuous vigilance. Although script kiddies are often seen as less sophisticated than other cyber threat actors, their actions can still lead to substantial disruption and damage.

One of the primary impacts of script kiddies on cybersecurity culture is the increased awareness of the importance of patch management. Script kiddies often exploit outdated software with known vulnerabilities, which can be easily mitigated by timely updates and patches. This drives home the necessity for organizations to implement rigorous patch management policies and ensure that all systems are up-to-date with the latest security fixes. Furthermore, the activities of script kiddies emphasize the need for basic cybersecurity hygiene among individuals and smaller organizations that may otherwise consider themselves low-risk targets. The ease with which script kiddies can find and use hacking tools means that no system, regardless of size or perceived insignificance, is entirely safe from attack. This has led to a cultural shift toward more inclusive and widespread cybersecurity education, ensuring that even those outside of large, high-profile organizations understand the risks and necessary precautions. In addition to encouraging better security practices, the actions of script kiddies can also lead to improved incident response strategies. Since script kiddies often perform low-level attacks that are relatively easy to detect, they provide real-world scenarios for cybersecurity teams to practice and refine their incident response processes. This can help organizations develop more effective strategies for identifying, containing, and mitigating cyber threats, ultimately leading to a more resilient cybersecurity posture.

In summary, while script kiddies may lack the advanced skills of more sophisticated cybercriminals, their impact on cybersecurity culture is significant. They serve as a constant reminder of the importance of basic security measures, continuous education, and vigilant incident response. By addressing the threats posed by script kiddies, organizations can build a stronger, more proactive cybersecurity culture that is better equipped to handle a wide range of cyber threats.

Script kiddies represent a unique challenge within the cybersecurity landscape. Their reliance on preexisting tools and lack of deep, technical knowledge does not diminish the potential harm they can cause. Addressing the threat posed by script kiddies requires focusing on strengthening basic security practices and fostering a culture of continuous vigilance. By understanding who script kiddies are, what they do, and their motivations, organizations can better prepare to defend against these and other low-level cyber threats.

5.6 LONE WOLVES

5.6.1 Who are they?

Lone wolves are individuals who operate independently without the backing of any organization, group, or nation-state. Unlike organized cybercriminal groups or state-sponsored actors, lone wolves conduct cyberattacks on their own. They leverage their own skills and resources. These individuals often possess a high level of technical expertise and can be motivated by various personal, ideological, or financial reasons.

5.6.2 What do they do?

Lone wolves engage in a variety of cyber activities, including hacking, phishing, and deploying malware. They may steal sensitive data, disrupt services, deface websites, or launch ransomware attacks. Because they operate alone, their attacks can be unpredictable and highly innovative. These actors often exploit vulnerabilities in systems and networks, bypass security measures, and gain unauthorized access to critical data. Their actions can cause significant damage, both financially and reputationally, to targeted organizations and individuals.

5.6.3 How do they operate?

Lone wolves typically use sophisticated techniques to carry out their attacks. They often begin by conducting reconnaissance to gather information about their target's vulnerabilities. They may use tools such as malware, ransomware, and exploit kits available on the dark web. They also use social engineering tactics to deceive and manipulate individuals into divulging sensitive information. They operate under the radar, making it difficult for authorities to detect and attribute their actions. The anonymity provided by the internet allows them to cover their tracks effectively.

5.6.4 Who do they target?

Lone wolves can target a wide range of entities, including individuals, businesses, government agencies, and critical infrastructure. Their choice of targets often depends on their motivations. For example, financially motivated lone wolves may target businesses and financial institutions to steal money or sensitive information that can be sold. Ideologically motivated actors may target government agencies or organizations they perceive as adversaries. They may also target high-profile individuals or entities to gain notoriety or achieve a specific agenda.

5.6.5 What motivates them?

Lone wolves are driven by diverse motivations. Financial gain is a common motivator, with some attackers seeking to profit from stolen data or ransom payments. Others may be driven by ideological beliefs, such as political or social causes, leading them to engage in hacktivism. Personal grievances, such as revenge against a former employer or individual, can also motivate lone wolves. The thrill of the challenge and the desire for recognition within the hacker community can drive these individuals to conduct cyberattacks.

5.6.6 Effects on cybersecurity culture

The presence of lone wolves poses significant challenges to cybersecurity culture. Their unpredictable and diverse attack methods require organizations to adopt a proactive and comprehensive approach to cybersecurity. This includes regular updates to security protocols, continuous monitoring of unusual activity, and educating employees about the latest threats and social engineering tactics. The existence of lone wolves also underscores the importance of fostering a security-conscious culture within organizations, where every individual understands his or her role in protecting sensitive information and systems from potential threats.

5.7 WHITE HAT HACKERS

5.7.1 Who are they?

White hat hackers, also known as ethical hackers, are cybersecurity professionals who use their skills to improve security systems rather than exploit them. Unlike black hat hackers who have malicious intent, white hats work within the law and often collaborate with organizations to identify and fix security vulnerabilities. They play a crucial role in protecting data and systems from cybersecurity threats by finding and addressing weaknesses before malicious actors can exploit them.

5.7.2 What do they do?

White hat hackers conduct authorized penetration testing, vulnerability assessments, and security audits to evaluate an organization's security posture. They simulate cyberattacks to uncover potential vulnerabilities and provide recommendations for improving security measures. Their work helps organizations strengthen their defenses, comply with regulations, and protect sensitive information from unauthorized access. Additionally, white hats may participate in bug bounty programs where they report security flaws in exchange for rewards.

5.7.3 How do they operate?

White hat hackers operate by using the same tools and techniques as malicious hackers but within a legal and ethical framework. They follow a structured approach, starting with reconnaissance to gather information about the target system. Next, they scan for vulnerabilities and attempt to exploit them in a controlled manner. After identifying security gaps, they document their findings and suggest remediation measures. Throughout the process, white hats adhere to strict ethical guidelines and ensure they do not cause any harm to the systems they are testing.

5.7.4 Who do they target?

White hat hackers target systems, networks, and applications with the explicit permission of the owner. Their primary targets include corporate networks, government systems, financial institutions, and critical infrastructure. They may also focus on consumer applications and products, such as software and Internet of Things (IoT) devices, to ensure they meet security standards. By targeting a wide range of systems, white hats help protect a broad spectrum of industries from cyber threats.

5.7.5 What motivates them?

White hat hackers are motivated by various factors, including a desire to improve cybersecurity, protect sensitive information, and contribute to the safety and security of the digital world. Financial incentives, such as salaries and rewards from bug bounty programs, also play a role. Many white hats are driven by a sense of ethical responsibility and a passion for solving complex security challenges. Their work is often recognized and valued by the cybersecurity community and society at large.

5.7.6 Effects on cybersecurity culture

White hat hackers have a profound impact on cybersecurity culture by promoting proactive security practices and continuous improvement. Their work raises awareness about the importance of identifying and addressing vulnerabilities before they can be exploited. Organizations that engage with white hats demonstrate a commitment to security and build trust with customers and stakeholders. Furthermore, white hat activities encourage a culture of ethical hacking and responsible disclosure, which is essential for the ongoing development of secure technologies and systems.

5.8 BLACK HAT HACKERS

5.8.1 Who are they?

Black hat hackers are groups or individuals who use their technical skills to gain unauthorized access to systems, networks, or data for malicious purposes. Unlike white hat hackers who work to improve security, black hats engage in illegal activities, often causing harm to individuals, businesses, or governments. They are motivated by various factors, including financial gain, political motives, personal satisfaction, or revenge.

5.8.2 What do they do?

Black hat hackers engage in a range of malicious activities, such as stealing sensitive data, deploying malware, launching ransomware attacks, and defacing websites. They may also conduct DDoS attacks to disrupt services or sell stolen data on the dark web. These hackers are constantly looking for vulnerabilities to exploit in order to achieve their objectives, which can include financial theft, espionage, or causing operational disruptions.

5.8.3 How do they operate?

Black hat hackers operate using a variety of sophisticated techniques and tools. They often begin by conducting reconnaissance to identify potential vulnerabilities in their target's systems. Common methods include phishing to steal credentials, exploiting software vulnerabilities, and using malware to gain access and control over systems. They may also use brute force attacks to crack passwords or employ social engineering to manipulate individuals into divulging sensitive information. Once inside a system, they may install backdoors to maintain persistent access, exfiltrate data, and cover their tracks to avoid detection.

5.8.4 Who do they target?

Black hat hackers can target virtually anyone, but they often focus on entities where the potential reward is highest. Common targets include financial institutions, large corporations, government agencies, healthcare organizations, and high-profile individuals. They may also target small- and medium-sized businesses, which often have fewer resources dedicated to cybersecurity. The choice of target is typically driven by the hacker's motive, whether it be financial gain, political impact, or personal vendetta.

5.8.5 What motivates them?

Black hat hackers are driven by a variety of motivations. Financial gain is one of the primary drivers, with hackers stealing and selling sensitive information, engaging in fraud, or demanding ransom. Other motivations include political or ideological beliefs, leading to hacktivism against entities they oppose. Some hackers are motivated by personal grievances, seeking revenge against former employers or adversaries. Additionally, the thrill of the challenge and the desire for notoriety within the hacker community can also motivate black hat activities.

5.8.6 Effects on cybersecurity culture

The presence of black hat hackers has significant implications for cybersecurity culture. Their actions create a constant threat environment that necessitates vigilance and proactive measures. Organizations must invest in robust cybersecurity frameworks, including regular security audits, advanced threat detection systems, and comprehensive employee training programs. The threat posed by black hat hackers also highlights the importance of fostering a culture of security awareness, where all employees understand the risks and their roles in mitigating them. Additionally, the activities of black hat hackers drive innovation in cybersecurity technologies and practices as organizations continuously adapt to counteract evolving threats.

5.9 GRAY HAT HACKERS

5.9.1 Who are they?

Gray hat hackers are individuals who straddle the line between white hat and black hat hacking. They often exploit security vulnerabilities without malicious intent and sometimes without explicit permission. Unlike black hat hackers, gray hats do not usually exploit vulnerabilities for personal gain, but unlike white hats may not always strictly follow ethical or legal standards. They often identify and expose security flaws in systems and networks, sometimes notifying the affected parties afterward.

5.9.2 What do they do?

Gray hat hackers identify and exploit vulnerabilities in computer systems, networks, or applications, but their motivations are not purely malicious or ethical. They may access systems without authorization to uncover flaws and later disclose these vulnerabilities to the affected organizations or the public. Their actions can include penetration testing, security audits, and vulnerability assessments performed without prior consent. In some cases, they may request compensation for their findings after the fact.

5.9.3 How do they operate?

Gray hat hackers operate by scanning and probing networks and systems for vulnerabilities, much like black hat and white hat hackers. They often use a combination of automated tools and manual techniques to discover weaknesses. Once a vulnerability is found, they may exploit it to demonstrate its severity; however, their approach to disclosure can vary: Some may inform the affected organization directly, while others might publish their findings online or in forums, potentially exposing the vulnerability to malicious actors.

5.9.4 Who do they target?

Gray hat hackers can target any entity, from large corporations and government agencies to small businesses and individuals. Their targets often include systems and networks they perceive as insecure or inadequately protected. Unlike black hat hackers, their choice of target is not necessarily driven by potential financial gain but rather by the challenge of finding and exposing security flaws.

5.9.5 What motivates them?

Gray hat hackers' motivations are diverse and complex. Many are driven by a sense of curiosity and the desire to improve cybersecurity by identifying and reporting vulnerabilities. Some are motivated by the challenge and technical skills required to discover security flaws. Others seek recognition within the cybersecurity community or aim to push organizations toward better security practices. In some cases, they might also be motivated by the potential for financial reward through bug bounty programs or other forms of compensation.

5.9.6 Effects on cybersecurity culture

Gray hat hackers have a nuanced impact on cybersecurity culture. On the one hand, their activities highlight the importance of proactive security measures and the need for continuous monitoring and improvement of systems. Their findings can lead to the patching of critical vulnerabilities and the strengthening of security protocols. On the other hand, their methods of disclosure can sometimes cause more harm than good, especially if vulnerabilities are made public before they can be patched. This duality reinforces the need for ethical guidelines and frameworks for vulnerability disclosure, encouraging a collaborative approach to improving cybersecurity while minimizing potential risks.

5.10 BLUE HAT HACKERS

5.10.1 Who are they?

Blue hat hackers are individuals who are often invited by companies to test their security systems and identify vulnerabilities before a product launch. They are not typically employed by the company but are contracted specifically for their expertise in finding and mitigating security threats. Blue hats can be thought of as external security consultants who help to fortify an organization's defenses against potential cyber threats.

5.10.2 What do they do?

Blue hat hackers perform security testing and vulnerability assessments on software, networks, and systems. They simulate cyberattacks to uncover weaknesses that could be exploited by malicious actors. By identifying these vulnerabilities, blue hat hackers help organizations patch and strengthen their security measures before they are exposed to the public. Their work is crucial in ensuring that products and systems are secure upon release.

5.10.3 How do they operate?

Blue hat hackers operate by using a combination of automated tools and manual techniques to test the security of systems. They often work under specific guidelines provided by the organization, focusing on particular areas of concern. Blue hats may conduct penetration testing, code reviews, and security audits. They report their findings to the organization, providing detailed analysis and recommendations for remediation. Their operations are conducted in a controlled environment, ensuring that no real harm is done during the testing phase.

5.10.4 Who do they target?

Blue hat hackers target the systems, networks, and applications of the organizations that hire them. Their targets are predetermined by the scope of the engagement and the organization's specific security concerns. Unlike black hat or gray hat hackers, blue hat hackers do not choose targets independently but work on designated systems to improve security measures.

5.10.5 What motivates them?

Blue hat hackers are motivated by a variety of factors, including financial compensation, professional recognition, and the intellectual challenge of finding and fixing security vulnerabilities. Many blue hats are driven by a desire to contribute positively to cybersecurity and to help organizations protect their data and systems. The contractual nature of their work provides both a financial incentive and an opportunity to showcase their skills in a professional setting.

5.10.6 Effects on cybersecurity culture

Blue hat hackers have a positive impact on cybersecurity culture by fostering a proactive approach to security. Their involvement highlights the importance of thorough security testing and the value of external perspectives in identifying vulnerabilities. By working with blue hats, organizations demonstrate a commitment to security and a willingness to invest in preventive measures. This collaboration helps to build a culture of continuous improvement and vigilance, encouraging organizations to regularly test and update their security protocols.

In summary, understanding the roles of various threat actors is crucial for developing effective defense strategies. White hat hackers contribute positively by identifying and addressing vulnerabilities, serving as ethical guardians of cyberspace. In contrast, black hat hackers seek to exploit weaknesses for personal or financial gain, posing significant risks to organizations and individuals. Gray hat hackers operate in a moral gray area, sometimes crossing ethical boundaries while aiming to improve security, but their actions can have unintended consequences. Blue hat hackers, typically external security testers, play a role in identifying weaknesses before they can be exploited. Together, these actors represent the spectrum of ethical and unethical behavior in cybersecurity, emphasizing the importance of cultivating a culture of vigilance, ethical hacking, and proactive defense to protect digital environments.

5.11 CYBERTERRORISTS

5.11.1 Who are they?

Unlike traditional cybercriminals motivated by financial gain, cyberterrorists are groups or individuals who use digital attacks to achieve political, religious, or ideological objectives. Cyberterrorists aim to instill fear, cause disruption, and advance their causes through targeted cyberattacks. These actors can be state-sponsored, part of organized groups, or even lone wolves driven by extremist ideologies.

5.11.2 What do they do?

Cyberterrorists engage in activities designed to create chaos, spread fear, and disrupt critical services. They often target essential infrastructure such as power grids, communication networks, transportation systems, and financial institutions. By compromising these critical systems, they can cause widespread panic, economic damage, and potentially physical harm to civilians. Cyberterrorists also use cyber espionage to steal sensitive information and cyber propaganda to spread their messages and recruit new members.

5.11.3 How do they operate?

Cyberterrorists use various methods to carry out their attacks. They exploit vulnerabilities in software and hardware, deploy malware such as ransomware and spyware, and launch DDoS attacks to overwhelm systems. Phishing campaigns and social engineering tactics are also common, tricking individuals into revealing sensitive information or granting access to secure systems. Cyberterrorists often use encrypted communication channels and the dark web to coordinate their activities and evade detection by authorities.

5.11.4 Who do they target?

Cyberterrorists primarily target critical infrastructure to maximize disruption and panic. This includes power plants, water supply systems, hospitals, and government institutions. They may also target financial institutions to destabilize economies and steal funds to finance their operations. Additionally, cyberterrorists can attack private corporations and media outlets to disrupt services, steal data, and spread disinformation. The ultimate goal is to undermine public trust and create widespread fear.

5.11.5 What motivates them?

The motivations behind cyberterrorism are deeply rooted in political, religious, or ideological beliefs. Cyberterrorists aim to advance their causes by creating fear and uncertainty among the general population and governments. They seek to draw attention to their grievances, coerce political change, or retaliate against perceived enemies. For some groups, cyberterrorism is a tool to demonstrate power and capability, potentially attracting more followers and increasing their influence.

5.11.6 Effects on cybersecurity culture

Cyberterrorism significantly impacts cybersecurity culture by heightening awareness and urgency around cyber threats. Organizations and governments recognize the potentially devastating effects of cyberterrorist activities, which can target critical infrastructure, financial systems, and communication networks. This recognition drives a shift toward prioritizing cybersecurity measures and adopting a proactive stance against potential threats.

The threat of cyberterrorism also fosters a culture of continuous vigilance and adaptation within cybersecurity practices. It encourages developing and implementing advanced security protocols, comprehensive risk assessments, and incident response strategies. Additionally, it promotes collaboration between private and public sectors, as well as international cooperation, to combat cyberterrorism's global nature. This cultural shift underscores the importance of maintaining a strong, resilient, and adaptive cybersecurity posture to protect against evolving threats and ensure the security and stability of essential services and infrastructure.

In conclusion, cyberterrorism represents a significant and growing threat in the age. Cyberterrorists seek to inflict fear, disruption, and damage through attacks on critical infrastructure, government systems, and private sector networks. Their motivations often stem from ideological, political, or religious beliefs, aiming to achieve their objectives through the destabilization of their targets. Understanding their methods, which range from sophisticated cyberattacks to simple yet effective disruption tactics, is essential for developing sophisticated defense mechanisms. The threat of cyberterrorism underscores the need for enhanced cybersecurity measures, international cooperation, and ongoing vigilance to protect against these malicious actors.

5.12 COMPETITORS (CORPORATE ESPIONAGE)

5.12.1 Who are they?

In the cybersecurity context, competitors are rival businesses that engage in unethical or illegal activities for the purpose of gaining an advantage over their industry counterparts. These entities seek to outmaneuver their competitors by accessing sensitive information, trade secrets, intellectual property, or proprietary technologies. Unlike traditional business competition, which relies on legitimate strategies such as marketing and innovation, competitors in this realm use underhanded tactics to undermine their rivals.

5.12.2 What do they do?

Competitors conduct cyber espionage to steal valuable information that can give them a strategic edge. This includes accessing confidential business plans, client databases, financial records, and research and development (R&D) data. By acquiring such information, they can anticipate and counter their competitors' moves, reduce their own R&D costs, and swiftly adapt to market changes. These activities disrupt the victim organization's operations, erode trust, and can lead to significant financial and reputational damage.

5.12.3 How do they operate?

Competitors employ a variety of methods to infiltrate their target's systems. They may use phishing attacks to trick employees into divulging login credentials or implanting malware through seemingly benign emails or software updates. Social engineering is another common tactic where attackers manipulate individuals into breaking security protocols. Additionally, competitors may exploit vulnerabilities in outdated software or poorly configured systems to gain unauthorized access. Advanced Persistent Threats (APTs) are particularly insidious, involving long-term, targeted cyberattacks where the intruder remains undetected while extracting valuable information over time.

5.12.4 Who do they target?

Competitors primarily target businesses within the same industry. They focus on companies that are perceived as direct rivals or those leading in innovation and market share. High-value targets often include technology firms, pharmaceutical companies, financial institutions, and manufacturing giants. These sectors hold critical intellectual property and sensitive data that can provide a substantial competitive advantage if compromised.

5.12.5 What motivates them?

The primary motivation for competitors engaging in cyber espionage is financial gain. By stealing proprietary information, they can reduce their R&D expenses, accelerate product development, and improve their market positioning. Gaining access to competitor strategies allows them to anticipate and counter market moves, securing a larger market share and increasing profitability. In some cases, the motivation might also be to inflict reputational harm on the rival, causing customers and partners to lose trust in the victim organization, thereby weakening its market position.

5.12.6 Effects on cybersecurity culture

Competitors and corporate espionage significantly impact cybersecurity culture within organizations. These threats necessitate a heightened focus on vigilance and proactive defense mechanisms. Companies targeted by corporate espionage often develop a stronger cybersecurity posture, emphasizing the importance of protecting intellectual property and sensitive data. This results in implementing advanced security measures such as encryption, intrusion detection systems, and rigorous access controls. Furthermore, the constant threat of espionage fosters a culture of continuous improvement where security protocols are regularly updated and tested to withstand sophisticated attacks.

The presence of competitors engaging in corporate espionage also instills a sense of urgency and awareness among employees. Training programs become more frequent and comprehensive, focusing on recognizing and responding to phishing attempts, social engineering, and other common tactics corporate spies use. Employees are educated on the importance of safeguarding proprietary information and are encouraged to report suspicious activities. Awareness and active participation from all levels of the organization contribute to a more resilient cybersecurity culture, where every member understands his or her role in protecting the company's assets.

In summary, the threat posed by competitors and corporate espionage drives organizations to adopt a more rigorous and comprehensive approach to cybersecurity. This includes advanced technological defenses, continuous employee education, and a culture of vigilance and proactive risk management. These efforts collectively enhance the organization's resilience against espionage attempts and contribute to a stronger, more secure business environment. Understanding the nature and methods of competitors in cybersecurity is crucial for organizations aiming to protect their assets and maintain a competitive edge. By recognizing the tactics employed and the motivations driving these actors, businesses can better prepare their defenses, implement necessary security measures, and foster a culture of vigilance and proactive security practices. Addressing these threats head-on ensures not only the protection of sensitive information but also the long-term stability and success of the organization in a highly competitive market.

5.13 CONCLUSION

This chapter examined the diverse landscape of threat actors, exploring who they are, what they do, how they operate, their targets, their motivations, and how they affect the cybersecurity culture of an organization. Table 5.1 summarizes the types of threat actors, their motivations, targets, and methods. From cybercriminals driven by financial gain to nation-states engaging in cyber espionage for strategic advantages, the spectrum of threat actors is clearly vast and varied. Hacktivists pursue ideological goals, insiders exploit their privileged

Table 5.1 Summary of types, motivations, target, and methods of threat actors

SUMMARY OF CYBER THREAT ACTORS: TYPES, MOTIVATIONS, TARGETS, AND METHODS

THREAT ACTOR TYPES	PRIMARY MOTIVATION	COMMON TARGETS	METHODS OF OPERATION
Cyber Criminals	Financial Gain	Individuals, businesses, financial institutions	Phishing, malware distribution, ransomware, identity theft, DDoS attacks
Nation States	Political, Economic, Military Gain	Government agencies, military, critical infrastructure, corporations	APTs (Advanced Persistent Threats), cyber espionage, sabotage, misinformation campaigns
Hacktivists	Political or Social Change	Government agencies, corporations, law enforcement	DDoS attacks, website defacement, data breaches, information leaks
Insiders	Financial Gain, Revenge, Coercion	Internal organization (employees, partners)	Data theft, sabotage, unauthorized access, misuse of credentials
Script Kiddies	Thrill, Recognition	Low-security websites, small businesses	Pre-written scripts, DDoS attacks, website defacements
Lone Wolves	Ideological, Financial Gain, Revenge	Individuals, businesses, government agencies	Phishing, malware, ransomware, social engineering
White Hat Hackers	Improve Security, Financial Rewards	Organizations that hire them	Penetration testing, vulnerability assessments, security audits
Black Hat Hackers	Financial Gain, Personal Satisfaction	Any organization with valuable data or assets	Hacking, malware, ransomware, DDoS attacks, data theft
Gray Hat Hackers	Improve Security, Personal Challenge	Various entities (without permission)	Vulnerability scanning, penetration testing, public disclosure
Blue Hat Hackers	Improve Security, Financial Compensation	Organizations that hire them	Security testing, vulnerability assessments, simulated attacks
Cyber Terrorists	Political, Ideological Goals	Critical infrastructure, government, financial institutions	DDoS attacks, malware, cyber espionage, cyber propaganda
Competitors (Corporate Espionage)	Financial gain, competitive advantage	Rival businesses, industry leaders	Phishing, social engineering, APTs, data theft, malware

access for personal or financial reasons, and script kiddies disrupt systems for the thrill of it. Cyberterrorists aim to incite fear and disruption, while competitors and corporate espionage actors seek to gain a competitive edge through illicit means.

This chapter also delved into the roles of lone wolves who act independently, white hat hackers who work ethically to improve security, and black hat hackers who engage in illegal activities. Also discussed were gray hat hackers who operate in a legal and ethical gray area and blue hat hackers who are often invited by organizations to test security systems. Each of these actors brings unique challenges and dynamics to the cybersecurity landscape.

Understanding these threat actors is crucial for organizations to develop effective cybersecurity strategies. By identifying the specific methods and motivations behind each type of threat, organizations can tailor their defenses to address the most relevant risks. This targeted approach allows for more efficient allocation of resources and better preparation against potential attacks. Recognizing the impact of these threat actors on cybersecurity culture highlights the importance of fostering an environment of vigilance, continuous improvement, and proactive risk management. By doing so, organizations can build a refined cybersecurity framework that protects their assets and strengthens their overall resilience in the face of evolving cyber threats.

By comprehensively understanding the various threat actors, from black hats to lone wolves, and leveraging the skills of white and blue hat hackers, organizations can enhance their cybersecurity posture. This multifaceted approach ensures that they are better equipped to anticipate, defend against, and recover from cyberattacks, ultimately leading to a more secure and resilient digital environment.

DISCUSSION QUESTIONS

1. Among the different types of threat actors discussed (e.g., cybercriminals, nation-states, hacktivists), which do you think poses the most significant challenge to cybersecurity professionals, and why?
2. How do the motivations of different threat actors (financial gain, political goals, ideological beliefs) influence the methods and tactics they use in their cyber attacks?
3. Considering the impact of insider threats, what are the most effective strategies an organization can use to mitigate the risks associated with insiders?
4. Do you believe hacktivists serve a positive role in society by exposing unethical practices, or do their actions cause more harm than good? Provide examples to support your argument.
5. How do nation-state cyber operations differ from those of other threat actors in terms of sophistication, scale, and objectives? What are the implications for global cybersecurity?
6. Why should organizations still be concerned about less sophisticated attackers like script kiddies, and how can these actors highlight the need for basic cybersecurity hygiene?
7. How does cyberterrorism differ from other forms of terrorism, and what are the unique challenges it presents to national security?
8. What role do white hat hackers play in strengthening cybersecurity culture, and how can organizations best utilize their skills to enhance security measures?
9. Should gray hat hackers be encouraged for their potential contributions to cybersecurity, or should their actions be regulated to prevent potential harm? Discuss the ethical implications.
10. How can understanding different threat actors and their tactics help organizations develop a more robust cybersecurity culture and better defense strategies?

BIBLIOGRAPHY

Akinola, A., & Afonja, A. (2022). *Introduction to cyber-security*. Chudace Publishing.

Alsowail, R. A., & Al-Shehari, T. (2020). Empirical detection techniques of insider threat incidents. IEEE Access, 8, 78385–78402. https://doi.org/10.1109/ACCESS.2020.2989739

Beretas, C. P. (2023). Analysis of white and black hat hacker roles, practices and techniques, considering ethical and legal issues, including bug bounty programs. SunText Review of Economics & Business, 4(4). https://suntextreviews.org/uploads/journals/pdfs/1700148397.pdf

Brancik, K. (2007). Insider computer fraud (1st ed.). CRC Press. https://www.perlego.com/book/1516517/insider-computer-fraud-an-indepth-framework-for-detecting-and-defending-against-insider-it-attacks-pdf (Original work published 2007)

Civuli, A., Luma-Osmani, S., Rufati, E., & Arifi, G. (2022). Cyber espionage consequences as a growing threat. *Journal of Natural Sciences & Mathematics (JNSM)*, 7. UDC: 327.84:004.493. https://www.researchgate.net/profile/Shkurte-Luma-Osmani/publication/368461675_Cyber_Espionage_Consequences_as_a_Growing_Threat/links/63e94f18c002331f72745ee8/Cyber-Espionage-Consequences-as-a-Growing-Threat.pdf

Clifton, A. (2024). Strategies for insider threat mitigation and detection (doctoral dissertation, Walden University). Walden Dissertations and Doctoral Studies, 15446. Retrieved from https://scholarworks.waldenu.edu/dissertations/15446

Cybersecurity and Infrastructure Security Agency. (n.d.). Nation-state cyber actors. CISA. https://www.cisa.gov/nation-state-cyber-actors

Gaia, J., Sanders, G., Sanders, S., Upadhyaya, S., Wang, X., & Woo, C. (2021). Dark traits and hacking potential. *Journal of Organizational Psychology*, *21*(3), 23–46. https://par.nsf.gov/servlets/purl/10335905

Gandhi, F., Pansaniya, D., & Naik, S. (2022). Ethical hacking: Types of hackers, cyber attacks and security. *International Research Journal of Innovations in Engineering and Technology*, *6*(1), 28–32. https://www.proquest.com/openview/99b27c29320e151b9d151305dedef0d5/1?pq-origsite=gscholar&cbl=5314840

George, J. J., & Leidner, D. E. (2019). From clicktivism to hacktivism: Understanding digital activism. *Information and Organization*, *29*(3), 100249. https://doi.org/10.1016/j.infoandorg.2019.04.001

Graphus. (2022, September 16). 10 nation-state cyberattack facts you need to know. Graphus. https://www.graphus.ai/blog/10-nation-state-cyberattack-facts-you-need-to-know/

Hosford, K. (n.d.). Hacker generations, subcultures and hat colours: A more practical approach to classification. https://www.researchgate.net/profile/Kevin-Hosford/publication/356285258_Hacker_Generations_Subcultures_and_Hat_Colours_A_More_Practical_Approach_to_Classification/links/62cd8d4ab261d22751e9cb96/Hacker-Generations-Subcultures-and-Hat-Colours-A-More-Practical-Approach-to-Classification.pdf

Jain, N., Tiwari, I., Patil, C. H., Solankar, D., Dubey, H., Roy, K., & Dhar, A. (n.d.). Hacking and its vulnerabilities. *3rd National Level Students' Research Conference on "Innovative Ideas and Inventions in Computer Science & IT with Its Sustainability"*, Dr. Vishwanath Karad MIT World Peace University, Pune, Maharashtra, India. https://www.researchgate.net/profile/Chandrashekhar-Patil-8/publication/361558831_Hacking_and_Its_Vulnerabilities/links/62b93eead49f803365bdabdb/Hacking-and-Its-Vulnerabilities.pdf

Jeong, M., & Zo, H. (2021). Preventing insider threats to enhance organizational security: The role of opportunity-reducing techniques. *Telematics and Informatics*, 63, 101670. https://doi.org/10.1016/j.tele.2021.101670

Joshi, S., Singh, S. K., & Sharma, M. (2023). Cybercrime by minors. In Pradeep Kumar Roy & Asis Kumar Tripathy (Eds.), *Cybercrime in social media* (pp. 143–166). Chapman and Hall/CRC.

Karagiannopoulos, V. (2021). A short history of hacktivism: Its past and present and what can we learn from it. In T. Owen & J. Marshall (Eds.), *Rethinking cybercrime: Critical debates* (pp. 63–86). Springer International Publishing. https://doi.org/10.1007/978-3-030-55841-3_4

Khan, N., Houghton, R. J., & Sharples, S. (2022). Understanding factors that influence unintentional insider threat: A framework to counteract unintentional risks. *Cognition, Technology & Work*, 24, 393–421. https://doi.org/10.1007/s10111-021-00690-z

Lutkevich, B. (2021, October). Script kiddie. TechTarget. https://www.techtarget.com/searchsecurity/definition/script-kiddy-or-script-kiddie

Macdonald, S., Jarvis, L., & Lavis, S. M. (2019). Cyberterrorism today? Findings from a follow-on survey of researchers. *Studies in Conflict & Terrorism*, *45*(8), 727–752. https://doi.org/10.1080/1057610X.2019.1696444

Mitchell, B. (2020). Corporate cyberespionage: Identification and prevention part 1. *EDPACS*, *62*(5), 1–14. https://doi.org/10.1080/07366981.2020.1798594

Montenegro, K. R. (n.d.). Ethical perspectives on hacktivism: The roles and actions of hacker activist groups [Doctoral dissertation]. De La Salle University. https://www.researchgate.net/profile/Kyla-Montenegro-2/publication/380874397_ETHICAL_PERSPECTIVES_ON_HACKTIVISMMontenegro_Kyla_R/links/6651e9e60b0d2845745ae90a/ETHICAL-PERSPECTIVES-ON-HACKTIVISMMontenegro-Kyla-R.pdf

Poudel, B., & Karna, S. K. (2024). What influences a hacker to be a black hat? *Medicon Engineering Themes*, 6(6). https://doi.org/10.55162/MCET.06.215

Ramdinmawii, E., Ghisingh, S., & Sharma, U. M. (2014). A study on the cyber-crime and cyber criminals: A global problem. *International Journal of Web Technology*, 3, 172–179. http://www.ijwebt.com/documents/%20IIR_IJWT_042.pdf

Romagna, M. (2020). *Evolution of hacktivism: From origins to now. From Sit-Ins to# revolutions: Media and the changing nature of protests*. Bloomsbury Publishing, 65–76.

Ruohonen, J., & Saddiqa, M. (2024). What do we know about the psychology of insider threats? https://doi.org/10.48550/arXiv.2407.05943

Sailio, M., Latvala, O.-M., & Szanto, A. (2020). Cyber threat actors for the factory of the future. *Applied Sciences*, *10*(12), 4334. https://doi.org/10.3390/app10124334

Security Staff. (2024, April 29). Experts weigh in on the MITRE nation-state cyberattack. Security Magazine. https://www.securitymagazine.com/articles/100616-experts-weigh-in-on-the-mitre-nation-state-cyberattack

Sinha, S., & Arora, Y. (2020). Ethical hacking: The story of a white hat hacker. *International Journal of Innovative Research in Computer Science & Technology (IJIRCST)*, *8*(3). https://elsevier-ssrn-document-store-prod.s3.amazonaws.com/20/08/10/ssrn_id3670801_code3665699.pdf

Snyder, O. (2022). Hacktivism's threat to cyber security today. Available at SSRN 4073748. https://elsevier-ssrn-document-store-prod.s3.amazonaws.com/22/04/02/ssrn_id4073748_code4549250.pdf

Soesanto, S. (2020). *Cyber terrorism: Why it exists, why it doesn't, and why it will.* Real Instituto Elcano, ARI 47/2020. https://media.realinstitutoelcano.org/wp-content/uploads/2021/11/ari47-2020-soesanto-cyber-terrorism-why-it-exists-why-it-doesnt-and-why-it-will.pdf

The Cyber Post. (2021, October 22). 'Lone Wolf' hacker group targeting Afghanistan and India with commodity RATs. The Cyber Post. https://thecyberpost.com/news/hackers/attacks/lone-wolf-hacker-group-targeting-afghanistan-and-india-with-commodity-rats/

Ulianizky, Z., & Segev Moyal, O. (2022). Understanding 'Lone Wolf' attacks: Dissecting and modeling 2022's most powerful cyber attacks [Video]. XM Cyber. https://info.xmcyber.com/understanding-lone-wolf-attacks

Vaishy, S., & Gupta, H. (2021). Cybercriminals' motivations for targeting government organizations. *2021 9th International Conference on Reliability, Infocom Technologies and Optimization (Trends and Future Directions) (ICRITO)*, Noida, India (pp. 1–6). https://doi.org/10.1109/ICRITO51393.2021.9596104

Vandervelden, S., Chowdhury, M. M., & Latif, S. (2021). Managing the cyber world: Hacker edition. 2021 *International Conference on Electrical, Computer, Communications and Mechatronics Engineering (ICECCME)* (pp. 1–6). IEEE. https://doi.org/10.1109/ICECCME52200.2021.9590870

Veerasamy, N. (2020). Cyberterrorism – The spectre that is the convergence of the physical and virtual worlds. In V. Benson & J. Mcalaney (Eds.), *Emerging cyber threats and cognitive vulnerabilities* (pp. 27–52). Academic Press. https://doi.org/10.1016/B978-0-12-816203-3.00002-2

Vishnuram, G., Tripathi, K., & Tyagi, A. K. (2022). Ethical hacking: Importance, controversies and scope in the future. *2022 International Conference on Computer Communication and Informatics (ICCCI)* (pp. 01–06). IEEE. https://doi.org/10.1109/ICCCI54379.2022.9740860

Weimann, G. (n.d.). Cyberterrorism: How real is the threat? United States Institute of Peace Special Report, 1–12. https://www.usip.org/sites/default/files/sr119.pdf

Chapter 6

Education, training, and awareness (ETA) in cybersecurity culture

As cyber threats become more complex and frequent, the need for a strong cybersecurity culture has never been more critical. Key to this culture are the pillars of education, training, and awareness (ETA) (Figure 6.1). These form the foundation for developing and maintaining a secure environment. It is not just a necessity but a tool for empowerment in building a strong cybersecurity culture.

ETA are three important parts that strengthen an organization's cybersecurity efforts. Education includes formal learning, such as school programs and professional certifications. It gives people a strong knowledge of cybersecurity and ensures a steady flow of knowledgeable professionals who can confidently tackle any threat. Training involves hands-on activities to teach employees the skills they need to respond to cyber incidents. It is essential to develop practical skills to handle security incidents quickly and effectively. Awareness means keeping everyone in the organization informed about cybersecurity threats and best practices, helping create a culture of alertness and proactive defense. Awareness campaigns

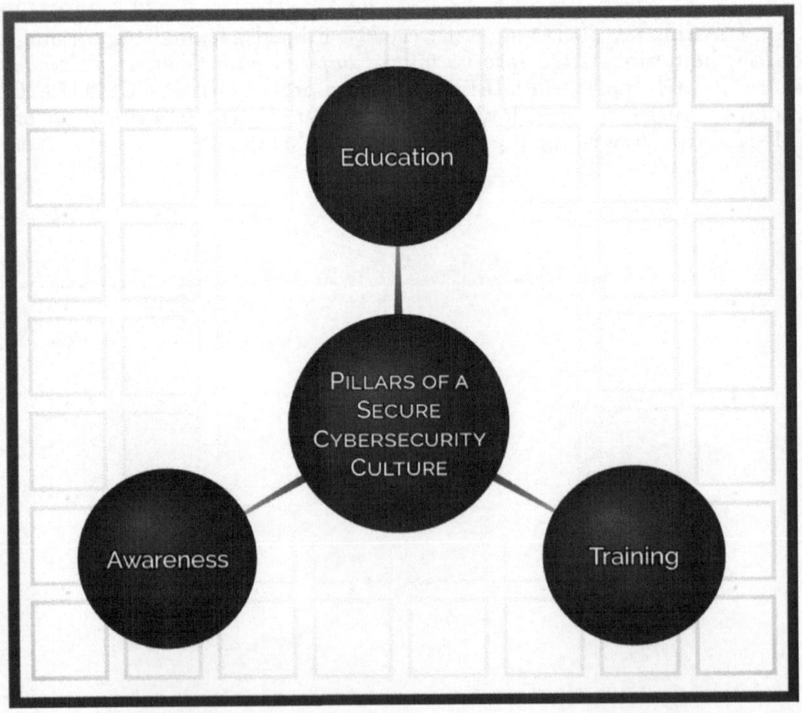

Figure 6.1 Pillars of cybersecurity training.

DOI: 10.1201/9781003368496-6

make cybersecurity a part of everyone's daily routine and reduce the risk of mistakes that can lead to security breaches. This comprehensive approach instills a sense of capability and confidence in the workforce, making ETA an integral part of the cybersecurity culture.

By integrating ETA into an organization's daily life, companies can improve their defense systems and encourage employees to think proactively about security. This holistic approach is essential for identifying and mitigating threats before they can cause major problems. Also, focusing on ETA builds resilience, so the organization is ready to handle cyber incidents and recover quickly from any disruptions.

In summary, ETA is a key part of a comprehensive cybersecurity strategy. By investing in these areas, organizations can create a security-conscious culture that protects against current threats and prepares for future challenges.

In the following sections, the role of education in cybersecurity will be presented. This chapter will examine different training programs and discuss how to run effective awareness campaigns. It will also cover how to integrate ETA into organizational culture and address common challenges. You will look at some solutions with examples and best practices. Finally, the chapter will explore future trends in ETA, including emerging technologies, the evolution of cyber threats, and global perspectives.

6.1 THE ROLE OF EDUCATION

Education is the cornerstone of a strong cybersecurity culture. In an era where cyber threats are constantly evolving, having a well-educated workforce is crucial for any organization. Education in cybersecurity encompasses a range of learning opportunities. Whether it is formal academic programs or professional certifications, these learning opportunities play a vital role in equipping individuals with the knowledge and skills necessary to respond effectively to cyber incidents. By investing in employee education, organizations can construct a shield against cyberattacks while fostering a security-conscious workforce.

A comprehensive approach to cybersecurity education, as shown in Figure 6.2, is multifaceted and includes formal education, certifications, and professional development. Continuous learning, on the other hand, emphasizes the importance of staying updated with the latest trends and advancements in the field. Together, these elements create a well-rounded educational framework that supports the ongoing development of cybersecurity professionals and strengthens an organization's overall security posture.

6.1.1 Formal education

Formal education is essential in developing a strong foundation in cybersecurity. Universities and colleges offer structured programs, such as bachelor's and master's degrees in cybersecurity, information technology, or computer science. These programs cover a wide range of topics, including network security, ethical hacking, and cryptography. Formal education provides students with both theoretical knowledge and practical skills, ensuring they are well-prepared to tackle the challenges of the cybersecurity field. The structured nature of these programs allows for a deep dive into complex subjects, fostering critical thinking and problem-solving abilities that are crucial for cybersecurity professionals.

For example, a bachelor's degree in cybersecurity might include courses like Introduction to Cybersecurity, Network Security, and Ethical Hacking. In these courses, students learn to protect computer networks, identify vulnerabilities, and respond to cyber incidents. At the graduate level, programs frequently offer more specialized subjects such as Cyber Threat Intelligence and Advanced Cryptography. Students engage in research projects and

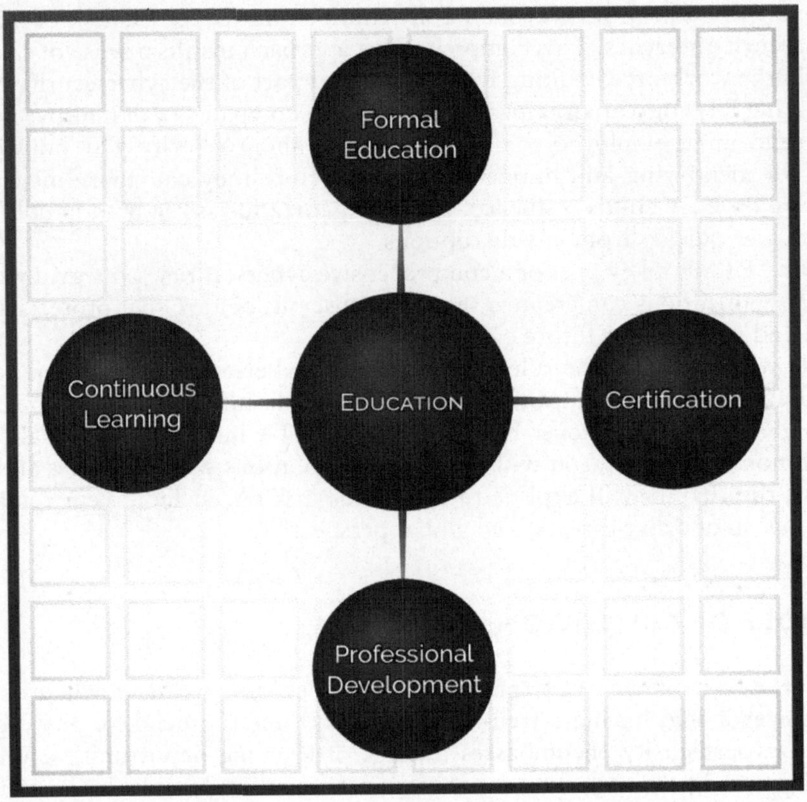

Figure 6.2 Cybersecurity education.

hands-on labs to apply their knowledge practically. These programs not only prepare students for immediate entry into the cybersecurity workforce but also lay the groundwork for advanced study and research in the field.

6.1.2 Certifications

Certifications are professional credentials that validate an individual's expertise and skills in specific areas of cybersecurity. They are essential for career advancement and are often required by employers to ensure that their staff has the necessary competencies to handle cybersecurity tasks effectively. Certifications provide a standardized measure of knowledge and skills. This is particularly important in a field as dynamic and complex as cybersecurity. By obtaining certifications, professionals demonstrate their commitment to maintaining high standards of practice and staying current with the latest developments in the field.

Popular cybersecurity certifications include the Certified Information Systems Security Professional (CISSP), Certified Ethical Hacker (CEH), and CompTIA Security+. Each of these certifications focuses on different aspects of cybersecurity. The CISSP certification covers broad topics like risk management and security operations, making it ideal for experienced security practitioners. The CEH certification focuses on ethical hacking and penetration testing, teaching professionals how to identify and exploit vulnerabilities ethically. CompTIA Security+ is an entry-level certification that covers essential cybersecurity knowledge and skills suitable for those new to the field. These certifications often require passing rigorous exams and ongoing education to maintain them. They ensure that certified professionals remain knowledgeable and skilled.

6.1.3 Professional development

Professional development involves continuous learning and skill enhancement for individuals already working in the cybersecurity field. It is crucial to stay updated on new technologies, emerging threats, and best practices. Professional development opportunities include attending conferences, workshops, webinars, and training sessions. These events provide valuable insights from industry experts, hands-on experiences, and opportunities to network with peers. They help cybersecurity professionals to stay current and adapt to the rapidly changing threat landscape.

There are many opportunities for cybersecurity professionals. Conferences like Black Hat and DEF CON (Defense Readiness Condition or Defense Condition) offer sessions on the latest trends and technologies in cybersecurity. Participants can attend expert talks, participate in hands-on workshops, and network with peers. Webinars and online training courses are also valuable resources. They allow professionals to learn at their own pace and from any location. Many organizations provide in-house training programs to keep their staff updated on the latest security practices and threats. A company might offer quarterly training sessions on recognizing phishing attacks, complete with simulations to practice responding to such incidents. These ongoing learning opportunities ensure that cybersecurity professionals and staff maintain their expertise and are prepared to handle new challenges.

6.1.4 Continuous learning

Continuous learning is essential for cybersecurity professionals to keep up with the rapidly changing threat landscape. It involves regularly updating their knowledge and skills through online courses, reading industry reports, and participating in professional communities. Continuous learning helps professionals stay ahead of new threats and technologies, ensuring they can effectively protect their organizations.

Online platforms like Coursera and LinkedIn Learning offer a wide range of cybersecurity courses that professionals can take at their own pace. These courses cover topics from basic cybersecurity awareness to advanced threat intelligence in cybersecurity. Staying current with the latest research papers, industry reports, and cybersecurity news is also important. Regularly reading sites like Krebs on Security, SANS Cyber Security Newsletters, or Threatpost helps professionals understand new threats and technologies. Joining professional communities and forums, such as ISACA or $(ISC)^2$, allows individuals to share knowledge, ask questions, and stay informed about industry developments. Continuous learning ensures that cybersecurity professionals remain knowledgeable and skilled, ready to tackle new challenges as they arise.

Education is the bedrock of a strong cybersecurity culture. From formal education programs that build foundational knowledge to certifications that validate specific skills, each plays a crucial role in preparing individuals to face the complicated threat landscape. Professional development ensures that those already in the field stay current with new technologies and emerging threats, while continuous learning emphasizes the importance of ongoing education to maintain a proactive security mindset.

In the next section, you will explore the training programs. The section will discuss why training is important, the different types of training available, and how to develop effective training programs. You will also see the role of hands-on training and simulations and how to measure the effectiveness of these programs.

6.2 TRAINING PROGRAMS

Training programs are another critical aspect of a strong cybersecurity culture. While education provides the foundational knowledge and certifications to validate specific skills, training programs bridge the gap between theory and practice. They offer practical, hands-on experiences that enable individuals to apply what they have learned in real-world scenarios. This is particularly important in cybersecurity, where threats are constantly evolving, and the ability to respond quickly and effectively can mean the difference between a minor incident and a major security breach.

The importance of training programs cannot be overstated. They help ensure that all members of an organization, from entry-level employees to top executives, understand their roles in maintaining security. Regular training keeps everyone informed about the latest threats and best practices. It reduces the risk of human error, a common factor in security breaches. By investing in comprehensive training programs, organizations can build a proactive security culture where employees are prepared to identify, respond to, and recover from cyber incidents.

Training is essential for several reasons. It helps employees develop the skills needed to identify and mitigate cyber threats. This is crucial because the cyber threat landscape is constantly changing, with new types of attacks emerging regularly. Without proper training, employees may not recognize these threats, leaving the organization vulnerable. Training also ensures that employees are familiar with the organization's security policies and procedures, which is essential for maintaining a consistent security stance.

Moreover, regular training fosters a culture of security awareness. When employees understand the importance of cybersecurity and how they can contribute to it, they are more likely to follow best practices and less likely to engage in risky behaviors. This cultural shift can significantly enhance an organization's overall security. In addition, training can boost employee morale and confidence, as they feel more competent and prepared to handle potential security incidents.

6.2.1 Types of training

There are several types of training that organizations can implement to enhance their cybersecurity posture, as shown in Figure 6.3. One common type is awareness training, which educates employees about basic security principles and best practices. This type of training is typically aimed at all employees and covers topics such as password management, phishing awareness, and safe internet usage. Awareness training is essential for creating a baseline level of security knowledge across the organization.

Another type is role-specific training, which focuses on the specific needs and responsibilities of different job roles. For example, IT staff might receive training on advanced threat detection and response techniques, while managers might learn about risk management and compliance requirements. This targeted approach ensures that each employee receives the training most relevant to his or her position. Additionally, scenario-based training uses real-world scenarios to teach employees how to respond to specific types of cyber incidents. This hands-on approach can be particularly effective in helping employees develop practical skills and confidence.

6.2.2 Developing training programs

Developing effective training programs involves several key steps, as summarized in Figure 6.4. First, it is important to conduct a needs assessment to identify the specific training needs of the organization. This might involve interviewing the employees, reviewing past security incidents, and consulting with security experts.

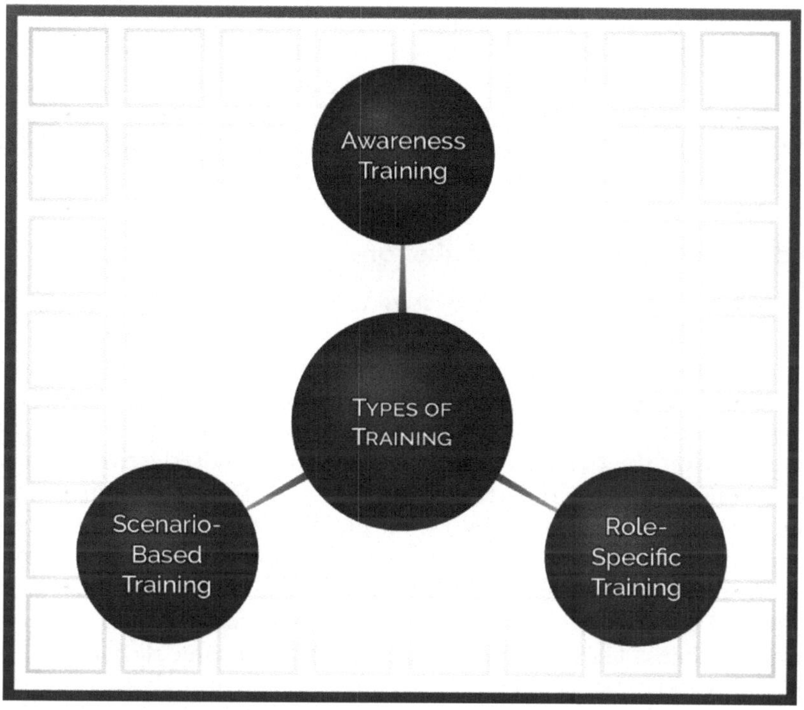

Figure 6.3 Types of training.

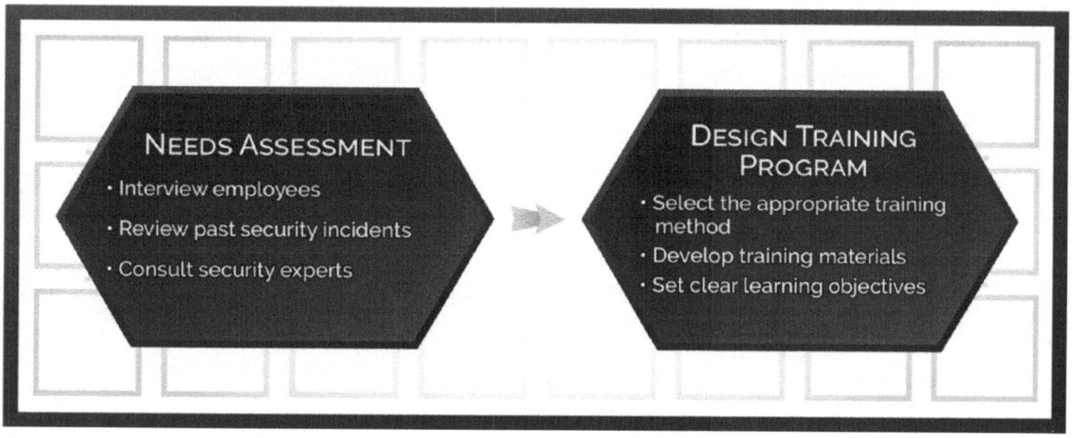

Figure 6.4 Key steps in developing effective training programs.

Once the training needs are identified, the next step is to design a training program that addresses these needs. This includes selecting the appropriate training methods, developing training materials, and setting clear learning objectives. Organizations must choose from various approaches, including instructor-led, online, or blended learning formats, based on learner needs and budget constraints. For example, a company might identify that phishing is a significant threat and decide to implement a comprehensive phishing awareness program. This program could include interactive e-learning modules, simulated phishing attacks, or workshops on recognizing phishing emails. The company might also provide ongoing support and resources, such as a dedicated email address for reporting suspicious emails and regular updates on new phishing tactics. By taking a structured and targeted approach, the company can effectively address its specific training needs and enhance its overall security posture. Implementing training programs can be challenging. Time constraints, employee resistance, and limited resources could be roadblocks. Addressing these challenges through strategic planning and prioritization is crucial.

6.2.3 Hands-on training and simulation

Hands-on training and simulation are effective components of cybersecurity training programs. These methods provide practical experience and allow employees to apply their knowledge in a controlled environment. Hands-on training might involve using cybersecurity tools and technologies, while simulation exercises replicate real-world scenarios to test employees' responses to cyber incidents. This type of training helps employees build confidence and develop the practical skills needed to respond effectively to cyber threats. For example, a company might conduct a simulated cyberattack to test its incident response plan. During the simulation, employees would practice identifying the threat, containing the attack, and restoring affected systems. This exercise allows the company to identify any weaknesses in its response plan and make improvements. Similarly, hands-on training sessions might involve using network monitoring tools to detect unusual activity or practice data recovery techniques. These practical experiences are invaluable for preparing employees to handle real-world cyber incidents.

6.2.4 Metrics and evaluation

Measuring the effectiveness of training programs is crucial for ensuring that they achieve their intended goals. A summary is shown in Table 6.1. Metrics and evaluations help organizations assess whether employees have acquired the necessary knowledge and skills and

Table 6.1 Metrics for evaluating training effectiveness

METRICS FOR EVALUATING TRAINING EFFECTIVENESS

METRIC TYPE	DESCRIPTION	HOW TO MEASURE
Pre-and Post-Training Assessments	Assess the knowledge level of employees before and after training sessions.	Administer quizzes or tests before and after training sessions.
Employee Feedback	Collect feedback from employees about their training experience and perceived value.	Use surveys or feedback forms distributed to employees post-training.
Number of Incidents Reported	Track the number of security incidents reported by employees after training.	Use incident tracking systems to log reports and responses.
Reduction in Phishing Attacks	Monitor the decrease in successful phishing attempts after training implementation.	Compare the rate of phishing incidents before and after training.
Behavioral Change Metrics	Measure changes in employee behavior towards security protocols and procedures.	Monitor adherence to security policies and reduction in risky behaviors.
Completion Rates of Training Modules	Evaluate the percentage of employees completing required training modules.	Use LMS or training platform data to track module completion.
Response Time to Incidents	Measure the time taken by employees to respond to security incidents post-training.	Use incident response logs to measure response times.

whether the training has had a positive impact on overall security. Common metrics include pre- and post-training assessments, employee feedback surveys, and tracking the number of security incidents before and after training. For example, an organization might use quizzes and tests to evaluate employees' understanding of training material. Employee feedback surveys can provide insights into the perceived value of the training and identify areas for improvement. Tracking security incidents, such as the number of successful phishing attacks, can help measure the training's impact on employee behavior. By regularly evaluating training programs and using metrics to assess their effectiveness, organizations can make data-driven decisions to enhance their cybersecurity training efforts.

Training programs are crucial in bridging the gap between cybersecurity theory and practice. By offering a variety of training, from foundational awareness to role-specific and scenario-based exercises, organizations can tailor their approaches to meet the specific needs of their workforce and bolster overall security. Hands-on learning and simulations provide invaluable practical experience, empowering employees to apply their knowledge confidently. Regular evaluation and feedback ensure training programs remain effective and adaptable to the evolving threat landscape. Ultimately, a comprehensive training program is essential for fostering a strong cybersecurity culture that equips employees to handle real-world cyber incidents.

Building a culture of awareness is equally vital. The next section will explore strategies for creating and maintaining a security-conscious workforce through awareness campaigns. This includes effective communication, the use of engaging techniques like gamification, and incentives to encourage employee participation. By fostering a heightened awareness of cybersecurity risks, organizations can further strengthen their defenses and create a more resilient security posture.

6.3 AWARENESS CAMPAIGNS

While education and training programs equip employees with the knowledge and skills needed to combat cyber threats, awareness campaigns ensure that cybersecurity remains a priority in their daily activities. These campaigns aim to create a culture of vigilance where every employee understands his or her role in maintaining security and feels responsible for protecting the organization's assets. By raising awareness, organizations can reduce the risk of human error, which is often a significant factor in security breaches.

The importance of awareness campaigns lies in their ability to engage employees continuously and keep them informed about the latest threats and best practices. Cybersecurity is not a one-time effort but an ongoing process that requires constant attention and adaptation. Awareness campaigns help to reinforce training, remind employees of critical security practices, and update them on new threats and policies. Through effective communication and innovative strategies like gamification and incentives, these campaigns can make cybersecurity an integral part of the organizational culture.

6.3.1 Building awareness

Building awareness is the first step in creating a security-conscious workforce. This involves educating employees about the importance of cybersecurity and their roles in protecting the organization. Awareness programs should cover basic security principles, such as recognizing social engineering attempts, using strong passwords, and understanding data privacy policies. The goal is to ensure that every employee, regardless of his or her role, understands the potential risks and knows how to act responsibly to mitigate them. For example, an organization might start with a series of introductory workshops or seminars that explain the basics of cybersecurity. These sessions can be supplemented with regular updates, newsletters, and reminders that highlight current threats and best practices. Creating an accessible resource center where employees can find information about cybersecurity policies and guidelines can help reinforce the importance of staying vigilant. By consistently communicating the importance of cybersecurity, organizations can foster a culture where employees are always mindful of security risks and proactive in their efforts to address them; however, one downside of this approach is awareness fatigue. To prevent awareness fatigue, it's crucial to vary messaging, use different communication channels, and provide tangible benefits to employees for engaging with security initiatives. Continuously refreshing content and tailoring messages to specific audiences can help maintain employee interest and effectiveness.

6.3.2 Communication channels

Effective communication is key to the success of awareness campaigns. Organizations must use a variety of communication channels to reach all employees and ensure the message is understood and retained. These channels can include emails, intranet posts, newsletters, posters, and meetings. The goal is to consistently reinforce the importance of cybersecurity by reminding employees of their crucial role in protecting the organization. For instance, a company might use monthly newsletters to highlight recent security incidents, provide tips for staying safe online, and share success stories of employees who have helped prevent security breaches. Posters in common areas can serve as visual reminders of key security practices, such as locking computers when not in use or verifying the sender before clicking on email links. Regular meetings or town halls can provide opportunities for more interactive discussions about cybersecurity, allowing employees to ask questions and share their experiences. By using multiple communication channels, organizations can ensure that their message reaches everyone, and that cybersecurity remains a constant focus.

6.3.3 Gamification

Gamification is an innovative approach to making cybersecurity awareness more engaging and effective. By incorporating game-like elements into awareness campaigns, organizations can motivate employees to participate actively and make learning about cybersecurity more enjoyable. Gamification can include challenges, quizzes, competitions, and reward systems that encourage employees to practice good security habits. For example, a company might create a cybersecurity quiz that employees can take to test their knowledge. Those who score well can earn points or badges, which can be displayed on an internal leaderboard. Competitions, such as phishing simulations where employees compete to identify phishing emails, can also be an effective way to reinforce learning. Additionally, offering small rewards, such as gift cards or extra time off, can incentivize participation and make the process more fun. By turning cybersecurity awareness into a game, organizations can increase engagement and help employees internalize important security practices.

6.3.4 Incentives

Incentives can be a powerful tool for encouraging employees to adopt and maintain good cybersecurity practices. By rewarding positive behavior, organizations can reinforce the importance of cybersecurity and motivate employees to stay vigilant. Incentives can take many forms, from financial rewards and recognition programs to professional development opportunities. For instance, a company might offer bonuses or gift cards to employees who complete cybersecurity training or participate in awareness activities. Recognition programs, such as "Employee of the Month" awards for those who demonstrate exceptional security awareness, can also be effective. Providing opportunities for professional development, such as funding for relevant courses or certifications, can incentivize employees to improve their cybersecurity skills. By offering meaningful rewards, companies can create a culture where employees are motivated to prioritize security and take proactive steps to protect the organization.

Awareness campaigns are instrumental in fostering a strong cybersecurity culture. By combining effective communication, engaging elements like gamification, and incentive programs, organizations can successfully elevate cybersecurity to a top priority across all levels. These campaigns serve as powerful complements to training initiatives, ensuring employees stay informed about emerging threats and reinforcing the importance of adhering to best practices.

As we move forward, it is important to integrate ETA into the broader organizational culture. In the next section, we will explore how leadership, employee involvement, and well-defined policies and procedures can help embed ETA into the fabric of the organization. This integration is crucial for sustaining a proactive and resilient cybersecurity culture.

6.4 INTEGRATING ETA INTO CULTURE

Integrating ETA into the organizational culture is crucial for creating a sustainable and proactive cybersecurity environment. While individual efforts in education and training are important, embedding these practices into the core values and daily operations of the organization ensures long-term effectiveness. When ETA becomes a fundamental part of the organizational culture, employees at all levels are more likely to internalize cybersecurity principles and apply them consistently. This integration helps in building a security-first mindset, where every action and decision is made with cybersecurity in mind.

The importance of integrating ETA into culture lies in its ability to create a cohesive and unified approach to cybersecurity. It transforms security from a set of isolated activities into a continuous, organization-wide effort. This cultural shift not only enhances the overall security posture but also improves collaboration and communication across departments. Employees feel more engaged and responsible, knowing that their actions are contributing to the organization's security. Moreover, a strong security culture can act as a deterrent to potential threats, as attackers are less likely to target organizations with well-implemented security practices.

6.4.1 Leadership

Leadership plays a pivotal role in integrating ETA into the organizational culture. Leaders set the tone for the entire organization. Their commitment to cybersecurity significantly influences how employees perceive and prioritize security. When leaders actively promote and participate in ETA initiatives, they demonstrate that cybersecurity is a top priority and that everyone, from top management to entry-level staff, has a role to play. This top-down approach ensures that security practices are taken seriously and embedded into the organization's operations and values. For example, executives can lead by example by participating in cybersecurity training sessions and promoting security awareness through regular communications. They can allocate resources and budget for continuous education and training programs, ensuring that these initiatives are well-supported. They can establish clear security policies and procedures and encourage employees to follow them diligently. By creating a culture of transparency and accountability, leaders can foster an environment where cybersecurity is viewed as a collective responsibility and an integral part of the organization's success.

6.4.2 Employee involvement

Employee involvement is a must for the successful integration of ETA into the organizational culture. When employees are actively engaged in cybersecurity initiatives, they are more likely to take ownership of their roles in maintaining security. This involvement can be achieved through regular training sessions, workshops, and interactive activities that make cybersecurity relevant and accessible to all employees. Encouraging feedback and suggestions from employees can also help identify potential security gaps and improve existing practices. For instance, organizations can create cybersecurity ambassador programs, where selected employees act as champions for security initiatives within their departments. These ambassadors can help promote best practices, organize awareness events, and serve as a point of contact for security-related questions. Most importantly, involving employees in simulated cyberattack exercises can provide valuable hands-on experience and help them understand the importance of their roles in preventing security breaches. By fostering a culture of participation and collaboration, organizations can ensure that cybersecurity becomes a shared responsibility and a key part of their daily operations.

6.4.3 Policy and procedures

Well-defined policies and procedures are the backbone of an effective cybersecurity culture. They provide a clear framework for employees to follow and ensure consistency in how security measures are implemented across the organization. Policies and procedures should cover a wide range of topics, including data protection, access control, incident response, and acceptable use of technology. They should be regularly reviewed and updated to reflect the evolving threat landscape and changes in the organization's operations. For example, a comprehensive data protection policy might outline how sensitive information should be handled, stored, and transmitted. An incident response procedure could detail the steps employees should take in the event of a security breach, including whom to contact and how to document the incident. These documents should be easily accessible and communicated to all employees through training sessions and regular reminders. Additionally, organizations can conduct periodic audits and compliance checks to ensure that policies and procedures are being followed correctly. By establishing clear and enforceable guidelines, organizations can create a structured and disciplined approach to cybersecurity that supports the overall security culture.

Integrating ETA into the organizational culture is essential for building a resilient and proactive cybersecurity environment. Leadership, employee involvement, and well-defined policies and procedures are key components of this integration. By setting a strong example, engaging employees, and providing clear guidelines, organizations can create a culture where cybersecurity is a shared responsibility and a core value.

Moving forward, it is important to recognize and address the challenges that may arise in implementing ETA initiatives. In the next section, you will explore the challenges and provide solutions supported by case studies and best practices. This will help organizations navigate potential obstacles and continue to strengthen their cybersecurity posture.

6.5 CHALLENGES AND SOLUTIONS

Implementing ETA initiatives in cybersecurity is not without its challenges. Organizations often face numerous obstacles, from limited resources to employee resistance. Understanding these common challenges and finding effective solutions are crucial for creating a resilient cybersecurity culture. By addressing these issues head-on, organizations can improve their security postures and ensure that their ETA initiatives are successful and sustainable.

Case studies and best practices provide valuable insights into how organizations have overcome these challenges and achieved success in their cybersecurity efforts. Analyzing real-world examples helps identify strategies that have been effective in different contexts. These case studies offer practical guidance for others facing similar issues. Additionally, best practices derived from industry standards and successful implementations serve as a roadmap for organizations looking to enhance their ETA programs. By learning from the experiences of others and adhering to proven strategies, organizations can navigate challenges more effectively and build a strong and resilient cybersecurity culture.

6.5.1 Common challenges and solutions

Organizations face many challenges when discussing ETAs. Addressing these challenges is crucial to creating a sustainable cybersecurity culture. Here are four common challenges and their possible solutions, with a summary in Table 6.2.

Challenge 1-Limited resources: Many organizations, particularly small- and medium-sized enterprises, struggle with limited resources for cybersecurity initiatives. This can include budget constraints, lack of dedicated cybersecurity staff, and insufficient access to training materials.

Solution: Organizations can maximize their resources by prioritizing the most critical aspects of their cybersecurity programs and seeking cost-effective solutions.

Table 6.2 Common challenges and solutions of implementing ETA

IMPLEMENTING ETA: COMMON CHALLENGES AND SOLUTIONS

CHALLENGE	DESCRIPTION	SOLUTION
Limited Resources	Organizations may face budget constraints, lack of dedicated staff, or insufficient access to training materials.	Prioritize critical aspects of the cybersecurity program and use cost-effective resources like free online courses or managed security services.
Employee Resistance	Employees may resist cybersecurity training due to perceived irrelevance or additional workload.	Communicate the importance of cybersecurity, make training engaging with gamification, and provide incentives for participation.
Keeping Up with Evolving Threats	The rapid evolution of cyber threats makes it challenging to keep training programs up to date.	Implement continuous learning with regularly updated materials, simulations, and partnerships with cybersecurity experts.
Measuring Effectiveness	It can be difficult to assess the impact of ETA initiatives and identify areas for improvement.	Establish clear metrics for assessment, such as pre-and post-training evaluations, employee feedback surveys, and tracking security incidents.

Leveraging free or low-cost training resources, such as online courses and webinars, can provide valuable education without significant financial investment. Partnering with external cybersecurity experts or utilizing managed security services can help augment internal capabilities without the need for extensive in-house staff.

Challenge 2-Employee resistance: Employees may resist participating in cybersecurity training and awareness programs due to a perceived lack of relevance or added workload. This resistance can undermine the effectiveness of ETA initiatives.

Solution: To overcome resistance, organizations should communicate the importance of cybersecurity and how it directly impacts each employee's role and the overall security of the organization. Making training engaging and relevant through gamification and interactive sessions can also help increase participation. Providing incentives, such as recognition and rewards for completing training, can further motivate employees to engage with cybersecurity initiatives.

Challenge 3-Keeping up with evolving threats: The cybersecurity landscape is constantly changing, with new threats emerging regularly. Keeping training programs and awareness campaigns up to date can be challenging for organizations.

Solution: Implementing a continuous learning approach can help address this challenge. Organizations should regularly update their training materials and awareness campaigns to reflect the latest threats and best practices. Partnering with cybersecurity experts and participating in industry forums can provide access to the latest information and trends. Incorporating simulated cyberattacks and hands-on exercises can help employees stay prepared for new types of threats.

Challenge 4-Measuring effectiveness: Assessing the impact of ETA initiatives can be difficult, making it challenging to determine their effectiveness and identify areas for improvement.

Solution: Organizations should establish clear metrics and evaluation methods to measure the effectiveness of their ETA programs. This can include pre- and post-training assessments, employee feedback surveys, and tracking the number of security incidents before and after training. Regularly reviewing these metrics and making data-driven adjustments to the programs can help ensure continuous improvement.

6.5.2 Case studies

As mentioned before, real-world examples provide valuable insight into how different organizations dealt with various issues they faced. Learning from these organizations provides much-needed insight. These might include the answers to improve ETA initiatives. Following are four simple case studies that show how companies dealt with four common problems.

Case Study 1-Princeton University: In 2016, Princeton University embarked on a mission to enhance its cybersecurity culture through a comprehensive awareness and training program. Led by CISO David Sherry and Training Program Manager Tara Schaufler, the Information Security Office (ISO) aimed to integrate information security into the campus culture. The program faced significant challenges, including reaching a diverse audience of students, staff, and faculty, overcoming resistance to mandatory training, and establishing strong relationships with security influencers. The team adopted a gradual approach, creating high-quality, engaging content and leveraging computing support professionals across campus to disseminate information effectively. By addressing the reality of cyber threats through relevant stories and imagery, they successfully garnered support and increased engagement.

The program significantly matured over the years, achieving widespread acceptance of mandatory training and improving security behaviors across the campus. The ISO implemented various tools and processes, such as Proofpoint Email Protection solutions and The Phish Bowl website, to enhance awareness and provide resources on phishing attempts. As a result, Princeton's security culture evolved, leading to better audit outcomes and increased requests for training from various departments. The program's success highlights the importance of tailored, contextually relevant content and continuous engagement to foster a strong cybersecurity culture in complex, open environments like universities.

Case Study 2-Kverneland Group: Kverneland Group, a global leader in agricultural technology, faced the challenge of onboarding all computer users into a continuous cybersecurity training program. They sought an automated solution with a managed service component to achieve sustainable results. They selected Hoxhunt's automated phishing simulation platform, which provided continuous updates on content and adaptable phishing simulations that became progressively harder based on user performance. This approach, coupled with gamification elements like stars and shields for successful behaviors, maintained high user engagement and performance.

The implementation of Hoxhunt at Kverneland Group yielded impressive results. The company achieved an 87.8% onboarding rate across its locations in 10 countries, with an 81.8% engagement rate and a resilience score of 24.75, well above the industry benchmark. Kverneland Group also saw high participation in advanced training levels, such as the optional "Spicy Mode," which offers highly targeted phishing simulations. The continuous improvements and localized content in multiple languages have kept the training relevant and challenging. This case study highlights the importance of adaptive learning models and positive reinforcement in building a robust security culture and preparing users for increasingly sophisticated phishing threats.

Case Study 3-Neoway: In 2018, Neoway, a leading B2B technology firm in Latin America, recognized the need to enhance its cybersecurity posture amidst rapid growth and increasing cyber threats. Initially operating with a small InfoSec team under the engineering department, Neoway strategically shifted this team to report directly to the CEO, emphasizing the importance of security at the highest level. The company initiated a comprehensive security awareness training program using KnowBe4's platform. This move aimed to transition Neoway from a startup mindset to a strategic, security-focused culture.

Under the new program, Neoway implemented monthly training sessions, frequent phishing tests, and continuous employee education. These efforts led to significant improvements: the organization's phish-prone percentage dropped from 20% to 3%, and the click-to-report ratio improved dramatically, indicating a heightened ability to recognize and report phishing attempts. This transformation highlights the critical role of structured, ongoing security awareness programs in fostering a resilient cybersecurity culture within growing organizations.

Case Study 4-People First Federal Credit Union: In 2012, People First Federal Credit Union (FCU) recognized the increasing cyber threats and the limitations of mere regulatory compliance for security. To address this, they conducted comprehensive social engineering assessments, both remotely and onsite, with the help of Digital Defense. The remote assessments involved phishing attacks that revealed many employees were susceptible to such threats, demonstrating a significant vulnerability in their security awareness. Onsite assessments saw an analyst successfully infiltrate secure areas by posing as a telecom provider employee, highlighting physical security weaknesses.

In response to these findings, the company implemented the SecurED® program developed by Digital Defense. This innovative security awareness education program, created in collaboration with an Emmy® award-winning comedy sketch writer, featured engaging and memorable characters to enhance employee retention of critical security practices. The corporate security campaign generated excitement with SecurED posters and mandatory participation in training. Seven of the 12 available modules were selected based on assessment findings, covering topics such as acceptable computer use, social engineering, password security, malware prevention, safe web browsing, and social media dangers. Employees were required to view training videos and pass test questions to ensure comprehension and application of security best practices. The training program was a success and, in 2013, they received excellent results from the ongoing training.

6.5.3 Best Practices

Best practices are proven methods and strategies that have been shown to be effective in achieving desired outcomes. In cybersecurity, they provide a roadmap for implementing successful ETA initiatives. By following these best practices, organizations can enhance their overall security, ensure consistency, and create a strong culture of cybersecurity awareness and responsibility. Although only a few of these best practices are mentioned for implementing successful ETAs, there are many more.

Engage leadership: Leadership commitment is essential for the success of ETA initiatives. Leaders should actively participate in training and awareness programs, set clear expectations for cybersecurity behavior, and allocate necessary resources. Executives can underscore the importance of cybersecurity by leading by example and fostering a culture of security from the top down.

Tailor training to roles: Customized training that addresses the specific needs and responsibilities of different job roles is more effective than a one-size-fits-all approach. Tailoring content ensures that employees receive relevant information that applies to their daily tasks, making the training more engaging and practical.

Incorporate interactive elements: Interactive training methods, such as simulations, hands-on exercises, and gamification, enhance learning and retention. These methods provide practical experience and keep employees engaged, making it easier for them to apply what they have learned in real-world situations.

Foster a continuous learning environment: Cybersecurity education should not be a one-time event but an ongoing process. Regular updates, refresher courses, and continuous learning opportunities help employees stay current with evolving threats and best practices. Encouraging a culture of continuous improvement ensures that the organization remains resilient against new challenges.

Evaluate and adapt: Regularly assessing the effectiveness of ETA initiatives through metrics and feedback is crucial for continuous improvement. Organizations should use this data to identify areas for enhancement and adapt their programs accordingly. This proactive approach helps maintain the relevance and impact of cybersecurity training and awareness efforts.

Addressing common challenges and learning from successful case studies are vital for the effective implementation of ETA initiatives. By understanding the obstacles and applying best practices, organizations can build a strong cybersecurity culture that is resilient and adaptable. Looking to the future, it is essential to stay ahead of emerging trends and evolving threats. In the next section, you will explore future trends in ETA, including the impact of emerging technologies, the evolution of cyber threats, and global perspectives. By anticipating these changes, organizations can continue to enhance their cybersecurity posture and maintain a proactive approach to security.

6.6 FUTURE TRENDS IN ETA

As the digital landscape continues to evolve, it is crucial for organizations to stay ahead of the curve by understanding and adapting to future trends in education, training, and awareness (ETA) in cybersecurity. Emerging technologies, the evolution of cyber threats, and global perspectives are three key areas that significantly impact the effectiveness of ETA initiatives. By studying these trends, organizations can proactively enhance their cybersecurity strategies and how they are going to approach new threats.

First, emerging technologies bring both opportunities and challenges to the cybersecurity field. Technologies such as artificial intelligence, machine learning, and blockchain are revolutionizing the way organizations detect and respond to threats. At the same time, the evolution of cyber threats means that attackers are continually developing new methods to exploit vulnerabilities. Understanding these evolving threats is essential for staying one step ahead of cybercriminals. Finally, a global perspective on cybersecurity provides valuable insights about how different countries address common challenges and, most importantly, the question of whether or not it is possible to foster a collaborative approach to enhancing security worldwide.

6.6.1 Emerging technologies

Emerging technologies are transforming the cybersecurity landscape by providing advanced tools and methods for detecting, preventing, and responding to threats. Artificial intelligence (AI) and machine learning (ML) are at the forefront of this transformation, offering capabilities to analyze vast amounts of data quickly and identify patterns that may indicate cyber threats. These technologies can automate many aspects of cybersecurity, from monitoring network traffic to identifying unusual behavior, making it easier for organizations to respond quickly to potential attacks.

For instance, AI-powered security systems can learn from past incidents to predict and prevent future attacks. Machine learning algorithms can analyze network traffic in real time to detect anomalies that might indicate a cyberattack. Blockchain technology is also gaining traction in cybersecurity, providing a secure and transparent way to record transactions and verify identities. For instance, blockchain can be used to enhance data integrity and prevent tampering by creating an immutable record of all transactions. Another emerging technology is the Internet of Things (IoT). While introducing new vulnerabilities, IoT also offers opportunities for advanced security measures through interconnected devices that can communicate and respond to threats autonomously.

Other emerging technologies are quantum computing, biometrics, and 5G. Quantum computing has the potential to revolutionize cybersecurity both positively and negatively. On the one hand, it could break current encryption standards, posing a significant threat. On the other hand, it could also lead to the development of quantum-resistant encryption and new security protocols. Biometrics offers a more secure form of authentication by relying on unique physical characteristics. As technology advances, biometric systems become increasingly accurate and accessible, making them a popular choice for protecting sensitive data and systems. 5G and beyond bring faster speeds and increased connectivity but also introduce new security challenges. The expanded attack surface and potential for IoT device vulnerabilities require security measures to protect networks and data from threats like DDoS attacks and data breaches.

6.6.2 Evolution of cyber threats

The evolution of cyber threats is a continuous process, with attackers constantly developing new methods to exploit vulnerabilities. As technology advances, so do the techniques used by cybercriminals, making it imperative for organizations to stay informed about the latest trends in cyber threats. Traditional threats, like phishing and malware, are becoming more sophisticated, while new types of attacks, such as ransomware and advanced persistent threats (APTs), are on the rise. Understanding these evolving threats is crucial for developing effective defensive strategies. For example, phishing attacks have evolved from simple email scams to highly targeted spear-phishing campaigns that use social engineering to deceive specific individuals. Ransomware attacks have also become more prevalent and damaging, with attackers encrypting critical data and demanding ransom payments for its release. APTs involve prolonged and targeted attacks where cybercriminals gain unauthorized access to a network and remain undetected for an extended period of time. The rise of state-sponsored cyberattacks and the use of artificial intelligence by cybercriminals to automate and scale their operations are other significant trends in the evolution of cyber threats. By staying aware of these developments, organizations can better prepare and defend against future attacks.

6.6.3 Global perspectives

A global perspective on cybersecurity provides valuable insights into how different regions and countries address common challenges and implement effective ETA initiatives. Cyber threats are not confined by geographic boundaries, and a collaborative approach to cybersecurity can enhance the overall security posture of organizations worldwide. Understanding the strategies and practices used in different parts of the world can help organizations adopt best practices and innovate in their own ETA programs. For example, countries in Europe have been at the forefront of implementing strict data protection regulations, such as the General Data Protection Regulation (GDPR), which has significantly influenced cybersecurity practices globally. In Asia, countries like Singapore and Japan have developed comprehensive national cybersecurity strategies that emphasize public-private partnerships and continuous education and training. The United States has focused on critical infrastructure protection and the integration of cybersecurity into national defense strategies. By examining these global approaches, organizations can learn from diverse experiences and apply relevant strategies to enhance their cybersecurity efforts.

To stay ahead in the ever-changing field of cybersecurity, it is essential to study emerging technologies, the evolution of cyber threats, and global perspectives. These trends provide valuable insights that can help organizations enhance their ETA initiatives, ensuring they remain adaptable in the face of new challenges. By embracing these trends, organizations can build a proactive and strong cybersecurity culture that is prepared for the future.

6.7 CONCLUSION

ETA are an organization's foundation for a strong cybersecurity culture. It is not just a strategic initiative anymore but a fundamental necessity in today's digital age. This chapter explored the multifaceted aspects of ETA, emphasizing the crucial roles of formal education, certifications, professional development, and continuous learning. By fostering a culture of continuous education and vigilance, organizations can significantly enhance their ability to anticipate, identify, and mitigate cyber threats. The investment in training programs and comprehensive awareness campaigns is essential for providing employees with the knowledge and skills needed to protect organizational assets and maintain a secure environment.

Furthermore, the ETA in an organizational culture relies heavily on strong leadership, active employee involvement, and well-defined policies and procedures. Overcoming common challenges through practical solutions and learning from real-world case studies and best practices have highlighted the pathways to effective cybersecurity practices. Looking to the future, understanding the impact of emerging technologies, the evolution of cyber threats, and the importance of global perspectives will be crucial in staying ahead of potential risks. By adopting a proactive approach and continuously evolving their ETA strategies, organizations can build a resilient and adaptable cybersecurity culture that not only defends against current threats but also prepares for future challenges.

DISCUSSION QUESTIONS

1. Why is continuous learning essential for cybersecurity professionals, and how can organizations effectively implement it to stay ahead of evolving threats?
2. How do formal education and professional certifications complement each other in building a solid cybersecurity workforce? Which do you think is more important for career advancement in cybersecurity?
3. What are the key elements of an effective cybersecurity awareness campaign, and how can organizations ensure these campaigns remain engaging and impactful over time?
4. How can organizational leaders set the tone for a cybersecurity-focused culture? What specific actions can they take to demonstrate their commitment to Education, Training, and Awareness (ETA)?
5. What are some common challenges organizations face when implementing ETA initiatives, and what strategies can be used to overcome them?
6. How does gamification enhance cybersecurity awareness training, and what are some examples of gamification techniques that could be effective in an organization?
7. What are the benefits of integrating Education, Training, and Awareness into the daily operations of an organization, and how can this be achieved effectively?
8. What are some of the most effective metrics for evaluating the success of cybersecurity training programs, and why are these metrics important?
9. How do you think emerging technologies and evolving cyber threats will shape the future of cybersecurity education and training? What new approaches might become necessary?
10. How can organizations benefit from understanding global approaches to cybersecurity education and awareness? What lessons can be learned from other countries or regions?

BIBLIOGRAPHY

Abrahams, T. O., Farayola, O. A., Kaggwa, S., Uwaoma, P. U., Hassan, A. O., & Dawodu, S. O. (2024). Cybersecurity awareness and education programs: A review of employee engagement and accountability. *Computer Science & IT Research Journal*, *5*(1), 100–119. https://www.fepbl.com/index.php/csitrj/article/view/708

Adams, M. (2019, June 27–29). *How to measure the effectiveness of cybersecurity training and awareness programs*. In FISSEA 32nd Annual Conference. https://csrc.nist.gov/CSRC/media/Events/FISSEA-32nd-Annual-Conference/documents/Track_3/How%20to%20Measure%20the%20Effectiveness%20of%20Cybersecurity%20Training%20and%20Awareness%20Program_Michael%20Adams.pdf

Andronache, A. (2021). Increasing security awareness through lenses of cybersecurity culture. *Journal of Information Systems & Operations Management*, *15*(1). https://www.researchgate.net/profile/Alina-Andronache-2/publication/353322243_Increasing_Security_Awarenesss_Through_Lenses_of_Cybersecurity_Culture/links/613c994f4e1df271062b528b/Increasing-Security-Awarenesss-Through-Lenses-of-Cybersecurity-Culture.pdf

Barletta, V. S., Caruso, F., Di Mascio, T., Greco, F., Islam, T., Rossano, V., & Xiao, H. (2024). CSE4IA 2024-2nd International Workshop on CyberSecurity Education for Industry and Academia. In *Proceedings of the 2024 International Conference on Advanced Visual Interfaces, AVI2024* (pp. 1–4). ACM International Conference Proceeding Series. ACM. https://doi.org/10.1145/3656650.3660536

Blackburn, A., Chen, I. L., & Pfeffer, R. (Eds.) (2018). *Emerging trends in cyber ethics and education*. IGI Global.

Blum, D., Sherry, D., & Schaufler, T. (2020). Case study: Transforming Princeton's security culture through awareness. *ISACA Journal*, *1*, 2021. https://www.isaca.org/resources/isaca-journal/issues/2021/volume-1/case-study-transforming-princetons-security-culture-through-awareness

Crabb, J., Hundhausen, C., & Gebremedhin, A. (2024). A critical review of cybersecurity education in the United States. In *SIGCSE 2024: Proceedings of the 55th ACM Technical Symposium on Computer Science Education V. 1* (pp. 241–247). Association for Computing Machinery. https://doi.org/10.1145/3626252.3630757

Crowdstrike. (2022, November 9). How to create an employee cybersecurity awareness training program (with examples). https://www.crowdstrike.com/solutions/small-business/employee-cybersecurity-training-program/

Daimi, K., & Francia, G. (Eds.) (2020). *Innovations in cybersecurity education*. Springer.

Dani, G. (2023). The future of cyber security: Cybersecurity in a post-pandemic world. Independently published.

Dash, B., & Ansari, M. F. (2022). An effective cybersecurity awareness training model: First defense of an organizational security strategy. *International Research Journal of Engineering and Technology (IRJET)*, *9*(04), 974–979. https://www.researchgate.net/publication/359772764_An_Effective_Cybersecurity_Awareness_Training_Model_First_Defense_of_an_Organizational_Security_Strategy

Digital Defense. (n.d.). Security awareness case study: People First Federal Credit Union. Digital Defense. https://static.fortra.com/digital-defense/pdfs/case-study/dd-security-awareness-people-first-federal-credit-union-cs.pdf

Georgiadou, A., Mouzakitis, S., Bounas, K., & Askounis, D. (2020). A cyber-security culture framework for assessing organization readiness. *Journal of Computer Information Systems*, *62*(3), 452–462. https://doi.org/10.1080/08874417.2020.1845583

Guimaraes, J. (2021). *Information security awareness: Learning for effectiveness* [Doctoral dissertation]. St. Thomas University. ProQuest Dissertations & Theses. (28720178). https://www.proquest.com/openview/d2a8de705479ad3be176483b13881c00/1?pq-origsite=gscholar&cbl=18750&diss=y

He, W., & Zhang, Z. (2019). Enterprise cybersecurity training and awareness programs: Recommendations for success. *Journal of Organizational Computing and Electronic Commerce*, 29(4), 249–257. https://doi.org/10.1080/10919392.2019.1611528

Hoxhunt. (n.d.). How agricultural technology leader, Kverneland Group sewed awareness training and reaped resilience. https://www.hoxhunt.com/case-studies/how-kverneland-group-sewed-awareness-training-and-reaped-resilience

Jawhar, S., Miller, J., & Bitar, Z. (2024). AI-driven customized cyber security training and awareness. In *2024 IEEE 3rd International Conference on AI in Cybersecurity (ICAIC)* (pp. 1–5). IEEE. https://doi.org/10.1109/ICAIC60265.2024.10433829

KnowBe4. (2023). Neoway and KnowBe4—Building a culture of security. https://www.knowbe4.com/hubfs/KMSAT-PhishER-Technology-Neoway-CS_EN-US.pdf?hsLang=en

Koutsouris, N., Vassilakis, C., & Kolokotronis, N. (2021). Cyber-security training evaluation metrics. In *2021 IEEE International Conference on Cyber Security and Resilience (CSR)* (pp. 192–197). IEEE. https://doi.org/10.1109/CSR51186.2021.9527946

McIlwraith, A. (2021). *Information security and employee behaviour: How to reduce risk through employee education, training and awareness* (2nd ed.). Routledge. https://doi.org/10.4324/9780429281785

Mungo, J. (2023). Self-paced cybersecurity awareness training educating retail employees to identify phishing attacks. *Journal of Cyber Security Technology*, *8*(2), 71–119. https://doi.org/10.1080/23742917.2023.2244210

Nasir, S. (2023). Exploring the effectiveness of cybersecurity training programs: Factors, best practices, and future directions. *Advances in Multidisciplinary & Scientific Research Journal Publication*, *2*(1), 151–160. https://doi.org/10.22624/AIMS/CSEAN-SMART2023P18

Qawasmeh, S. A.-D., AlQahtani, A. A. S., & Khan, M. K. (2024, January 20). Navigating cybersecurity training: A comprehensive review. https://doi.org/10.48550/arXiv.2401.11326

Reeves, A., Pittas (Nee Calic), D., & Delfabbro, P. (n.d.). Employees are sick of cybersecurity: Can the industry decipher how to respond? SSRN: https://ssrn.com/abstract=4884508

Rubeck, T. J. (2023, October 31). Building a culture of cybersecurity: Strategies for training and awareness. IdenHaus. https://www.idenhaus.com/building-a-culture-of-cybersecurity-strategies-for-training-and-awareness/

Saldana II (2023). *The effect of cybersecurity training on government employee's knowledge of cybersecurity issues and practices* [Doctoral dissertation]. The University of Texas Rio Grande Valley). ProQuest Dissertations & Theses. (30314775).

Walton, H. (2024). *Security culture: A how-to guide for improving security culture and dealing with people risk in your organisation* (1st ed.). Routledge.

Chapter 7

Psychological aspects of cybersecurity culture

Today, cybersecurity is not just about technology; it's also about people. Understanding human behavior and psychology is essential for creating a strong cybersecurity culture. Not only human errors and poor decisions but also manipulation and deceit can undermine the best technical defenses; therefore, understanding the psychological factors that influence employee behavior is crucial for building a strong security culture. This chapter will explore just that.

By examining motivations, cognitive biases, and the effects of stress, it will uncover the vulnerabilities that cybercriminals exploit. This knowledge will empower organizations to develop effective education, training, and awareness (ETA) programs that foster a security-conscious mindset. Discussions will include strategies for changing habits, encouraging a supportive work environment, and creating a proactive security culture where everyone takes ownership of protecting organizational assets.

To begin, the content must explore the foundational aspects of human behavior in the context of cybersecurity. Understanding these psychological principles is the first step toward building a resilient organization that can withstand evolving threats. By bridging the gap between technology and human psychology, a more secure digital landscape can be created.

To build a security-conscious culture, it is crucial to first understand human behavior. This involves examining why people act in certain ways and identifying common errors and vulnerabilities. The next section will explore the foundational aspects of human behavior in cybersecurity.

7.1 UNDERSTANDING HUMAN BEHAVIOR

Human behavior plays a crucial role in cybersecurity. While technology provides the tools to protect information, it is ultimately people who use these tools and make decisions that impact security. Understanding how and why people behave in certain ways helps to create better security practices and reduce risks.

Cyberattacks often exploit human vulnerabilities rather than technical flaws. Phishing attacks, for example, rely on deceiving individuals into revealing sensitive information. Even the most sophisticated security systems can be compromised if users are not vigilant or informed; therefore, addressing the human element is essential for a comprehensive cybersecurity strategy.

What also needs to be taken into consideration is that people's behaviors are shaped by various factors, including their perceptions, emotions, and social interactions. These behaviors can be influenced by cognitive biases, stress, and organizational culture. By understanding these factors, organizations can develop more effective training and awareness programs that can put them ahead of the game.

DOI: 10.1201/9781003368496-7

To better understand this behavior, this chapter will further investigate these two key areas: the basics of cyberpsychology and the common human factors in cybersecurity.

7.1.1 Introduction to cyberpsychology

Cyberpsychology is the study of how psychological factors influence cybersecurity practices, focusing on the human elements that can either fortify or undermine an organization's security. Studying it is essential for fostering a robust cybersecurity culture. By examining the human element, organizations can develop more effective strategies to protect against cyber threats and enhance their overall security posture. In the quest to examine cyberpsychology, three factors, as shown in Figure 7.1, will be examined: cognitive processes, emotional influences, and social interactions.

Cognitive processes such as perception, memory, and decision-making are fundamental to how individuals interact with security measures. For instance, perception determines how a person recognizes and assesses the threat level of a phishing email. Effective cybersecurity training programs aim to enhance cognitive awareness by teaching employees to identify red flags and suspicious activities. Memory also plays a critical role; repetitive training helps reinforce security protocols and ensure they are second nature to employees. Decision-making, influenced by these cognitive processes, dictates the actions individuals take when faced with potential security threats. Understanding cognition in cybersecurity helps organizations design training programs that improve employees' ability to detect and respond to threats. By focusing on enhancing cognitive skills, organizations can reduce the likelihood of human error, which is often a significant factor in security breaches.

Emotions significantly impact cybersecurity behaviors. Fear, stress, and anxiety can impair judgment and lead to mistakes. For example, an employee under stress might click on a malicious link without fully considering the consequences. Conversely, positive emotions

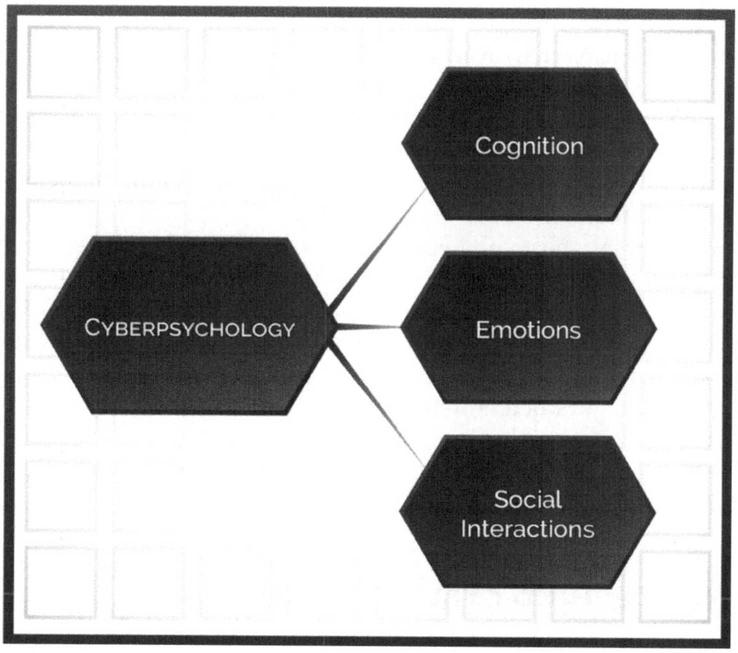

Figure 7.1 Elements of cyberpsychology.

like satisfaction from successfully thwarting a phishing attempt can reinforce good practices. Organizations that recognize the emotional components of cybersecurity can implement better support systems and stress management strategies, creating a work environment where employees feel confident and vigilant.

Social dynamics within an organization also play a crucial role in cybersecurity. Social engineering attacks exploit human trust and social norms to gain unauthorized access to information. Attackers often use tactics that prey on people's inherent trust in authority figures or colleagues. Educating employees about these tactics and promoting a culture of healthy skepticism can reduce the effectiveness of social engineering attacks. Encouraging a verification-first mindset, where employees are trained to verify the identity of anyone requesting sensitive information, can significantly strengthen an organization's defenses.

Understanding these aspects of cyberpsychology provides a solid foundation for addressing the human factors in cybersecurity. It is possible to develop targeted strategies to mitigate these risks and strengthen the overall security posture by examining common errors and vulnerabilities.

The next section will delve into the human factors in cybersecurity, exploring how specific behaviors and attitudes can impact security and what can be done to address them.

7.1.2 Human factors in cybersecurity

Human factors are common errors and vulnerabilities that people exhibit in cybersecurity contexts. These include fear of authority, boredom and attention, gullibility, and trust. By recognizing these factors, organizations can create strategies to mitigate risks.

Fear of authority in the context of cybersecurity refers to the anxiety employees might feel about reporting security incidents, admitting mistakes, or questioning directives from superiors. Employees might fear these because they worry about repercussions. This fear can prevent timely responses to security threats. To mitigate this, organizations should foster a culture of openness and support where employees feel safe to report issues without fear of blame. Encouraging anonymous reporting and ensuring that there are no negative consequences for it can help alleviate this fear.

Boredom and attention refer to routine tasks that can become monotonous, leading to lapses in vigilance. This can result in overlooked security protocols and increased vulnerability to attacks. To address this, organizations can introduce varied and engaging methods for completing security tasks, such as interactive training sessions and gamified security exercises. Regularly rotating responsibilities and incorporating new challenges can also help maintain attention and interest.

Gullibility and trust can be exploited by attackers through social engineering tactics. Understanding why people are gullible can help in designing better awareness programs. Training employees to recognize and respond to social engineering attacks is essential in mitigating this risk. Simulated phishing attacks and role-playing exercises can help employees develop the skills needed to identify and avoid these threats.

Addressing these few mentioned human factors can help organizations create a more resilient security culture. Some ways to mitigate these vulnerabilities are to encourage open communication, make security tasks engaging, and educate employees about social engineering tactics. Later, this chapter will cover human factors in detail.

7.2 MOTIVATIONS BEHIND CYBER BEHAVIOR

Understanding the motivations behind cyber behavior is essential for creating effective cybersecurity strategies. People's actions in the cybersecurity context are influenced by various factors, both positive and negative. By identifying and addressing these motivations, organizations can encourage secure behaviors and reduce risky ones. These two categories will be further examined.

Positive motivations include factors that encourage individuals to engage in good cybersecurity practices. These motivations leverage employees' natural inclinations and desires to protect the organization and improve their own skills. Positive reinforcement and creating an environment that rewards good behavior can significantly enhance the overall security culture.

Negative motivations, on the other hand, are factors that lead individuals to neglect or bypass cybersecurity measures. These motivations often stem from a lack of knowledge, fear, or convenience. By understanding these negative motivations, organizations can develop strategies to counteract them and promote a more secure environment.

This section will explore both positive and negative motivations behind cyber behavior. It will discuss how each type of motivation influences actions and provide examples of how organizations can harness positive motivations while mitigating negative ones.

7.2.1 Positive motivations

Positive motivations, as summarized in Figure 7.2, are factors that encourage individuals to engage in good cybersecurity practices. By leveraging these motivations, organizations can foster a proactive and secure cybersecurity culture. In this section, you will see what they are, their impact, and how to mitigate them.

- **Love of winning** is leveraging the competitive spirit to encourage secure behavior. For example, implementing gamification in cybersecurity training, where employees earn points, badges, or rewards for completing security-related tasks, reporting phishing attempts, or participating in security drills can create a friendly competitive environment. By tapping into employees' natural competitive instincts, organizations can make cybersecurity engaging and fun. This not only increases participation in security activities but also reinforces positive behavior, making security practices more habitual and ingrained in the daily routine. Organizations can ensure that the competition remains healthy and inclusive by rotating the challenges regularly to keep the activities

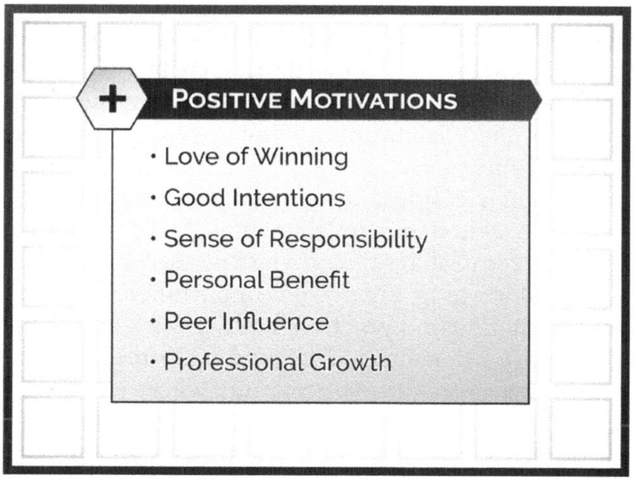

Figure 7.2 Positive motivations.

fresh and engaging or providing various rewards to cater to different interests and motivations.

- **Good intentions** involve encouraging and harnessing employees' natural inclination to help. Promoting a company-wide initiative where employees can volunteer to be part of a "security ambassador" program, helping educate their peers, and supporting security initiatives are excellent examples. By recognizing employees' goodwill, organizations can build a supportive and collaborative environment. Employees who are motivated by good intentions are more likely to go above and beyond in following security protocols, assisting others, and ultimately adhering to safety measures.

  Some mitigating strategies organizations could use to harness good intentions are providing clear guidelines and support to security ambassadors. This ensures that the ambassadors have the resources needed to be effective. Organizations can recognize and reward volunteers' efforts to keep them motivated and appreciated. They can also ensure that the extra responsibilities do not become overwhelming, which could lead to burnout.
- **Sense of responsibility** is instilling a sense of duty toward protecting the organization. For example, regular communication of the importance of cybersecurity and how each employee's actions contribute to the overall safety of the organization can reinforce this. This can also be reinforced through workshops, meetings, and internal communications that highlight the role of everyone in maintaining security. When employees feel a personal sense of responsibility, they are more likely to take proactive measures to protect the organization. This collective sense of duty enhances vigilance and accountability, leading to a more resilient security posture.

  Effective mitigation strategies include ensuring that employees are not overwhelmed with responsibilities and that they receive the necessary training and tools to perform their roles successfully. Fostering a supportive environment where employees feel comfortable asking for help and reporting issues can also be a good way to create this sense of responsibility. Regular reinforcement of the importance of each person's role in maintaining engagement and commitment is a must.
- **Personal benefit** highlights how good cybersecurity practices can protect employees' personal information. Some examples of providing employees with personal benefits could be offering training sessions that not only cover workplace security but also provide tips on protecting personal devices and information at home. Demonstrating how skills learned at work can be applied to personal cybersecurity could be an additional benefit. When employees see the direct benefits of cybersecurity practices in their personal lives, they will be more motivated to adopt these practices at work. This dual benefit reinforces good habits and promotes a culture of continuous learning and application of security measures.

  Some mitigating strategies could include ensuring that the training is relevant and practical and providing actionable tips that employees can easily implement. You can also encourage employees to share their own experiences and tips, fostering a sense of community and shared learning. Finally, it is important to provide follow-up resources to help employees maintain good practices both at work and at home.
- **Peer influence** is positive behavior modeled and reinforced by colleagues. To promote this, try to establish peer recognition programs where employees can nominate colleagues who demonstrate exemplary security practices. Highlighting these role models in company newsletters or meetings can also be an influencing factor. Positive peer influence creates a supportive environment where good security practices are

normalized and valued. Employees are more likely to adopt secure behaviors when they see their peers doing the same, leading to a collective enhancement of security awareness and practices.

To keep this positive motivation going, ensure that recognition programs are inclusive and fair, providing opportunities for all employees to be acknowledged. You can promote a culture of mutual respect and collaboration where the employees will feel valued for their contributions. It is important to regularly update the recognition criteria to reflect evolving security challenges and practices.

- **Professional growth** emphasizes the career benefits of developing strong cybersecurity skills. By providing opportunities for employees to attend cybersecurity conferences and workshops, earn certifications, and participate in advanced training programs, you can promote this benefit. Offering career development plans that include a focus on cybersecurity expertise can also motivate employees. When employees understand that cybersecurity skills can enhance their career prospects, they are more likely to invest time and effort in learning and applying these skills. This type of motivation not only benefits the individual but also strengthens the organization's overall security capabilities.

  It is possible to mitigate these opportunities by ensuring that opportunities for professional growth are accessible to all employees, regardless of their current role or level. Another option is to provide financial support for employees pursuing certifications or attending conferences, workshops, and training. Recognizing and rewarding the achievements of employees who invest in their professional growth reinforces the value of their contributions to the organization.

By leveraging these positive motivations and addressing potential challenges, organizations can create a proactive, engaged, and resilient cybersecurity culture. Encouraging these behaviors helps build a strong foundation for a secure organizational environment where every employee plays a crucial role in maintaining security.

7.2.2 Negative motivations

Negative motivations, as summarized in Figure 7.3, are factors that lead individuals to neglect or bypass cybersecurity measures. These motivations often stem from a lack of knowledge, fear of consequences, or the desire for convenience. A lack of knowledge occurs when individuals are unaware of cybersecurity risks or don't understand the importance of following security protocols, making them more likely to engage in risky behaviors. Fear of consequences can drive individuals to avoid reporting incidents or following procedures because they worry about disciplinary actions, job security, or legal implications, even if it leads to larger issues later. The desire for convenience plays a role when people choose shortcuts, such as weak passwords, reusing credentials, or skipping security steps, because it saves time or effort, even though it exposes systems to vulnerabilities. By understanding these negative motivations, organizations can develop strategies to counteract them and promote a more secure environment.

- **Lack of knowledge and awareness** is the impact of insufficient knowledge on security behavior. For example, employees who do not understand the importance of strong passwords might use simple, easily guessable passwords for convenience. Lack of knowledge and awareness can lead to poor security practices, increasing the risk of breaches. Employees who are unaware of the latest threats and security protocols are more likely to make mistakes that compromise the organization's security.

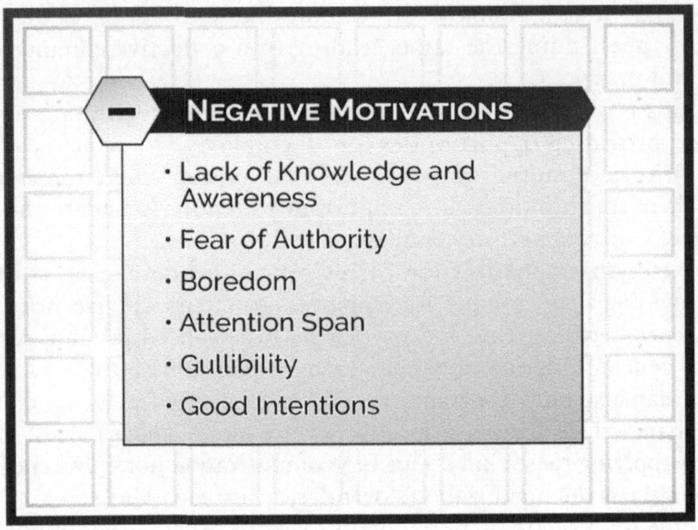

Figure 7.3 Negative motivations.

This negative motivation can be mitigated by providing regular, comprehensive training sessions that cover the basics of cybersecurity and introduce advanced topics over time. Diverse training methods, including online courses, in-person workshops, and interactive simulations, can engage all learning styles. Newsletters, alerts, and regular communications can be excellent ways to keep employees updated on the latest threats and best practices.

- **Fear of authority** stems from the fear of reporting security incidents or admitting mistakes due to potential negative consequences. A good example is when an employee accidentally clicks on a phishing link and might not report the incident out of fear of reprimand or punishment. Fear of authority can lead to unreported incidents and missed opportunities to promptly address security threats. It can also create a culture of silence and mistrust, where employees are reluctant to share information or seek help.

  One way to mitigate this motivation is to foster a blame-free culture where reporting incidents is encouraged and valued. Implementing anonymous reporting channels to make it easier for employees to report issues without fear is an excellent way to have employees report incidents. Regularly reinforcing that reporting mistakes is a critical part of maintaining security and that there will be no negative consequences for honest mistakes can help eliminate the fear.
- **Boredom** refers to the feeling of disinterest and monotony that employees may experience when performing routine and repetitive security tasks. These tasks, while essential, can become tedious and lead to disengagement if not managed properly.

  For example, an employee might find the routine task of updating passwords or regularly reviewing security policies dull and unengaging. This might lead them to perform these tasks with less care or to ignore them altogether.

  Boredom can have several negative impacts on an organization's cybersecurity posture. When employees are bored, they are more likely to become distracted and make mistakes, such as missing important security updates or failing to recognize phishing attempts. Disinterest in security tasks can lead to noncompliance with security protocols and policies, increasing the risk of security breaches. Bored employees can be less vigilant, resulting in overlooked threats and vulnerabilities.

In order to alleviate boredom, it is suggested to employ interactive training methods, such as gamification, simulations, and hands-on exercises, to make learning about cybersecurity more engaging. You can rotate responsibilities among employees to keep tasks fresh and interesting. This also ensures that more employees are knowledgeable about different tasks. Try incorporating new challenges, for example, advanced training opportunities to keep employees intellectually stimulated and invested in improving their cybersecurity skills.

Regularly recognizing and rewarding employees who consistently follow security protocols and contribute to a secure environment can maintain motivation and interest in security tasks. Feedback from employees on security processes and continuous improvements to keep the procedures relevant and engaging can benefit the organization tremendously.

- **Attention span** refers to a temporary period during which an individual's focus and concentration diminish, leading to a decreased ability to notice or respond to important security-related tasks or threats. This can occur due to various factors, such as fatigue, distraction, or the monotonous nature of routine tasks. For example, an employee might experience an attention lapse while quickly scanning through a large volume of emails, causing them to overlook a phishing email that appears slightly suspicious. Another example is an employee performing routine system checks without fully engaging, thereby missing critical signs of a potential security breach.

  Attention lapses can significantly negatively impact an organization's cybersecurity posture. Employees can miss threats or critical signs of phishing attacks, malware, or unauthorized access attempts. They can also make errors in judgment or fail to follow security protocols correctly, leading to vulnerabilities. Delayed responses can slow down the identification and response to security incidents, allowing threats to escalate.

  In order to mitigate these negative motivations, encourage employees to take regular breaks to avoid fatigue and maintain high levels of attention and focus. Implement task rotation to regularly rotate security-related responsibilities among employees to keep tasks from becoming too monotonous and to maintain high engagement levels. Use interactive and engaging training methods that require active participation, such as simulations and role-playing exercises, to maintain attention during learning sessions. Incorporating mindfulness practices and techniques can help employees improve their focus and concentration, such as brief meditation sessions or focus-enhancing exercises. Implementing automated alert systems can assist employees by highlighting potential threats and ensuring that critical information is not missed, even during brief periods of inattention.
- **Gullibility** refers to a person's tendency to be easily deceived or tricked into believing something that is not true. In the context of cybersecurity, gullibility often manifests as a susceptibility to social engineering attacks, where attackers manipulate individuals into revealing confidential information or performing actions that compromise security. For example, an employee might receive a convincing email that appears to be from a trusted source, such as a company executive or well-known vendor. This email might ask for sensitive information or instruct them to click on a malicious link. Due to their gullibility, the employee might comply with the request without verifying its authenticity, thereby falling victim to a phishing attack.

  Gullibility can significantly undermine an organization's security by increasing the risk of social engineering attacks. Employees who are easily deceived can become entry points for attackers, leading to data breaches. Gullible employees may inadvertently share confidential information, such as login credentials or financial data, with unauthorized individuals. Frequent incidents resulting from gullibility can erode trust within the organization and among its stakeholders.

The good news is there are some mitigating strategies that organizations can utilize. Conducting regular training sessions that educate employees about common social engineering tactics, such as pretexting and baiting, can be very useful. Using real-life examples and case studies can illustrate the risks. You can implement simulated phishing attacks to test employees' responses and provide immediate feedback and additional training to those who fall for the simulations. This helps employees recognize and resist real attacks. Encourage a culture where employees are urged to verify the identity of anyone requesting sensitive information, even if the request appears to come from a known or trusted source. You can provide clear procedures for verification and implement multifactor authentication to add an extra layer of security, making it harder for attackers to gain access even if they obtain login credentials through deception.

- **Good intentions** refer to employees' natural inclination to help others and do the right thing. In the context of cybersecurity, this well-meaning behavior can sometimes be exploited by attackers. Employees who are eager to assist may unknowingly compromise security by not adhering to protocols or by being overly trusting. An employee might hold open a secure door for someone they don't recognize because they want to be polite, not realizing that the person is an unauthorized individual trying to gain access. Similarly, an employee might quickly respond to an urgent-sounding email from a "colleague" requesting sensitive information, wanting to be helpful without verifying the authenticity of the request.

  While good intentions are generally positive, they can inadvertently lead to security breaches. Acts of kindness, such as letting someone into a secure area without proper identification, can lead to unauthorized access. Employees might leak information by sharing sensitive information too readily when they believe they are helping a trusted individual. Well-intentioned actions can sometimes bypass established security protocols, weakening the overall security framework.

  There are several actions that can be taken to mitigate these situations. Awareness training can educate employees about how attackers can exploit good intentions. By using real-life scenarios, one can illustrate how seemingly innocent actions can lead to security breaches. You can establish clear protocols and procedures for verifying requests for sensitive information and access to secure areas. This will ensure that all employees understand and follow these protocols, even in situations where they want to help.

  By conducting role-playing exercises where employees practice responding to requests for help in a secure manner, it can reinforce the importance of following security protocols while still being helpful. It is imperative to create an environment where employees feel comfortable reporting any unusual or suspicious requests for assistance.

  Encouraging a mindset where security is prioritized and reminding employees that while it's important to be helpful, it's equally important to ensure that security protocols are always followed.

In conclusion, understanding the motivations behind cyber behavior is crucial for developing effective cybersecurity strategies. By identifying both positive and negative motivations, organizations can create targeted programs and policies that encourage secure behaviors and mitigate risks. Positive motivations tap into employees' natural inclinations and desires, promoting engagement and vigilance in security practices. By recognizing and harnessing these positive motivations, organizations can build a supportive and collaborative environment where security is a shared priority. Negative motivations are factors that often lead to noncompliance with security protocols and increase the risk of breaches. Understanding these negative motivations allows organizations to develop strategies to counteract them, such as providing comprehensive training, fostering a blame-free culture, introducing engaging tasks, promoting skepticism and verification, and reinforcing the importance of security protocols.

By addressing both positive and negative motivations, organizations can create a balanced approach to cybersecurity. Encouraging positive behaviors while mitigating negative ones helps build a resilient security culture where employees are informed, engaged, and committed to protecting the organization. This comprehensive understanding of human behavior and motivations is essential for developing effective ETA programs that strengthen the overall cybersecurity posture.

7.3 THE ROLE OF ORGANIZATIONAL CULTURE

Organizational culture plays a critical role in shaping cybersecurity behaviors and practices. It includes the values, beliefs, and norms shared by members of an organization, which influence how they perceive and respond to cybersecurity threats. A strong and positive cybersecurity culture is essential for fostering an environment where security is prioritized and integrated into everyday activities. A supportive environment, clear communication, and recognition and rewards, as shown in Figure 7.4, are three important aspects of how organizational culture contributes to shaping a strong cybersecurity culture.

7.3.1 A supportive environment

When classifying an environment as supportive, this is one where employees feel encouraged and empowered to follow security protocols and report incidents without fear of repercussions. For example, an organization might have an open-door policy where employees can freely discuss security concerns with their managers or the IT department. Regular town hall meetings to discuss cybersecurity issues and improvements can also foster a supportive environment. This reduces fear and promotes transparency, ensuring that security incidents are reported promptly and handled effectively. It encourages employees to be proactive about security and fosters a sense of shared responsibility. To create a supportive environment, organizations can implement anonymous reporting systems, encourage open communication, and provide training that emphasizes the importance of reporting incidents without fear of negative consequences.

7.3.2 Clear communication

Clear communication involves effectively conveying security policies, procedures, and expectations to all employees. An organization might use multiple channels, such as emails, intranet posts, and training sessions, to communicate security updates and protocols. Regular newsletters highlighting recent threats and how to mitigate them can also be effective. Clear communication ensures that all employees are aware of and understand security policies and procedures, reducing confusion and ensuring consistent application of security measures across the organization. To achieve this, organizations should use simple,

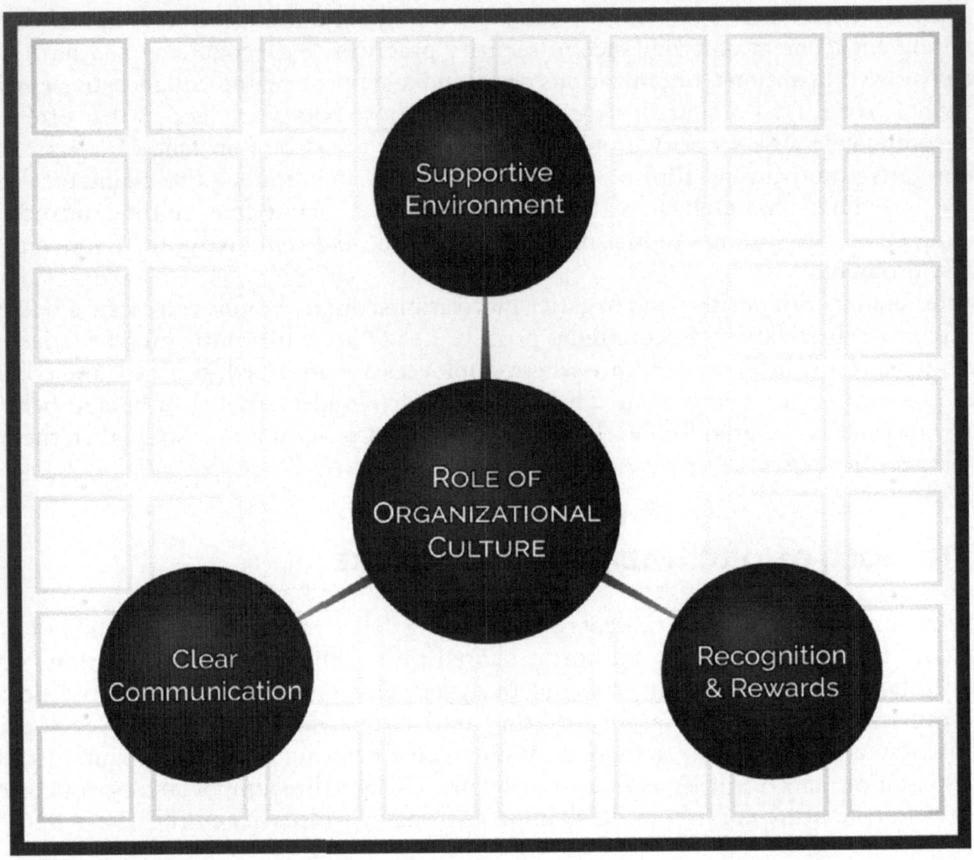

Figure 7.4 Role of organizational culture.

jargon-free language, regularly update employees on new threats, and ensure that security messages are consistent and reinforced by leaders within the organization.

7.3.3 Recognition and rewards

Recognition and rewards involve acknowledging and rewarding employees who demonstrate exemplary security behaviors and contribute to the organization's cybersecurity efforts. For instance, an organization might have a recognition program where employees are awarded for identifying security threats, following best practices, or suggesting improvements to security protocols. Recognition and rewards motivate employees to adhere to security policies and actively participate in improving the organization's security posture. They reinforce positive behavior and encourage a culture of continuous improvement. Organizations can establish a formal recognition program, provide both tangible and intangible rewards, and encourage peer recognition where employees can nominate their colleagues for their security efforts.

In conclusion, organizational culture is a powerful driver of cybersecurity behaviors and practices. By fostering a supportive environment, ensuring clear communication, and recognizing and rewarding positive behaviors, organizations can create a culture where security is a shared priority. A strong cybersecurity culture not only enhances compliance with security policies but also empowers employees to take proactive steps in safeguarding the organization's assets. The next section will explore the impact of cognitive biases on decision-making in cybersecurity and strategies to mitigate these biases.

7.4 COGNITIVE BIASES AND DECISION-MAKING

Cognitive biases are systematic patterns of deviation from rationality in judgment and decision-making. These biases occur because our brains use mental shortcuts to process information quickly. While these shortcuts are useful in many situations, they can also lead to errors and misjudgments. In the context of cybersecurity, cognitive biases can significantly impact how individuals perceive threats, assess risks, and make security-related decisions.

Understanding cognitive biases is crucial for improving cybersecurity practices. Biases can cause employees to underestimate risks, overlook critical information, or make inconsistent decisions. By recognizing these biases, organizations can develop strategies to mitigate their effects and enhance decision-making processes. This, in turn, can lead to more robust and effective security measures.

This section will explore common cognitive biases that affect cybersecurity decision-making, including overconfidence, confirmation, anchoring, availability, and groupthink biases, as summarized in Table 7.1. It will also address strategies to mitigate these biases and improve the overall security posture of the organization. By addressing cognitive biases, organizations can foster a more rational and evidence-based approach to cybersecurity, reducing the risk of human error and enhancing the effectiveness of their security efforts.

7.4.1 Overconfidence bias

Overconfidence bias occurs when individuals overestimate their knowledge, skills, or the accuracy of their predictions. For example, employees might believe they are highly

Table 7.1 Summary of cognitive biases

Cognitive Bias	Description	Impact on Cybersecurity	Mitigation Strategies
Overconfidence Bias	Overestimating one's knowledge or skills, leading to complacency.	Can lead to errors in judgment, such as underestimating threats or not following protocols.	Regular training, simulated attacks, promoting humility and continuous learning.
Confirmation Bias	Focusing on information that confirms pre-existing beliefs while ignoring contradictory evidence.	May cause overlooking of potential vulnerabilities and a false sense of security.	Encourage critical thinking, independent audits, valuing diverse perspectives.
Anchoring Bias	Relying heavily on the first piece of information encountered when making decisions.	Results in outdated or incorrect threat assessments and slow adaptation to new threats.	Regularly update threat assessments, encourage dynamic decision-making.
Availability Bias	Basing judgments on immediate examples or recent experiences rather than a broad perspective.	Overemphasis on certain threats, potentially neglecting others and creating an unbalanced security strategy.	Provide comprehensive threat intelligence, use balanced threat assessments.
Groupthink	Desire for group harmony that leads to irrational or suboptimal decision-making.	Leads to poor decision-making, lack of critical evaluation, and potential overlook of key threats.	Promote open dialogue, rotate team roles, bring in external perspectives.

proficient at identifying phishing emails and, therefore, might not take necessary precautions. This can lead to an increased risk of falling for a sophisticated phishing attack.

Overconfidence can result in complacency and a lack of vigilance, making it easier for attackers to exploit weaknesses. By providing regular training and updates on emerging threats, it is possible to keep the employees aware of their limitations. You can conduct simulated attacks and assessments to highlight areas where overconfidence might lead to errors and also encourage a culture of continuous learning and humility regarding security skills.

7.4.2 Confirmation bias

Confirmation bias is the tendency to search for, interpret, and remember information that confirms one's preconceptions while ignoring contradictory evidence. For example, an IT professional might focus on evidence that supports his or her belief that a network is secure while disregarding signs of potential vulnerabilities. This bias can lead to a false sense of security and missed opportunities to identify and address weaknesses.

In order to mitigate confirmation bias, you can encourage critical thinking and healthy skepticism, where employees regularly question and test their assumptions. Implementing regular, independent security audits and reviews can provide an objective assessment of security. Fostering an environment where diverse perspectives are valued and considered is by far the best remedy.

7.4.3 Anchoring bias

Anchoring bias occurs when individuals rely too heavily on the first piece of information encountered (the "anchor") when making decisions. A good example of this type of bias is when an employee might overly depend on initial information about a security threat and fail to adjust his or her understanding based on new evidence. The impacts of anchoring bias can be severalfold. It can result in outdated or incorrect responses to threats, as initial assessments are not revised when new information becomes available.

To mitigate anchoring bias, your organization must train employees to continuously seek out and consider new information and establish protocols for regularly updating threat assessments and security measures. You should also encourage a dynamic and flexible approach to security management, where decisions are revisited and revised as new data emerges.

7.4.4 Availability bias

Availability bias occurs when individuals rely on immediate examples when evaluating a topic, concept, method, or decision. For example, an employee might focus on a recent phishing attack he or she heard about and overestimate the likelihood of that specific type of attack while underestimating other potential threats. The impact of this bias on cybersecurity culture can lead to an overemphasis on certain threats while neglecting others, resulting in an unbalanced security strategy.

To mitigate availability bias, it is suggested to provide comprehensive threat intelligence that covers a wide range of potential risks and regularly update training materials to include diverse examples of different types of attacks. A balanced approach to threat assessment that considers both recent and historical data is encouraged.

7.4.5 Groupthink

Groupthink occurs when a group's desire for harmony or conformity results in irrational or dysfunctional decision-making. For example, a cybersecurity team might agree on a particular security strategy without critically evaluating alternative approaches because it wants to maintain group cohesion. The impact of this bias can lead to poor decision-making and overlook critical security measures or innovations.

It is possible to mitigate this bias by promoting a culture of open dialogue where dissenting opinions are encouraged and valued. You can rotate team roles and invite external perspectives to challenge existing assumptions. Use structured decision-making processes that require the consideration of multiple viewpoints. By understanding and addressing these cognitive biases, organizations can enhance the quality of decision-making in cybersecurity. This leads to more effective security practices, reducing the risk of human error and improving the overall security posture.

Biases play a significant role in how individuals perceive and respond to cybersecurity threats. Biases such as overconfidence, confirmation, anchoring, availability, and groupthink can lead to suboptimal decisions and increased vulnerabilities. By recognizing these biases and implementing strategies to mitigate their effects, organizations can improve their decision-making processes and enhance their overall security posture. Addressing cognitive biases fosters a more rational and evidence-based approach to cybersecurity, reducing the risk of human error and strengthening the organization's defenses against evolving threats.

7.5 STRESS AND CYBERSECURITY CULTURE

Stress is a significant factor that can influence behavior and decision-making in cybersecurity. High levels of stress can impair cognitive functions, reduce attention to detail, and increase the likelihood of errors. Understanding the impact of stress on cybersecurity professionals and employees is essential for creating a resilient cybersecurity culture.

7.5.1 Impact of stress

Stress is the body's response to challenging or threatening situations. In the context of cybersecurity, stress can arise from high-pressure environments, tight deadlines, constant vigilance, and the ever-present threat of cyberattacks. For example, a cybersecurity analyst working long hours to respond to a major security breach may experience high levels of stress, leading to fatigue and reduced cognitive functioning. High-stress levels can impair judgment, reduce concentration, and slow reaction times, increasing the risk of mistakes. Stressed employees may overlook critical security measures or fail to follow protocols correctly, making the organization more susceptible to attacks. Prolonged stress can lead to burnout, resulting in high turnover rates among cybersecurity professionals, which can weaken the organization's security posture.

For employees, stress can also be significant due to the need to maintain cybersecurity awareness while performing their regular job duties. For instance, employees might feel overwhelmed by the constant need to recognize phishing emails, remember complex passwords, and adhere to stringent security protocols. This ongoing vigilance can lead to stress, particularly if employees are not adequately trained or if the security measures are perceived as overly burdensome. Stressed employees may become complacent, leading to lapses in security practices, such as using weak passwords or failing to report suspicious activities. Ensuring that all employees have the training and tools necessary to understand and mitigate cybersecurity risks is crucial. Promoting a supportive environment where employees feel comfortable reporting potential threats without fear of punishment can help reduce stress and enhance overall security.

7.5.2 Sources of stress

Common sources of stress for cybersecurity professionals and employees, as summarized in Table 7.2, include heavy workloads, the constant threat of cyberattacks, rapid changes in technology, and the need for continuous learning and adaptation. Cybersecurity teams often face a high volume of incidents and alerts, leading to long hours and high-pressure situations. The ever-evolving landscape of cyber threats requires continuous vigilance, creating a persistent state of alertness and anxiety. Rapid advancements in technology necessitate ongoing training and adaptation, which can be stressful for employees trying to keep up. Responding to security breaches or incidents often involves high-stress, time-sensitive situations that require immediate and effective action.

For general employees, stress can stem from the pressure to adhere to strict security protocols. They may feel overwhelmed by the need to constantly recognize and respond to potential threats such as phishing emails, suspicious attachments, or unusual network activity. The fear of making mistakes that could lead to a security breach creates a high-stakes environment, further contributing to anxiety and stress. The rapid pace of technological change means that employees must continually update their knowledge and skills, which can be challenging for those who are less tech-savvy. This ongoing need for adaptation can be a significant source of stress, especially if employees feel they lack the necessary support or resources to keep up.

7.5.3 Stress management

Organizations can implement various techniques to manage stress. Encouraging a healthy work-life balance by promoting regular breaks, flexible working hours, and limiting overtime ensures that employees have time to rest and recharge. Providing access to mental health resources, such as counseling services and stress management workshops, creates a supportive work environment where employees feel comfortable seeking help. Offering

Table 7.2 Managing stress in cybersecurity culture

Managing Stress in Cybersecurity Culture: Sources, Impacts, and Strategies			
Source of Stress	**Impact**	**Example**	**Management Strategy**
High Workload	Leads to fatigue, reduced cognitive functioning, and errors in judgment.	Employees making mistakes due to exhaustion from overtime work.	Encourage regular breaks, flexible hours, and limit overtime.
Constant Threat of Cyber Attacks	Creates anxiety, hypervigilance, and decision paralysis.	Cybersecurity analysts overreacting or missing threats due to stress.	Provide access to mental health resources and support systems.
Rapid Technological Changes	Causes stress due to the constant need to adapt and learn.	Employees feeling overwhelmed by new software or systems.	Offer ongoing training and support for new technologies.
Need for Continuous Learning	Leads to burnout from the ongoing effort to stay up to date.	Staff struggling to keep up with new threats and security protocols.	Foster a continuous learning culture with adequate support.
Incident Response Pressure	Increases stress levels due to high-pressure, time-sensitive situations.	Employees under pressure to quickly contain a breach while being scrutinized.	Implement team support systems and provide clear incident protocols.
Fear of Making Mistakes	Leads to anxiety and reluctance to take necessary actions.	Employees hesitant to report incidents or mistakes due to fear of repercussions.	Promote a blame-free culture and encourage open communication.

regular training sessions helps employees stay up-to-date with the latest cybersecurity trends and technologies. This will reduce the stress associated with feeling unprepared or overwhelmed. Fostering a sense of community and teamwork through team-building activities and regular check-ins helps mitigate the effects of stress. Introducing mindfulness practices, such as meditation and deep-breathing exercises, can also help employees manage stress and maintain focus.

By understanding the impact of stress on cybersecurity professionals and implementing effective stress management techniques, organizations can enhance the well-being of their employees and improve their overall security posture. Reducing stress helps maintain high performance, vigilance, and a proactive approach to cybersecurity, contributing to a more resilient and effective security culture. Stress is an unavoidable aspect of work, but its impact can be managed through thoughtful strategies and support systems. By recognizing the sources of stress and implementing effective management techniques, organizations can protect the well-being of their employees and strengthen their cybersecurity defenses. A culture that prioritizes stress management fosters a more focused, alert, and resilient workforce better equipped to handle the challenges of the dynamic cybersecurity landscape.

7.6 CONCLUSION

This chapter explained the complex interplay between human psychology and cybersecurity. By examining motivations, cognitive biases, organizational culture, and stress, a spotlight has shone upon the critical role of the human element in safeguarding digital assets. Understanding the intricacies of human behavior is essential for developing effective cybersecurity strategies. When leveraging positive motivations, addressing negative influences, mitigating cognitive biases, fostering a supportive culture, and managing stress, organizations can create a more resilient security posture.

A holistic approach that integrates technology, processes, and people is paramount. When organizations invest in employee well-being, enhance cybersecurity awareness, and cultivate a security-conscious culture, they can significantly reduce their vulnerability to cyberattacks. To truly harness the power of the human factor, organizations must prioritize the development of comprehensive cybersecurity training programs, conduct regular security assessments, and foster a culture of continuous learning and improvement. By doing so, a workforce will be built that is not only knowledgeable about security threats but also empowered to make sound decisions and contribute to a safer digital environment.

DISCUSSION QUESTIONS

1. How does human behavior impact an organization's cybersecurity posture? Discuss specific examples where human behavior, rather than technological flaws, has been a critical factor in a security breach.
2. Why is understanding cognitive biases important in cybersecurity decision-making? Identify common cognitive biases and how they may affect the effectiveness of cybersecurity strategies.
3. What role do emotions play in cybersecurity practices? How can organizations address the emotional components, such as fear or overconfidence, to improve security behaviors?
4. How can organizations leverage positive motivations, like a sense of responsibility or personal benefit, to enhance cybersecurity culture? Discuss practical examples of initiatives that could be implemented to encourage these positive motivations.

5. What are the potential drawbacks of focusing only on technology and neglecting the human element in cybersecurity? How might this approach leave an organization vulnerable to certain types of attacks?
6. What are some effective strategies for mitigating the negative impacts of stress on cybersecurity practices? Consider both organizational-level strategies and individual-level practices.
7. How can a supportive organizational culture help foster a proactive cybersecurity mindset? Discuss the role of leadership, communication, and employee involvement in building this culture.
8. Why might employees fear reporting security incidents, and how can organizations address this fear? Explore the psychological and organizational factors contributing to this fear and propose solutions.
9. What are the risks of overconfidence and confirmation biases in cybersecurity teams? How can organizations train employees to recognize and overcome these biases in their decision-making?
10. How do stress and cognitive overload impact the attention span of cybersecurity professionals? Discuss practical steps that can be taken to reduce cognitive overload and maintain vigilance.

BIBLIOGRAPHY

Ali, N. (2023, November 23). *20 cognitive biases that hackers target and strategies to train them out.* The Security Company. https://thesecuritycompany.com/the-insider/20-cognitive-biases-that-hackers-target-and-strategies-to-train-them-out/

Bowen, B. M., Devarajan, R., & Stolfo, S. (2011). Measuring the human factor of cyber security. In *2011 IEEE International Conference on Technologies for Homeland Security (HST)* (pp. 230–235). IEEE. https://doi.org/10.1109/THS.2011.6107876

Carpenter, P. (2021, December 30). Five cognitive biases that can threaten your cybersecurity efforts. Forbes Business Council. Retrieved, 21 April 2022, from https://www.forbes.com/sites/forbesbusinesscouncil/2021/12/30/five-cognitive-biases-that-can-threaten-your-cybersecurity-efforts/

Ertan, A., Crossland, G., Heath, C., Denny, D., & Jensen, R. (2020). Cyber security behaviour in organisations. https://doi.org/10.48550/arXiv.2004.11768

Jeong, J., Mihelcic, J., Oliver, G., & Rudolph, C. (2019). Towards an improved understanding of human factors in cybersecurity. In *2019 IEEE 5th International Conference on Collaboration and Internet Computing (CIC)* (pp. 338–345). IEEE. https://doi.org/10.1109/CIC48465.2019.00047

Johnson, C. K., Gutzwiller, R. S., Gervais, J., & Ferguson-Walter, K. J. (2021). Decision-making biases and cyber attackers. In *2021 36th IEEE/ACM International Conference on Automated Software Engineering Workshops (ASEW)* (pp. 140–144). IEEE. https://doi.org/10.1109/ASEW52652.2021.00038

McAlaney, J., Frumkin, L. A., & Benson, V. (Eds.). (2018). *Psychological and behavioral examinations in cyber security (ebook).* IGI Global.

McAlaney, J., Hills, P. J., & Cole, T. (2024). *Forensic perspectives on cybercrime: Human behaviour and cybersecurity (ebook).* Taylor & Francis.

Monev, V. (2018, August). Cognitive biases in information security: Causes, examples, and mitigation. *Cyber Security Review.* https://www.cybersecurity-review.com/wp-content/uploads/2018/08/COGNITIVE-BIASES-IN-INFORMATION-SECURITY-CAUSES-EXAMPLES-AND-MITIGATION-By-Veselin-Monev-CSR.pdf

Moustafa, A. (Ed.). (2022). *Cybersecurity and cognitive science (ebook).* Elsevier Science.

Nobles, C. (2022). Stress, burnout, and security fatigue in cybersecurity: A human factors problem. *Holistica Journal of Business and Public Administration, 13*(1), 49–72. https://doi.org/10.2478/hjbpa-2022-0003

Patterson, W., & Winston-Proctor, C. E. (2020). *Behavioral cybersecurity: Fundamental principles and applications of personality psychology (ebook)*. CRC Press.
Robinson, N. (2023). Human factors security engineering: The future of cybersecurity teams. *EDPACS*, *67*(5), 1–17. https://doi.org/10.1080/07366981.2023.2211429
Ruohonen, J., & Saddiqa, M. (2024). What do we know about the psychology of insider threats? https://doi.org/10.48550/arXiv.2407.05943
Ting, D. (2022). Why cognitive biases and heuristics lead to an under-investment in cybersecurity. https://www.cs.tufts.edu/comp/116/archive/fall2019/dting.pdf
Triplett, W. J. (2022). Addressing human factors in cybersecurity leadership. *Journal of Cybersecurity and Privacy*, 2(3), 573–586. https://doi.org/10.3390/jcp2030029
Willie, M. (2023). *The role of organizational culture in cybersecurity: Building a security-first culture*. ResearchGate. https://www.researchgate.net/publication/371399113_The_Role_of_Organizational_Culture_in_Cybersecurity_Building_a_Security-First_Culture

Chapter 8

Importance of leadership in cybersecurity culture

Cybersecurity is a fundamental component of organizational strategy. Effective leadership is crucial in establishing and maintaining a strong cybersecurity culture. Leaders play a vital role in setting the tone and ensuring that cybersecurity practices are integrated into the daily operations of the organization. Without strong leadership, even the most advanced technical defenses can be rendered ineffective by human error and organizational vulnerabilities.

It is imperative to explore the multifaceted role of leadership in fostering a cybersecurity-conscious culture and see how leaders at various levels—from executive leadership to middle management—can influence the organization's approach to cybersecurity. Their unique vision, communication styles, integrity, and adaptability will be key elements of effective cybersecurity leadership. They can also build a cybersecurity-conscious organization through a top-down approach where they set strong examples by fostering collaboration and communication.

This chapter will consider the challenges of change management and the strategies leaders can use to facilitate successful transitions. It will also consider how organizational culture can be changed to enhance cybersecurity, providing practical steps and insights. Finally, it will identify common challenges faced by cybersecurity leaders and provide solutions to overcome them, ensuring a resilient and proactive approach to cybersecurity within organizations.

By the end of this chapter, readers will have a comprehensive understanding of the critical role of leadership in cybersecurity culture and will be equipped with strategies to strengthen their organization's security posture through effective leadership.

8.1 LEADERSHIP ROLES AND RESPONSIBILITIES

Leadership plays a pivotal role in shaping an organization's security stance. Effective leadership ensures that cybersecurity is not viewed merely as a technical necessity but as an integral part of the organization's strategic vision. Leaders at all levels, as shown in Figure 8.1—executive, IT, and middle management—carry distinct responsibilities that collectively contribute to a strong cybersecurity culture. Executive leaders set the strategic direction and priorities for cybersecurity. They make high-level decisions about resource allocation and risk management, integrating cybersecurity into the overall business strategy. They set the tone from the top and foster a culture where cybersecurity is a shared responsibility across the organization. They ensure that necessary resources and support are provided for effective security measures.

IT leadership translates the executive vision into actionable cybersecurity strategies. These leaders develop and implement technical solutions that protect the organization's information assets. They bridge the gap between high-level strategic goals and practical day-to-day

DOI: 10.1201/9781003368496-8

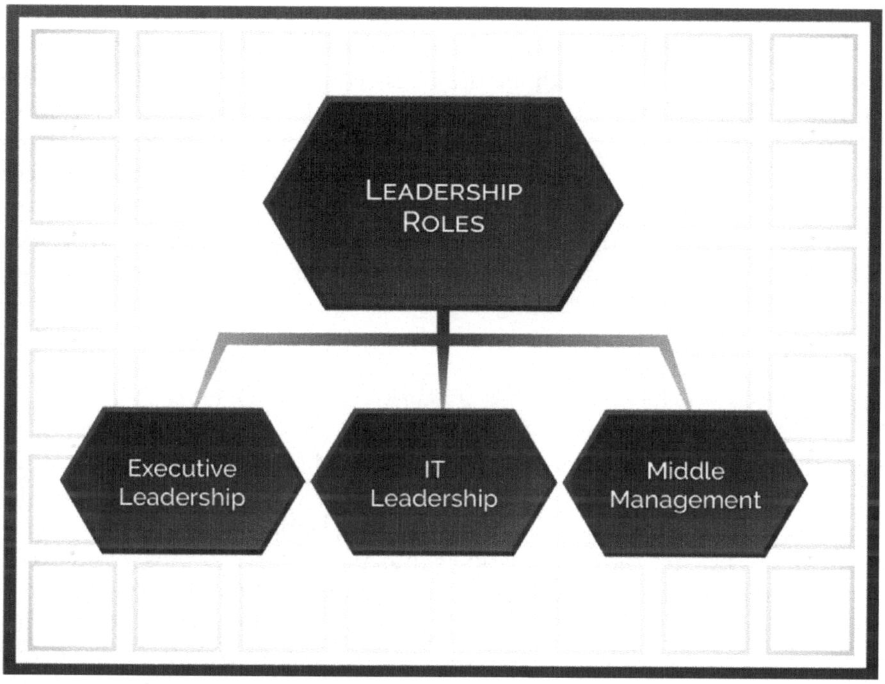

Figure 8.1 Leadership roles.

security operations by staying abreast of emerging threats, ensuring compliance with security policies, and maintaining the organization's security infrastructure.

Middle management acts as the link between upper management and frontline employees. These leaders ensure security policies, procedures, and protocols are communicated clearly and adhered to consistently. This is the key to fostering a security-aware culture within their departments, addressing compliance issues, and providing support and training to their teams.

Understanding these distinct roles is essential for building a unified and effective cybersecurity strategy. The following sections will examine the specific roles of executive leadership, IT leadership, and middle management, exploring how each contributes to a comprehensive approach to cybersecurity.

8.1.1 Executive leadership

Executive leadership is pivotal in establishing and maintaining a strong cybersecurity culture within an organization. Executives, such as chief executive officers (CEOs) and chief financial officers (CFOs), set strategic directions and priorities for cybersecurity and signal its importance to all employees. They are the highest level of authority in an organization, and their commitment helps embed a security-first mindset throughout. They accomplish this by making clear statements about the importance of cybersecurity in company communications and leading by example when adhering to security protocols themselves. Executives must balance cybersecurity measures with other business priorities, ensuring the organization is protected without hindering operational efficiency. This includes effective resource allocation and investing in cybersecurity technologies, personnel, and training programs to maintain and improve the organization's security posture.

Moreover, executives foster a culture of accountability and continuous improvement in cybersecurity by establishing clear policies and ensuring consistent enforcement across the organization. They stay informed about the latest cybersecurity trends and threats, supporting initiatives that enhance security capabilities. These include cybersecurity audits, innovation in security practices, and cross-functional collaboration between departments. A CEO who wants to set an example might review security policies regularly, participate in cybersecurity training sessions alongside employees, and include cybersecurity as a standing agenda item in executive meetings. By setting the strategic direction, making informed resource decisions, and fostering a culture of accountability, they can ensure that cybersecurity is deeply integrated into the organization's operations, resulting in a resilient and proactive cybersecurity culture.

8.1.2 IT leadership

IT leaders, such as chief information officers (CIOs) and chief information security officers (CISOs), play a crucial role in translating the strategic vision set by executive leadership into actionable cybersecurity measures. They develop, implement, and manage the technical infrastructure to protect the organization's information assets. This involves conducting risk assessments to identify potential threats and crafting dynamic strategies to mitigate these risks. IT leaders oversee the deployment of security technologies like firewalls, intrusion detection systems, encryption, and access controls. One of their most important roles is to ensure that these technologies integrate seamlessly into the organization's infrastructure and function effectively to protect sensitive data and systems.

IT leaders also act as intermediaries between executive leadership and technical teams. Communicating the strategic importance of cybersecurity initiatives and ensuring their efficient execution can be challenging. They must have a deep understanding of both the technical and business aspects of cybersecurity. Regularly reporting on security metrics and the effectiveness of current measures to executives helps them make informed decisions about resource allocation and strategic adjustments. IT leaders ensure compliance with relevant cybersecurity regulations and standards by staying updated with legal requirements and integrating them into the organization's policies, covering areas such as data protection, access controls, incident response, and employee training.

Moreover, IT leaders stay abreast of the constantly evolving cybersecurity landscape, which includes emerging threats and technologies. This involves continuous learning and engagement with the broader cybersecurity community through conferences, professional networks, and ongoing education. They are required to foster a culture of innovation within their teams, encouraging the exploration and adoption of new security technologies and practices. For instance, a good example would be a CIO leading the implementation of advanced threat detection systems that use machine learning to identify and respond to real-time anomalies. Through their leadership, IT leaders build a solid and adaptive cybersecurity posture that protects the organization's critical assets and enhances its resilience against cyberattacks.

8.1.3 Middle management

Middle management plays a vital role in ensuring departmental adherence to cybersecurity policies and procedures. Acting as the bridge between upper management's strategic directives and the daily activities of frontline employees, middle managers are tasked with clearly communicating cybersecurity policies and procedures, ensuring consistent adherence. They must be well versed in the organization's cybersecurity policies and procedures. They should monitor compliance within their teams and address deviations from established protocols. They must ensure all employees understand and follow security guidelines through regular check-ins, audits, and reviews.

The key responsibility of middle managers lies in effective communication and enforcement of security measures. They must break down complex security protocols into understandable steps, so the operational staff fully understands and abides by them. They ensure team members are aware of the latest security threats and know how to respond appropriately. All things considered, their most important job is to create an environment where employees feel comfortable reporting security incidents or potential vulnerabilities without fear of retribution.

Middle managers lead by example, strictly adhering to cybersecurity protocols and reinforcing their importance through regular training sessions and drills to keep security practices fresh in employees' minds. They also test their staff's readiness to respond to potential threats to identify vulnerabilities and improve incident response capabilities.

Middle managers are also vital in supporting ongoing cybersecurity training and development. They identify the training needs of their teams and ensure employees receive the necessary education and resources to stay updated on cybersecurity best practices. When compliance issues arise, middle managers respond first, identifying the root causes of noncompliance and taking corrective actions. They provide critical support during security incidents, acting as their teams' first point of contact. They are the ones who coordinate with IT and executive leadership to manage and mitigate the impact of security breaches. By actively engaging their teams in cybersecurity activities and fostering a culture of continuous learning, middle managers ensure that cybersecurity practices are consistently and effectively implemented throughout the organization.

Overall, the effective implementation of cybersecurity within an organization hinges on the collaboration and commitment of leaders at all levels. Each tier of leadership carries distinct but complementary responsibilities vital for promoting a strong cybersecurity culture. The successful execution of these roles is deeply intertwined with essential leadership traits and qualities.

Moving forward in this chapter, you will see these critical leadership traits and explore how they enhance leaders' abilities to fulfill their roles and responsibilities. By understanding and cultivating these traits, leaders can strengthen their effectiveness and inspire a culture of security and vigilance throughout the organization.

8.2 LEADERSHIP TRAITS AND QUALITIES IN CYBERSECURITY

Effective leadership in cybersecurity requires more than just technical knowledge and strategic vision. It demands a set of specific traits and qualities. These enable leaders to inspire and guide to maintain a strong security culture. They are essential for navigating the complex and ever-evolving landscape of cybersecurity threats, ensuring that security measures are not only implemented but also embraced by the entire organization.

This section will explore the key traits, as depicted in Figure 8.2, that distinguish successful cybersecurity leaders. Effective cybersecurity leaders possess vision and strategic thinking. They have strong communication skills to share their vision and strategic plans. Integrity, ethical leadership, adaptability, and resilience enable them to excel and earn respect.

By examining these traits in detail, the goal is to provide a comprehensive understanding of effective cybersecurity leadership. Whether you are an executive setting strategy, an IT leader implementing measures, or a middle manager ensuring compliance, these qualities are critical for cultivating a proactive and resilient cybersecurity culture.

Figure 8.2 Leadership traits and qualities.

8.2.1 Vision and strategic thinking

Vision and strategic thinking are foundational for effective cybersecurity leadership, providing direction and purpose. Leaders with a clear cybersecurity vision can articulate a future state where the organization is resilient against cyber threats, adopting a shared commitment to this goal. This vision aligns cybersecurity initiatives with the organization's overall objectives, ensuring integration into all aspects of the business and enabling the anticipation of potential challenges and opportunities.

Strategic thinking involves effective planning and foresight. It is essential for addressing current threats and preparing for future risks. Leaders must conduct thorough risk assessments to identify vulnerabilities and prioritize actions. These include technical measures, process improvements, policy updates, and employee training programs. Foresight allows leaders to stay informed about emerging technologies, evolving attack vectors, and regulatory changes. It enables proactive strategy adjustments to maintain protection.

Proactive threat hunting, integrating cybersecurity into business strategy, and long-term investment in advanced security technologies are examples of vision and strategic thinking in action. A strategic CISO might implement a threat-hunting program, forming a team to actively search for and mitigate network threats before causing damage. An executive leader could integrate cybersecurity into business decisions, ensuring it's prioritized in new initiatives and mergers. Meanwhile, a forward-thinking IT leader might advocate for investments in AI and machine learning, leveraging these technologies for enhanced threat detection and response, strengthening the organization's security posture.

Developing these skills requires continuous learning, professional development, and engaging with peers and experts. Encouraging a culture of innovation within the organization can help foster strategic thinking. Leaders can tap into diverse perspectives and solutions by promoting cross-functional collaboration and empowering employees to contribute ideas. This collaborative approach not only strengthens the organization's cybersecurity strategy but also reinforces the importance of a shared vision. These leadership qualities enable organizations to navigate cybersecurity complexities and remain resilient against evolving threats.

8.2.2 Communication skills

Effective communication is a critical leadership trait. It enables leaders to convey policies, procedures, and the importance of security practices to all employees. Clear communication ensures that everyone understands his or her role in maintaining security and is aware of potential risks and mitigation strategies. Leaders must translate complex technical information into easily understood language. This will enable them to foster a culture where cybersecurity is seen as a shared responsibility. Consistent, clear, and accessible messages are essential for all employees, regardless of their technical expertise.

Raising awareness and educating employees about potential threats and best practices is a key aspect of effective communication in cybersecurity. Leaders must regularly update employees on new threats, emerging trends, and changes in security policies. These updates can be done through training sessions, workshops, newsletters, and intranet posts. Encouraging open dialogue where employees feel comfortable asking questions and discussing security concerns, reinforces learning and promotes a more engaged and security-conscious workforce.

Building trust and encouraging openness are also crucial for effective communication. Employees need to feel confident in reporting security incidents or potential vulnerabilities without fear of blame or retribution. Leaders must create an environment where reporting issues is encouraged and seen as a positive contribution to the organization's security. Trust is built through consistent and transparent communication, where leaders regularly share updates on the organization's security posture, including successes and challenges. They can build credibility and trust within their teams by being open about security issues. Some examples of effective communication in cybersecurity include regular security briefings, clear incident reporting procedures, and interactive training sessions.

Developing strong communication skills requires continuous learning and practice. Leaders can enhance their abilities by seeking team feedback, participating in workshops, and learning from effective communicators. They can ensure their messages are clear and impactful by actively listening and addressing employee concerns. Effective communication is essential for cybersecurity leaders to convey policies, create awareness, build trust, and encourage openness. This is imperative for developing a security-conscious culture where all employees are informed and committed to maintaining security.

8.2.3 Integrity and ethical leadership

Integrity and ethical management are essential for effective cybersecurity leadership, promoting a culture of honesty, transparency, and accountability. Leaders who demonstrate these qualities set a standard for the entire organization. Promoting a culture of honesty means being transparent about security issues and how they are being addressed. Transparency about security issues and open communication about the organization's security posture build trust and encourage employees to report incidents or vulnerabilities without fear of retribution. When employees see their leaders acting with clarity and integrity, they are more likely to adopt similar behaviors, and this leads to a more cohesive and security-conscious organization.

Ethical decision-making in cybersecurity involves considering the impact on all stakeholders and balancing security measures with individual rights and privacy. Leaders must navigate complex situations where the right course of action is not always clear. They ensure that security measures comply with legal and regulatory requirements, and they should always consider the ethical implications. One example is when implementing surveillance technologies in an organization, leaders should respect employee privacy.

Trust is a critical component of an effective cybersecurity culture. Employees need to trust that their leaders prioritize their safety and privacy. This trust is built through consistent ethical behavior and transparent communication from supervisors. Leaders who act with integrity and demonstrate a commitment to ethical principles earn the trust and respect of their teams. Being accountable for their actions, admitting mistakes, and taking responsibility for decisions further reinforce the importance of integrity and ethical behavior throughout the organization.

Developing integrity and ethical leadership involves self-reflection, continuous learning, and a commitment to upholding ethical standards. Leaders can enhance these qualities by seeking mentorship from respected leaders, participating in ethics training programs, and staying informed about legal and regulatory changes impacting cybersecurity. Their encouragement of open dialogue about ethics within the organization helps reinforce these values. This encouragement can create opportunities for employees to discuss ethical dilemmas and share perspectives on handling challenging situations. By establishing a culture of ethical awareness and mutual respect, leaders can strengthen the organization's commitment to integrity.

Ethical leadership and integrity are essential for building and maintaining a strong cybersecurity culture. Promoting honesty, transparency, and ethical decision-making enables leaders to earn the trust and respect of their teams, ensuring security measures are effective and aligned with organizational values. These qualities are critical for navigating the complex and evolving landscape of cybersecurity, where trust and accountability are paramount.

8.2.4 Adaptability and resilience

Adaptability and resilience are vital traits for leaders in the ever-evolving field of cybersecurity. As new vulnerabilities, attack vectors, and technologies emerge, adaptable leaders can swiftly respond to these changes. This adaptability ensures their organization remains protected against the latest threats. Being adaptable means being open to new information, willing to change strategies as needed, and capable of quickly pivoting in response to unforeseen challenges. Resilient leaders maintain a positive and proactive attitude even in setbacks, demonstrating the ability to recover from incidents and learn from them.

Crises are inevitable in cybersecurity, such as data breaches or ransomware attacks requiring immediate attention. Resilient leaders can guide their teams through these challenging times, maintaining focus and morale. They manage the immediate response to a crisis and lead recovery efforts. They ensure that their organization emerges stronger. During a crisis, adaptable leaders quickly assess the situation, make informed decisions, and implement effective response strategies. They handle the stress and pressure of high-stakes situations, keeping their teams motivated and focused on resolving the issues. Postcrisis, resilient leaders conduct thorough analyses to identify lessons learned and implement improvements to prevent future incidents.

To cultivate adaptability and resilience within an organization, leaders must welcome a culture that encourages flexibility and continuous improvement. This involves creating an environment where employees feel empowered to suggest changes and improvements and where experimentation and innovation are valued. Leaders should promote continuous learning by encouraging teams to stay informed about the latest developments in cybersecurity and providing opportunities for professional development, such as attending conferences, participating in training programs, and obtaining certifications. Resilience can be enhanced by building strong support systems within the organization, including access to mental health resources, promoting work-life balance, and encouraging open communication about challenges and stressors. By supporting their teams' well-being, leaders can enhance their resilience and ability to cope with adversity.

Table 8.1 Leadership traits and their impact on cybersecurity culture

Leadership Traits and Their Impact on Cybersecurity Culture			
Trait	Description	Impact on Cybersecurity Culture	Examples
Vision & Strategic Thinking	Ability to set a clear cybersecurity vision and strategically plan for future threats and opportunities.	Aligns cybersecurity initiatives with business objectives and fosters a proactive approach.	A CEO integrating cybersecurity into overall business strategy and prioritizing investments.
Communication Skills	Skill in conveying complex security concepts in accessible language and ensuring open dialogue.	Ensures all employees understand their role in security and promotes a shared responsibility.	A CISO conducting regular training sessions and promoting open communication channels.
Integrity & Ethical Leadership	Commitment to honesty, transparency, and ethical decision-making in all cybersecurity actions.	Builds trust within the organization and ensures a strong ethical foundation in security practices.	An IT leader admitting mistakes and openly sharing lessons learned from security breaches.
Adaptability & Resilience	Flexibility to respond to emerging threats and resilience to recover from incidents.	Enables the organization to quickly adapt to new threats and strengthens overall security posture.	A CIO quickly reallocating resources in response to a new cyber threat.

In order to develop adaptability and resilience, leaders must maintain an open mindset, take calculated risks, and learn from failures. They should regularly seek feedback, reflect on their experiences, and promote a growth mindset within their teams, viewing challenges as opportunities for learning. By celebrating successes and acknowledging team efforts, leaders can encourage a culture of resilience and adaptability. These qualities are essential for staying flexible and proactive amid changing threats; therefore, guiding teams through crises and ensuring organizational security and recovery. Fostering continuous learning and support further strengthens these leadership traits, contributing to a dynamic cybersecurity posture.

In closing, as summarized in Table 8.1, we can say that effective cybersecurity leadership hinges on a blend of vision, strategic thinking, communication skills, integrity, ethical decision-making, adaptability, and resilience. Leaders who embody these traits can inspire and guide their organizations to maintain a strong security posture, navigate complex challenges, and embrace a culture of continuous improvement. These traits ensure cybersecurity is a fundamental part of the organizational culture, not just a technical concern. Moving forward, you will see how these leadership qualities contribute to building a cybersecurity-conscious organization. A security-first mindset, supported by comprehensive policies, continuous training, and a collaborative environment, is essential for a resilient and proactive cybersecurity approach. Strong leadership creates a culture where every employee understands his or her role in protecting the organization from cyber threats.

8.3 BUILDING A CYBERSECURITY-CONSCIOUS ORGANIZATION

The foundation of a strong security posture lies in creating an environment where every employee understands and prioritizes security. This section, as shown in Figure 8.3, explores the key strategies leaders can use to build such an organization, focusing on setting the tone

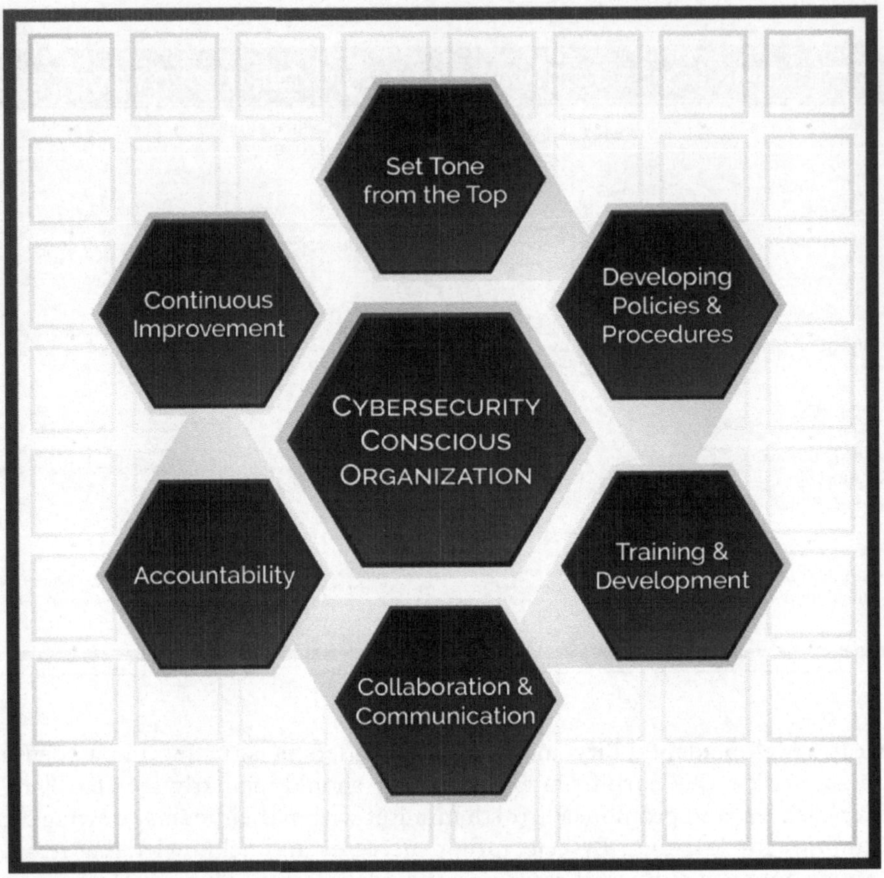

Figure 8.3 Cybersecurity conscious organization.

from the top, developing comprehensive policies and procedures, investing in continuous training and development, and encouraging collaboration and communication. By effectively implementing these strategies, organizations can create a security-conscious workforce that is equipped to identify, report, and mitigate risks, ultimately enhancing the organization's overall resilience against cyber threats.

8.3.1 Setting the tone from the top

Creating a cybersecurity-conscious organization begins with leadership. Leaders set the tone for the entire organization by demonstrating a strong commitment to cybersecurity. This involves integrating cybersecurity into the organization's core values and business strategy, making it clear that security is a priority at every level. Leaders must model the behaviors they expect from their employees, such as adhering to security protocols and participating in regular cybersecurity training.

When executives and senior managers prioritize cybersecurity, it sends a powerful message to the rest of the organization. This top-down approach ensures that cybersecurity is seen as an essential aspect of the organization's operations rather than an afterthought. By visibly supporting and engaging in cybersecurity initiatives, leaders can promote a culture where security is everyone's responsibility.

8.3.2 Developing policies and procedures

Effective cybersecurity policies and procedures are the backbone of a cybersecurity-conscious organization. These policies should be comprehensive, covering all aspects of security, including data protection, access controls, incident response, and employee responsibilities. Clear, well-documented policies provide a framework for consistent security practices across the organization.

Leaders must ensure that these policies are not only thorough but also practical and enforceable. This involves regularly reviewing and updating policies to reflect new threats, technological advancements, and regulatory changes. Engaging employees in the development and refinement of these policies can also enhance their relevance and effectiveness.

Communication is key to the successful implementation of security policies. Leaders should ensure that all employees are aware of and understand the policies, providing training and resources to support compliance. Regular audits and assessments can help identify areas for improvement and ensure that policies are being followed correctly.

8.3.3 Training and development

Continuous training and development are essential for maintaining a cybersecurity-conscious organization. Employees must stay informed about the latest risks and best practices. Regular training sessions, workshops, and online courses can help employees develop the skills and knowledge needed to protect the organization from cyber threats.

Leaders should invest in training programs that are engaging, relevant, and accessible to all employees. This includes role-specific training that addresses the unique security challenges faced by different departments. For example, training for IT staff might focus on technical defenses and threat detection, while training for HR might emphasize protecting sensitive employee data and recognizing social engineering tactics.

In addition to formal training, leaders should encourage a culture of continuous learning and improvement. This can involve staying updated on the latest cybersecurity trends, sharing insights from industry conferences, and promoting a collaborative environment where employees feel comfortable discussing security concerns and sharing knowledge.

8.3.4 Encouraging collaboration and communication

A collaborative and communicative environment is essential for a cybersecurity-conscious organization. Cybersecurity is a shared responsibility, and effective collaboration across departments can enhance the organization's overall security posture. Leaders should welcome open communication channels where employees can report security incidents, share concerns, and suggest improvements without fear of retribution.

Regular cross-departmental meetings and workshops can facilitate collaboration and ensure that security practices are aligned across the organization. Encouraging teamwork and collective problem solving can help identify and address vulnerabilities more effectively. Leaders should also recognize and reward collaborative efforts that contribute to the organization's cybersecurity goals. One example of fostering collaboration might include forming cross-functional security teams that bring together members from IT, HR, and other departments. These teams can work on specific security projects, conduct risk assessments, and develop comprehensive incident response plans. By leveraging the diverse expertise within the organization, these teams can create effective security strategies.

8.3.5 Building a culture of accountability and continuous improvement

Building a cybersecurity-conscious organization also involves establishing a culture of accountability and continuous improvement. Leaders should hold themselves and their teams accountable for adhering to security policies and achieving security goals. This includes conducting regular performance reviews, setting clear expectations, and providing constructive feedback.

Continuous improvement requires a proactive approach to identifying and addressing security challenges. Leaders should encourage innovation and experimentation, allowing employees to explore new security technologies and practices. Regularly reviewing and updating security measures, based on lessons learned from incidents and feedback, can help the organization stay ahead of emerging threats. A good example of promoting continuous improvement could be implementing a security innovation program where employees are encouraged to propose new security solutions or improvements to existing practices. This program could include a formal process for evaluating and implementing suggestions, with recognition and rewards for successful contributions.

Building a cybersecurity-conscious organization requires strong leadership, comprehensive policies, continuous training, and a collaborative culture. When the tone is set from the top, leaders can act as role models for the employees. By developing practical and enforceable policies, leaders can set their staff up for success. When investing in ongoing training and development, leaders can prevent incidences, and by fostering open communication and collaboration, leaders can create an environment where cybersecurity is a shared responsibility. This holistic approach ensures that the organization is resilient, proactive, and well prepared to face the ever-evolving landscape of cyber threats.

8.4 CHANGE MANAGEMENT IN CYBERSECURITY CULTURE

Change management is a structured approach to transitioning individuals, teams, and organizations from a current state to a desired future state. In the context of cybersecurity, change management is critical for implementing new security measures and updating policies. Effective change management ensures that changes are smoothly integrated and that all stakeholders are on board, minimizing resistance and maximizing adoption.

Since cybersecurity threats are constantly evolving, organizations must be agile in their responses. This requires not only technical changes but also cultural shifts. Employees must understand and embrace new security practices, which can be challenging without proper guidance and support. Change management helps to align organizational practices with the latest security standards and fosters a proactive approach to cybersecurity. To successfully manage change in cybersecurity, leaders must employ a range of strategies.

Clear and consistent communication is vital to successful change management. Leaders must explain the reasons for the change, the benefits it will bring, and how it will impact employees. Transparency helps build trust and reduces resistance. Regular updates and open forums for discussion can ensure that everyone is informed and has the opportunity to voice concerns.

Visible and active support from leadership is crucial. Leaders should champion the change, demonstrate their commitment, and address any concerns that arise. When employees see that leaders are fully invested in the change, they are more likely to follow suit.

Engaging employees early in the process fosters ownership and reduces resistance. Involving employees in planning and decision-making helps them feel valued and increases their commitment to the new cybersecurity measures. This can include forming committees or working in groups that represent different departments and levels within the organization.

Providing comprehensive training is essential to ensure that employees understand the new security measures and how to implement them. Ongoing education helps reinforce these changes and keeps employees updated on the latest threats and best practices. Training programs should be tailored to address the specific needs and roles of different employees.

Establishing channels for feedback and concerns is crucial. Listening to employees and addressing their issues can improve the change process and increase buy-in. Regular surveys, suggestion boxes, and feedback sessions can help gather valuable input from employees. Continuously monitoring the implementation of changes and being prepared to make adjustments as needed is a must. Flexibility is key to responding to unforeseen challenges and ensuring that the change is effectively integrated into the organization's culture.

Let's consider the example of implementing a new security protocol. Initially, employees who are accustomed to the old way of doing things may resist. By clearly communicating the reasons for the change, providing thorough training, and involving employees in the planning process, leaders can ease the transition. Regular feedback sessions can help identify any issues and allow adjustments to be made, ensuring that the new protocol is successfully adopted.

8.5 CAN ORGANIZATIONAL CULTURE BE CHANGED?

Organizational culture is the set of shared values, beliefs, and practices that shape how work is done. Changing an established culture, especially in the context of cybersecurity, can be challenging but is not impossible. A shift toward a cybersecurity-conscious culture requires sustained effort, strategic planning, and strong leadership. To change organizational culture, it is essential to understand the current culture and how it influences cybersecurity practices. This involves assessing the existing values and behaviors, identifying areas that need change, and understanding the underlying reasons for these behaviors. Leaders must recognize the cultural barriers to effective cybersecurity and address them directly.

Change starts at the top. Leaders must be committed to the cultural shift and lead by example. Their behavior sets the tone for the rest of the organization. Consistent and visible commitment from leadership reinforces the importance of change. They must articulate the desired cultural values and behaviors and make it clear what is expected and why it's important for cybersecurity. This involves creating a clear vision of the future state and the steps needed to get there. Reinforcing the desired culture through consistent messaging, using every opportunity to communicate the importance of cybersecurity and the role of each employee, with internal communication, training sessions, and everyday interactions can contribute to this change process.

Recognizing and rewarding behaviors that align with the desired culture and positive reinforcement helps embed new practices. This can include formal recognition programs, performance incentives, and informal acknowledgment of employees' efforts. Empowering employees to take ownership of security and providing them with the tools and authority to make decisions will encourage initiative and innovation, which can lead to more effective security practices. Building an environment where employees feel safe to report security issues and share their concerns will encourage open dialogue and collaboration. This will help create a culture of psychological safety and ensure that employees can speak up without fear of repercussion. For example, a successful cultural change might involve transforming a reactive cybersecurity culture into a proactive one. Initially, the organization only responds to security incidents after they occur. Through a structured change management approach, leaders communicated the benefits of a proactive stance. They provide training on threat detection and reward teams for identifying and mitigating potential threats before they escalate; this shift can result in a more vigilant and responsive organization, with employees actively participating in maintaining and improving cybersecurity measures.

In conclusion, one can say that change management is essential for implementing new cybersecurity measures and fostering a security-conscious culture. This can only be done using clear communication, strong leadership support, and employee involvement. With comprehensive training, effective feedback mechanisms, and ongoing monitoring, organizations can successfully navigate changes and enhance their cybersecurity posture. While challenging, changing organizational culture is achievable with sustained effort and strategic planning. By understanding the current culture, defining clear values, and empowering employees, leaders can foster a proactive and resilient cybersecurity culture that is well prepared to face evolving threats.

8.6 CHALLENGES AND SOLUTIONS IN CYBERSECURITY LEADERSHIP

Given the dynamic and complex nature of cyber threats, cybersecurity leadership is loaded with challenges. Leaders must navigate a constantly changing landscape, balancing the need for strong security measures with business objectives, regulatory compliance, and resource constraints. This section explores some of the common challenges faced by cybersecurity leaders and provides practical solutions to address these issues effectively, as summarized in Table 8.2.

Table 8.2 Leadership challenges and solutions

LEADERSHIP CHALLENGES & SOLUTIONS

CHALLENGE	DESCRIPTION	SOLUTION
Balancing Security & Business Goals	The need to align stringent security measures with business objectives without causing friction.	Implement a risk-based approach to prioritize resources where they are most needed.
Keeping Up with Evolving Threats	Constantly changing cyber threats require proactive adaptation and strategy adjustment.	Invest in continuous learning, threat intelligence programs, and collaboration with peers.
Managing Limited Resources	Limited budget and personnel for cybersecurity initiatives.	Prioritize investments based on critical assets and utilize automation for routine tasks.
Ensuring Regulatory Compliance	Adapting to evolving regulations and standards in different regions.	Conduct regular compliance audits and implement compliance management systems.
Building & Maintaining Trust	Developing trust with employees, customers, and stakeholders regarding data security.	Practice transparency in security measures and demonstrate ethical leadership.

8.6.1 Common challenges and solutions

- **Balancing security and business goals:** One of the primary challenges for cybersecurity leaders is balancing the need for stringent security measures with the organization's business objectives. Security measures can sometimes hinder business operations, leading to resistance from other departments. Implementing a risk-based approach to cybersecurity, focusing on the most critical assets and threats, will allow for the prioritization of resources where they are needed most, minimizing disruptions to business operations. Engaging business leaders and stakeholders in cybersecurity discussions to ensure alignment between security and business goals will bring up innovative ideas. Regular meetings and collaborative planning can help bridge the gap between security and business priorities.
- **Keeping up with evolving threats:** The cyber threat landscape is continually evolving, with new vulnerabilities, attack vectors, and technologies emerging regularly. Staying ahead of these threats is a significant challenge for cybersecurity leaders. Investing in continuous learning and training programs for cybersecurity teams to keep them updated on the latest threats and technologies is paramount. This includes attending conferences, participating in webinars, and obtaining relevant certifications. Implementing threat intelligence programs to monitor and analyze emerging threats will help in staying informed about the latest attack techniques and preparing defenses accordingly.

  Encouraging collaboration with industry peers, government agencies, and cybersecurity organizations to share information and best practices is an effective approach that enhances the ability to anticipate and respond to new threats.
- **Managing limited resources:** Cybersecurity often competes with other business priorities for limited resources. Leaders must manage these constraints while ensuring that security measures are effective and comprehensive.

  Efficient resource allocation is the solution to this challenge. Prioritizing security investments based on risk assessments and business impact analyses, focusing on the most critical areas, and allocating resources accordingly are imperative solutions. Utilizing automation and advanced technologies to enhance security operations can help manage routine tasks, freeing up resources for more strategic activities. Building a security-conscious culture where cybersecurity is everyone's responsibility should be a priority. By educating and engaging employees, organizations can extend their security efforts beyond the cybersecurity team.
- **Ensuring regulatory compliance:** Compliance with regulations is a major challenge for organizations. Regulatory requirements for cybersecurity are continually evolving, and noncompliance can result in severe penalties. Keeping up with these regulations and ensuring compliance is a complex task. Conduct regular audits and assessments to ensure compliance with relevant regulations. This includes both internal audits and third-party assessments. Implement compliance management systems to track regulatory requirements and manage compliance activities. These systems can help automate compliance processes and provide real-time insights into compliance status. Providing training and awareness programs for employees to ensure they understand the importance of compliance and their roles in maintaining is also an effective solution.
- **Building and maintaining trust:** This can be a difficult challenge. Trust is a critical component of a successful cybersecurity program. Leaders must build and maintain trust with employees, customers, and stakeholders. Transparency about cybersecurity practices and incidents and open communication build trust and demonstrate a

commitment to security. So does engaging with employees and stakeholders regularly to gather feedback and address concerns. This inclusive approach fosters a sense of shared responsibility and trust. Demonstrating ethical leadership by prioritizing the privacy and security of data helps to uphold ethical standards and reinforces trust and integrity.

8.6.2 Best practices in cybersecurity leadership

Effective cybersecurity leadership is essential for protecting organizational assets and ensuring business continuity. By adopting best practices, as shown in Table 8.3, such as risk assessments, continuous improvement, innovation, collaboration, and ethical conduct, cybersecurity leaders can build a strong security posture. This approach supports organizational goals and protects against potential threats.

- **Conducting regular risk assessments:** Conducting regular risk assessments to identify potential vulnerabilities and threats is a fundamental practice in cybersecurity leadership. These assessments provide a comprehensive understanding of the organization's risk landscape, allowing leaders to allocate resources effectively and prioritize security measures. Regular vulnerability scans and penetration testing are also essential, as they help uncover weaknesses in the security infrastructure that could be exploited by attackers. A well-developed incident response plan is crucial, outlining clear procedures for detecting, responding to, and recovering from security incidents, thereby minimizing damage and ensuring swift recovery.
- **Fostering a culture of continuous improvement and innovation:** These are another cornerstone of effective leadership in cybersecurity practices. Leaders should encourage employees to stay informed about the latest cybersecurity trends and technologies,

Table 8.3 Best practices in cybersecurity leadership

Best Practices in Cybersecurity Leadership	
Best Practice	**Description**
Regular Risk Assessments	Regular checks to find weaknesses and create a plan to quickly respond to incidents.
Continuous Improvement & Innovation	Encourage learning and new ideas to stay ahead of threats.
Collaboration & Information Sharing	Work with different departments and share information with others to improve security.
Clear Policies & Procedures	Create and update rules for security, making sure everyone knows their role.
Accountability & Ethics	Set a good example as a leader, be transparent, and ensure everyone follows security practices.
Advanced Technologies & Monitoring	Use tools like AI to detect threats and constantly watch for problems.
Effective Change Management	Implement new security measures by involving everyone and offering support during changes.

promoting continuous learning through training programs, certifications, and professional development opportunities. Implementing innovation programs that incentivize employees to propose and develop new security solutions can drive progress and enhance the organization's security posture. Regular reviews and updates of security policies, procedures, and technologies are necessary to keep them relevant and effective against evolving threats. By creating an environment that values learning and innovation, cybersecurity leaders can ensure their organizations remain resilient and adaptive in the face of emerging challenges.

- **Collaboration and information sharing:** These are critical components of cybersecurity leadership. Promoting cross-departmental collaboration ensures that cybersecurity is integrated into all business processes, fostering a unified approach to security. Establishing partnerships with industry peers, government agencies, and cybersecurity organizations facilitates the sharing of information and best practices, enhancing the organization's ability to anticipate and respond to threats. Participation in threat intelligence sharing programs keeps the organization informed about the latest attack techniques and vulnerabilities. By embracing a collaborative approach, cybersecurity leaders can build a stronger, more informed defense against cyber threats.
- **Development of comprehensive policies and procedures:** Effective cybersecurity leadership necessitates the development of comprehensive policies and procedures that align with the organization's goals and regulatory requirements. These policies should encompass all aspects of cybersecurity, from data protection and access controls to incident response and employee training. Leaders must ensure these policies are clearly communicated and regularly updated to reflect the changing threat landscape. Establishing clear guidelines and expectations helps create a security-conscious culture where employees understand their roles and responsibilities in safeguarding organizational assets.
- **Accountability and ethical conduct:** A culture of **accountability and ethical conduct** is fundamental to robust cybersecurity leadership. Leaders must model ethical behavior and hold themselves and their teams accountable for adhering to security policies and practices. This involves setting clear performance metrics and conducting regular audits to ensure compliance. Encouraging transparency and open communication about security practices and incidents promotes trust and reinforces the importance of integrity in cybersecurity. By promoting ethical conduct and accountability, leaders can build a strong foundation for a resilient and trustworthy security environment.
- **Advanced technologies and continuous monitoring:** Incorporating advanced technologies and continuous monitoring into cybersecurity strategies is another best practice for leaders. Tools such as artificial intelligence, machine learning, and automation can enhance threat detection and response capabilities. Continuous monitoring of network activity and systems helps identify potential threats in real time, allowing for swift intervention. Leaders must ensure their teams are equipped with the latest technologies and are trained to leverage these tools effectively.
- **Change management:** This is critical in cybersecurity as new threats and technologies continuously emerge. Leaders should implement proactive change management strategies to ensure smooth transitions and the adoption of new security measures. This involves engaging stakeholders across the organization, providing adequate training and support, and addressing potential resistance to change. By managing changes effectively, leaders can minimize disruptions and enhance the overall security framework.

Best practices in cybersecurity leadership are multifaceted and dynamic, requiring a blend of strategic planning, continuous improvement, collaboration, and ethical conduct. Performing regular risk assessments helps identify vulnerabilities. Encouraging a culture of learning and innovation keeps the organization adaptable. Implementing clear policies and promoting accountability ensure everyone understands his or her role. Using advanced technologies enhances security measures. Managing changes proactively builds resilience in the face of evolving threats. These practices not only protect the organization's assets but also ensure its long-term success in an increasingly complex cyber landscape.

8.7 CONCLUSION

Leadership plays a pivotal role in shaping and maintaining the culture within an organization. From executive leaders setting the strategic vision to IT leaders implementing technical measures and middle managers ensuring compliance, each level of leadership contributes to the overall security posture. Effective cybersecurity leadership involves a blend of key traits and qualities, including vision, strategic thinking, communication skills, integrity, ethical behavior, adaptability, and resilience.

Building a cybersecurity-conscious organization requires leaders to set the tone from the top, develop comprehensive policies and procedures, invest in continuous training and development, and foster a collaborative and communicative environment. Change management is crucial for integrating new security measures and fostering a proactive security culture, and this can be achieved through clear communication, strong leadership support, employee involvement, and continuous monitoring and adjustment.

Cybersecurity leaders face numerous challenges, including balancing security with business objectives, keeping up with evolving threats, managing resource constraints, ensuring regulatory compliance, and building trust; however, these challenges can be effectively addressed through proactive risk management, continuous improvement, collaboration, and information sharing.

In conclusion, effective cybersecurity leadership is essential for protecting an organization against evolving cyber threats. By embodying the right traits and qualities, promoting a strong security culture, and implementing strategic change management, leaders can ensure their organizations are resilient, proactive, and well prepared to face the complexities of the digital landscape. Cybersecurity leaders can build a strong security framework that supports the organization's goals and safeguards its assets through continuous learning, innovation, and ethical practices.

DISCUSSION QUESTIONS

1. What role does leadership play in shaping cybersecurity culture? How do different levels of leadership (executive, IT, and middle management) contribute to building a strong cybersecurity culture within an organization?
2. Why are vision and strategic thinking important for cybersecurity leaders? How can a clear vision and strategic thinking help them navigate the complex and evolving landscape of cybersecurity threats?
3. How can leaders effectively communicate cybersecurity priorities? What are some best practices for ensuring that cybersecurity policies and procedures are clearly communicated to all employees?
4. What traits are essential for effective cybersecurity leadership? Why are traits like integrity, adaptability, and resilience critical for leaders in the cybersecurity field?

5. How can organizations foster a cybersecurity-conscious culture? What steps can leaders take to set the tone from the top and ensure that cybersecurity is a priority for all employees?
6. What strategies can be used to manage change in cybersecurity practices? How can change management strategies help in the smooth implementation of new cybersecurity measures and policies?
7. What common challenges do cybersecurity leaders face? How can these challenges, such as balancing security with business objectives or keeping up with evolving threats, be effectively addressed?
8. How can ethical leadership influence cybersecurity practices? What roles do integrity and ethical behavior play in building trust and fostering a proactive security culture?
9. Why is collaboration important in cybersecurity leadership? How can leaders promote cross-departmental collaboration to enhance the organization's overall security posture?
10. What are the benefits of continuous learning and development in cybersecurity leadership? How can leaders ensure that their teams stay informed about the latest threats and technologies?

BIBLIOGRAPHY

Aslaner, M. (2024). *Cybersecurity strategies and best practices: A comprehensive guide to mastering enterprise cyber defense tactics and techniques.* Packt Publishing.

Baines, A., Ahmad, A., & Chang, S. (2022, December 12). Competencies of cybersecurity leaders: A review and research agenda. In *Proceedings of the ICIS 2022: Cybersecurity, Privacy and Ethics in AI* (pp. 1–19). Association for Information Systems AIS Electronic Library (AISeL).

Blum, D. (Year). *Rational cybersecurity for business: The security leaders' guide to business alignment.* Apress. https://doi.org/10.1007/978-1-4842-5952-1

Borkovich, D. J., Skovira, R. J., & Kohun, F. (2023). Foundation of cybersecurity infoscapes: It's all about the culture. *Issues in Information Systems*, *24*(3), 1–14. https://doi.org/10.48009/3_iis_2023_101

Brown, J. W. (2021). *The security leader's communication playbook: Bridging the gap between security and the business* (1st ed.). CRC Press.

Chatterjee, D. (2021). *Cybersecurity readiness: A holistic and high-performance approach.* SAGE Publications.

Corradini, I. (2020). Building a cybersecurity culture. In I. Corradini (Ed.), *Building a cybersecurity culture in organizations: How to bridge the gap between people and digital technology* (pp. 63–86). Springer.

Dent, P. (2021). *Cybersecurity failures of small and medium-sized businesses: Circumventing leadership failure* [Doctoral dissertation]. Utica College. ProQuest Dissertations & Theses, 28718619.

Dyché, J. (2015). *The new IT.* McGraw Hill.

Fitzgerald, T. (2018). *CISO compass: Navigating cybersecurity leadership challenges with insights from pioneers* (1st ed.). Auerbach Publications.

Furnell, S. (2021). The cybersecurity workforce and skills. *Computers & Security*, *100*, 102080. https://doi.org/10.1016/j.cose.2020.102080

Gaillard, J.-C. (2023). *The cybersecurity leadership handbook for the CISO and the CEO: How to fix decade-old issues and protect your organization from cyber threats.* Leaders Press.

Gururaj, H. L., Spoorthi, M., Ravi, V., Shreyas, J., & Roy, K. S. (2024). *Securing the future: Introduction to Zero Trust in cybersecurity.* Springer.

Hasib, M. (2022). *Cybersecurity leadership: Powering the modern organization.* Tomorrow's Strategy Today.

Hubbard, D. W., & Seiersen, R. (2016). *How to measure anything in cybersecurity risk.* Wiley.

Kárász, B., & Kollár, C. (2021). Leadership responsibilities in information security awareness development. *AARMS – Academic and Applied Research in Military and Public Management Science*, *19*(2), 79–91. https://doi.org/10.32565/aarms.2020.2.6

Karpiuk, M., Pizło, W., & Kaczmarek, K., et al. (2023). Cybersecurity management – Current state and directions of change. *International Journal of Legal Studies (IJOLS)*, *14*(2), 645–663. https://doi.org/10.5604/01.3001.0054.2880

King, N. (2023). *The cybersecurity mindset: Cultivating a culture of vigilance*. Aude Publishing.

Kleinberg, H., Reinicke, B., & Cummings, J. (2015). Cyber security best practices: What to do? *Journal of Information Systems Applied Research*, *8*(2), 52–59. http://jisar.org/2015-8/

Lehto, M., & Limnéll, J. (2020). Strategic leadership in cyber security, case Finland. *Information Security Journal: A Global Perspective*, *30*(3), 139–148. https://doi.org/10.1080/19393555.2020.1813851

Mandal, D. K., Singhal, N., & Tyagi, M. D. (2023). *Cybersecurity in the era of emerging technology*. Manglam Publications.

McHale, S. (2021). *Insiders guide to culture change: Creating a workplace that delivers, grows, and adapts*. HarperCollins Publishers.

Mohamed, H., & Ali, H. (2021). Finding solutions to cybersecurity challenges in the digital economy. In Aneta Bobenič Hintošová, Pawel Marszalek, Wolf-Georg Ringe, & Annarita Trotta (Eds.), *Fostering innovation and competitiveness with FinTech, RegTech, and SupTech* (pp. 80–96). IGI Global.

Mwim, E. N., & Mtsweni, J. (2022). Systematic review of factors that influence the cybersecurity culture. In N. Clarke & S. Furnell (Eds.), *Human aspects of information security and assurance* (pp. 147–172). Springer International Publishing. https://doi.org/10.1007/978-3-031-12172-2_12

Ogden, S. E. (2021). *Cybersecurity: Creating a cybersecurity culture* [Master's project]. California State University - San Bernardino, Department of Information and Decision Sciences. https://scholarworks.lib.csusb.edu/cgi/viewcontent.cgi?article=2425&context=etd

Parenty, T. J., & Domet, J. J. (2019). *A leader's guide to cybersecurity: Why boards need to lead—and how to do it*. Harvard Business Review Press.

Penchev, G. (2021). Planning and implementing change in cyber security network organisations. *Information & Security*, *50*(1), 89–101. https://connections-qj.org/system/files/5008_transforming_cno.pdf

Pöyhönen, J., & Lehto, M. (2020, June). Cyber security: Trust based architecture in the management of an organization security. In *Proceedings of the 18th European Conference on Cyber Warfare and Security ECCWS2020, 25–26 June 2020, Chester, UK* (pp. 304–313). Academic Conferences and Publishing International Limited.

Ramluckan, T., van Niekerk, B., & Martins, I. (2020, June). A change management perspective to implementing a cyber security culture. In *ECCWS 2020 20th European Conference on Cyber Warfare and Security* (p. 442).

Saeed, S., Altamimi, S. A., Alkayyal, N. A., Alshehri, E., & Alabbad, D. A. (2023). Digital transformation and cybersecurity challenges for business resilience: Issues and recommendations. *Sensors*, *23*(15), 6666. https://doi.org/10.3390/s23156666

Schein, E. H. (2022). *Corporate culture: What it is and how to change it*. Creative Media Partners, LLC.

Shoemaker, D., Laidlaw, G., & Kohnke, A. (2019). Positioning cybersecurity in the C-suite: How to build a joint security operations center. *EDPACS*, *60*(6), 1–7. https://d1wqtxts1xzle7.cloudfront.net/111366953/07366981.2019.169113920240211-1-iems4d-libre.pdf

Swerdlow, A. (2023). *Tech leadership: The blueprint for evolving from individual contributor to tech leader*. Base Two Publishing.

Tarun, R. (2021). *Fight fire with fire: Proactive cybersecurity strategies for today's leaders*. Wiley.

Uchendu, B., Nurse, J. R. C., Bada, M., & Furnell, S. (2021). Developing a cyber security culture: Current practices and future needs. *Computers & Security*, 109, 102387. https://doi.org/10.1016/j.cose.2021.102387

Chapter 9

Importance of policies, procedures, and compliance in cybersecurity culture

Cyber threats that can compromise sensitive information, disrupt operations, and damage reputations are increasingly targeting organizations. To combat these threats effectively, it is essential to establish a strong cybersecurity culture, which is underpinned by policies, procedures, and compliance with regulatory standards.

Policies and procedures form the backbone of an organization's cybersecurity framework. They provide clear guidelines on how to protect information assets, manage risks, and respond to security incidents. Effective policies and procedures not only enhance an organization's security posture but also foster a culture of security awareness and responsibility among employees.

Compliance with regulatory standards is equally important. These regulations set the minimum requirements for protecting sensitive data and ensuring the confidentiality, integrity, and availability of information. Adhering to these standards helps organizations avoid legal penalties, build trust with stakeholders, and maintain a competitive edge in the market.

As the exploration of cybersecurity policies and procedures begins, it is crucial to understand their foundational role in an organization's overall security strategy. This section will explore the importance of having well-defined policies and procedures and examining how they are crafted, implemented, and maintained. By understanding these critical components, organizations can better prepare themselves to navigate the complex landscape of cybersecurity.

9.1 UNDERSTANDING POLICIES AND PROCEDURES

Policies and procedures are essential for a strong cybersecurity framework. They provide clear guidelines and actions that help protect an organization's data and systems. Understanding how to create and implement these policies is key to building a secure and compliant workplace.

Policies and procedures are formal guidelines that outline how tasks and processes should be performed. They help manage and protect information assets and ensure that all employees know their roles and responsibilities in maintaining security. They help ensure consistency across the organization in security practices and provide clear instructions for handling security tasks. They also ensure adherence to laws and regulations and help manage potential security risks through established protocols.

Effective cybersecurity policies include several key components. A purpose statement explains why the policy exists and what it aims to achieve. The scope defines who the policy applies to and what systems or processes it covers. Roles and responsibilities outline the duties of various stakeholders, including employees, managers, and staff. Policy statements provide detailed rules that must be followed to ensure security. A good example of a cybersecurity policy includes data protection policies. These policies guide the handling

DOI: 10.1201/9781003368496-9

and protection of sensitive data. Access control policies set rules for granting and managing user access to systems and data. Incident response policies outline procedures for detecting, responding to, and recovering from security incidents.

Procedures, on the other hand, describe the specific steps required to implement the policy. Creating effective cybersecurity procedures is challenging since the process needs to be clear and guide the individual to follow it precisely. This involves several steps. First, we need to assess the organization's specific security needs and risks. This needs to be done by engaging key stakeholders, which, when done in the development process, ensures the procedures are practical and comprehensive. Only after that, each policy is broken down into detailed, actionable steps that are easy to follow and written in clear, concise language to avoid confusion. Testing the procedures to ensure they are accurate and effective is a must. Providing training and resources will help all employees to understand and execute the procedures. New threats, technologies, and business processes are addressed by regularly reviewing and updating procedures.

In conclusion, understanding and implementing effective policies and procedures are crucial for any organization's cybersecurity efforts. They provide a clear framework for managing and protecting information assets and ensure that all employees know their roles in maintaining security. By developing and regularly updating these policies and procedures, organizations can create a solid foundation for a secure and compliant workplace. This leads to the next critical aspect: the role of compliance in maintaining security standards and protecting sensitive information.

9.2 ROLE OF COMPLIANCE IN CYBERSECURITY

Compliance with cybersecurity regulations and standards is essential for protecting sensitive information and maintaining a secure organizational environment. Regulatory requirements provide a framework for managing risks and ensuring that organizations implement best practices to safeguard data. Understanding the role of compliance in cybersecurity helps organizations avoid legal penalties, build trust with stakeholders, and enhance their overall security posture.

Compliance in cybersecurity refers to the adherence to laws, regulations, and standards that govern how organizations protect and manage information. It involves implementing necessary measures to ensure the confidentiality, integrity, and availability of data. Compliance helps organizations mitigate risks, prevent data breaches, and effectively respond to security incidents. Regulatory bodies and industry standards set these requirements to ensure that organizations maintain a high level of security. Noncompliance can result in significant penalties, legal actions, and reputational damage; therefore, understanding and adhering to compliance requirements is crucial for maintaining a secure organizational environment.

Compliance ensures the following of best practices and guidelines by involving regular audits, assessments, and updates to keep up with evolving threats and regulatory changes. By adhering to these standards, organizations demonstrate their commitment to security, which helps build trust with customers, partners, and stakeholders. Compliance is not just about avoiding penalties but also about fostering a culture of security within the organization. It ensures that security measures are consistently applied and that everyone understands his or her role in maintaining the organization's security posture. Compliance frameworks provide a structured approach to managing security risks and protecting valuable information assets.

A compliance framework is a structured set of guidelines, standards, and practices that organizations follow to meet regulatory and industry requirements for cybersecurity and

Figure 9.1 Compliance framework.

data protection. These frameworks provide a comprehensive approach to managing security risks and ensuring that organizations implement effective measures to protect sensitive information. Frameworks have several aspects, as seen in Figure 9.1, such as guidelines and standards, risk assessment and management, and policies and procedures. Training and awareness, monitoring and reporting, auditing and assessment, and incident response and recovery are also important parts of frameworks.

Guidelines and standards refer to a set of rules and best practices that organizations must follow to ensure data security. They are often developed by regulatory bodies, industry groups, or international organizations. They are designed to address various aspects of cybersecurity, such as data protection, access control, and incident response.

Risk assessment and management are core components of many compliance frameworks. Organizations are required to conduct regular risk assessments, which involve identifying potential security threats, evaluating their impact, and implementing measures to mitigate these risks. Effective risk management helps organizations prioritize their security efforts and allocate resources appropriately.

Policies and procedures are developed as a requirement of the framework. Comprehensive policies and procedures that outline how security measures will be applied are imperative. These documents provide clear instructions for employees and ensure that security practices are consistently followed across the organization.

Training and awareness, which ensure that employees are aware of their security responsibilities and are trained in best practices, are critical aspects of compliance frameworks. Regular training sessions and awareness programs help create a security-conscious culture within the organization.

Compliance frameworks often mandate monitoring and reporting. They require continuous monitoring of security systems and regular reporting on compliance status. This involves tracking security incidents, assessing the effectiveness of security measures, and providing documentation to regulatory authorities or industry auditors.

Regular audits and assessments are essential components of compliance frameworks. These evaluations help ensure that organizations adhere to the required standards and identify areas for improvement. Internal audits, third-party assessments, and regulatory inspections are common methods used to verify compliance.

Effective incident response and recovery plans are necessary for minimizing the impact of security breaches. Compliance frameworks typically require organizations to have documented procedures for detecting, responding to, and recovering from security incidents. These plans ensure that organizations can quickly and effectively address security threats and restore normal operations.

In summary, the compliance frameworks provide a structured approach to managing cybersecurity and data protection. They help organizations implement best practices, meet regulatory requirements, and mitigate security risks. By following these frameworks, organizations can enhance their security posture, build trust with stakeholders, and ensure the confidentiality, integrity, and availability of their information assets. Understanding and adhering to a compliance framework is essential for maintaining a secure and compliant organizational environment.

9.3 COMPLIANCE REQUIREMENTS AND STANDARDS

Compliance requirements and standards are essential for establishing a secure and resilient cybersecurity environment. These frameworks provide structured guidelines and regulations that organizations must follow to protect sensitive information, comply with legal obligations, and enhance their overall security posture. By understanding and implementing these frameworks, businesses can safeguard their data, ensure legal compliance, and build trust with stakeholders.

In this section, several frameworks will be sampled, including:

1. Payment Card Industry Data Security Standard (PCI DSS)
2. Health Insurance Portability and Accountability Act (HIPAA)
3. National Institute of Standards and Technology (NIST) Cybersecurity Framework
4. General Data Protection Regulation (GDPR)
5. ISO/IEC 27001
6. Canada's Personal Information Protection and Electronic Documents Act (PIPEDA)

Understanding these frameworks is crucial because each provides a unique set of guidelines and requirements that help organizations address specific aspects of cybersecurity. By examining these frameworks, it is possible to illustrate how they shape business practices, drive compliance efforts, and contribute to a stronger cybersecurity culture.

9.3.1 Payment Card Industry Data Security Standard (PCI DSS)

The PCI DSS framework is designed to protect credit card information and prevent data breaches. It applies to all organizations that handle cardholder data, including merchants and service providers. Key requirements include building and maintaining a secure network, protecting cardholder data through encryption, and implementing strong access control measures. Businesses must also conduct regular security tests and maintain an information security policy.

Compliance with PCI DSS helps businesses protect against credit card fraud and data breaches, which can lead to significant financial losses and damage to reputation. Adhering to PCI DSS standards not only secures cardholder information but also builds customer trust and avoids penalties from card networks.

9.3.2 Health Insurance Portability and Accountability Act (HIPAA)

HIPAA sets standards for protecting patient health information in the healthcare industry. It requires organizations to implement administrative, physical, and technical safeguards to ensure the confidentiality, integrity, and availability of electronic protected health information (ePHI). Key requirements include risk assessments, secure storage of ePHI, and staff training on data protection. HIPAA compliance helps healthcare organizations protect patient information, which is crucial for maintaining patient trust and avoiding legal and financial penalties. It also ensures that healthcare providers can operate effectively within the regulatory framework.

9.3.3 National Institute of Standards and Technology (NIST) cybersecurity framework

The NIST cybersecurity framework offers a flexible and comprehensive approach to managing cybersecurity risks. It consists of five core functions: Identify, Protect, Detect, Respond, and Recover. Organizations are expected to develop a thorough understanding of their cybersecurity risks, implement protective measures, and establish procedures for detecting and responding to security incidents. Following the NIST framework helps organizations build a solid cybersecurity foundation and improve their ability to manage risks. It supports organizations in creating security programs that are adaptable to evolving threats, thus enhancing their overall resilience.

The NIST cybersecurity framework is a valuable resource for organizations seeking to improve their cybersecurity posture. Providing a structured approach to managing cybersecurity risks helps organizations prioritize their efforts, allocate resources effectively, and demonstrate their commitment to cybersecurity to stakeholders. Additionally, the framework aligns with other cybersecurity standards and regulations, making it easier for organizations to comply with multiple requirements.

9.3.4 General Data Protection Regulation (GDPR)

GDPR is a regulation that governs data protection and privacy for individuals in the European Union (EU). It requires organizations to obtain explicit consent for data processing, ensure data protection through measures like encryption, and provide individuals with rights to access, correct, and delete their data. It mandates timely reporting of data breaches. GDPR compliance is essential for organizations that handle the data of EU residents, helping them avoid hefty fines and legal issues. It also demonstrates a commitment to protecting user privacy, which can enhance the organization's reputation and customer trust.

Beyond the immediate legal requirements, GDPR also encourages organizations to adopt a privacy-by-design approach, integrating data protection principles into the development of new technologies and business processes from the outset. This proactive stance not only helps in achieving compliance but also fosters innovation in creating secure and privacy-respecting products and services. Additionally, GDPR's emphasis on accountability requires businesses to maintain detailed records of their data processing activities and conduct regular impact assessments, ensuring continuous monitoring and improvement of their data protection practices. These comprehensive measures contribute to a more transparent and trustworthy relationship between organizations and their stakeholders.

9.3.5 ISO/IEC 27001

ISO/IEC 27001 is an international standard for managing information security through an information security management system (ISMS). It requires organizations to establish, implement, and continually improve an ISMS by conducting risk assessments and implementing controls to manage security risks. Achieving ISO/IEC 27001 certification helps organizations demonstrate their commitment to information security, build trust with customers, and meet regulatory requirements. It also supports a structured approach to managing security risks and improving security practices.

ISO/IEC 27001 certification also promotes a culture of continuous improvement within an organization. By requiring regular internal audits and management reviews, the standard ensures that security practices are consistently evaluated and enhanced. This ongoing process helps organizations stay ahead of emerging threats and adapt to changes in the cybersecurity landscape. Moreover, the comprehensive nature of this standard, covering physical, technical, and organizational controls, ensures a holistic approach to information security. This not only mitigates risks but also fosters a security-aware culture among employees, encouraging them to take an active role in protecting the organization's information assets.

9.3.6 Personal Information Protection and Electronic Documents Act (PIPEDA)

PIPEDA is a Canadian law that governs how private sector organizations collect, use, and disclose personal information in the course of commercial business. It requires organizations to obtain consent when collecting personal data, implement appropriate safeguards to protect the information, and provide individuals with access to their data. It also mandates that organizations be transparent about their privacy practices and provide mechanisms for individuals to challenge compliance.

PIPEDA compliance is essential for businesses operating in Canada or handling the personal information of Canadian residents. It helps organizations build trust with consumers by demonstrating a commitment to privacy and data protection. Compliance also helps avoid legal penalties and enhances the organization's reputation.

Understanding and implementing these compliance requirements and standards are crucial for establishing a secure and trustworthy cybersecurity framework. Each framework, as summarized in Table 9.1, offers specific guidelines that help organizations protect sensitive data, comply with legal obligations, and build strong security practices. Effective adherence to these frameworks not only mitigates risks but also supports business objectives and enhances organizational resilience.

Table 9.1 Compliance standards and requirements

Framework/Standard	Description	Key Requirements	Benefits
Payment Card Industry Data Security Standard (PCI DSS)	• Designed to protect credit card information and prevent data breaches. • Applies to all entities handling cardholder data, including merchants and service providers.	• Secure network • Protect cardholder data • Access control • Regular testing • Maintain security policy	• Protects against credit card fraud • Builds customer trust • Avoid penalties
Health Insurance Portability & Accountability Act (HIPAA)	• Sets standards for protecting patient health information. • Requires administrative, physical, and technical safeguards to ensure confidentiality, integrity, and availability of electronic protected health information (ePHI).	• Risk assessments • Secure ePHI storage • Staff training • Breach notification	• Protects patient information • Ensures trust • Avoid legal penalties
National Institute of Standards and Technology (NIST) Cybersecurity Framework	• Offers a flexible and comprehensive approach to managing cybersecurity risks. • Consists of five core functions: Identify, Protect, Detect, Respond, and Recover.	• Risk management • Implement protective measures • Establish detection and response capabilities	• Improves risk management • Supports adaptable security programs Enhances resilience.
General Data Protection Regulation (GDPR)	• Regulation governing data protection and privacy for individuals in the EU. • Requires explicit consent for data processing, data protection measures, and rights for individuals over their data.	• Consent for data use • Data protection measures • Breach notification • User rights	• Avoids fines • Builds customer trust • Enhances reputation
ISO/IEC 27001	• An international standard for managing information security through an Information Security Management System (ISMS). • Requires risk assessments and controls to manage security risks.	• Establish ISMS • Conduct risk assessments • Continuous improvement	• Demonstrates commitment to security • Builds trust • Ensures regulatory compliance
PIPEDA (Personal Information Protection and Electronic Documents Act)	• Canadian law that governs how private sector organizations collect, use, and disclose personal information during commercial activities.	• Obtain consent for data collection • Implement data protection safeguards • Ensure transparency in privacy practices • Provide individuals access to their data.	• Builds consumer trust • Enhances transparency • Ensure legal compliance • Prevents penalties

With a solid foundation in compliance, the next step is to focus on developing and implementing cybersecurity policies and procedures. This involves creating comprehensive policies, establishing procedures for adherence, and ensuring ongoing management to align with these standards and support a strong cybersecurity culture.

9.4 BENEFITS OF COMPLIANCE

Compliance with cybersecurity regulations and standards provides numerous benefits that extend beyond merely avoiding legal penalties. These benefits encompass enhanced security, improved business operations, and increased trust from stakeholders. By adhering to compliance requirements, as shown in Figure 9.2, organizations can build a strong cybersecurity framework that supports their overall business goals.

Compliance frameworks first require organizations to implement stringent security mea sures, such as encryption, access controls, and incident response plans. These measures help protect sensitive information from unauthorized access, data breaches, and cyberattacks. A well-implemented compliance program ensures that security practices are consistently

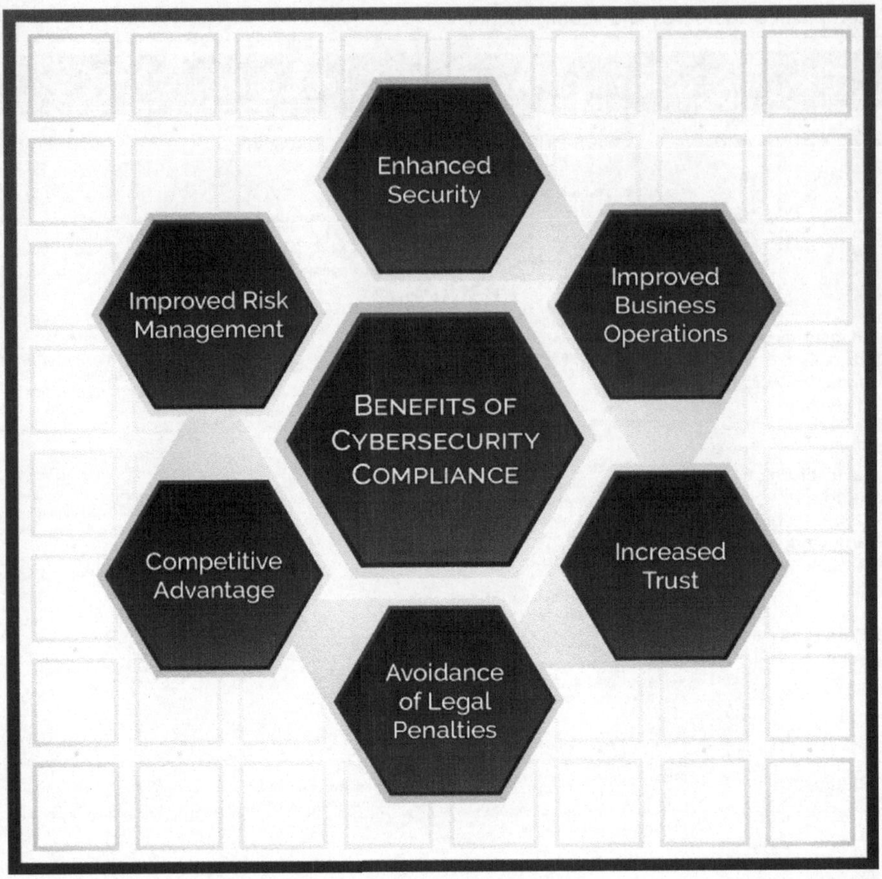

Figure 9.2 Benefits of cybersecurity compliance.

applied across the organization, reducing vulnerabilities and enhancing the overall resilience to cyber threats.

Adhering to compliance standards often necessitates a thorough review and improvement of existing business processes. This leads to more efficient and streamlined operations. For instance, conducting regular risk assessments and audits helps organizations identify inefficiencies and areas for improvement. Implementing best practices from compliance frameworks can also lead to better resource allocation and more effective management of security-related tasks. As a result, organizations can operate more smoothly and respond to security incidents more swiftly and effectively.

Compliance demonstrates an organization's commitment to protecting sensitive information and maintaining high-security standards. This commitment is crucial for building trust with customers, partners, and other stakeholders. When stakeholders know that an organization adheres to recognized security standards, they are more likely to trust that their data is being handled securely. This trust can enhance the organization's reputation and lead to stronger business relationships. For example, businesses that comply with PCI DSS can assure customers that their payment card information is secure, fostering customer confidence and loyalty.

Noncompliance with regulations such as PCI DSS, HIPAA, and GDPR can result in significant fines and legal penalties. By adhering to these regulations, organizations can avoid these costly repercussions. For instance, GDPR noncompliance can lead to fines of up to €20 million or 4% of the global annual turnover, whichever is higher. Compliance not only helps avoid financial penalties but also reduces the risk of legal disputes and reputational damage that can arise from data breaches and security incidents.

Organizations that achieve compliance with recognized standards can use this as a differentiator in the marketplace. Compliance certifications, such as ISO/IEC 27001, signal to customers and partners that the organization takes security seriously and has implemented rigorous measures to protect data. This can provide a competitive advantage by attracting customers who prioritize security and by enabling partnerships with other organizations that require compliance as a prerequisite. In highly regulated industries, compliance can also be a requirement for doing business, making it essential for market access.

Finally, compliance frameworks often include components for risk assessment and management, which help organizations identify, assess, and mitigate potential security risks more effectively. Regular risk assessments ensure that organizations stay aware of new and evolving threats, allowing them to adapt their security measures accordingly. This proactive approach to risk management helps prevent security incidents and minimizes the impact of any breaches that do occur.

The benefits of compliance with cybersecurity regulations and standards are far-reaching and significant. Enhanced security, improved business operations, increased trust from stakeholders, avoidance of legal penalties, competitive advantage, and improved risk management are just some of the key advantages. By prioritizing compliance, organizations not only protect their data and systems but also support their broader business objectives and build a strong foundation for long-term success. With a solid understanding of the benefits of compliance, the next step is to focus on developing and implementing cybersecurity policies and procedures to ensure ongoing adherence to these critical standards.

9.5 DEVELOPING AND IMPLEMENTING CYBERSECURITY POLICIES AND PROCEDURES

Developing and implementing cybersecurity policies and procedures is a critical step in building a security framework. These policies provide clear guidelines and actions that employees must follow to protect the organization's information assets and ensure compliance with relevant regulations. Effective policies and procedures help create a culture of security where everyone understands his or her role in safeguarding data and maintaining a secure environment.

The first step in developing cybersecurity policies, as indicated in Figure 9.3, is to identify the specific needs of the organization. This involves assessing the organization's current security posture, understanding the types of data it handles, and identifying potential threats. By conducting a thorough risk assessment, organizations can pinpoint areas where policies are needed to address vulnerabilities and protect critical information.

Understanding the regulatory requirements relevant to the organization is also important. For example, healthcare organizations must comply with HIPAA, while financial institutions need to adhere to regulations like PCI DSS. Tailoring policies to meet these requirements ensure that the organizations stay compliant and protect sensitive data.

Effective cybersecurity policies are clear, concise, and actionable. They should provide specific instructions on how to handle various aspects of security, from data protection to incident response. When writing policies, it is essential to involve key stakeholders, including IT staff, legal advisors, and department heads, to ensure that the policies are comprehensive and practical. A well-crafted policy should include a purpose statement explaining

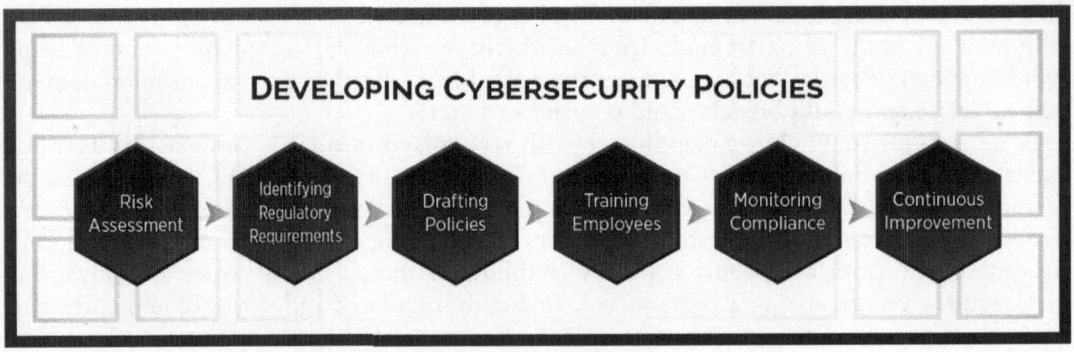

Figure 9.3 Developing cybersecurity policies.

the rationale behind the policy and its intended outcomes as well as a scope that defines who the policy applies to and what systems or processes it covers. Roles and responsibilities should clearly outline the duties and obligations of various stakeholders. The compliance and enforcement should explain in detail how compliance will be monitored and the consequences of noncompliance. There should be a schedule established for regular review and updates to keep the policy current with evolving threats and regulatory requirements.

Implementing cybersecurity policies effectively requires a strategic approach to ensure that all employees understand and adhere to the guidelines. Training and communication are two important elements to the successful implementation of policies. Once policies are developed, they must be communicated clearly to all employees. Training sessions, workshops, and regular updates help ensure that everyone understands his or her responsibilities and how to follow the policies. Providing accessible resources, such as manuals and online modules, can also aid in reinforcing the policies. To ensure compliance, organizations must establish mechanisms for monitoring adherence to policies. This includes regular audits, assessments, and real-time monitoring of security practices. Enforcement measures help maintain the integrity of the policies and emphasize their importance.

Cybersecurity is an evolving field, and policies must be regularly reviewed and updated to address new threats and regulatory changes. Organizations should establish a process for continuous improvement, incorporating feedback from employees and lessons learned from security incidents. Regularly updating policies ensures they remain effective and relevant.

A strong cybersecurity framework is essential for safeguarding organizational assets and achieving long-term success. By meticulously developing and implementing comprehensive policies and procedures aligned with specific organizational needs, businesses can effectively mitigate risks, ensure compliance, and cultivate a security-conscious culture. This strategic approach not only protects sensitive information but also strengthens the organization's overall resilience and competitive advantage; however, it all depends on how compliance is ensured. The next section will explore ensuring compliance with these policies through regular audits, assessments, and continuous monitoring.

9.6 ENSURING COMPLIANCE

Ensuring compliance with cybersecurity policies and procedures is critical to maintaining a secure organizational environment. Compliance involves not only adhering to established guidelines but also continuously monitoring, assessing, and improving security practices. Regular audits, assessments, and effective reporting mechanisms help organizations identify

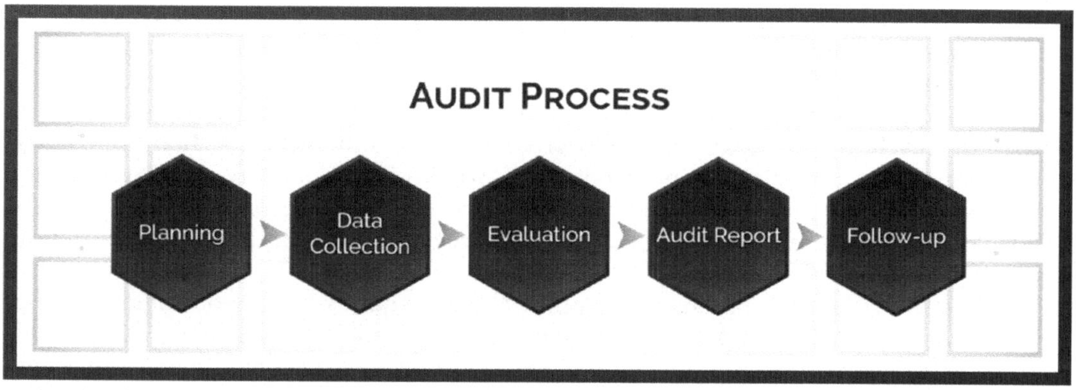

Figure 9.4 Audit process.

noncompliance issues and address them promptly. This section explores the strategies and tools necessary for ensuring ongoing compliance with cybersecurity policies.

Regular internal audits are essential for verifying that cybersecurity policies and procedures are being followed. These audits involve a systematic examination of the organization's security practices, identifying areas of noncompliance and potential vulnerabilities. Audits should be conducted by an internal audit team or external auditors to provide an objective assessment of the organization's adherence to policies. The process begins with planning, as shown in Figure 9.4, where the scope and objectives of the audit are defined. Data collection involves gathering relevant documentation, such as access logs, incident reports, and employee training records. The evaluation phase assesses the effectiveness of existing security measures and identifies gaps or areas for improvement. The findings are then documented in a detailed audit report, highlighting noncompliance issues and recommending corrective actions. Finally, follow-up ensures that corrective actions are implemented and verified for their effectiveness in subsequent audits.

In addition to audits, regular assessments are crucial for identifying and mitigating security risks. These risk assessments involve evaluating the likelihood and impact of various threats and vulnerabilities, helping organizations prioritize their security efforts. The process includes identifying potential threats, assessing the likelihood and impact of each identified risk, and determining the level of risk for each threat. This prioritization allows organizations to develop and implement strategies to effectively mitigate high-priority risks.

Continuous monitoring involves the real-time tracking of security activities and events to detect and respond to potential incidents promptly. By implementing automated monitoring tools, organizations can gain visibility into their security environment and identify noncompliance issues as they arise. Key aspects of continuous monitoring include intrusion detection systems (IDS) that monitor network traffic for suspicious activity, security information and event management (SIEM) systems that collect and analyze security data from various sources, and endpoint detection and response (EDR) tools that monitor and respond to threats on individual devices within the network.

Establishing effective reporting mechanisms is essential for identifying and addressing noncompliance issues. Employees should be encouraged to report security incidents, vulnerabilities, and suspicious activities without fear of retribution. Clear reporting channels and procedures help ensure that issues are promptly addressed and resolved. Effective reporting strategies include providing anonymous reporting options, developing and communicating clear procedures for reporting security incidents, and establishing a dedicated incident response team to handle reported incidents and ensure timely resolution.

Identifying noncompliance issues is the first step in addressing them. Regular audits, risk assessments, and continuous monitoring help uncover areas where policies and procedures are not being followed. Once noncompliance issues are identified, organizations must take corrective actions to address them. This involves implementing measures to resolve the issues and prevent future occurrences. The process begins with root cause analysis to determine the underlying causes of noncompliance. Corrective measures are then implemented to address the issues, such as updating policies, improving training, or enhancing controls. Follow-up ensures that corrective measures have been successfully implemented and are effective in preventing recurrence.

Ensuring compliance is an ongoing process that requires continuous improvement. Organizations should regularly review and update their policies, procedures, and controls to adapt to evolving threats and regulatory changes. Strategies for continuous improvement include conducting periodic reviews of policies and procedures, soliciting feedback from employees to identify areas for improvement, and continuously updating training programs to reflect new policies, procedures, and emerging threats.

In the end, ensuring compliance with cybersecurity policies and procedures is essential for maintaining a secure and resilient organizational environment, as summarized in Table 9.2. With a strong compliance framework in place, organizations are better equipped to protect their information assets and support their broader business objectives. This leads to the next section, where case studies and best practices in successful policy implementation and compliance will be explored.

Table 9.2 Steps to ensuring compliance

Strategy	Description	Tools/Methods	Purpose
Internal Audits	Regular examination of adherence to cybersecurity policies.	· Internal audit teams · External auditors · Detailed audit reports · Corrective actions · Follow-ups	Verify policy adherence and identify vulnerabilities.
Risk Assessments	Evaluating potential risks and vulnerabilities to prioritize security efforts.	· Threat modeling · Risk likelihood and impact evaluation · Prioritization of high-risk areas	Identify and mitigate risks effectively.
Continuous Monitoring	Real-time tracking of security activities to detect and respond to incidents promptly.	· Intrusion Detection Systems (IDS) · Security Information and Event Management (SIEM) · Endpoint Detection (EDR)	Monitor for compliance issues and security threats.
Effective Reporting Mechanisms	Providing clear channels for reporting security incidents and vulnerabilities.	· Anonymous reporting systems · Incident response teams · Clear communication protocols	Encourage transparency and quick resolution.
Corrective Actions	Taking measures to resolve noncompliance issues and prevent future occurrences.	· Root cause analysis · Policy updates · Additional training · Improved security controls	Address and prevent noncompliance issues.
Continuous Improvement	Regularly updating and reviewing policies, procedures, and training to adapt to emerging threats.	· Policy reviews · Employee feedback · Periodic training updates · Regular system updates	Ensure ongoing compliance and adaptability.

9.7 CASE STUDIES IN COMPLIANCE

Examining real-world examples of cybersecurity compliance provides valuable insights into the challenges and successes organizations face in implementing effective security measures. These case studies highlight practical applications of policies and procedures, showcasing both benefits and difficulties encountered. This section presents case studies of successful compliance implementations and the lessons learned from these experiences.

Our first case study is Microsoft. A global leader in technology recognized the need to strengthen its cybersecurity framework in response to increasing cyber threats. The company decided to adopt a proactive approach to compliance, focusing on continuous improvement and rigorous adherence to international standards. Microsoft implemented the ISO/IEC 27001 standard across its operations to manage and protect sensitive information. Regular risk assessments were conducted to identify potential vulnerabilities, and detailed policies and procedures were developed to address these risks. This proactive compliance approach led to a significant reduction in security incidents. The ISO/IEC 27001 certification enhanced Microsoft's reputation, building trust with customers and partners. Regular audits and continuous monitoring ensured that security measures remained effective, adapting to new threats and regulatory changes. Lessons learned from Microsoft's experience include the importance of adopting international standards, continuous improvement, and comprehensive risk assessments.

Our second case study comes from an organization facing significant regulatory scrutiny and public concern over data privacy. Google aimed to bolster its compliance with global data protection regulations, particularly the GDPR. They implemented measures to enhance data privacy, including obtaining explicit consent from users for data processing, anonymizing data, and providing users with tools to manage their privacy settings. The company also established a dedicated Data Protection Office to oversee compliance with GDPR and other privacy regulations. Google's commitment to data privacy improved its compliance posture and enhanced user trust. The company successfully avoided major fines associated with noncompliance and set a standard for data privacy practices in the tech industry.

Our final case study is the Mayo Clinic, a renowned healthcare provider that needed to ensure strict compliance with HIPAA to protect patient information and maintain its reputation for excellence in healthcare. Mayo Clinic developed comprehensive administrative, physical, and technical safeguards to secure electronic protected health information (ePHI). Regular training programs were conducted for staff to ensure they understood HIPAA requirements and their responsibilities. Additionally, the Mayo Clinic implemented advanced encryption methods and access controls to protect sensitive data. The clinic's improved compliance program resulted in enhanced data protection, significantly reducing the risk of data breaches. Continuous training and adherence to HIPAA standards strengthened patient trust and supported Mayo Clinic's commitment to high-quality healthcare. Lessons learned from the Mayo Clinic's experience include the importance of regular training programs, advanced encryption and access controls, and comprehensive safeguards.

Microsoft, Google, and Mayo Clinic's real-world case studies demonstrate the importance of proactive compliance measures and continuous improvement in cybersecurity practices. These examples highlight how organizations can successfully implement international standards, strengthen data privacy, and ensure regulatory compliance to protect sensitive information and build trust with stakeholders. Adopting best practices such as regular training, comprehensive risk assessments, and data protection measures, can enhance an organization's cybersecurity posture and effectively navigate the complexities of compliance.

9.8 BEST PRACTICES IN COMPLIANCE

Implementing best practices in cybersecurity compliance is crucial for ensuring that organizations not only meet regulatory requirements but also create a strong security framework that protects sensitive information and builds trust with stakeholders. These practices help organizations navigate the complexities of compliance and reduce vulnerabilities. This section outlines several key best practices for achieving and maintaining compliance, as summarized in Table 9.3.

Active engagement and support from leadership are fundamental for overcoming compliance challenges. Leaders must prioritize cybersecurity, allocate necessary resources, and promote a culture of compliance throughout the organization. Clear communication from the top reinforces the importance of compliance and motivates employees to adhere to established policies and procedures. Leadership commitment ensures that compliance initiatives receive the attention and investment needed for success.

Regular training programs are essential for keeping employees informed about compliance requirements and best practices. Training should be tailored to different roles within the organization, ensuring that everyone understands their responsibilities. Training helps employees stay up-to-date with evolving threats and regulatory changes. Effective training programs should include simulations and practical exercises to enhance understanding and retention of cybersecurity practices.

Table 9.3 Best practices in cybersecurity compliance

BEST PRACTICES IN CYBERSECURITY COMPLIANCE		
STRATEGY	DESCRIPTION	TOOLS/METHODS
Leadership Engagement	Active leadership support, resource allocation, and communication.	• Reinforces the importance of compliance • Ensures necessary resources are allocated
Regular Training	Tailored training programs that keep employees informed of compliance requirements.	• Increases awareness • Reduces human errors • Helps employees stay updated with threats and regulations
Leveraging Technology	Using compliance management software, SIEM, and automated monitoring tools.	• Streamlines compliance • Real-time insights • Improves detection of incidents
Regular Audits & Risk Assessments	Conducting internal and external audits, as well as ongoing risk assessments.	• Identifies noncompliance • Provides objective assessment • Improves security measures
Clear Policies & Procedures	Developing and maintaining clear, practical, and comprehensive policies.	• Ensures employee understanding • Increases adherence to compliance requirements
Automated Monitoring & Reporting	Implementing tools to detect security incidents and setting up clear reporting channels.	• Enhances incident detection • Quick response times • Encourages reporting
Continuous Improvement	Reviewing and updating policies regularly, incorporating feedback, and refining practices.	• Adapts to evolving threats • Improves compliance • Ensures security resilience
Culture of Compliance	Promoting accountability and awareness across all organizational levels.	• Strengthens cybersecurity culture • Improves adherence to policies • Ensures a secure environment

Leveraging technology solutions, such as compliance management software and automated monitoring tools, can streamline compliance efforts and reduce the burden on staff. These tools help organizations track compliance status, identify gaps, and generate reports, making it easier to manage and maintain compliance. Automated monitoring tools, such as security information and event management (SIEM) systems, provide real-time insights into security activities and help promptly detect potential incidents.

Conducting regular audits and risk assessments helps identify areas of noncompliance and potential vulnerabilities. These evaluations provide valuable insights that can be used to improve security measures and ensure ongoing adherence to policies. External audits can also provide an objective assessment of the organization's compliance status. Regular assessments ensure that security practices are consistently applied and that any gaps are promptly addressed.

Developing clear and comprehensive policies and procedures is essential for ensuring that employees understand and follow compliance requirements. Policies should be written in plain language and provide specific guidance on how to handle various security issues. Involving key stakeholders in the policy development process ensures that the policies are practical and address the organization's specific needs and risks. Regularly reviewing and updating policies and procedures helps keep them relevant and effective.

Implementing automated monitoring tools to track security activities and detect potential incidents in real time is crucial for maintaining compliance. Establishing clear reporting mechanisms encourages employees to promptly report security incidents and vulnerabilities. Effective monitoring and reporting help organizations respond quickly to threats and maintain compliance. Providing anonymous reporting options can further encourage employees to report issues without fear of retribution.

Cybersecurity is an evolving field, and continuous improvement is necessary to stay ahead of emerging threats. Organizations should regularly review and update their policies, procedures, and controls to ensure they remain effective and relevant. Incorporating feedback from audits, assessments, and employees helps continually refine security practices. A culture of ongoing improvement ensures that organizations adapt to new challenges and maintain a high level of security.

Fostering a culture of compliance involves promoting awareness and accountability at all levels of the organization. Regular communication about the importance of compliance, celebrating successes, and promptly addressing noncompliance are key components of this culture. Encouraging employee participation in compliance efforts and recognizing their contributions can further strengthen this culture.

Implementing best practices in cybersecurity compliance is essential for creating a secure and resilient organizational environment. These not only enhance the organization's security and ensure regulatory compliance but also play a vital role in shaping a strong cybersecurity culture. This comprehensive approach to compliance supports the organization's broader business objectives and prepares it to face the ever-evolving cyber threat landscape, ultimately embedding security deeply into the organizational culture.

9.9 COMPLIANCE CHALLENGES AND SOLUTIONS

While compliance with cybersecurity regulations is imperative, organizations often face significant challenges in achieving and maintaining compliance. These challenges can arise from various factors, including evolving regulatory requirements, resource constraints, and the complexity of implementing comprehensive security measures. This section will explore common compliance challenges and provide practical solutions to address them effectively, as summarized in Table 9.4.

Table 9.4 Common compliance challenges and solutions

COMMON COMPLIANCE CHALLENGES AND SOLUTIONS		
CHALLENGE	DESCRIPTION	SOLUTION
Evolving Regulatory Requirements	Constant updates to frameworks like GDPR, HIPAA, and PCI DSS.	· Establish a compliance team · Review policies regularly · Stay informed about updates
Resource Constraints	Limited resources make it difficult to meet all compliance requirements.	· Prioritize based on risk · Use automated tools · Outsource to compliance experts if needed
Complex Implementation	Technical requirements of compliance frameworks are hard to understand and apply.	· Provide comprehensive training · Use simple language in policies · Engage external experts as needed
Consistency Compliance Across Departments	Ensuring policies are consistently applied across all locations and departments.	· Use centralized compliance management systems · Conduct regular audits · Promote a culture of accountability
Balancing Security and Usability	Security measures can hinder usability, leading to resistance from employees.	· Involve users in policy development · Provide training · Find solutions that balance security with usability

One of the primary challenges organizations face is **keeping up with evolving regulatory requirements**. Regulations such as GDPR, HIPAA, and PCI DSS are continually updated to address new threats and vulnerabilities. This constant change requires organizations to stay informed and adapt their policies and procedures accordingly. To manage this, organizations can establish a dedicated compliance team responsible for monitoring regulatory changes. Regularly reviewing and updating policies to ensure they align with current requirements is essential.

Implementing and maintaining compliance can be resource intensive, requiring significant time, effort, and financial investment. **Resource constraints**, especially in smaller organizations, may cause a struggle with limited resources, making it challenging to meet all compliance requirements. To address this, organizations can prioritize compliance efforts based on risk assessments, focusing on the most critical areas first. Leveraging technology solutions, such as automated compliance management tools, can streamline processes and reduce the burden on staff. Outsourcing compliance to specialized service providers can be a viable option if internal resources are insufficient.

Cybersecurity compliance frameworks often involve **complex implementation.** The technical requirements can make implementation difficult. Organizations may struggle with understanding and applying these requirements, leading to gaps in compliance. Providing comprehensive training and education for employees involved in compliance efforts is crucial to ensure they understand the requirements and how to implement them. Using clear and straightforward language in policies and procedures can make them more accessible. Engaging external experts or consultants to assist with complex compliance requirements can also help bridge the knowledge gap.

Maintaining **consistent compliance** across all departments and locations can be challenging, especially for large organizations with diverse operations. Inconsistent application of policies and procedures can lead to vulnerabilities and noncompliance. Developing a centralized compliance management system can ensure the consistent application of policies and procedures across the organization. Regular internal audits and assessments can help identify and address inconsistencies. Fostering a culture of compliance by promoting awareness and accountability at all levels of the organization is also vital for achieving consistent compliance.

Implementing **stringent security** measures to achieve compliance can sometimes impact the usability of systems and hinder business operations. Employees may resist security controls that they perceive as cumbersome or disruptive. To mitigate this, it is essential to involve users in the development of security policies and procedures to ensure they are practical and user friendly. Providing training to demonstrate the importance of security measures and how they protect both the organization and employees can help gain buy-in. Striving to find a balance between security and usability by implementing flexible solutions that accommodate business needs without compromising security is key.

Achieving and maintaining cybersecurity compliance can be challenging, but understanding these challenges and implementing effective solutions are essential for protecting sensitive information and maintaining a secure organizational environment. By addressing evolving regulatory requirements, resource constraints, implementation complexities, consistency in compliance, and balancing security with usability, organizations can enhance their compliance efforts. This comprehensive approach not only supports regulatory adherence but also strengthens the organization's overall cybersecurity posture, nurturing a culture of security and resilience.

9.10 CONCLUSION

The landscape of cybersecurity is constantly evolving, presenting organizations with new challenges and opportunities to protect their information assets and maintain compliance with regulatory requirements. This chapter has explored the critical components of cybersecurity policies, procedures, and compliance, highlighting their importance in building a healthy cybersecurity culture.

In conclusion, it should now be clear that the integration of comprehensive cybersecurity policies, proactive compliance measures, and continuous improvement is essential for building a secure and resilient organizational environment. By adopting a culture of security and compliance, organizations can protect their information assets, build trust with stakeholders, and ensure their preparedness for the ever-evolving cyber threat landscape. Embracing these principles and staying ahead of emerging trends will enable organizations to create a strong cybersecurity culture that supports their broader business objectives and secures their future in the digital age; however, embracing these principles and staying ahead of emerging threats is not enough. There needs to be a way to measure success in building a cybersecurity culture. We can only be sure we have accomplished our goal by creating these measurements. The next chapter will investigate the metrics and measurements and see if a truly solid cybersecurity culture was accomplished.

DISCUSSION QUESTIONS

1. Why are policies and procedures critical to building a strong cybersecurity culture in an organization? Discuss how well-defined policies contribute to security awareness and responsibility among employees.
2. How does compliance with regulatory standards like GDPR, HIPAA, and PCI DSS enhance an organization's security posture? Explore the benefits of adhering to these standards beyond avoiding legal penalties.

3. What challenges do organizations face when developing and implementing cybersecurity policies and procedures? Consider factors like resource constraints, complexity of requirements, and user resistance.
4. How can organizations ensure that their cybersecurity policies remain effective and relevant over time? Discuss strategies such as continuous monitoring, regular reviews, and employee feedback.
5. What roles do leadership and employee engagement play in ensuring compliance with cybersecurity policies? Examine how leadership commitment and employee involvement can foster a culture of compliance.
6. Why is it important for organizations to understand and adhere to multiple cybersecurity frameworks (e.g., PCI DSS, NIST, GDPR)? Discuss the need for a multi-layered approach to cybersecurity compliance.
7. How can automated monitoring tools and compliance management software help organizations meet their cybersecurity compliance requirements? Evaluate the benefits and potential drawbacks of using technology to streamline compliance efforts.
8. What are some best practices for creating a culture of continuous improvement in cybersecurity compliance? Consider methods like regular training, audits, risk assessments, and employee recognition programs.
9. How should an organization handle non-compliance issues that arise despite established policies and procedures? Discuss the steps for addressing non-compliance, from root cause analysis to corrective actions.
10. What lessons can be learned from real-world case studies, such as those of Microsoft, Google, and Mayo Clinic, regarding effective cybersecurity compliance? Reflect on the strategies used by these organizations to enhance their security and build trust with stakeholders.

BIBLIOGRAPHY

Calder, A. (2018). *NIST cybersecurity framework: A pocket guide*. Walter de Gruyter GmbH.

Edwards, J., & Weaver, G. (2024). *The cybersecurity guide to governance, risk, and compliance*. Wiley.

Federal Trade Commission. (n.d.). Understanding the NIST cybersecurity framework. Retrieved, 3 August 2024, from https://www.ftc.gov/business-guidance/small-businesses/cybersecurity/nist-framework

GDPR.EU. (2024). Complete guide to GDPR compliance. https://gdpr.eu/

Google Cloud. (n.d.). GDPR and Google Cloud. https://cloud.google.com/privacy/gdpr

Google. (n.d.). GDPR. https://business.safety.google/gdpr/

Intersoft Consulting. (n.d.). General Data Protection Regulation GDPR. https://gdpr-info.eu/

International Organization for Standardization. (2022). *ISO/IEC 27001:2022: Information security, cybersecurity and privacy protection—Information security management systems—Requirements* (3rd ed.). ISO. https://www.iso.org/standard/27001

Jaar, D., & Zeller, P. E. (2009). Canadian privacy law: The Personal Information Protection and Electronic Documents Act (PIPEDA). *International In-House Counsel Journal*, 2(7), 1135–1146. https://www.iicj.net/subscribersonly/09june/iicj4jun-dataprotection-patrickzeller-guidancesoftware-USA.pdf

Knowles, J. (2020). *Cybersecurity for beginners: How to apply the NIST risk management framework*. Amazon Digital Services LLC - KDP Print US.

Mayo Clinic. (2003). HIPAA policy: Using, disclosing, and requesting the minimum necessary amount of protected health information (Policy No. 2023). MCH, MCS, PCC. Date effective: April 14, 2003. https://www.mayoclinic.org/documents/mcsusedisclosure-pdf/doc-20079524

Microsoft. (2023). *ISO/IEC 27001:2013 information security management standards*. Microsoft Compliance. https://learn.microsoft.com/en-us/compliance/regulatory/offering-iso-27001

Microsoft. (2023). *General data protection regulation*. Microsoft GDPR. https://learn.microsoft.com/en-us/compliance/regulatory/gdpr#what-is-the-gdpr

Miller, M. (2024, June 21). Best practices for a culture of security compliance. AuditBoard. https://www.auditboard.com/blog/best-practices-for-a-culture-of-security-compliance/
National Institute of Standards and Technology. (2024, February 26). The NIST Cybersecurity Framework (CSF) 2.0. https://doi.org/10.6028/NIST.CSWP.29
Office of the Privacy Commissioner of Canada. (2021, December 8). *The Personal Information Protection and Electronic Documents Act (PIPEDA)*. https://www.priv.gc.ca/en/privacy-topics/privacy-laws-in-canada/the-personal-information-protection-and-electronic-documents-act-pipeda/
Seaman, J. (2020). *PCI DSS: An integrated data security standard guide*. Apress.
Srivastav, N., & Saxena, S. (2023). *Security and compliance: A must-have visual guide for everyone!*. CyberEdx.
Thompson, E. C. (2017). *Building a HIPAA-compliant cybersecurity program: Using NIST 800-30 and CSF to secure protected health information*. Apress.
Vasileiou, I., & Furnell, S. (Eds.) (2019). *Cybersecurity education for awareness and compliance*. IGI Global.

Chapter 10

Measuring organizational success in cybersecurity culture

Measuring success in cybersecurity culture is not just about having the right technology but ensuring that everyone in the organization understands his or her role in maintaining security. Without clear measurements, it's impossible to know if cybersecurity efforts are working or where improvements are needed. Regularly checking the effectiveness of these efforts helps organizations stay ahead of new threats and improve their security strategies.

Using a variety of metrics is key to gaining a comprehensive understanding of an organization's security effectiveness. Incident metrics track how often security breaches happen and how severe they are. Employee engagement metrics show how well employees follow security practices. Policy and compliance metrics measure how well the organization adheres to security policies and regulations. Technical metrics assess the effectiveness of security controls. Financial metrics look at the costs and savings related to security measures. By using these various metrics, organizations can get a detailed understanding of their cybersecurity environment.

This chapter will look at key elements that make a successful cybersecurity culture and discuss the importance of measuring these elements. It will also examine different metrics and tools for effective measurement. By understanding and applying these concepts, organizations can build a strong, adaptive cybersecurity culture that supports their overall security goals.

10.1 DEFINING SUCCESS IN CYBERSECURITY CULTURE

How is success defined in cybersecurity culture? This will vary from organization to organization. Success can be measured by several factors. For example, the reduction in the number of security incidents, increased employee awareness and adherence to security protocols, the effectiveness of incident response strategies, and compliance with relevant regulations and standards are just to name a few. Other indicators might include the organization's ability to quickly adapt to emerging threats, the strength of its security training programs, and the overall improvement in risk management practices. Ultimately, defining success involves setting clear, measurable goals that align with the organization's unique risk landscape and business objectives.

Measuring the success of cybersecurity initiatives is important because, first, it allows organizations to understand the impact of their security programs and identify areas for improvement. Without measurement, it is challenging to determine whether the initiatives are effective or if adjustments are needed. Metrics provide concrete data that can guide decision-making and resource allocation. For instance, tracking the number of security incidents over time can reveal trends and highlight areas that require more focus. Similarly, monitoring employee compliance with security protocols can help identify whether additional training or more stringent enforcement measures are needed.

 DOI: 10.1201/9781003368496-10

Continuous measurement supports the ongoing improvement and adaptation of cybersecurity strategies. Regularly evaluating the effectiveness of security measures ensures that they remain relevant and effective in addressing new threats. This ongoing assessment helps organizations stay ahead of potential risks and enhances their overall security effectiveness. Metrics such as the time taken to detect and respond to incidents, the effectiveness of security patches, and the level of employee engagement with security initiatives can all provide valuable insights. These insights can then be used to refine and enhance the organization's cybersecurity strategy, ensuring it evolves in line with emerging threats and best practices.

Measuring success helps build a culture of accountability and transparency. By tracking progress and sharing results, organizations can demonstrate their commitment to security and engage employees in the process. This fosters a sense of shared responsibility and encourages everyone to contribute to the organization's security efforts. Transparency in reporting and celebrating achievements in cybersecurity can further solidify a positive security culture within the organization. Regular reports on cybersecurity performance should be shared with all employees. Celebrating achievements, such as a significant reduction in phishing incidents or successful completion of a cybersecurity audit, reinforces the importance of cybersecurity and motivates employees to continue following best practices; moreover, involving employees in the measurement process can provide additional benefits. Employees can offer valuable feedback on the effectiveness of training programs and security policies, helping to identify gaps. By creating opportunities for employees to share their insights and experiences, organizations can foster a collaborative environment where everyone feels invested in maintaining a strong cybersecurity culture.

In conclusion, defining success in cybersecurity culture involves understanding and implementing key elements, such as awareness and education, employee engagement and behavior, and incident response and resilience. Measuring these elements through various metrics provides the data needed to assess effectiveness and support continuous adaptation. By building a culture of accountability and transparency, organizations can engage employees in the cybersecurity process and create a resilient, adaptive security environment that protects against evolving threats. This comprehensive approach not only enhances security but also strengthens the overall organizational culture, fostering a shared commitment to maintaining a secure and trustworthy environment.

To effectively measure the success of these elements, organizations must use a variety of metrics tailored to different aspects of cybersecurity culture. The following section will explore the specific metrics that organizations can use to evaluate their cybersecurity initiatives and ensure they are meeting their security goals.

10.2 METRICS FOR MEASURING SUCCESS

Measuring success in cybersecurity culture requires a comprehensive approach that encompasses various aspects of the organization's security environment. Metrics provide the data needed to evaluate the effectiveness of cybersecurity initiatives. They identify areas for improvement and ensure continuous adaptation to evolving threats. Organizations can gain a detailed understanding of their security status and make informed decisions by using a diverse set of metrics. This section will explore key metrics for measuring success, as listed in Figure 10.1. Areas covered include incident metrics, employee engagement, and behavior metrics. Other metrics will also be utilized, such as policy and compliance metrics, technical metrics, and continuous improvement metrics to gain a comprehensive understanding of security efforts.

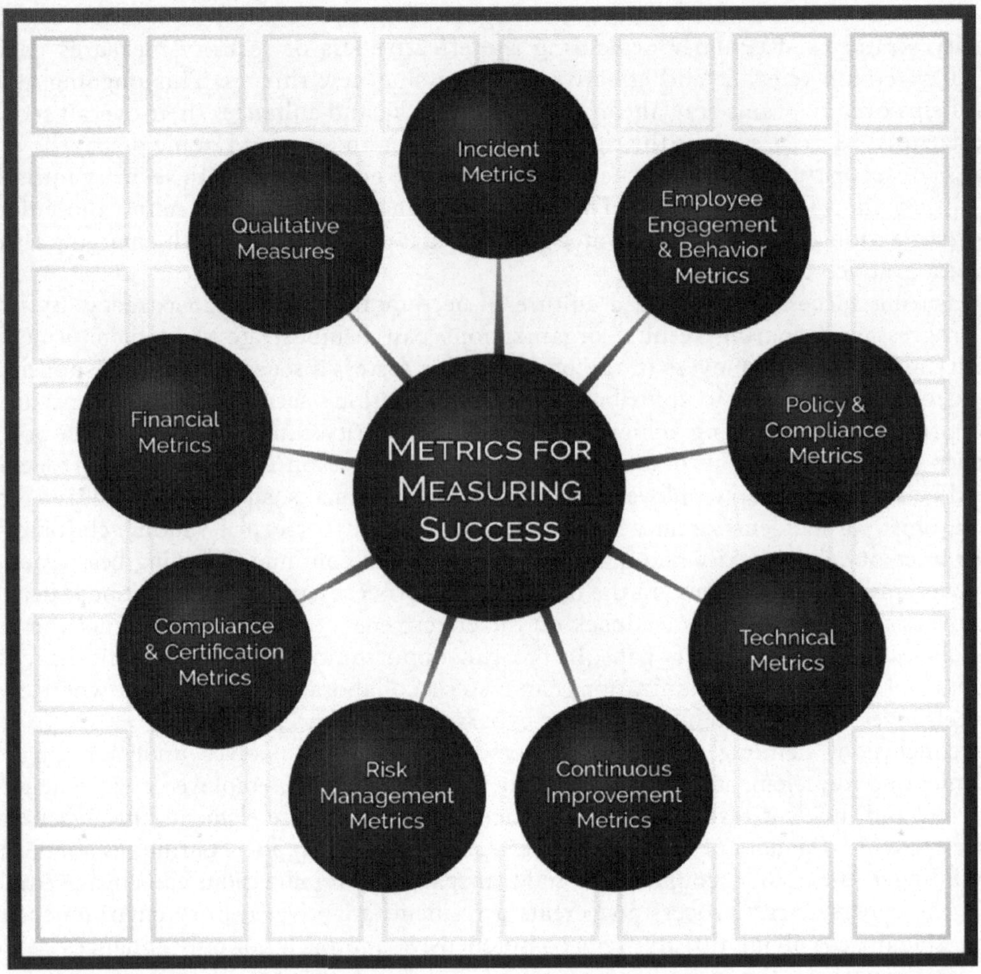

Figure 10.1 Metrics for measuring success.

10.2.1 Incident metrics

Incident metrics are important for understanding the frequency, severity, and impact of security incidents within an organization. These metrics help evaluate the effectiveness of incident response strategies and identify trends that may indicate underlying vulnerabilities. Tracking the total number of security incidents and breaches over time provides insight into the organization's overall security effectiveness. A decrease in incidents over time may indicate improved security measures, while an increase could signal the need for additional resources or changes in strategy.

Measuring the time taken to detect, respond to, and recover from security incidents is essential for assessing the efficiency of incident response plans. Faster response times typically indicate a more prepared and capable incident response team. Evaluating the impact and severity of security incidents helps prioritize response efforts and allocate resources effectively. Metrics such as the financial cost of incidents, the number of affected systems, and the duration of disruptions provide a comprehensive view of the incident's impact. For example, an organization that experiences a significant drop in the number of successful phishing attacks after implementing a new email filtering system can use this metric to demonstrate the effectiveness of the new system and justify continued investment in similar technologies. By monitoring these metrics, organizations can gain valuable insights into their incident response capabilities and make data-driven decisions to enhance their security.

10.2.2 Employee engagement and behavior metrics

Employee engagement and behavior metrics provide valuable insights into how well employees understand and stick to cybersecurity policies and practices. These metrics highlight the human element of cybersecurity, which is often the most challenging to manage. Tracking participation rates in security training programs indicates the level of engagement and commitment to cybersecurity training. High participation rates suggest that employees recognize the importance of cybersecurity and are willing to invest time in learning best practices.

Monitoring changes in behavior, such as increased reporting of suspicious activities or adherence to security protocols, reflects the effectiveness of training and awareness initiatives. Positive changes in behavior can reduce the risk of security incidents caused by human error. Conducting regular surveys to assess employees' knowledge and attitudes toward cybersecurity helps identify gaps in awareness and areas for improvement. Survey results can guide the development of targeted training programs and communication strategies. A good example would be a company that sees a significant increase in the number of employees reporting phishing attempts after conducting a phishing awareness campaign. This metric highlights the campaign's success and the importance of ongoing awareness efforts. By focusing on these metrics, organizations can better understand their employees' engagement and behavior, ultimately strengthening their cybersecurity culture.

10.2.3 Policy and compliance metrics

Policy and compliance metrics measure the organization's adherence to internal policies and external regulations. These metrics are essential for maintaining a strong security framework and avoiding legal and financial penalties. Evaluating compliance with internal security policies and procedures ensures that employees follow established guidelines. Regular audits and assessments can help identify areas where policies may not be fully implemented or understood.

Tracking the frequency and nature of policy violations helps identify areas where additional training or enforcement may be needed. Reducing policy violations over time indicates improved adherence to security standards. Conducting regular compliance audits provides an objective assessment of the organization's adherence to regulatory requirements and internal policies. Audit results can highlight strengths and weaknesses in the security program.

10.2.4 Technical metrics

Technical metrics assess the effectiveness of technical controls and security measures implemented within the organization. These metrics provide a detailed view of the organization's technical security landscape. Regular vulnerability scans identify potential weaknesses in the organization's systems and networks. Tracking the number of vulnerabilities detected and remediated helps measure the effectiveness of vulnerability management efforts.

Measuring the timeliness and effectiveness of patch management practices helps ensure that systems are protected against known vulnerabilities. High patching rates indicate a proactive approach to maintaining system security. Evaluating the performance of security controls, such as firewalls, intrusion detection systems, and encryption, helps determine their effectiveness in preventing and mitigating threats. Regular testing and monitoring of these controls are essential for maintaining a strong security posture.

10.2.5 Continuous improvement metrics

Continuous improvement metrics track the organization's progress in addressing identified security gaps and implementing recommendations from audits and assessments. These metrics support the ongoing enhancement of the security program. Monitoring the implementation of recommendations from security audits and assessments ensures that identified gaps are addressed promptly. This metric demonstrates the organization's commitment to continuous improvement.

Evaluating the progress made in addressing security gaps over time helps measure the organization's dedication to improving its security. Regular updates to security measures indicate a proactive approach to risk management. Tracking updates and enhancements to security policies and procedures ensures that they remain relevant and effective in addressing new threats. Regular reviews and revisions of policies are essential for maintaining a strong security framework.

10.2.6 Risk management metrics

Risk management metrics measure the organization's ability to identify, assess, and mitigate security risks. These metrics are crucial for maintaining a comprehensive risk management strategy. Tracking the identification and mitigation of security risks provides insight into the organization's risk management capabilities. Effective risk management practices reduce the likelihood of security incidents.

Evaluating the effectiveness of risk management strategies helps determine their impact on reducing overall risk. Metrics such as the number of mitigated risks and the success of risk mitigation efforts provide valuable insights. Conducting regular and comprehensive risk assessments ensures that the organization remains aware of potential threats and vulnerabilities. Regular assessments help maintain a proactive approach to risk management.

10.2.7 Compliance and certification metrics

Compliance and certification metrics measure the organization's adherence to regulatory requirements and achievement of cybersecurity certifications. These metrics are essential for maintaining legal compliance and building trust with stakeholders. Tracking the achievement of certifications, such as ISO/IEC 27001 and PCI DSS, demonstrates the organization's commitment to maintaining high-security standards. Certifications provide external validation of the organization's security efforts.

Regular external compliance audits provide an objective assessment of the organization's adherence to regulatory requirements. Audit results can highlight strengths and weaknesses in the security program. Evaluating adherence to regulatory requirements ensures that the organization remains compliant with applicable laws and standards. Compliance metrics help avoid legal and financial penalties.

10.2.8 Financial metrics

Financial metrics assess the financial impact of cybersecurity initiatives and incidents. These metrics help organizations understand the costs associated with maintaining security and the financial benefits of effective security measures. Monitoring budget allocation for cybersecurity initiatives helps ensure that adequate resources are dedicated to maintaining security. Comparing budget allocations with actual expenditures provides insights into the organization's financial commitment to cybersecurity.

Assessing the financial impact of security incidents and breaches will help quantify the cost of inadequate security measures. Metrics such as the cost of remediation, lost revenue, and regulatory fines provide a comprehensive view of the financial impact. Measuring the ROI for security investments helps determine the effectiveness of allocated resources in improving security posture. Positive ROI indicates that security investments are yielding financial benefits, such as reduced incident costs and improved operational efficiency.

10.2.9 Qualitative measures

Qualitative measures provide insights into the perceptions and attitudes of employees toward cybersecurity. These metrics complement quantitative data by offering a deeper understanding of the human factors influencing cybersecurity culture. Gathering feedback from security training sessions helps identify areas for improvement and ensures that training is effective. Qualitative feedback provides insights into employee perceptions of the training content and delivery.

Conducting surveys and interviews to assess employees' perceptions of the cybersecurity culture provides valuable insights into the effectiveness of security initiatives. Qualitative data helps identify areas where the culture can be strengthened. Utilizing interviews and focus groups to gather detailed feedback on security practices and culture helps identify strengths and areas for improvement.

In conclusion, employing a variety of metrics is essential for gaining a comprehensive understanding of an organization's cybersecurity culture. All of the metrics discussed in this chapter, as summarized in Table 10.1, provide unique insights into different aspects of cybersecurity. Regularly monitoring these metrics can help organizations evaluate the effectiveness of their cybersecurity initiatives, identify the gaps, and make informed decisions to enhance their security.

The next section will examine the tools and techniques for effectively measuring these metrics. By utilizing appropriate tools and methods, organizations can gather accurate data, analyze it effectively, and use it to drive continuous improvement in their cybersecurity culture.

10.3 TOOLS AND TECHNIQUES FOR MEASUREMENT

Organizations need the right tools and techniques to effectively measure cybersecurity initiatives' success. These tools, summarized in Table 10.2, help gather accurate data, analyze it, and provide insights. This section will explore various tools and techniques for measuring cybersecurity metrics, including surveys and questionnaires, security audits and assessments, incident analysis, and benchmarking and comparative analysis.

10.3.1 Surveys and questionnaires

Surveys and questionnaires are valuable tools for assessing employee awareness, attitudes, and behaviors toward cybersecurity. They can provide both qualitative and quantitative data, helping organizations understand how well employees comprehend and adhere to security practices. By regularly conducting these surveys, organizations can track changes over time and measure the impact of training and awareness programs.

Table 10.1 Metrics for measuring success

Metrics for Measuring Success		
Metric	**Definition**	**Purpose**
Incident Frequency	The total number of security incidents occurring within a given time period.	To assess the effectiveness of overall security measures and identify trends.
Response Time	The time taken to detect, respond to, and recover from a security incident.	To evaluate the efficiency of incident response and recovery processes.
Employee Compliance Rate	The percentage of employees adhering to established security policies and procedures.	To measure adherence to security protocols and identify areas for additional training.
Policy Violation Rate	The number of times security policies are violated within a given period.	To identify weak points in policy enforcement and areas needing stronger controls.
Vulnerability Remediation Time	The average time taken to fix or patch known vulnerabilities.	To gauge the efficiency of vulnerability management efforts.
Security Awareness Training Completion	The percentage of employees completing mandatory security awareness training.	To ensure all employees are educated on security threats and best practices.
Regulatory Compliance Rate	The extent to which the organization adheres to regulatory requirements and standards.	To maintain compliance with laws and avoid legal penalties.
Financial Impact of Incidents	The total financial cost associated with security incidents, including remediation and lost revenue.	To understand the financial impact of incidents and justify cybersecurity investments.
Risk Mitigation Rate	The rate at which identified security risks are mitigated or reduced.	To track progress in reducing security risks.
Employee Security Feedback	Feedback from employees on security policies, training, and overall security culture.	To gather insights for improving the organization's security culture.

Table 10.2 Tools for measuring success

Tools for Measuring Success		
Tool	**Description**	**Purpose**
Surveys and Questionnaires	Tools used to assess employee awareness, attitudes, and behaviors toward cybersecurity.	To gather both qualitative and quantitative data on employee engagement and understanding of security practices.
Security Audits & Assessments	Systematic evaluations of an organization's security status to identify vulnerabilities and ensure compliance.	To verify adherence to policies, identify areas of non-compliance, and assess the effectiveness of security controls.
Incident Analysis & Reporting	Tools and processes for tracking and examining security incidents to understand their causes, impacts, and handling.	To improve incident response plans and prevent future incidents by learning from past events.
Benchmarking & Comparative Analysis	Comparing an organization's cybersecurity performance against industry standards or peers.	To set goals, identify best practices, and understand how the organization compares to similar entities.

Surveys must be well-designed to collect useful data. This involves asking clear, concise questions that directly relate to the metrics being measured. Avoiding ambiguous or leading questions is crucial to ensuring the accuracy of the responses. Surveys should cover a range of topics, including awareness of security policies, understanding of common threats, and confidence in reporting suspicious activities.

Once collected, survey data will be analyzed to identify trends, gaps in knowledge, and areas for improvement. This can involve statistical analysis to find correlations between different responses or qualitative analysis to interpret open-ended answers. The insights gained from these analyses can guide the development of targeted training programs and communication strategies.

An organization could conduct an annual cybersecurity awareness survey to measure employees' understanding of phishing threats. The survey results show a significant increase in awareness after a comprehensive phishing training program, indicating the program's success and the effectiveness of ongoing awareness efforts.

10.3.2 Security audits and assessments

Security audits and assessments are systematic evaluations of an organization's security status. They help identify vulnerabilities, ensure compliance with policies and regulations, and provide a clear picture of the effectiveness of security controls. Regular audits and assessments are critical for maintaining a security environment.

Regular audits involve reviewing security policies, examining the effectiveness of security controls, and testing systems for vulnerabilities. These audits can be internal, conducted by the organization's staff, or external, conducted by third-party experts. Internal audits help maintain ongoing vigilance, while external audits provide an unbiased assessment.

Assessments focus on specific aspects of the security program, such as compliance with regulatory requirements or the effectiveness of incident response procedures. They provide detailed insights that can guide improvements and ensure that security measures are functioning as intended. Assessments can also help organizations prepare for certifications and regulatory inspections. A company can perform quarterly security audits and biannual assessments to ensure compliance with ISO/IEC 27001 standards. The audits can reveal a gap in patch management, leading to the implementation of a new patch management policy that addresses the identified vulnerabilities.

10.3.3 Incident analysis and reporting

Incident analysis and reporting involve tracking and examining security incidents to understand their causes, impacts, and handling. This helps improve incident response plans and prevent future incidents. Maintaining detailed records of all security incidents is crucial for effective analysis.

Organizations should keep records of the nature of the incident, how it was detected, the response actions taken, and the final resolution. This data is crucial for understanding trends and patterns in security breaches. Detailed records allow for thorough analysis and better preparation for future incidents.

By analyzing incidents, organizations can identify common vulnerabilities and areas where response procedures can be improved. This might involve conducting root cause analyses to determine how and why an incident occurred and what changes can prevent similar incidents in the future. This proactive approach helps in continuously improving security measures.

10.3.4 Benchmarking and comparative analysis

Benchmarking and comparative analysis involve comparing an organization's cybersecurity performance against industry standards or peers. This helps set goals, identify best practices, and understand how an organization stacks up against similar entities. Benchmarking provides a clear reference point for evaluating performance.

Organizations can use benchmarking to compare their performance with industry standards, such as those set by NIST or ISO. This comparison can highlight areas where the organization excels or needs improvement. It also helps in setting realistic and achievable goals for cybersecurity initiatives.

By setting benchmarks, organizations can establish clear goals for their cybersecurity programs. Regularly measuring progress against these benchmarks helps track improvements and adjust strategies as needed. This continuous evaluation process ensures that the organization remains aligned with industry best practices.

In closing, employing the right tools and techniques for measuring cybersecurity metrics is essential for gaining accurate and actionable insights. All tools play a critical role in understanding and improving an organization's cybersecurity effectiveness. By effectively utilizing these tools, organizations can ensure that their cybersecurity initiatives are on track and continually evolving to meet new challenges.

The next section will explore best practices for measuring success. It will explore how to set clear objectives, regularly review and adapt strategies, and involve employees in the measurement process to create a comprehensive and effective approach to cybersecurity measurement.

10.4 BEST PRACTICES FOR MEASURING SUCCESS

Measuring the success of a cybersecurity culture involves more than just tracking incidents and compliance. It requires a comprehensive approach that considers various aspects of the organization's security outlook and its alignment with business objectives. This section will explore best practices, as depicted in Figure 10.2, for effectively measuring success in cybersecurity culture. By adopting these practices, organizations can ensure that their metrics provide meaningful insights and support continuous improvement. From setting clear objectives to employee involvement, these best practices will guide organizations in developing measurement frameworks that drive strategic decision-making and enhance overall cybersecurity effectiveness.

10.4.1 Setting clear objectives

Defining clear, measurable goals for cybersecurity initiatives is the first step in ensuring their success. Objectives should be specific, attainable, relevant, and time bound. Clear objectives provide direction and focus for the organization's cybersecurity efforts, ensuring that all activities align with the overall security strategy. When setting objectives, organizations should consider the specific risks they face and the resources available to address these risks. Objectives should cover various aspects of cybersecurity, including threat prevention, incident response, compliance, and employee engagement. By having well-defined goals, organizations can measure progress accurately and make informed decisions about where to allocate resources.

10.4.2 Regular review and adaptation

Cybersecurity is a dynamic field with constantly evolving threats. Regularly reviewing and adapting cybersecurity strategies are essential to stay ahead of potential risks. This involves

Figure 10.2 Best practices for measuring success.

periodically evaluating the effectiveness of security measures, analyzing incident data, and staying informed about new threats and best practices.

Organizations should establish a schedule for reviewing cybersecurity metrics and performance. This might involve monthly reviews of incident metrics, quarterly audits of compliance with security policies, and annual assessments of overall security posture. Regular reviews help identify trends and emerging threats, allowing organizations to adjust their strategies accordingly.

Adaptation is also crucial. Based on the findings from regular reviews, organizations should be prepared to update their security policies, adopt new technologies, and refine their training programs. This continuous improvement cycle ensures that the organization's cybersecurity measures remain effective and relevant.

10.4.3 Employee involvement

Involving employees in the measurement and feedback processes is vital for building a strong cybersecurity culture. Employees are on the front lines of cybersecurity and can provide valuable insights into the effectiveness of security measures and areas for improvement.

Organizations should encourage employees to participate in security training, report suspicious activities, and provide feedback on security policies and procedures. Creating channels for employees to voice their concerns and suggestions can lead to valuable improvements in the organization's cybersecurity practices.

Regular communication and engagement with employees help reinforce the importance of cybersecurity and build a culture of shared responsibility. Recognition and rewards for employees who demonstrate exemplary security practices can further motivate others to follow suit.

Incorporating best practices for measuring success is essential for developing a resilient and adaptive cybersecurity culture. By setting clear objectives, regularly reviewing and adapting strategies, and involving employees in the process, organizations can create a comprehensive framework for evaluating and enhancing their cybersecurity initiatives. These practices ensure that cybersecurity efforts are aligned with organizational goals, responsive to new threats, and supported by all members of the organization.

10.5 CONCLUSION

Measuring organizational success in cybersecurity culture is essential for understanding the effectiveness of security initiatives and identifying areas for improvement. This chapter has highlighted the importance of defining success in cybersecurity culture by focusing on key elements such as awareness and education, employee engagement and behavior, and incident response and resilience. By setting clear objectives and utilizing various metrics, organizations can gain a comprehensive understanding of their cybersecurity effectiveness. These metrics, ranging from incident metrics to financial metrics, provide valuable insights that guide decision-making and resource allocation.

Tools and techniques for measurement, including surveys and questionnaires, security audits and assessments, incident analysis and reporting, and benchmarking and comparative analysis, are critical for gathering accurate and actionable data. Each tool plays a unique role in helping organizations evaluate different aspects of their cybersecurity culture. Regular use of these tools ensures that the data collected is current and relevant, enabling organizations to make timely adjustments to their cybersecurity strategies. This ongoing process of evaluation and adjustment is vital in a field where threats are constantly evolving.

Implementing best practices for measuring success, such as setting clear objectives, regularly reviewing and adapting strategies, and involving employees in the measurement process, further strengthens an organization's cybersecurity culture. These practices foster a culture of continuous improvement, accountability, and shared responsibility. By engaging employees and making them active participants in cybersecurity efforts, organizations can build a more resilient and adaptive security environment. Ultimately, the continuous cycle of measurement, feedback, and adaptation ensures that cybersecurity measures are effective and aligned with the organization's overall goals, creating a proactive approach to protecting against cyber threats.

As the discussion moves beyond the confines of the organization, it is crucial to explore broader aspects of cybersecurity that extend outside the immediate workplace. The next chapter, "Beyond the Organization: National Initiatives," will guide the reader through the role of government and talk about national cybersecurity initiatives. Understanding these external factors is vital for developing a comprehensive cybersecurity strategy that not only protects the organization but also contributes to the broader security landscape.

DISCUSSION QUESTIONS

1. Why is it important to define success in cybersecurity culture? How can organizations ensure that their definition of success aligns with their specific risks and business objectives?
2. What role do incident metrics play in evaluating an organization's cybersecurity effectiveness? How can tracking incident response times help improve an organization's security posture?

3. How do employee engagement and behavior metrics contribute to a strong cybersecurity culture? What strategies can organizations use to increase employee participation in security awareness training?
4. Why are policy and compliance metrics critical for maintaining a strong cybersecurity framework? How can regular compliance audits help identify gaps in an organization's security measures?
5. What are the benefits of using technical metrics to assess the effectiveness of security controls? Can you provide examples of technical metrics that organizations might use to evaluate their cybersecurity posture?
6. How does continuous improvement in cybersecurity culture rely on effective measurement? What continuous improvement metrics should organizations prioritize to ensure ongoing adaptation to new threats?
7. What challenges might organizations face when implementing risk management metrics, and how can they overcome them? How can regular risk assessments support a proactive approach to cybersecurity?
8. What is the significance of financial metrics in measuring the success of cybersecurity initiatives? How can organizations calculate the return on investment (ROI) for their cybersecurity investments?
9. How do qualitative measures complement quantitative data in assessing cybersecurity culture? How can organizations gather qualitative feedback on security practices and culture?
10. What are the best practices for involving employees in measuring and improving cybersecurity culture? How can organizations foster a culture of continuous improvement and shared responsibility among employees?

BIBLIOGRAPHY

Bodeau, D. J., Graubart, R. D., McQuaid, R. M., & Woodill, J. (2018, September). *Cyber resiliency metrics, measures of effectiveness, and scoring: Enabling systems engineers and program managers to select the most useful assessment methods* (MITRE Technical Report MTR180314). MITRE. https://www.mitre.org/sites/default/files/2021-11/prs-18-2579-cyber-resiliency-metrics-measures-of-effectiveness-and-scoring.pdf

Black, P., Scarfone, K., & Souppaya, M. (2008). Cyber security metrics and measures. https://doi.org/10.1002/9780470087923.hhs440

Davidovič, Š. (2021). Incident metrics in SRE: Critically evaluating MTTR and friends. https://static.googleusercontent.com/media/sre.google/en//static/pdf/IncidentMeticsInSre.pdf

DayBlink. (2021). Introduction to metrics in cybersecurity. https://dayblinkconsulting.com/wp-content/uploads/2021/02/Introduction-to-Metrics-in-Cybersecurity.pdf

Dornheim, P., & Zarnekow, R. (2023). Determining cybersecurity culture maturity and deriving verifiable improvement measures. *Information & Computer Security*, *32*(2), 179–196. Emerald Publishing Limited. https://doi.org/10.1108/ICS-07-2023-0116

Herrmann, D. S. (2007). *Complete guide to security and privacy metrics: Measuring regulatory compliance, operational resilience, and ROI*. CRC Press.

McIlwraith, A. (2016). *Information security and employee behaviour: How to reduce risk through employee education, training and awareness*. Taylor & Francis.

Chapter 11

Beyond the organization

National initiatives

National cybersecurity initiatives are crucial in safeguarding a country's digital infrastructure. They provide the foundation for protecting sensitive information, critical systems, and national security from evolving cyber threats. Through comprehensive policies, regulations, and programs, governments create a framework that enhances the nation's overall security.

In the United States, agencies like the National Institute of Standards and Technology (NIST), the Cybersecurity and Infrastructure Security Agency (CISA), and the Department of Homeland Security (DHS) lead these efforts. Their programs and frameworks address diverse cyber threats, ensuring that the public and private sectors are prepared to handle potential risks. Understanding these national efforts helps organizations align their security practices with broader strategies, enhancing their cybersecurity.

11.1 ROLE OF GOVERNMENTS

The government plays a fundamental role in shaping and maintaining a nation's cybersecurity landscape. Through developing and enforcing policies, regulations, and initiatives, various government agencies work collaboratively to protect critical infrastructure, national security, and the digital assets of both the public and private sectors. This section explores the pivotal roles of key government agencies in the United States.

Many government agencies have distinct responsibilities and areas of focus when it comes to protecting organizations and individuals from cyber threats, but they work collectively. Government policies and regulations form the foundation of national cybersecurity efforts. They provide a structured framework for protecting digital assets and ensure compliance with security standards. Several guidelines and regulations have been established in the United States to enhance cybersecurity across different sectors.

This chapter will focus on the nine government agencies and their roles, as listed in Figure 11.1. Understanding the roles of these government agencies is essential for several reasons. First, it helps organizations align their cybersecurity practices with national standards and guidelines.

This ensures they are well prepared to meet regulatory requirements and effectively protect their assets. Awareness of agency-specific initiatives enables businesses to utilize resources, such as threat intelligence, training, and best practice frameworks.

Second, these agencies facilitate better collaboration between the public and private sectors. If private organizations understand the responsibilities and capabilities of government entities, they can engage more effectively in information sharing and public-private partnerships. This collaboration is crucial for addressing complex cyber threats, sometimes requiring coordinated responses across different sectors.

DOI: 10.1201/9781003368496-11

Figure 11.1 U.S. government agencies.

Finally, being informed about the initiatives provided by these agencies helps organizations stay ahead of emerging threats and adapt to the evolving cybersecurity landscape. As government agencies continuously update their policies and frameworks in response to new challenges, businesses that remain engaged can proactively strengthen their defenses and mitigate risks more effectively.

11.2 NATIONAL CYBERSECURITY GOVERNMENT AGENCIES AND INITIATIVES IN THE UNITED STATES

National cybersecurity initiatives in the United States involve policies, frameworks, and programs from various government agencies. The goal is to create a resilient cybersecurity framework that protects critical infrastructure, government operations, and private-sector activities.

Several initiatives in the United States address cybersecurity challenges. These initiatives are spearheaded by prominent agencies such as the National Institute of Standards and

Technology (NIST), the Cybersecurity and Infrastructure Security Agency (CISA), and the Department of Homeland Security (DHS), to name a few. Each agency plays a vital role in developing and enforcing cybersecurity standards. They promote information sharing and coordinating responses to cybersecurity incidents. This chapter will explore nine government agencies and several major national cybersecurity initiatives in the United States.

11.2.1 National Institute of Standards and Technology (NIST)

The National Institute of Standards and Technology (NIST) is a government agency under the U.S. Department of Commerce. Its main goal is to help improve the security of the United States' digital infrastructure. NIST develops standards and guidelines for organizations to protect their information systems. One of its most important contributions is the NIST Cybersecurity Framework (CSF), which provides a structured approach to managing and reducing cybersecurity risks. Both public and private sectors widely use the framework because it is flexible and can be adapted to different types of organizations. Another significant resource from NIST is the Special Publication 800 Series, which offers detailed technical guidance on various cybersecurity topics, helping organizations effectively implement best practices.

NIST's work is crucial because it provides a common language and set of practices everyone can use to improve security. Organizations can better protect themselves against cyber threats and their sensitive information by following NIST's guidelines. This not only helps individual organizations but also strengthens the nation's overall security posture. Through its standards and guidelines, NIST plays a vital role in enhancing the resilience of the United States' digital ecosystem.

11.2.2 Cybersecurity and Infrastructure Security Agency (CISA)

The Cybersecurity and Infrastructure Security Agency (CISA) is another crucial U.S. government agency under the Department of Homeland Security. It is responsible for protecting the nation's critical infrastructure from cyber threats. Through the Cybersecurity Information Sharing Act, CISA promotes the sharing of cybersecurity threat information between the federal government and the private sector. This information sharing helps organizations stay informed about potential threats and vulnerabilities, enabling them to take proactive measures to protect their systems collectively. CISA also operates the National Cyber Awareness System (NCAS), which provides timely information on current security issues, vulnerabilities, and exploits. This helps organizations and individuals stay vigilant and informed about potential cyber risks.

CISA's initiatives are essential for creating a united front against cyber adversaries. The Continuous Diagnostics and Mitigation (CDM) program is another critical effort by CISA. The program provides federal agencies with the tools to identify, prioritize, and mitigate cybersecurity risks in real time. The program also helps agencies maintain a strong security posture by continuously monitoring their networks for vulnerabilities. Through these initiatives, CISA plays a vital role in enhancing the cybersecurity resilience of both public and private sectors, ensuring that critical infrastructure and services are protected from cyber threats.

11.2.3 Department of Homeland Security (DHS)

The Department of Homeland Security (DHS) plays a critical role in safeguarding the United States against cyber threats through its comprehensive cybersecurity initiatives. One of the most important DHS initiatives is the National Cybersecurity and Communications Integration Center (NCCIC), which serves as the central hub for cyber defense operations and incident response, coordinating efforts across federal, state, and local governments, as well as with private-sector partners. This center is vital for real-time information sharing and collaboration, ensuring a coordinated response to cyber incidents and threats. The NCCIC helps to enhance the overall security posture of the nation's digital infrastructure, acting as a central point for cyber defense.

DHS focuses on protecting critical infrastructure sectors, such as electricity, water, and transportation, through various initiatives to identify and mitigate cyber risks. These efforts are part of DHS's broader mission to secure the nation's essential services from cyber threats. By working closely with other government agencies and private-sector stakeholders, DHS ensures that critical infrastructure is resilient and capable of withstanding cyberattacks. Through its comprehensive approach to cybersecurity, DHS plays a crucial role in defending the nation against a wide range of cyber threats, thereby contributing to the overall safety and security of the United States.

11.2.4 Federal Bureau of Investigation (FBI)

The Federal Bureau of Investigation (FBI) plays a vital role in the United States' cybersecurity efforts, focusing on identifying and combating cyber threats. Through its Cyber Division, the FBI conducts investigations into a wide range of cybercrimes, including identity thefts, ransomware attacks, and nation-state-sponsored cyber espionage. The Cyber Division employs specialized teams of agents and analysts who use advanced techniques to track and neutralize cyber threats.

The FBI also collaborates extensively with other federal agencies, international partners, and private-sector organizations to enhance its cybersecurity efforts. The FBI gathers and disseminates critical threat intelligence through partnerships and information-sharing initiatives. They enable a coordinated response to cybersecurity incidents. The FBI's involvement in joint cyber task forces, such as the National Cyber Investigative Joint Task Force (NCIJTF), further strengthens its ability to address complex and multifaceted cyber threats. The FBI plays an important role in enhancing the overall cybersecurity of the United States, ensuring that cyber threats are effectively identified, investigated, and mitigated by working closely with various stakeholders.

11.2.5 Office of the Director of National Intelligence (ODNI)

The Office of the Director of National Intelligence (ODNI) plays a crucial role in the cybersecurity framework by integrating and coordinating cyber threat intelligence across various government agencies. Through its Cyber Threat Intelligence Integration Center (CTIIC), ODNI provides a comprehensive view of the cyber threat landscape, ensuring that actionable intelligence is shared among federal entities. The CTIIC serves as a central hub for analyzing cyber threats, combining information from multiple sources to create a holistic understanding of potential risks and vulnerabilities.

The integration of intelligence facilitated by ODNI helps inform strategic decision-making and operational responses to cybersecurity incidents. The ODNI supports the efforts of other agencies, such as the FBI, DHS, and CISA, providing timely and accurate intelligence. This enables them to respond more effectively to cyber threats. The coordination and dissemination of threat intelligence ensures that all relevant parties are aware of emerging threats and can take proactive measures to protect their systems and infrastructure. The ODNI's efforts strengthen the nation's cybersecurity, keeping the United States vigilant and prepared against various cyber threats.

11.2.6 Federal Trade Commission (FTC)

The Federal Trade Commission (FTC) plays a fundamental role in protecting consumer information and ensuring businesses adhere to best practices in cybersecurity. The FTC is responsible for enforcing regulations that safeguard consumer data and prevent deceptive or unfair business practices related to data security. Through its guidelines and enforcement actions, the FTC helps maintain a high standard of cybersecurity across various industries.

One key aspect of the FTC's role is providing guidelines for businesses on how to protect consumer information effectively. These guidelines cover a range of practices, including implementing strong access controls, using encryption to protect sensitive data, regularly updating and patching software, and conducting ongoing security assessments. By following these guidelines, businesses can better protect their customers' personal information from cyber threats.

The FTC also conducts investigations and takes enforcement actions against companies that fail to adequately protect consumer data. When a business's data security practices are found to be lacking, resulting in breaches that expose consumer information, the FTC can impose fines and mandate corrective actions. These enforcement actions serve as a deterrent to other businesses and emphasize the importance of maintaining robust cybersecurity measures.

Additionally, the FTC engages in consumer education efforts to raise awareness about cybersecurity threats and best practices for protecting personal information. By providing resources and information to the public, the FTC helps consumers make informed decisions and take proactive steps to safeguard their data. Through its multifaceted approach, the FTC contributes to the overall cybersecurity landscape by promoting better business practices, protecting consumer information, and enhancing public awareness of cybersecurity issues.

11.2.7 Department of Defense (DoD)

The Department of Defense (DoD) plays a pivotal role in the United States cybersecurity landscape, focusing on protecting the nation's military networks and critical infrastructure. The DoD's cybersecurity efforts are driven by its overarching cyber strategy, which aims to defend DoD networks, secure critical infrastructure, and maintain military advantages in cyberspace.

A key component of the DoD's cybersecurity framework is the U.S. Cyber Command (USCYBERCOM). The USCYBERCOM conducts cyber operations to deter and defend against cyber threats targeting military and national security assets. This includes both offensive and defensive cyber operations designed to protect DoD information systems and to counteract potential cyber adversaries. USCYBERCOM ensures that the DoD can carry out its missions securely and effectively, even in the face of sophisticated cyberattacks.

The DoD also works to secure national defense infrastructure, including sectors like energy, transportation, and communications. Through various initiatives and collaborations with other government agencies and private-sector partners, the DoD enhances infrastructure sectors against cyber threats. This collaborative approach is crucial for ensuring the nation's defense capabilities are not compromised by vulnerabilities.

Furthermore, the DoD places a strong emphasis on cybersecurity research and development. By investing in advanced technologies and innovative solutions, the DoD aims to stay ahead of emerging cyber threats and to develop new capabilities that can enhance national security. This includes initiatives to improve cyber threat intelligence, develop advanced encryption methods, and create more secure network architectures.

In addition to its operational and technological efforts, the DoD also focuses on cybersecurity education and workforce development. Through various programs, the DoD ensures that its personnel is well trained and equipped with the necessary skills to address the complex challenges of cybersecurity. Fostering a culture of cybersecurity awareness and continuous learning enables the DoD to enhance its ability to defend against a wide range of cyber threats.

Overall, the DoD's comprehensive approach to cybersecurity is essential for protecting the United States' military capabilities and national security interests. Through its cyber strategy, USCYBERCOM, and collaborative efforts, the DoD plays a critical role in safeguarding the nation's defense infrastructure from cyber adversaries.

11.2.8 National Security Agency (NSA)

The National Security Agency (NSA) is a key player in the United States' national cybersecurity efforts. It primarily focuses on signals intelligence, cryptographic solutions, and information assurance to protect national security systems. The NSA's role in cybersecurity is multifaceted, involving both offensive and defensive operations to safeguard the nation's critical information infrastructure.

One of the NSA's primary responsibilities is to develop and implement cryptographic solutions that secure sensitive communications and data. The Information Assurance Directorate (IAD) within the NSA provides guidance on cryptographic standards and techniques. This ensures that government agencies and military organizations use encryption to protect classified and sensitive information. This work is critical for maintaining the confidentiality, integrity, and availability of national security information in the face of sophisticated cyber threats.

The NSA also conducts signals intelligence (SIGINT) operations to gather information on foreign entities and potential cyber adversaries. By monitoring and analyzing electronic communications and data flows, the NSA can identify emerging threats and provide valuable intelligence to other government agencies and decision-makers. This intelligence is crucial for informing strategic and operational responses to cyber threats, enabling the United States to stay ahead of adversaries.

In addition to its intelligence-gathering efforts, the NSA plays a significant role in securing national security systems and networks. Through various cybersecurity programs and initiatives, the NSA works to identify vulnerabilities, develop mitigation strategies, and enhance the overall resilience of the nation's critical infrastructure. This is done through collaborating with other federal agencies, private-sector partners, and international allies to share threat intelligence and best practices.

The NSA is also involved in advanced research and development efforts aimed at addressing future cybersecurity challenges. Investing in cutting-edge technologies and fostering innovation, the NSA makes sure that the United States remains at the forefront of cybersecurity capabilities. This includes exploring new methods for detecting and countering cyber threats, developing advanced encryption techniques, and improving the overall security of information systems.

Overall, the NSA's comprehensive approach to cybersecurity, encompassing cryptographic solutions, signals intelligence, information assurance, and advanced research, plays a vital role in protecting the United States' national security interests. Leveraging its expertise and resources, the NSA helps secure the nation's critical information infrastructure and maintain a strong defense against cyber adversaries.

11.2.9 National Cybersecurity Center of Excellence (NCCoE)

The National Cybersecurity Center of Excellence (NCCoE) was created through a partnership with the National Institute of Standards and Technology (NIST). The NCCoE brings together experts from industry, government, and academia to address complex cybersecurity challenges and develop practical, standards-based solutions.

One of the NCCoE's primary goals is to accelerate the adoption of secure technologies by providing organizations with guidance and resources. The center focuses on creating easily deployable cybersecurity solutions that can be implemented across various sectors. The center works on a wide range of projects that address specific cybersecurity issues faced by different industries. These projects involve building, testing, and demonstrating integrated solutions that address real-world challenges. For example, the NCCoE has developed solutions for securing medical devices, protecting industrial control systems, and enhancing the security of financial transactions. Providing these sector-specific solutions, the NCCoE helps organizations implement effective cybersecurity measures tailored to their unique needs.

Collaboration is at the heart of the NCCoE's mission. The center partners with technology vendors, industry leaders, and academic institutions to leverage their expertise and resources. These partnerships enable the agency to stay at the forefront of cybersecurity innovation and ensure that its solutions are practical and effective. The center fosters a collaborative environment, bridging the gap between research and real-world applications and making advanced cybersecurity technologies more accessible to organizations of all sizes.

Overall, the NCCoE plays an important role in advancing the nation's cybersecurity capabilities. Through its collaborative approach, the agency develops practical, standards-based solutions that help organizations and respond to emerging cyber threats. The NCCoE contributes to building a more secure and resilient digital ecosystem by promoting best practices and fostering innovation.

U.S. government agencies safeguard national security and critical infrastructure; and play a vital role in shaping and enforcing cybersecurity policies. Each agency brings unique expertise and responsibilities, ranging from regulatory enforcement and intelligence gathering to incident response and infrastructure protection. Together, these agencies collaborate to create a comprehensive defense strategy against emerging cyber threats. While the efforts of individual agencies are critical, it is through broader cybersecurity initiatives and programs that these agencies can unite their strengths. Table 11.1 summarizes the key U.S. government agencies involved in cybersecurity, setting the stage for a deeper exploration of the national initiatives that further strengthen collective cyber defenses.

11.2.10 Comprehensive National Cybersecurity Initiative (CNCI)

The Comprehensive National Cybersecurity Initiative (CNCI) was launched in 2008 to enhance the cybersecurity posture of the United States. This initiative tackles growing cyber threats with a range of strategies and programs. CNCI's key goals include enhancing situational awareness, securing federal cyber infrastructure, improving network security, and advancing cybersecurity research. It also emphasizes cybersecurity education, coordinating federal research, and deterring malicious online activity.

One of the cornerstone programs under CNCI is the Einstein Program, an intrusion detection and prevention system designed to protect federal executive branch civilian networks. Einstein monitors network traffic for malicious activity and provides automated responses to detected threats, significantly enhancing the government's ability to defend against cyberattacks. Another important initiative is the Trusted Internet Connections (TIC) program, which aims to optimize and standardize the security of the federal government's external

Table 11.1 U.S. government agencies

THE U.S. GOVERNMENT AGENCIES		
AGENCY	KEY RESPONSIBILITIES	KEY INITIATIVES
National Institute of Standards and Technology (NIST)	Developing cybersecurity standards and guidelines; Managing the NIST Cybersecurity Framework.	• NIST Cybersecurity Framework • Special Publication 800 Series
Cybersecurity and Infrastructure Security Agency (CISA)	Protecting the nation's critical infrastructure; Promoting information sharing between public and private sectors.	• Cybersecurity Information Sharing Act (CISA) • National Cyber Awareness System (NCAS) • Continuous Diagnostics and Mitigation (CDM) program
Department of Homeland Security (DHS)	Coordinating national efforts to protect critical infrastructure; Enhancing the security of federal networks.	• National Cybersecurity and Communications Integration Center (NCCIC) • Various critical infrastructure protection programs
Federal Bureau of Investigation (FBI)	Investigating cybercrimes and nation-state threats; Coordinating with other federal agencies and international partners.	• Cyber Division • National Cyber Investigative Joint Task Force (NCIJTF)
Office of the Director of National Intelligence (ODNI)	Integrating and coordinating cyber threat intelligence across government agencies; Supporting decision-making with actionable intelligence.	• Cyber Threat Intelligence Integration Center (CTIIC)
Department of Defense (DoD)	Defending military networks and national security assets; Conducting offensive and defensive cyber operations.	• U.S. Cyber Command (USCYBERCOM) • Cyber Strategy, Cybersecurity research and development
National Security Agency (NSA)	Securing national security systems through cryptographic solutions; Gathering signals intelligence and analyzing cyber threats.	• Information Assurance Directorate (IAD) • Cryptographic standards • Signals intelligence operations
National Cybersecurity Center of Excellence (NCCoE)	Developing practical cybersecurity solutions; Collaborating with industry and academia to address real-world cybersecurity challenges.	• Cybersecurity projects in healthcare, financial services, and industrial control systems
Federal Trade Commission (FTC)	Protecting consumer data; Enforcing regulations to prevent deceptive or unfair business practices related to cybersecurity.	• Guidelines for protecting consumer information • Enforcement actions against companies with inadequate data security

network connections. Reducing the number of access points to the internet and implementing stringent security controls helps to strengthen the overall security of federal networks.

The CNCI also promotes collaboration between various government agencies and the private sector to improve information sharing and develop advanced cybersecurity technologies. Through these coordinated efforts, the CNCI aims to create a more resilient national cybersecurity infrastructure capable of defending against both current and future cyber threats. The CNCI plays a vital role in enhancing the cybersecurity posture of the United States, ensuring that critical systems and information are well protected.

11.2.11 Cybersecurity education and workforce development initiatives

Cybersecurity education and workforce development initiatives are components of the United States' national strategy to enhance its cybersecurity. These initiatives aim to cultivate a skilled and knowledgeable workforce capable of addressing the complex and evolving challenges posed by cyber threats.

One of the most significant efforts in this area is the **National Initiative for Cybersecurity Education (NICE)**. It is led by the National Institute of Standards and Technology (NIST) and focuses on promoting education, training, and workforce development in cybersecurity.

NICE's mission is to energize and promote a healthy network, as well as an ecosystem of cybersecurity education, training, and workforce development. The NICE aims to build a skilled cybersecurity workforce that can protect the nation's information systems and critical infrastructure. This is accomplished by fostering collaboration among government, academia, and industry.

The NICE's efforts include developing and promoting a comprehensive cybersecurity workforce framework known as the NICE Cybersecurity Workforce Framework, which provides a common language to describe cybersecurity work and its required skills. It helps educators design curricula that align with industry needs. It also assists employers in identifying and hiring qualified professionals and guides individuals in pursuing careers in cybersecurity. By standardizing the way cybersecurity roles and skills are defined, the NICE Framework helps bridge the gap between education and employment in the cybersecurity field.

In addition to the NICE Framework, several other initiatives aim to enhance cybersecurity education and workforce development. The **CyberCorps®: Scholarship for Service (SFS)** program provides scholarships to students pursuing cybersecurity degrees in exchange for their commitment to work for government agencies after graduation. This program helps ensure that federal, state, local, and tribal governments have access to highly skilled cybersecurity professionals.

Another initiative is the **National Centers of Academic Excellence in Cybersecurity (NCAE-C)** program, which designates and supports colleges and universities that offer high-quality cybersecurity education. These institutions are recognized for their commitment to producing skilled cybersecurity professionals and for their contributions to cybersecurity research and development. Promoting excellence in cybersecurity education helps a steady pipeline of qualified professionals entering the workforce; moreover, the National Centers of Academic Excellence in Cyber Defense (CAE-CD) and the National Centers of Academic Excellence in Cyber Operations (CAE-CO) programs aim to reduce vulnerability in the national information infrastructure by promoting higher education and research in cyber defense.

These cybersecurity education and workforce development initiatives are vital for building a resilient cybersecurity ecosystem. Investing in education and training, the United States can develop a highly skilled workforce capable of defending against cyber threats and securing the nation's digital future. Through programs like NICE, CyberCorps: Scholarship for Service, and the Centers of Academic Excellence, the country is better prepared to address the growing demand for cybersecurity professionals and to protect its critical information infrastructure.

11.2.12 Additional federal cybersecurity programs and regulations

There are several federal cybersecurity programs and regulations that play a crucial role in protecting sensitive information and ensuring that organizations across various sectors adopt security measures. Key regulations such as FISMA, HIPAA, GLBA, SOX, and PCI DSS set the standards for managing and safeguarding data, helping to create a secure and resilient digital environment.

The **Federal Information Security Management Act (FISMA)**, enacted in 2002 and updated by the Federal Information Security Modernization Act of 2014, establishes comprehensive guidelines for federal agencies to protect their information systems. FISMA requires agencies to develop, document, and implement information security programs that address risk management, continuous monitoring, and incident response. Setting stringent security standards enables FISMA to ensure that federal agencies maintain a high level of cybersecurity, protecting sensitive government data from cyber threats.

The **Health Insurance Portability and Accountability Act (HIPAA)** focuses on safeguarding sensitive patient data in the healthcare sector. HIPAA mandates that healthcare providers, insurers, and their business associates implement strong security measures to safeguard electronic protected health information (ePHI). These measures include administrative, physical, and technical guardrails designed to ensure the confidentiality, integrity, and availability of patient data. Compliance with HIPAA is essential for maintaining patient trust and protecting healthcare information from unauthorized access and breaches. HIPAA was covered in detail in Chapter 9.

The **Gramm-Leach-Bliley Act (GLBA)** imposes data protection requirements on financial institutions. GLBA mandates that these institutions establish comprehensive information security programs to safeguard customer data against threats and unauthorized access. Some components of GLBA compliance include risk assessments, implementing appropriate security controls, and regularly reviewing and updating security measures. By ensuring that financial institutions adopt security practices, GLBA helps protect consumers' financial information from cyber threats.

The **Sarbanes-Oxley Act (SOX)**, enacted in response to corporate financial scandals, includes provisions to enhance corporate governance and financial transparency. While SOX primarily targets financial reporting, it also has significant implications for cybersecurity. SOX requires companies to implement internal controls for data integrity and security, ensuring that financial information is accurate and protected from tampering or unauthorized access. By enforcing stringent controls and audits, SOX helps maintain the integrity of financial data and protects against cyber threats.

The **Payment Card Industry Data Security Standard (PCI DSS)** sets the standards for securing payment card information. Organizations that handle payment card data must comply with PCI DSS requirements, which include implementing security management policies, access controls, network security measures, and regular security assessments. Compliance with PCI DSS is crucial for protecting cardholder data from breaches and fraud, ensuring the security of payment transactions, and maintaining consumer trust in the payment card industry. PCI DSS was covered in detail in Chapter 9.

Together, these federal cybersecurity programs and regulations provide a comprehensive framework for protecting sensitive information across various sectors. Adhering to these standards can help organizations enhance their security, mitigate risks, and ensure the privacy of critical data. These regulations not only help protect individual organizations but also contribute to the overall resilience of the nation's digital infrastructure.

While federal programs and regulations establish the foundation for national cybersecurity, the success of these initiatives relies heavily on collaboration between the public and private sectors. Public-private partnerships are essential for enhancing information sharing, developing best practices, and responding to cyber threats in a coordinated manner. By working together, government agencies and private organizations can leverage their combined resources and expertise to create a more secure cybersecurity environment. The next section explores the importance of these partnerships and highlights key initiatives that foster collaboration between public and private entities.

11.3 PUBLIC-PRIVATE PARTNERSHIPS

Collaboration between the public and private sectors is essential for strengthening national cybersecurity. These partnerships, as shown in Figure 11.2, combine the strengths and resources of both sectors to enhance cybersecurity. Government agencies and private organizations collaborate to share information, develop best practices, and respond to cyber threats.

One example of this collaboration is the **Information Sharing and Analysis Centers (ISACs)**, which facilitate the exchange of cybersecurity information among industry-specific organizations. The ISACs help companies in finance, healthcare, and energy share threat

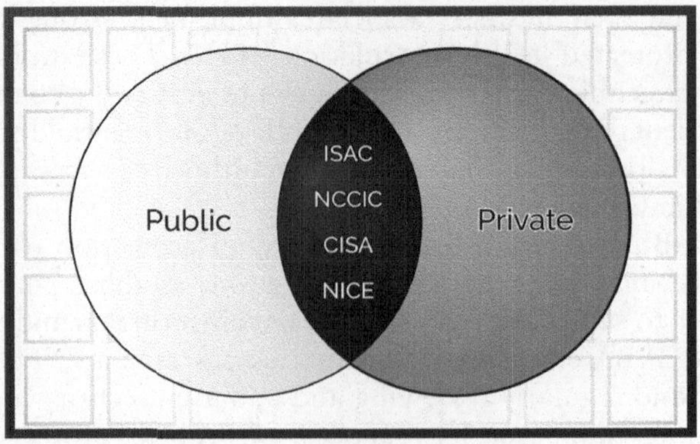

Figure 11.2 Participating agencies in public-private partnerships.

intelligence and coordinate responses to cybersecurity incidents. These centers play a crucial role in ensuring that relevant threat information is disseminated quickly and efficiently, enabling organizations to take proactive measures to protect their systems.

An initiative mentioned before is the **National Cybersecurity and Communications Integration Center** (NCCIC), which serves as a central hub for cyber threat information sharing and incident response coordination between civilian agencies, government entities, and the private sector. It enables a unified approach to addressing cybersecurity challenges by bringing together experts from various sectors. Furthermore, it helps to create a comprehensive understanding of the threat landscape and facilitates coordinated actions to mitigate risks.

The **Cybersecurity Information Sharing Act** (CISA) also promotes the sharing of cybersecurity threat information between the federal government and private-sector organizations. This act encourages companies to share threat data with the government, which can then be used to enhance national security. By fostering an environment of trust and collaboration, the CISA helps to ensure that critical threat information is shared in a timely manner, allowing for more effective responses to cyber threats.

Public-private partnerships also extend to joint training and education programs. Initiatives like the **National Initiative for Cybersecurity Education** (NICE) promote cybersecurity awareness and skill development across sectors. By working together, government and private organizations can ensure a well-trained workforce capable of addressing current and future cyber threats. Joint training exercises and workshops help to build relationships and improve coordination between public and private entities, enhancing overall cybersecurity readiness.

These partnerships are crucial for building a comprehensive and effective national cybersecurity strategy. Combining resources, expertise, and information, the public and private sectors can work together to protect critical infrastructure, secure sensitive data, and respond to cyber threats more effectively. Through collaboration, they can create a more resilient cybersecurity environment that is better equipped to handle the complexities of modern cyber threats.

11.4 CONCLUSION

National cybersecurity initiatives are essential for safeguarding the United States' digital infrastructure against the complicated landscape of cyber threats. Establishing comprehensive policies, frameworks, and programs can help governments play a pivotal role in protecting critical information and systems. The collaborative efforts of various government agencies, including NIST, CISA, DHS, FBI, and ODNI, ensure that standards and guidelines are in place to manage and mitigate cybersecurity risks effectively.

The importance of these initiatives is further amplified through public-private partnerships. By fostering collaboration between government entities and private organizations, the United States can leverage the collective strengths, resources, and expertise of both sectors. These partnerships facilitate information sharing, increase threat intelligence, and promote the development of best practices. Joint efforts in education and training also ensure that the workforce is well-equipped to address current and future cybersecurity challenges.

As cyber threats continue to evolve, there needs to be a coordinated and comprehensive approach to national cybersecurity. This is becoming increasingly critical. The initiatives and partnerships discussed in this chapter highlight the significance of a united front in defending against cyber adversaries. Maintaining a strong focus on collaboration, continuous improvement, and adherence to established standards, the United States can build a secure and resilient digital infrastructure capable of withstanding the complexities of the cyber world. This proactive and integrated approach not only protects organizations but also strengthens the overall security of the nation.

While national efforts are crucial, cybersecurity is a global challenge that requires international cooperation and collaboration. The next chapter will explore international cybersecurity initiatives, examining how different countries and global organizations work together to enhance cybersecurity worldwide. By understanding these international efforts, you will gain insights into best practices and strategies that transcend national boundaries, contributing to a more secure global digital environment.

DISCUSSION QUESTIONS

1. What is the role of the National Institute of Standards and Technology (NIST) in the US cybersecurity landscape, and how does its Cybersecurity Framework help both public and private sector organizations? Discuss the significance of the NIST Cybersecurity Framework and its flexibility in addressing various organizational needs.
2. How does the Cybersecurity and Infrastructure Security Agency (CISA) contribute to national cybersecurity efforts, particularly in protecting critical infrastructure? Explore the initiatives by CISA, such as the National Cyber Awareness System (NCAS) and Continuous Diagnostics and Mitigation (CDM) program.
3. What are the primary functions of the Department of Homeland Security (DHS) in managing cybersecurity threats, and how does the National Cybersecurity and Communications Integration Center (NCCIC) facilitate these efforts? Evaluate the role of NCCIC in coordinating cyber defense operations across federal, state, and private sectors.
4. How do federal agencies like the FBI and the Office of the Director of National Intelligence (ODNI) collaborate to enhance cybersecurity through intelligence sharing and threat analysis? Analyze the importance of joint efforts, such as the National Cyber Investigative Joint Task Force (NCIJTF).
5. In what ways does the Comprehensive National Cybersecurity Initiative (CNCI) strengthen the overall cybersecurity posture of the United States? Discuss the importance of programs like the Einstein Program and Trusted Internet Connections (TIC) in defending federal networks.
6. How does the Federal Trade Commission (FTC) enforce cybersecurity standards, and what impact do its regulations have on consumer protection? Reflect on the FTC's

role in protecting consumer data and its enforcement actions against companies with inadequate security measures.

7. Why is the Department of Defense (DoD) a critical player in national cybersecurity, and how does the US Cyber Command (USCYBERCOM) support its mission? Consider the DoD's role in protecting military networks and critical infrastructure through both offensive and defensive cyber operations.
8. What is the importance of public-private partnerships in strengthening national cybersecurity, and how do initiatives like Information Sharing and Analysis Centers (ISACs) facilitate these collaborations? Explore how information sharing and joint training programs enhance the overall cybersecurity ecosystem.
9. How do cybersecurity education and workforce development initiatives, such as the National Initiative for Cybersecurity Education (NICE), contribute to the national cybersecurity strategy? Examine the impact of programs like the Cyber Corps Scholarship for Service and the National Centers of Academic Excellence in fostering a skilled cybersecurity workforce.
10. What challenges do US government agencies face in coordinating a comprehensive national cybersecurity strategy, and how can public and private sector collaboration help overcome these challenges? Discuss the complexities of coordination and the role of shared responsibilities in addressing evolving cyber threats.

BIBLIOGRAPHY

Cybersecurity and Infrastructure Security Agency. (n.d.). NCCIC ICS Fact Sheet. U.S. Department of Homeland Security. https://www.cisa.gov/sites/default/files/FactSheets/NCCIC%20ICS_FactSheet_NCCIC%20ICS_S508C.pdf

Cybersecurity and Infrastructure Security Agency (CISA). (n.d.). Federal Information Security Modernization Act. U.S. Department of Homeland Security. https://www.cisa.gov/topics/cyber-threats-and-advisories/federal-information-security-modernization-act

De Groot, J. (2023, May 6). What is GLBA compliance? (Understand Requirements). Digital Guardian. https://digitalguardian.com/blog/what-glba-compliance-understand-requirements

Federal Bureau of Investigation. (n.d.). National Cyber Investigative Joint Task Force. https://www.fbi.gov/investigate/cyber/national-cyber-investigative-joint-task-force

Federal Trade Commission. (n.d.). Understanding the NIST cybersecurity framework. https://www.ftc.gov/business-guidance/small-businesses/cybersecurity/nist-framework

IBM. (n.d.). What is the NIST cybersecurity framework? https://www.ibm.com/topics/nist

IBM. (n.d.). What is SOX (Sarbanes-Oxley Act) compliance? https://www.ibm.com/topics/sox-compliance

Lord, N. (2023, May 6). What is FISMA compliance? (Definition, Requirements, Penalties, & More). Digital Guardian. https://www.digitalguardian.com/blog/what-fisma-compliance-fisma-definition-requirements-penalties-and-more

Nakashima, E. (2019, September 30). NSA launches new cyber defense directorate. The Washington Post. https://www.washingtonpost.com/national-security/nsa-launches-new-cyber-defense-directorate/2019/09/30/c18585f6-e219-11e9-be96-6adb81821e90_story.html

National Institute of Standards and Technology. (n.d.). About. https://www.nist.gov/itl/applied-cybersecurity/nice/about.

National Institute of Standards and Technology. (n.d.). Cybersecurity. https://www.nist.gov/cybersecurity

National Security Agency. (n.d.). Signals Intelligence (SIGINT) Overview. https://www.nsa.gov/Signals-Intelligence/Overview/

National Security Agency. (n.d.). NSA cybersecurity collaboration center. https://www.nsa.gov/About/Cybersecurity-Collaboration-Center/

National Security Agency (NSA). (n.d.). *National centers of academic excellence in cybersecurity*. U.S. Department of Defense. https://www.nsa.gov/Academics/Centers-of-Academic-Excellence/

Office of the Director of National Intelligence. (n.d.). Cyber Threat Intelligence Integration Center (CTIIC). https://www.dni.gov/index.php/ctiic-home

Office of the Director of National Intelligence. (n.d.). Who we are. https://www.dni.gov/index.php/who-we-are

Office of the Inspector General. (n.d.). *FISMA*. Federal Reserve. Retrieved, 29 July 2024, from https://oig.federalreserve.gov/fisma.htm

Rollins, J., & Henning, A. C. (2009, March 10). *Comprehensive national cybersecurity initiative: Legal authorities and policy considerations*. Congressional Research Service. https://sgp.fas.org/crs/natsec/R40427.pdf

The White House. (n.d.). The comprehensive national cybersecurity initiative. https://obamawhitehouse.archives.gov/sites/default/files/cybersecurity.pdf

U.S. Department of Commerce. (2011, August 11). National initiative for cybersecurity education strategic plan building a digital nation. https://scholar.google.com/scholar?q=national+initiative+for+cybersecurity+education+(nice)+education&hl=en&as_sdt=0&as_vis=1&oi=scholart

U.S. Department of Commerce. (2024, February 26). The NIST cybersecurity framework (CSF) 2.0. https://www.nist.gov/cyberframework

Zelvin, L. (2012). *National Cybersecurity & Communications Integration Center (NCCIC) overview*. National Cybersecurity & Communications Integration Center. https://csrc.nist.gov/CSRC/media/Events/ISPAB-OCTOBER-2012-MEETING/documents/ispab_oct2012_lzelvin_nccic-overview.pdf

ZenGRC. (2024, February 18). Complete guide to the NIST cybersecurity framework. reciprocity. https://reciprocity.com/resource-center/complete-guide-to-the-nist-cybersecurity-framework/

Chapter 12

Beyond the organization

International initiatives

Cyber threats are global in nature, and their impact can be felt across countries and continents. As a result, international cooperation and collaboration are essential in addressing these threats effectively. The global nature of cyber threats requires countries to work together. This can be done by sharing information, resources, and best practices to defend against common threats. International organizations, treaties, and alliances play a crucial role in facilitating this collaboration. Nations can strengthen their cybersecurity defenses and contribute to a more secure international digital environment if they understand and participate in these global efforts.

A strong international cybersecurity culture is built on cooperation, trust, and mutual understanding. Embracing international standards and participating in global cybersecurity frameworks can help organizations and nations improve their security practices and resistance against cyber threats. This chapter underscores the need for continued international collaboration.

12.1 INTERNATIONAL CYBERSECURITY INITIATIVES

Addressing cyber threats globally is crucial because these threats know no borders and can impact anyone, anywhere. In our interconnected world, a cyberattack on one country can quickly ripple across the globe, affecting economies, critical infrastructures, and individual lives. When nations collaborate, they pool their strengths, knowledge, and resources together, creating a strong defense against these relentless adversaries.

Imagine the power of shared intelligence, where one country's discovery of a new threat can instantly protect others from falling victim. Consider the collective expertise that emerges when the best minds from around the world unite to tackle the same problem. This global cooperation not only enhances our defenses but also fosters innovation, driving forward new technologies and strategies that can outpace even the most sophisticated cybercriminals; moreover, addressing cyber threats on a global scale builds a foundation of trust and mutual support among nations. This unity is vital in creating a secure digital environment where individuals can safely engage in online activities, businesses can innovate without fear, and governments can protect their citizens' data and privacy.

In essence, global collaboration in cybersecurity is not just about defense; it's about building a safer, more resilient world where the digital revolution can flourish without the looming shadow of cyber threats. It is about ensuring that the benefits of our interconnected world are safeguarded for everyone, everywhere.

Key international cybersecurity collaborations involve various organizations and initiatives that bring together countries to develop common standards and strategies. For instance, the European Union Agency for Cybersecurity (ENISA) plays a pivotal role in enhancing

DOI: 10.1201/9781003368496-12

Europe's cyber resilience, while the North Atlantic Treaty Organization's (NATO), and Cooperative Cyber Defense Centre of Excellence (CCDCOE) focus on improving the cyber defense capabilities of its member states. In addition to collaborative efforts, international treaties provide a legal framework for addressing cybercrime and protecting data privacy. The Budapest Convention on Cybercrime is a treaty designed to harmonize national laws, enhance investigative methods, and promote international collaboration in fighting cybercrime. Similarly, the General Data Protection Regulation (GDPR) sets stringent standards for data protection and privacy, impacting organizations worldwide and emphasizing the importance of safeguarding personal information.

Understanding these international collaborations and treaties is essential for developing a comprehensive approach to cybersecurity. Participating in these global efforts, nations can strengthen their defenses, improve their response to cybersecurity incidents, and contribute to a more secure and resilient international digital environment. This section explores these international cybersecurity collaborations and treaties, as shown in Figure 12.1, highlighting their significance and impact on global cybersecurity practices.

12.1.1 European Union

The European Union (EU) plays a significant role in shaping global cybersecurity standards and practices through various initiatives and regulatory frameworks. One of the most influential entities within the EU is the **European Union Agency for Cybersecurity (ENISA).** Established in 2004, ENISA's primary mission is to enhance the cybersecurity resilience of the EU and its member states. ENISA provides expertise and guidance to both the public and private sectors, helping them develop cybersecurity strategies and policies. The agency conducts cybersecurity exercises, offers training programs, and facilitates the exchange of best practices among EU member states.

Another critical aspect of the EU's approach to cybersecurity is the **General Data Protection Regulation (GDPR)**, which came into effect in May 2018. The GDPR is a comprehensive data protection regulation that sets stringent standards for the collection, processing, and storage of personal data. It applies not only to organizations within the EU but also to those outside the EU that handle the personal data of EU citizens. The GDPR emphasizes the importance of data privacy and security, mandating that organizations implement strong protective measures to safeguard personal information. Noncompliance with the GDPR can result in significant fines, making it a powerful tool for enforcing data protection standards globally.

The EU also collaborates with international partners to enhance global cybersecurity. Through initiatives such as the **EU Cyber Diplomacy Toolbox**, the EU engages in cyber diplomacy efforts to promote stability in cyberspace, advocate for international norms of responsible state behavior, and respond to malicious cyber activities. In addition, the **EU-U.S. Cyber Dialogue** fosters cooperation between the EU and the United States on cybersecurity issues, including the exchange of threat intelligence, coordination of cybersecurity incident responses, and development of joint cybersecurity standards.

Overall, the European Union's comprehensive approach to cybersecurity, through entities like ENISA, regulations like GDPR, and international collaborations, plays a crucial role in enhancing global cyber resilience. Setting high standards and fostering cooperation, the EU contributes to a safer and more secure digital environment, not only within Europe but across the globe.

12.1.2 Council of Europe

The Council of Europe is another participant in the international cybersecurity landscape. One of the Council's most significant contributions is the **Budapest Convention on Cybercrime,**

Figure 12.1 International cybersecurity initiatives.

also known as the Convention on Cybercrime. Adopted in 2001, it is the first international treaty that addresses crimes committed via the Internet and computer networks. The convention provides a comprehensive framework for aligning national laws, enhancing investigative methods, and promoting global cooperation to effectively combat cybercrime.

The Budapest Convention sets out specific requirements for the participating countries to establish laws against various forms of cybercrime, such as illegal access, data interference, and computer-related fraud. It also outlines procedures for the preservation of data and the collection of electronic evidence, which are critical for prosecuting cybercriminals. The convention facilitates collaboration between countries, enabling them to respond more effectively to transnational cybercrime by establishing a common legal framework.

In addition to the Budapest Convention, the **Council of Europe** promotes cybersecurity through various initiatives and training programs. These efforts aim to strengthen the capacity of member states to prevent and combat cybercrime. The council organizes workshops, seminars, and training sessions for law enforcement officials, judicial authorities, and policymakers, helping them stay abreast of the latest trends and techniques in cybercrime investigation and prosecution.

The Council of Europe also works closely with other international organizations, such as INTERPOL and Europol, to enhance global cooperation in the fight against cybercrime. They foster partnerships and facilitate the exchange of information and best practices; the council helps build a coordinated and effective global response to cyber threats.

Overall, the Council of Europe's initiatives, particularly the Budapest Convention on Cybercrime, play a crucial role in enhancing international cooperation and harmonizing efforts to combat cybercrime. They provide a common legal framework and promote capacity-building initiatives; the council contributes significantly to the global fight against cyber threats, ensuring a safer digital environment for all.

12.1.3 North Atlantic Treaty Organization (NATO)

The North Atlantic Treaty Organization (NATO) is a critical player in international cybersecurity efforts, focusing on enhancing the cyber defense capabilities of its member states. NATO recognizes that cyber threats pose a significant challenge to global security and stability; therefore, it has developed a comprehensive approach to address these challenges.

A cornerstone of NATO's cybersecurity efforts is the **NATO Cooperative Cyber Defense Centre of Excellence** (**CCDCOE**). Established in 2008, its headquarters are located in Tallinn, Estonia. The CCDCOE is a global cyber defense organization that conducts research, training, and exercises to enhance the cyber defense capabilities of NATO members. The organization also plays a vital role in developing strategic and operational concepts and policies related to cybersecurity. It facilitates collaboration and information sharing among member states, helping them to strengthen their cyber defenses collectively.

NATO also conducts **Cyber Coalition**, one of the largest and most comprehensive cyber defense exercises in the world. Cyber Coalition brings together participants from NATO member states, partner nations, and various organizations to test and enhance their abilities to defend against cyber threats in a coordinated manner. These exercises simulate real-world cybersecurity incidents, providing participants with valuable experience in responding to complex cyberattacks and improving their readiness.

In addition to its training and exercises, NATO has established the **NATO Cyber Rapid Reaction Teams (CRRTs)**, which can be deployed to assist member states in the event of a significant cybersecurity incident. These teams provide 24-hour technical assistance, support incident response efforts, and help restore affected systems. The CRRTs are a crucial component of NATO's collective defense strategy in cyberspace, ensuring that member states can rely on each other for support in times of crisis.

NATO also emphasizes the importance of cyber defense in its overall strategic framework. The **NATO Cyber Defense Policy**, first endorsed in 2011 and updated in subsequent years, outlines NATO's approach to protecting its communication and information systems, enhancing resilience, and supporting member states in their cyber defense efforts. This policy underscores NATO's commitment to integrating cyber defense into its broader defense and security strategy.

Through these initiatives and policies, NATO plays a crucial role in enhancing the cyber defense capabilities of its member states and promoting collective security in cyberspace. Fostering collaboration, conducting joint exercises, and providing rapid response capabilities, NATO contributes significantly to global cybersecurity resilience, ensuring that its members are better prepared to face cyber threats.

12.1.4 United Nations

The United Nations (UN) plays an important role in promoting international cooperation and establishing norms and standards in cybersecurity. It recognizes the global nature of cyber threats and the need for a coordinated international response and has developed several initiatives and frameworks for these challenges.

One of the efforts of the UN in cybersecurity is the **Group of Governmental Experts (GGE) on Developments in the Field of Information and Telecommunications in the Context of International Security.** The GGE, established by the UN General Assembly, brings together experts from various countries to discuss and develop norms, rules, and principles for responsible behavior in cyberspace. The GGE has produced several reports that outline voluntary, nonbinding norms for states, including recommendations on the protection of critical infrastructure and the importance of international cooperation to prevent cybersecurity incidents from escalating into conflicts.

In addition to the GGE, the UN has also established the **Open-Ended Working Group (OEWG)** on developments in the field of information and telecommunications in the context of international security. The OEWG is an inclusive platform that allows all UN member states to participate in discussions on cybersecurity. It aims to build consensus on key issues, such as responsible cyber conduct and enhancing mutual trust. The inclusive nature of the OEWG ensures that the voices of all member states, including those from developing countries, are heard in the global cybersecurity dialogue.

Furthermore, the **International Telecommunication Union (ITU)**, a specialized agency of the UN, focuses on issues related to information and communication technologies (ICTs). The ITU develops global standards for telecommunications and ICTs, including cybersecurity standards, to ensure the interoperability and security of communication networks. The union also organizes conferences and forums to facilitate dialogue and knowledge sharing among stakeholders, promoting best practices and international cooperation in cybersecurity.

Through these initiatives and efforts, the United Nations plays a crucial role in shaping the global cybersecurity landscape. Promoting international cooperation and establishing norms of responsible cyber conduct, the UN helps to enhance global cyber resilience and create a safer digital environment for all. The UN's comprehensive approach to cybersecurity underscores the importance of a coordinated and collaborative response to cyber threats.

12.1.5 Asia-Pacific Economic Cooperation (APEC)

The Asia-Pacific Economic Cooperation (APEC) was established in 1989 to promote free trade and economic cooperation throughout the Pacific region. In 2005, APEC created a cybersecurity initiative, a collaborative, multi-year effort to strengthen cybersecurity standards among APEC's 21 member economies, particularly in the context of the rapidly growing Internet of Things (IoT). The initiative emphasizes creating frameworks to address emerging cybersecurity risks, developing policies for data protection, and fostering cooperation among governments, industry, and academia.

One of APEC's initiatives is the **APEC Cybersecurity Strategy**, which provides a comprehensive approach to enhancing cybersecurity cooperation among member economies. The strategy focuses on several critical areas, including the protection of critical infrastructure, capacity building, information sharing, and the development of best practices. By promoting collaboration and mutual assistance, the APEC Cybersecurity Strategy aims to strengthen the collective cybersecurity posture of member economies and ensure the security of the region's digital infrastructure.

APEC also emphasizes the importance of public-private partnerships in addressing cybersecurity challenges. Through initiatives such as the **APEC Public-Private Dialogue on Cybersecurity**, APEC facilitates discussions between government officials, industry leaders, and cybersecurity experts to share insights, experiences, and best practices. These dialogues help build trust and cooperation between the public and private sectors, fostering a collaborative approach to tackling cyber threats.

Information sharing is a cornerstone of APEC's cybersecurity initiatives. They encourage member economies to share threat intelligence, incident reports, and best practices to improve their collective ability to detect, prevent, and respond to cyber threats. Member economies can collaborate on developing common standards and protocols for information sharing and ensuring effective responses to cyber incidents.

In summary, the Asia-Pacific Economic Cooperation (APEC) plays a vital role in enhancing cybersecurity across the Asia-Pacific region. Through its comprehensive cybersecurity strategy, emphasis on public-private partnerships, capacity-building initiatives, and commitment to information sharing, APEC fosters a secure and resilient digital environment. Promoting collaboration and mutual assistance among its member economies contributes to the overall stability and prosperity of the region's digital economy.

12.1.6 Organization of American States (OAS)

The Organization of American States (OAS) was founded in 2003. It is a regional organization that plays a significant role in promoting cybersecurity and enhancing the resilience of its member states in the Americas. The OAS is committed to strengthening cooperation among its member states to address the growing threats posed by cybercrime and to improve overall cybersecurity practices across the region.

One of the key components of the OAS's cybersecurity efforts is the **Inter-American Committee against Terrorism (CICTE)**. Founded in 1999, CICTE works to enhance the cybersecurity capabilities of member states through various initiatives, including capacity-building programs, technical assistance, and the promotion of best practices. CICTE's work focuses on several critical areas, such as the protection of critical infrastructure, cybersecurity incident response, and the development of national cybersecurity strategies. By providing member states with the necessary tools and knowledge, CICTE helps to build a more secure and resilient digital environment in the Americas.

Another important initiative led by the OAS is the **Cybersecurity Program.** This program aims to strengthen the institutional capacities of member states to prevent and respond to cybersecurity incidents. The program provides training and technical assistance to government officials, law enforcement agencies, and other relevant stakeholders. These efforts are designed to enhance the ability of member states to detect, investigate, and prosecute cybercrime, as well as to develop effective cybersecurity policies and frameworks.

The OAS also promotes regional cooperation and information sharing through the establishment of the **Inter-American Portal on Cybercrime.** This platform facilitates communication and collaboration among member states, enabling them to share threat intelligence, best practices, and lessons learned from cybersecurity incidents. By promoting a culture of cooperation and mutual assistance, the Inter-American Network on Cybercrime helps to improve the region's collective cybersecurity posture.

In addition to these efforts, the OAS has developed several important policy documents and frameworks to guide member states in their cybersecurity endeavors. One such document is the **Comprehensive Inter-American Strategy to Combat Threats to Cybersecurity**, which outlines a strategic approach to addressing cyber threats in the Americas. This strategy emphasizes the importance of international cooperation, the development of national cybersecurity capabilities, and the protection of critical infrastructure.

The OAS also collaborates with other international organizations and stakeholders to enhance cybersecurity in the region. For example, the OAS has partnered with the European Union Agency for Cybersecurity (ENISA), the International Telecommunication Union (ITU), and various private-sector entities to promote cybersecurity awareness and to develop joint initiatives aimed at improving cybersecurity practices.

Through these initiatives and collaborations, the Organization of American States (OAS) plays a crucial role in enhancing cybersecurity across the Americas. OAS helps its member states better protect their digital infrastructure and respond effectively to cyber threats. They accomplish this by providing capacity-building programs, promoting regional cooperation, and developing strategic frameworks. OAS's comprehensive approach to cybersecurity underscores the importance of a coordinated and collaborative effort in addressing the complex and evolving challenges posed by cybercrime and cyber threats.

12.1.7 African Union

The African Union (AU) is a continental organization that plays a significant role in promoting cybersecurity and enhancing digital resilience across its member states. Recognizing the importance of a secure digital environment for economic growth and development, the AU has undertaken several initiatives to strengthen cybersecurity frameworks and foster cooperation among African nations.

One of the key milestones in the AU's cybersecurity efforts is the adoption of the **African Union Convention on Cyber Security and Personal Data Protection**, commonly known as the **Malabo Convention**. Adopted in 2014, the Malabo Convention aims to establish a comprehensive legal framework for cybersecurity, electronic transactions, and data protection across the continent. The convention provides guidelines for member states to develop national cybersecurity policies, protect critical infrastructure, and ensure the security of personal data. The Malabo Convention facilitates cooperation and information sharing among African nations with uniform cybersecurity laws and regulations.

In addition to the Malabo Convention, the AU has established the **African Union Cyber Security Expert Group (AUCSEG)**. This group comprises cybersecurity experts from various member states who collaborate to develop strategies and policies to enhance cybersecurity in Africa. The AUCSEG provides technical assistance, shares best practices, and conducts capacity-building programs to help member states strengthen their cybersecurity capabilities. The expertise of its members is crucial for advancing the AU's cybersecurity agenda.

The AU also focuses on building the cybersecurity capacity of its member states through various training programs and workshops. These initiatives aim to equip government officials, law enforcement agencies, and other stakeholders with the knowledge and skills needed to address cyber threats effectively. Enhancing the capabilities of national institutions helps its member states to better protect their digital infrastructure and respond to cybersecurity incidents; moreover, the AU promotes regional and international cooperation in cybersecurity. Through partnerships with organizations such as the International Telecommunication Union (ITU), the European Union Agency for Cybersecurity (ENISA), and other international bodies, the AU facilitates the exchange of information, threat intelligence, and best practices. These collaborations help to create a more secure and resilient digital environment in Africa and beyond.

The AU has also launched initiatives to raise awareness about cybersecurity among its member states. The African Union Commission (AUC) regularly organizes conferences, seminars, and forums to discuss emerging cyber threats and to promote a culture of cybersecurity. These events provide a platform for policymakers, industry leaders, and cybersecurity professionals to share insights and develop strategies for enhancing cybersecurity in Africa.

Through these efforts, the African Union (AU) plays a crucial role in promoting cybersecurity and digital resilience across the continent. Fostering regional and international cooperation, the AU helps its member states to better protect their digital infrastructure and to respond effectively to cyber threats. The AU's comprehensive approach to cybersecurity underscores the importance of a coordinated and collaborative effort in addressing the complex and evolving challenges posed by cybercrime and cyber threats.

This chapter demonstrates that international collaborations and treaties are essential for addressing the borderless nature of cyber threats. They are summarized in Table 12.1. Working together, it is possible to develop standardized approaches to cybersecurity, share critical information, and coordinate responses to incidents. These collaborations help build a global digital environment by leveraging the strengths and resources of various countries.

Even though the benefits are undeniable, this collaboration has challenges. The next section will explore the difficulties countries face in aligning their policies, legal frameworks,

Table 12.1 Key initiatives of international cybersecurity organizations

KEY INITIATIVES OF INTERNATIONAL CYBERSECURITY ORGANIZATIONS

Organization	Region	Key Initiatives	Primary Focus	Collaboration Partners
European Union Agency for Cybersecurity (ENISA)	Europe	Cybersecurity resilience, GDPR support, training programs	Enhancing cybersecurity resilience, data protection, coordination	EU member states, United States, private sector entities
Council of Europe (CoE)	Europe	Budapest Convention on Cybercrime, capacity-building programs	Combatting cybercrime, harmonizing legal frameworks, training	INTERPOL, Europol, national governments
North Atlantic Treaty Organization (NATO)	North America Europe	CCDCOE, Cyber Coalition exercises, CRRTs	Cyber defense, joint exercises, strategic policy development	Member states, partner nations, private sector
United Nations (UN)	Global	GGE on cybersecurity norms, OEWG on information security	Establishing norms, promoting cooperation, capacity building	All UN member states, international organizations
Asia-Pacific Economic Cooperation (APEC)	Asia-Pacific	APEC Cybersecurity Strategy, public-private dialogues	Protecting digital economies, information sharing, capacity building	Member economies, private sector, cybersecurity experts
Organization of American States (OAS)	Americas	CICTE, Cybersecurity Program, Inter-American Portal on Cybercrime	Regional cooperation, enhancing cybersecurity capacities	Member states, EU, ITU, private sector
African Union (AU)	Africa	Malabo Convention, AUCSEG, capacity-building programs	Cybersecurity policy development, harmonization, cooperation	Member states, ITU, ENISA, international organizations

and operational practices. Understanding these challenges is important for developing strategies to overcome them and strengthen global cybersecurity efforts.

12.2 CHALLENGES OF INTERNATIONAL INITIATIVES

Aligning the efforts of various countries to create a unified defense against cyber threats presents significant challenges. These challenges, listed in Figure 12.2, stem from differences in legal frameworks, national interests, and varying levels of technological advancement. Understanding these obstacles is essential for developing effective strategies that can enhance global cybersecurity collaboration. Exploring these challenges will shed light on the complexities that hinder international cooperation.

One challenge is that countries have **different legal systems and regulations** regarding cybersecurity. These differences can create complications in cooperation, as what is considered a cybercrime in one country may not be in another. Aligning laws and regulations across countries is a significant challenge that requires extensive negotiations and compromises.

Nations have **varying priorities and interests** when it comes to cybersecurity. While some countries may prioritize protecting critical infrastructure, others might focus more on

Figure 12.2 Challenges of international initiatives.

combating cybercrime or securing government data. These differing priorities can lead to conflicts in collaborative efforts.

Cybersecurity incidents often span multiple jurisdictions, raising questions about which country has the authority to investigate and prosecute offenders. **Issues of sovereignty** can complicate cooperation, as countries are often reluctant to allow foreign entities to operate within their borders, even for the sake of cybersecurity.

Mutual trust is essential for effective international cooperation, but it is often lacking. Historical tensions, espionage fears, and geopolitical rivalries can lead to a lack of trust among nations, which can make them hesitant to share sensitive information or collaborate closely on cybersecurity initiatives.

Countries differ widely in their **levels of cybersecurity maturity.** While some nations have advanced cybersecurity infrastructure and capabilities, others are still developing their basic cyber defenses. This disparity can make cooperation challenging, as less advanced countries may struggle to keep up with the requirements of joint initiatives.

Effective cybersecurity cooperation relies on the timely and accurate sharing of information about threats, vulnerabilities, and incidents; however, various barriers, such as classification levels, privacy laws, and proprietary concerns, can impede information sharing. Organizations and nations may be reluctant to share data that could reveal their own weaknesses or competitive disadvantages.

Technological differences between countries can pose significant challenges. Nations with advanced cybersecurity technologies may find it difficult to integrate their systems with those of less technologically developed countries. This disparity can lead to inefficiencies and gaps in collective cybersecurity efforts.

Language barriers and cultural differences can also hinder international cybersecurity cooperation. Miscommunications and misunderstandings can occur, leading to ineffective coordination and collaboration. Efforts to bridge these gaps through translation services and cultural awareness training are essential but not always sufficient.

Coordinating international cybersecurity efforts involves managing a complex web of stakeholders, including government agencies, private-sector entities, and international organizations. Ensuring that all parties are aligned and working toward common goals requires significant effort and resources.

Many countries face **resource limitations** that affect their ability to participate in international cybersecurity initiatives. Financial constraints, lack of skilled personnel, and inadequate technological infrastructure can prevent nations from contributing effectively to cooperative efforts.

Political and economic pressures can also influence international cybersecurity cooperation. Sanctions, trade disputes, and other political issues can impact the willingness of countries to collaborate. Additionally, economic pressures may lead nations to prioritize immediate economic gains over long-term cybersecurity goals.

The concept of **cyber sovereignty**, where countries assert control over their own cyber infrastructure, can conflict with international cooperation efforts. Nations may prioritize their sovereignty over collaborative cybersecurity measures, leading to fragmented approaches and reduced effectiveness.

International cybersecurity cooperation is crucial for addressing the global nature of cyber threats, but it faces numerous challenges. All of the factors addressed above complicate efforts to work together. Overcoming these challenges requires sustained commitment and communication, as well as the development of mechanisms that facilitate effective collaboration while respecting national differences. Addressing these obstacles can enhance the collective cybersecurity efforts of countries and provide better protection against cyber threats globally.

12.3 CONCLUSION

International cybersecurity initiatives and collaborations are essential for addressing the complex and borderless nature of cyber threats. This chapter revealed a number of organizations, such as the Council of Europe, NATO, and the Asia-Pacific Economic Cooperation (APEC), that play pivotal roles in enhancing global cybersecurity resilience. These entities provide frameworks for cooperation, develop international standards, and promote best practices that collectively strengthen the global cybersecurity landscape.

Fostering international collaboration helps nations share critical information, resources, and expertise, enabling them to respond more effectively to cybersecurity incidents. Initiatives such as the Budapest Convention and the Malabo Convention highlight the importance of harmonizing cybersecurity laws and policies to combat cybercrime and protect critical infrastructure. Additionally, capacity-building programs and training workshops offered by these organizations equip stakeholders with the skills and knowledge necessary to defend against evolving cyber threats.

The comprehensive approach taken by these international organizations underscores the need for a coordinated global response to cybersecurity challenges. Participating in these efforts enhances countries' cybersecurity posture, protects their digital economies, and contributes to a more secure international digital environment.

Moving forward, it is crucial to recognize that cybersecurity culture varies significantly across different regions and countries. The next chapter will explore the diverse cybersecurity cultures around the world, examining how various nations approach cybersecurity and what lessons can be learned from their experiences. Understanding these cultural differences is vital for fostering a global cybersecurity culture that promotes collaboration, trust, and mutual assistance in the fight against cyber threats.

DISCUSSION QUESTIONS

1. Why is international collaboration critical in addressing cybersecurity threats, and what are the potential benefits of such cooperation? Discuss the advantages and challenges of global cooperation in cybersecurity.
2. How do organizations like the European Union Agency for Cybersecurity (ENISA) contribute to global cybersecurity efforts? Explore the role and impact of key international organizations on enhancing cybersecurity resilience.
3. What are the key provisions of the Budapest Convention on Cybercrime, and how have they influenced global cybersecurity practices? Evaluate the effectiveness of the Budapest Convention in harmonizing cybercrime laws across different nations.
4. In what ways does the General Data Protection Regulation (GDPR) set a global standard for data protection, and how has it impacted organizations worldwide? Analyze how GDPR has influenced global cybersecurity and privacy policies.
5. What are the main challenges faced by countries in aligning their legal frameworks for cybersecurity cooperation? Identify the obstacles to international collaboration and how they can be overcome.
6. How do regional organizations, like the African Union (AU) and Asia-Pacific Economic Cooperation (APEC), tailor their cybersecurity initiatives to address local and regional threats? Discuss the importance of regional approaches to cybersecurity and their effectiveness.
7. Why is capacity building crucial in global cybersecurity efforts, and what role do organizations like the United Nations play in this regard? Examine the significance

of training and knowledge-sharing in fostering a resilient global cybersecurity environment.

8. How do cultural and political differences among countries impact international cybersecurity cooperation? Debate the effects of cultural diversity on building a unified global response to cyber threats.
9. What strategies can be implemented to enhance trust and information sharing among nations in the field of cybersecurity? Propose methods for overcoming trust barriers in international cybersecurity partnerships.
10. How do treaties like the Malabo Convention and Budapest Convention help establish a unified approach to combating cybercrime, and what more can be done to strengthen these frameworks? Discuss the role of international treaties in promoting a cohesive global cybersecurity strategy and potential areas for improvement.

BIBLIOGRAPHY

ACT NATO. (n.d.). Cyber Coalition: NATO's flagship cyber exercise. https://www.act.nato.int/activities/cyber-coalition/

African Union. (2019, December 12). African Union Cybersecurity Expert Group holds its first inaugural meeting. https://au.int/en/pressreleases/20191212/african-union-cybersecurity-expert-group-holds-its-first-inaugural-meeting

APEC. (2024, July). History. https://www.apec.org/about-us/about-apec/history

Blakely, B., Billings, H., Evans, N., Landry, A., & Domingo, A. (2023, June 15). Evaluation of an autonomous intelligent cyberdefense agent at NATO cyber coalition exercise 2022. In *Proceedings Volume 12542, Disruptive Technologies in Information Sciences VII* (125420D). https://doi.org/10.1117/12.2662959

Burton, J. (2015). NATO's cyber defence: Strategic challenges and institutional adaptation. *Defence Studies*, *15*(4), 297–319. https://doi.org/10.1080/14702436.2015.1108108

Carstens, A. (2019, May 29). *A handful of cyber - five key issues for international cooperation.* Bank for International Settlements. https://www.bis.org/speeches/sp190529.htm.

Centre for Public Impact. (2017, September 29). General data protection regulation in the EU. https://www.centreforpublicimpact.org/case-study/general-data-protection-regulation-eu

Chernenko, E., & Demidov, O. (2018, February 23). *Increasing international cooperation in cybersecurity and adapting cyber norms.* Council on Foreign Relations. https://www.cfr.org/report/increasing-international-cooperation-cybersecurity-and-adapting-cyber-norms

Council of Europe. (n.d.). 20 years of the convention on cybercrime. https://www.coe.int/en/web/cybercrime/20th-anniversary-budapest-convention

DigWatch. (n.d.). European Union Agency for Cybersecurity. https://dig.watch/actor/european-union-agency-network-and-information-security

European Commission. (2024, January 31). EU and United States enhance cooperation on cybersecurity [Press release]. https://digital-strategy.ec.europa.eu/en/news/eu-and-united-states-enhance-cooperation-cybersecurity

European Union. (n.d.). European Union Agency for Cybersecurity (ENISA). https://european-union.europa.eu/institutions-law-budget/institutions-and-bodies/search-all-eu-institutions-and-bodies/european-union-agency-cybersecurity-enisa_en

Fonseca, L., & Delgado, T. (2014). Interdisciplinary Journal of the William J. Perry Center for Hemispheric Defense Studies (Vol. 16). https://wjpcenter.org/wp-content/uploads/2023/09/SDSR-Vol16.pdf

Hurel, L. M. (2022, September 6). The rocky road to cyber norms at the United Nations. Council on Foreign Relations. https://www.cfr.org/blog/rocky-road-cyber-norms-united-nations-0

International Telecommunication Union. (n.d.). About International Telecommunication Union (ITU). https://www.itu.int/en/about/Pages/default.aspx

Maigre, M. (2022). *NATO's role in global cyber security.* German Marshall Fund of the United States. https://scholar.google.com/scholar?as_ylo=2020&q=Nato+Cyber+coalition&hl=en&as_sdt=0,33&as_vis=1#d=gs_cit&t=1722915748550&u=%2Fscholar%3Fq%3Dinfo%3A1zI-5KjevPEJ%3Ascholar.google.com%2F%26output%3Dcite%26scirp%3D0%26hl%3Den

NATO. (2012, March 13). NATO Rapid Reaction Team to fight cyber attack. https://www.nato.int/cps/en/natolive/news_85161.htm

NATO. (2023, August 29). NATO Centres of Excellence – Cooperative Cyber Defence (CCD COE). https://www.act.nato.int/article/nato-centres-of-excellence-cooperative-cyber-defence-ccd-coe/

NATO. (2024, July 30). Cyber defence. https://www.nato.int/cps/en/natohq/topics_78170.htm?selectedLocale=en

Organization of American States. (n.d.). Cyber security. https://www.oas.org/en/topics/cyber_security.asp

Organization of American States. (n.d.). Cybersecurity program. https://www.oas.org/ext/en/security/prog-cyber

Richardson, J. (2002, August 19–23). *APEC cybersecurity strategy*. APEC Telecommunications and Information Working Group, 26th Meeting, Moscow, Russia. https://ccdcoe.org/uploads/2018/10/APEC-020823-CyberSecurityStrategy.pdf

Sheik, S. (2023, April 24). AU Convention on Cyber Security and Personal Data Protection | Malabo Convention. *Michalsons*. https://www.michalsons.com/blog/au-convention-on-cyber-security-and-personal-data-protection-malabo-convention/65281

SOM Steering Committee on Economic and Technical Cooperation (SCE), & Policy Partnership on Science, Technology and Innovation (PPSTI). (2024, April). APEC public-private dialogue on challenges, opportunities, and digitally-enabled recovery in the post-COVID era. APEC. https://www.apec.org/docs/default-source/publications/2024/4/224_ppsti_apec-public-private-dialogue-on-challenges-opportunities-and-digitally-enabled-recovery-in-the-post-covid-era.pdf?sfvrsn=fc454801_2

The Cyber Diplomacy Toolbox. (n.d.). https://www.cyber-diplomacy-toolbox.com/

United Nations. (n.d.). Cybersecurity and new technologies. https://www.un.org/counterterrorism/cybersecurity

UN. Secretary-General, & UN. Group of Governmental Experts on Developments in the Field of Information and Telecommunications in the Context of International Security. (2015, July 22). *Group of governmental experts on developments in the field of information and telecommunications in the context of international security: Note by the secretary-general*. UN. http://digitallibrary.un.org/record/799853

Chapter 13

Cybersecurity initiatives and culture around the world

Cybersecurity is a global concern. It requires a deep understanding of how different countries approach the challenge of protecting their digital environments. Cyber threats do not care about national borders. A strong global cybersecurity posture depends on the diverse strategies and cultural approaches that various nations bring to the table. Each country has developed its own unique blend of government initiatives, policies, and organizational practices to address cybersecurity challenges shaped by their political, economic, and social context.

Understanding these different cultures is not just a matter of academic interest, but a crucial step in fostering international cooperation and developing best practices that can be adapted across borders. This chapter examines the cybersecurity cultures of several countries. It will look at both their government-led initiatives and organizational practices. Understanding and appreciating the unique approaches of each country, one can learn how cybersecurity is managed and implemented. This knowledge can be used to build bridges and support collaboration in the global fight against cyber threats.

The chapter will start by looking at Canada, where collaboration and education are emphasized in both government and organizational approaches. Next, the United Kingdom will be explored, a country that has developed a comprehensive cybersecurity strategy supported by public-private partnerships. Germany's focus on critical infrastructure protection and compliance standards provides another unique perspective, while in Japan, technological innovation drives cybersecurity measures. As you will see, each country offers a unique perspective on securing its information assets, summarized in Figure 13.1. Understanding these variations is essential for developing effective, culturally attuned cybersecurity strategies and promoting a global culture of cybersecurity.

13.1 CANADA

13.1.1 Cybersecurity initiatives

Canada has developed a comprehensive approach to cybersecurity through various government-led initiatives. The **Canadian Centre for Cyber Security** (CCCS), established in 2018, is the national authority responsible for the country's cybersecurity. It provides trusted advice and guidance to Canadian citizens, businesses, and government organizations. The CCCS is part of the **Communications Security Establishment** (CSE) and plays a critical role in protecting Canada's cyber infrastructure.

One of the cornerstone documents guiding Canada's cybersecurity efforts is the **National Cyber Security Strategy**, released in 2018. This strategy represents Canada's vision for cybersecurity as ensuring secure and resilient Canadian systems, building an innovative and

DOI: 10.1201/9781003368496-13

Figure 13.1 Key government initiatives.

adaptive cyber ecosystem, and supporting effective leadership and collaboration. The strategy emphasizes the importance of public-private partnerships and encourages collaboration between government, industry, and academia to address cybersecurity challenges.

Canada has also implemented several specific programs and initiatives to support its cybersecurity strategy. **The Cyber Security Cooperation Program** provides funding to initiatives that enhance cybersecurity research and development. Additionally, the **Cyber Incident Response Centre (CIRC)** is responsible for coordinating the national response to significant cybersecurity incidents, working closely with both domestic and international partners to mitigate threats and recover from attacks.

13.1.2 Cybersecurity culture

The landscape of cybersecurity in Canada is evolving rapidly, reflecting the increasing complexity and frequency of cyber threats, as summarized in Table 13.1. Recent statistics report the pressing need for Canadian businesses to strengthen their cybersecurity measures and adopt a culture that prioritizes security.

The number of Canadian organizations that have experienced cybersecurity incidents is high. The 2023 Global Cybersecurity Leadership Insights Study reports that these organizations experienced at least 25 cybersecurity incidents in 2022. This high incidence rate indicates a need for strong cybersecurity frameworks and proactive measures to mitigate risks.

The frequency of cybersecurity incidents varies across different types of organizations as well. Larger organizations and those in critical sectors tend to report higher rates of incidents due to their more prominent digital footprints, which make them attractive targets for cybercriminals. In contrast, smaller organizations may report fewer incidents, not necessarily due to a lower frequency of attacks but often because of inadequate monitoring and detection capabilities.

One of the significant challenges is the preparedness of Canadian organizations to handle worst-case cyber threats. Many businesses, particularly smaller ones, often underestimate the sophistication and potential impact of cyberattacks. Economic pressures and competing priorities can lead to cybersecurity being deprioritized, leaving organizations vulnerable.

The survey indicates a troubling trend. The smaller organizations are identifying fewer cybersecurity incidents than in previous years. This decline in detection is not necessarily indicative of a decrease in attacks but rather a shift in focus away from cybersecurity.

Table 13.1 Summary of cybersecurity culture in Canada

SUMMARY OF CYBERSECURITY CULTURE IN CANADA

Aspect	Description
Government Initiatives	• Canadian Centre for Cyber Security (CCCS) • National Cyber Security Strategy • Cyber Security Cooperation Program
Primary Focus	• Public-private collaboration • Incident response • Cybersecurity education.
Cultural Influences	• High trust in government initiatives • Emphasis on collaborative approaches • Community involvement
Challenges	• Declining detection and reporting of incidents • Economic pressures diverting resources away from cybersecurity
Impact on National Cybersecurity	Strengthened collaboration across sectors, but with a need for more proactive threat identification and employee education.

Economic uncertainties and other immediate business concerns are diverting attention and resources away from maintaining cybersecurity measures.

Basic cyber hygiene practices are crucial for defending against common cyber threats. These measures include updated malware protection, regular software updates, and strong password policies. The EY survey shows that while a majority of businesses in Canada have these basic protections in place, there has been a decline in the adoption of some essential practices over the past few years. For instance, the use of password policies has decreased, reflecting a potential complacency or resource constraint among organizations. This decline is particularly notable among smaller businesses, which may lack the resources and expertise to maintain comprehensive cybersecurity measures.

To address the growing threat landscape, Canadian organizations must adopt a proactive approach to cybersecurity. This involves continuous learning, regular security assessments, and staying abreast of the latest developments in cyber threats and defense strategies. Proactive threat identification and response are critical to mitigating the impact of cybersecurity incidents.

Even though there are a number of initiatives, Canadian cybersecurity culture is currently facing significant challenges. Despite substantial spending on cybersecurity measures, Canadian organizations are experiencing frequent and costly incidents. Detection and response times are notably slow, because many organizations take months to identify and address breaches. There is a struggle to balance security with innovation, particularly with the rise of emerging technologies such as cloud computing and the Internet of Things (IoT), which introduce new risks.

One more important aspect of enhancing cybersecurity culture in Canada involves recognizing the importance of continuous learning and adaptation. As threats evolve, so too must the strategies to combat them. Organizations are encouraged to invest in training programs that keep employees informed about the latest threats and best practices in cybersecurity. This ongoing education helps to cultivate a vigilant and informed workforce, which is a critical line of defense against cyberattacks; moreover, cybersecurity integration at the leadership level is less mature in Canada compared to its global counterparts. Only a small percentage of CISOs and C-suite executives believe their cybersecurity efforts are effective, and many are dissatisfied with how cybersecurity is incorporated into business decisions.

To improve, Canadian organizations need to embed cybersecurity into all aspects of their operations, viewing it as a value driver rather than merely a risk mitigation strategy. With an average of 25 incidents per year, it is evident that there is a need for significant improvements in how these organizations approach cybersecurity. By adopting a culture of continuous learning, proactive threat management, and strong leadership, Canadian organizations can better prepare for and mitigate the impact of cyber threats.

13.2 UNITED KINGDOM

13.2.1 Cybersecurity initiatives

The United Kingdom has developed a comprehensive approach to cybersecurity with strong government initiatives and policies. Central to these efforts is the **National Cyber Security Centre** (NCSC), which was established in 2016 as part of the **Government Communications Headquarters** (GCHQ). The NCSC serves as the UK's authority on cybersecurity and provides support and guidance to public and private sector organizations and the general public.

The UK's cybersecurity efforts are primarily guided by the **Cyber Security Strategy.** The most recent iteration, the National Cyber Strategy 2022–2030, outlines the UK's vision for cybersecurity and sets forth five pillars of strategy. The first pillar is to manage cybersecurity risks. Effective cybersecurity risk management involves processes, governance, and accountability. It involves identifying, assessing, and managing cyber security risks at both the organizational and cross-government levels. The second pillar is protecting against cyberattacks. Understanding the risks helps with the adoption of proportionate security measures with strong defense mechanisms. The third pillar is the detection of cybersecurity events. Effective monitoring systems can detect cyber events promptly. Advanced technologies and intelligence can help identify threats quickly. The fourth pillar is to minimize the impact of incidences. A comprehensive incident response plan can soften the impact of a cyberattack. Efficient recovery efforts can also be of great help. The final pillar is developing cyber security capabilities, investing in the development of cyber security skills and capabilities across the workforce. Continuous training, education, and awareness programs ensure that individuals and teams are well-prepared to handle cyber threats.

The NCSC plays a pivotal role in implementing this strategy, coordinating national efforts to protect the UK's digital infrastructure. This includes providing incident response support, threat intelligence, and guidance on best practices. The NCSC also collaborates with other government agencies, private sector partners, and international allies to enhance the UK's cybersecurity posture.

The UK government has also introduced specific programs to support its cybersecurity objectives. The **Cyber Aware Campaign** aims to educate the public and small businesses about the importance of cybersecurity and provides practical advice on how to stay safe online. The **Cyber Essentials Scheme** offers a certification process for businesses to demonstrate their commitment to cybersecurity and to protect themselves against common cyber threats.

The **Cyber Security Export Strategy** aims to promote the UK's cybersecurity industry on the global stage, supporting businesses in exporting their cybersecurity products and services. This strategy underscores the importance of the cybersecurity sector to the UK's economy and its role in enhancing global cybersecurity.

13.2.2 Cybersecurity culture

The cybersecurity landscape in the UK has seen significant developments over recent years, reflecting both advancements in security measures and the increasing sophistication of cyber threats. According to 2024 cybercrime statistics, 32% of UK businesses reported suffering a cyberattack in 2023, with this figure rising to 59% for medium businesses and 69% for large businesses.

Phishing remains the most common cyber threat, accounting for 83% of identified attacks against UK businesses in 2022. This method is often used as a precursor for more damaging ransomware attacks, which have also seen an increase. Ransomware accounted for around 20% of cyber breaches in 2022, with phishing being the primary delivery method. The interconnection between phishing and ransomware underscores the importance of email security and employee training to recognize and respond to such threats.

Financially, the impact of cybercrime on UK businesses is substantial. It is estimated that cybercrime cost UK businesses around £736 million in 2021, with the average cost of a breach against medium and large businesses standing at £4,960 as of December 2023. These figures reflect both direct financial losses and the indirect costs associated with responding to and recovering from cyberattacks.

The Cyber Security Breaches Survey 2023 by the UK Department of Science, Innovation and Technology provides additional insights into the state of cybersecurity. According to the survey, while 82% of boards or senior management in UK businesses see cybersecurity as a high priority, there remains a gap in effective cybersecurity measures. For instance, only 19% of UK businesses have a formal incident response plan, and just 6% have Cyber Essentials certification, which is a basic level of cybersecurity assurance.

The survey also highlights the importance of integrating cybersecurity into the overall business strategy. Despite the high level of awareness among senior management, the implementation of comprehensive cybersecurity measures remains inconsistent. This inconsistency can be attributed to several factors, including budget constraints, lack of specialized knowledge, and the rapidly evolving nature of cyber threats; moreover, the UK's cybersecurity culture is influenced by global trends and threats. For instance, the growing cost-of-living crisis has provided fertile ground for cybercriminals to launch phishing campaigns, impersonating entities like the energy regulator Ofgem to harvest financial information. This trend emphasizes the need for continuous vigilance and adaptation to new threat vectors.

Looking ahead, the UK's cybersecurity landscape must evolve to address these challenges effectively. This includes fostering a culture of cybersecurity awareness, investing in advanced security technologies, and developing incident response plans. Additionally, as emerging technologies such as cloud computing and the Internet of Things (IoT) become more prevalent, businesses must balance innovation with security to mitigate new risks.

In conclusion, the cybersecurity culture in the UK, as depicted in Table 13.2, is marked by significant awareness and concern at the management level, but there are gaps in implementation and preparedness. Addressing these gaps requires a holistic approach that integrates cybersecurity into all aspects of business operations, continuous education and training for employees,

Table 13.2 Summary of cybersecurity culture in the United Kingdom

SUMMARY OF CYBERSECURITY CULTURE IN THE UNITED KINGDOM

ASPECT	DESCRIPTION
Government Initiatives	· National Cyber Security Centre (NCSC) · National Cyber Strategy · Cyber Essentials Scheme
Primary Focus	· Risk management · Public awareness · Capacity building · Certification standards
Cultural Influences	Strong emphasis on resilience and collaboration between public and private sectors.
Challenges	· High rates of phishing and ransomware · Gaps in formal incident response plans · Balancing innovation and security
Impact on National Cybersecurity	High awareness but inconsistent implementation of best practices, need for integration of cybersecurity into overall business strategies.

and proactive measures to stay ahead of evolving threats. By doing so, UK businesses can better protect themselves against the growing and ever-changing landscape of cyber threats.

13.3 GERMANY

13.3.1 Cybersecurity initiatives

Germany has established a comprehensive cybersecurity framework with a focus on protecting critical infrastructure, fostering public-private partnerships, and promoting cybersecurity innovation. **The Federal Office for Information Security (BSI)** is the central authority for cybersecurity in Germany. Founded in 1991, the BSI is responsible for enhancing and ensuring the security of information technology systems and networks within Germany.

A cornerstone of Germany's approach to cybersecurity is the **National Cybersecurity Strategy.** The most recent version, updated in 2021, outlines Germany's 30 strategic objectives for cybersecurity. These objectives include aims to enhance the critical infrastructures and IT systems against cyber threats. The strategy focuses on improving the detection, analysis, and response to cyberattacks. It ensures control over digital infrastructure and data and supports the development of new cybersecurity technologies. It also emphasizes international cooperation to tackle global cyber threats and establishes common standards while increasing public awareness and education on cybersecurity issues to build a security-conscious society. These objectives create a comprehensive framework to protect Germany's digital assets and environment.

The BSI plays a crucial role in implementing this strategy by providing guidance, conducting risk assessments, and coordinating cybersecurity efforts across different sectors. It also works closely with other government agencies, private sector entities, and international partners to share information and best practices.

Germany has also enacted specific laws and regulations to enhance cybersecurity. **The IT Security Act 2.0**, passed in 2021, mandates stricter security requirements for operators of critical infrastructure and increases the penalties for noncompliance. This law aims to enhance the critical infrastructure and ensure that operators implement strong cybersecurity measures.

Furthermore, Germany promotes cybersecurity through the **Alliance for Cyber Security**, an initiative launched by the BSI and the **German Association for Information Technology, Telecommunications and New Media (Bitkom)** in 2012. This alliance brings together organizations from various sectors to share knowledge, resources, and best practices in cybersecurity.

Germany has a well-established reputation for technological innovation and industrial strength; however, its cybersecurity culture is facing significant challenges that need urgent attention to maintain its competitive edge and national security. Germany's cybersecurity landscape is rooted in a strong regulatory framework and strategic initiatives. The German government has implemented several policies aimed at enhancing cybersecurity, including the **German IT Security Act** and the **National Cyber Security Strategy**, which we have seen previously. These measures emphasize the protection of critical infrastructure, promote collaboration between public and private sectors, and aim to enhance overall cybersecurity efforts.

13.3.2 Cybersecurity culture

Despite these measures, German organizations often have a false sense of security. Many businesses believe that their current cybersecurity measures are adequate, which often leads to complacency. This inflated sense of security can be attributed to several factors, including an overreliance on traditional security measures and a lack of awareness about the evolving nature of cyber threats. Complacency is dangerous, especially given the increasing sophistication of cyberattacks. German companies are not sufficiently prepared for the advanced persistent threats (APTs) that can penetrate traditional defenses. This gap in preparedness is particularly alarming in critical sectors such as manufacturing, energy, and finance, where the impact of a successful cyberattack can be devastating.

A critical aspect of enhancing cybersecurity culture in Germany involves promoting best practices across all organizational levels. This includes regular software updates, strong password policies, and robust incident response plans. Continuous education and training programs are also important for keeping employees informed about the latest threats and cybersecurity practices.

Furthermore, the adoption of advanced technologies such as artificial intelligence and machine learning for threat detection and response is essential. These technologies can help identify unusual patterns and potential threats more effectively than traditional methods; however, their implementation requires significant investment and a shift in the organizational mindset toward proactive cybersecurity measures.

The German government also promotes international collaboration. Cyber threats are borderless, and its participation in international cybersecurity efforts, such as those led by the European Union and NATO, is vital for a comprehensive defense strategy. These alliances facilitate the exchange of information and resources, enhancing Germany's ability to respond to global cyber threats.

Looking ahead, Germany must address several key areas to strengthen its cybersecurity culture. First, there needs to be a shift from a reactive cybersecurity approach to a proactive one. This includes investing in advanced threat detection technologies and fostering a culture of continuous improvement and vigilance. Second, small and medium-sized enterprises, which form the backbone of the German economy, need more support in enhancing their cybersecurity measures. Many of these enterprises lack the resources and expertise to implement cybersecurity frameworks, making them vulnerable targets for cybercriminals. Third, increasing public awareness about cybersecurity is crucial. Educational campaigns aimed at both businesses and the general public can help build a more security-conscious society. This includes understanding the risks associated with cyber threats and the steps that can be taken to mitigate them.

Germany's cybersecurity culture is at a crossroads. While the country has a strong regulatory framework and strategic initiatives in place, there is a pressing need to address the false sense of security that prevails among many organizations. Promoting proactive cybersecurity measures, enhancing collaboration, and increasing public awareness, can help Germany build a resilient cybersecurity culture capable of withstanding the evolving threat landscape. As cyber threats continue to grow in sophistication and frequency, a dynamic cybersecurity culture will be essential for safeguarding Germany's technological and industrial leadership. A summary of Germany's cybersecurity culture is represented in Table 13.3.

13.4 JAPAN

13.4.1 Cybersecurity initiatives

Japan has established a framework for cybersecurity driven by a strong commitment to technological innovation and the protection of critical infrastructure. **The National Center of Incident Readiness and Strategy for Cybersecurity** (NISC), established in 2015, is the central agency responsible for coordinating cybersecurity efforts across the nation. NISC plays

Table 13.3 Summary of cybersecurity culture in Germany

SUMMARY OF CYBERSECURITY CULTURE IN GERMANY	
Aspect	**Description**
Government Initiatives	• Federal Office for Information Security (BSI) • National Cybersecurity Strategy • IT Security Act 2.0
Primary Focus	• Protecting critical infrastructure • Compliance • Fostering innovation
Cultural Influences	• Emphasis on privacy • Strong regulatory framework • Sense of security complacency
Challenges	• False sense of security • Inadequate preparedness for advanced threats • Slow adoption of innovative solutions
Impact on National Cybersecurity	Need for more proactive measures and technological adoption to match the evolving threat landscape.

a crucial role in developing and implementing Japan's cybersecurity policies and strategies, by working with the public and private sectors.

A major document guiding Japan's cybersecurity efforts is the **Cybersecurity Strategy**, which is updated periodically to address emerging threats and technological advancements. The most recent strategy, released in 2021, outlines Japan's vision for cybersecurity and sets forth several strategic objectives. These objectives include protecting critical infrastructure, strengthening cyber defenses, coordinating responses to cybersecurity incidents, developing new technologies, improving public awareness through education, and promoting international cooperation.

In addition to the national strategy, Japan has implemented several specific initiatives to enhance cybersecurity, such as the **Basic Act on Cybersecurity.** Enacted in 2014, it provides a legal framework for cybersecurity policies and measures. This law defines the responsibilities of government agencies, businesses, and individuals in protecting cyberspace and establishes NISC as the central coordinating body.

13.4.2 Cybersecurity culture

Japan, a global leader in technology and innovation, faces significant challenges in cybersecurity despite its advanced digital landscape. The country's cybersecurity culture is evolving, driven by increasing cyber threats and the need for more protective measures.

Japan's rapid digital transformation has made it a target for cybercriminals. A staggering number of businesses in Japan experience cyberattacks. Despite this, many organizations still lack adequate cybersecurity measures. The awareness of cyber threats has increased, but the implementation of effective safeguards lags, leaving many businesses vulnerable to attacks such as ransomware, phishing, and data breaches.

Japan has made progress in its cybersecurity efforts, even though significant gaps remain. The country has improved its regulatory framework and incident response capabilities, but these measures are insufficient to address the rapidly evolving threat landscape. The reliance on outdated systems and insufficient investment in cybersecurity infrastructure are critical issues that need addressing.

One of the primary challenges in Japan's cybersecurity culture is the perception of cybersecurity as a secondary concern. Many businesses prioritize operational efficiency and cost saving over investing in cybersecurity measures. This mindset leaves them exposed to potential cyber threats. Even though a considerable number of businesses acknowledge the importance of cybersecurity, they fail to implement comprehensive safeguards due to budget constraints and a lack of expertise.

Another significant challenge Japan faces is the complexity and sophistication of modern cyber threats. Cybercriminals continually develop new methods to exploit vulnerabilities, making it difficult for organizations to keep up. Japan's approach to cybersecurity has historically been reactive rather than proactive, often addressing issues only after incidents occur. This reactive stance is inadequate in the face of sophisticated attacks that require advanced threat detection and prevention capabilities.

To enhance its cybersecurity culture, Japan must adopt a multifaceted approach that includes technological upgrades, regulatory improvements, and cultural shifts within organizations. A critical step is increasing investment in cybersecurity infrastructure. Upgrading outdated systems and implementing advanced security technologies, such as artificial intelligence and machine learning, can help detect and mitigate threats more effectively. These technologies enable organizations to identify patterns and anomalies that indicate potential cyberattacks, allowing for quicker and more effective responses.

Education and training are also vital components of a strong cybersecurity culture. Regular training sessions can help employees recognize phishing attempts, understand the importance of strong passwords, and follow proper data handling protocols. This proactive approach reduces the risk of human error, a common factor in many cybersecurity incidents.

The Japanese government plays a crucial role in shaping the country's cybersecurity landscape. Strengthening regulatory frameworks and enforcing compliance with cybersecurity standards is essential. The government should incentivize businesses to invest in cybersecurity through grants, tax breaks, and other financial support mechanisms. Additionally, public-private partnerships can facilitate the sharing of threat intelligence and best practices, helping organizations stay ahead of emerging threats.

Shifting from a reactive to a proactive cybersecurity mindset is critical for Japan. This involves not only responding to incidents but also anticipating potential threats and vulnerabilities. Regular security assessments and penetration testing can help identify weaknesses before they are exploited. Organizations should also develop and regularly update their incident response plans to ensure they can respond quickly and effectively when attacks occur.

Fostering a culture of security at all organizational levels is another important aspect. Leadership commitment is crucial in setting the tone and prioritizing cybersecurity investments. Executives and board members should understand the strategic importance of cybersecurity and allocate resources accordingly. Encouraging a top-down approach ensures that cybersecurity is integrated into the overall business strategy rather than being treated as an IT issue.

Japan's cybersecurity culture also needs improvements. While progress has been made, significant challenges remain that require immediate attention. Increasing investment in

Table 13.4 Summary of cybersecurity culture in Japan

SUMMARY OF CYBERSECURITY CULTURE IN JAPAN	
ASPECT	DESCRIPTION
Government Initiatives	• National Center of Incident Readiness and Strategy for Cybersecurity (NISC) • Cybersecurity Strategy
Primary Focus	• Technological innovation • Critical infrastructure protection • Public education
Cultural Influences	• Prioritization of operational efficiency over cybersecurity • Slow transition from reactive to proactive security
Challenges	• Inadequate cybersecurity investments • Outdated systems • Perception of cybersecurity as secondary
Impact on National Cybersecurity	Need for increased investment, continuous education, and proactive security postures to counter rapidly evolving cyber threats.

cybersecurity infrastructure, enhancing education and training, strengthening regulatory frameworks, and promoting a proactive cybersecurity mindset can help Japan build a cybersecurity culture capable of withstanding the evolving threat landscape. As cyber threats continue to grow in sophistication and frequency, a comprehensive and dynamic approach to cybersecurity will be essential for safeguarding Japan's technological and economic leadership in the digital age. A summary of Japan's cybersecurity culture is presented in Table 13.4.

13.5 CONCLUSION

This chapter has explored the diverse cybersecurity initiatives and cultures across the globe, examining how various countries approach the challenge of securing their digital environments. Unique government initiatives, policies, and organizational practices of key nations, such as Canada, the United Kingdom, Germany, and Japan, provide valuable insights into the best practices, innovative strategies, and critical roles of collaboration that enhance global cybersecurity resilience.

Understanding these varied approaches underscores the importance of tailoring cybersecurity efforts to cultural and regional contexts. Each country's unique blend of strategies reflects its political, economic, and social environment, highlighting that there is no one-size-fits-all solution to cybersecurity. By fostering a global culture of cybersecurity that promotes cooperation, trust, and mutual assistance, it will be possible to better combat the ever-evolving cyber threats that transcend national borders.

This exploration of global cybersecurity cultures reveals common themes and unique practices that can inform and inspire international cooperation and the development of best practices. The insights gained from examining these diverse approaches emphasize the need for continuous learning, adaptation, and collaboration in the global cybersecurity landscape.

As one looks toward the future, it is essential to consider how these cultural insights can shape the evolution of cybersecurity. The next chapter will look at the future of cybersecurity culture, exploring emerging trends, technologies, and ethical considerations that will influence the way we approach cybersecurity in the years to come. By doing so, one can create a more secure digital world for future generations, building on the foundations of diverse cybersecurity cultures.

DISCUSSION QUESTIONS

1. How do cultural factors influence the cybersecurity strategies of different countries, such as Canada and Japan? Discuss how cultural norms, values, and societal attitudes shape the approach to cybersecurity in these nations.
2. What role do public-private partnerships play in enhancing national cybersecurity in the countries discussed? Examine the effectiveness of these partnerships in countries like the United Kingdom and Germany, and how they contribute to overall cybersecurity resilience.
3. Why is it important to understand the cybersecurity culture of different countries when developing global cybersecurity strategies? Discuss the benefits and challenges of integrating diverse approaches into a cohesive global strategy.
4. What are the unique challenges faced by countries like Japan and Germany in developing a strong cybersecurity culture? Explore how these challenges impact their ability to respond to evolving cyber threats and what strategies might help overcome them.
5. How do government-led initiatives, such as the National Cyber Security Centre in the UK, shape the cybersecurity landscape in their respective countries? Analyze the effectiveness of these institutions and their impact on national cybersecurity efforts.
6. In what ways does the rapid adoption of new technologies impact the cybersecurity cultures of countries like Japan? Discuss the trade-offs between innovation and security, and how these countries manage the associated risks.
7. What lessons can other countries learn from Canada's emphasis on collaboration and education in cybersecurity? Consider how these elements contribute to a more resilient cybersecurity culture and whether they could be applied effectively in other contexts.
8. How does the cybersecurity culture in Germany reflect its regulatory framework and compliance-driven approach? Discuss the strengths and weaknesses of this approach in fostering a proactive cybersecurity culture.
9. How do different countries balance the need for technological innovation with the requirement for robust cybersecurity measures? Compare and contrast the approaches of countries like Japan, which prioritizes innovation, with those of other nations that emphasize regulatory compliance.
10. What are the potential benefits and drawbacks of a one-size-fits-all approach to global cybersecurity? Debate whether it is feasible or desirable to develop universal cybersecurity standards, given the diverse cultural, political, and economic contexts of different countries.

BIBLIOGRAPHY

Andronache, A. (2021). Increasing security awareness through lenses of cybersecurity culture. *Journal of Information Systems & Operations Management, 15*(1), 7. https://www.researchgate.net/profile/Alina-Andronache-2/publication/353322243_Increasing_Security_Awarenesss_Through_Lenses_of_Cybersecurity_Culture/links/613c994f4e1df271062b528b/Increasing-Security-Awarenesss-Through-Lenses-of-Cybersecurity-Culture.pdf

Appalraju, Y. (2023, October 19). Canadian organizations must prepare for worst-case cyber threats now. EY. https://www.ey.com/en_ca/cybersecurity/organizations-must-prepare-for-cyber-threats

Bhatt, S. (2023, September 1). Cybersecurity in the digital age: Fortifying businesses against cyber threats. tntra.io. https://www.tntra.io/blog/cybersecurity-digital-era-protecting-businesses/#:~:text=The%20fact%20that%2097.1%25%20of,acknowledged%20having%20no%20such%20safeguards

Carayannis, E. G., Campbell, D. F. J., & Efthymiopoulos, M. P. (Eds.). (2014). *Cyber-development, cyber-democracy and cyber-defense: Challenges, opportunities and implications for theory, policy and practice*. Springer. https://doi.org/10.1007/978-1-4939-1028-1

Department for International Trade. (n.d.). Cyber security export strategy. https://assets.publishing.service.gov.uk/media/5ab52043ed915d78bc23464e/CCS151_CCS0118810124-1_Cyber_Security_Export_Strategy_Brochure_Web_Accessible.pdf

Department of Science, Innovation and Technology. (2023, April 19). Cyber security breaches survey 2023. https://www.gov.uk/government/statistics/cyber-security-breaches-survey-2023/cyber-security-breaches-survey-2023

DigWatch. (September 2021). Cybersecurity for All Cybersecurity which leaves no-one behind. https://www.nisc.go.jp/pdf/policy/kihon-s/cs-senryaku2021-en-booklet.pdf

EY. (2023, October 19). Canadian organizations averaged 25 cybersecurity incidents in the past year, finds EY survey [Press release]. https://www.ey.com/en_ca/news/2023/10/canadian-organizations-averaged-twenty-five-cybersecurity-incidents-in-past-year

Federal Ministry of Interior, Building and Community. (2021). Cyber security strategy for Germany 2021. https://www.bmi.bund.de/SharedDocs/downloads/EN/themen/it-digital-policy/cybersecurity-strategy-for-germany2021.pdf?__blob=publicationFile

Federal Office of Information Security. (n.d.). Second act on increasing the security of IT systems (German IT Security Act 2.0). https://www.bsi.bund.de/EN/Das-BSI/Auftrag/Gesetze-und-Verordungen/IT-SiG/2-0/it_sig_2-0.html

Federal Office for Information Security. (n.d.). The BSI's mandate. https://www.bsi.bund.de/EN/Das-BSI/Auftrag/auftrag_node.html

Government Communications Headquarters (GCHQ). (n.d.). Government Communications Headquarters. https://www.gchq.gov.uk/

Government of Canada. (2024, May 31). Canadian Centre for Cyber Security. https://www.cyber.gc.ca/en

Government of Canada. (2024, July 15). Communications Security Establishment Canada. https://www.cse-cst.gc.ca/en

Government of Canada. (2022, December 23). Creating a culture of cybersecurity in your business. https://ised-isde.canada.ca/site/cybersecure-canada/en/node/46

Government of Canada. (2024, June 4). Parliamentary Committee Notes: National Cyber Security Strategy. https://www.securitepublique.gc.ca/cnt/trnsprnc/brfng-mtrls/prlmntry-bndrs/20240614/20-en.aspx.

Government of Canada. (2015, December 9). The Canadian Cyber Incident Response Center's (CCIRC) collection of digital information. https://www.publicsafety.gc.ca/cnt/trnsprnc/ccss-nfrmtn-prvc/prvc-mpct-ssssmnt/cndn-cbr-ncdnt-en.aspx

Government of Canada. (2020, December 15). The Cyber Security Cooperation Program. https://www.publicsafety.gc.ca/cnt/ntnl-scrt/cbr-scrt/cprtn-prgrm/index-en.aspx

Gov.UK. (2014, April 7). Cyber essentials scheme: Overview. https://www.gov.uk/government/publications/cyber-essentials-scheme-overview

Griffiths, C. (2024, July 1). The latest 2024 cyber crime statistics (updated July 2024). AAG-IT.com. https://aag-it.com/the-latest-cyber-crime-statistics/

Haapala, A. (2024, January 10). *Professor of practice Mikko Kiviharju: Businesses must develop their cyber skills continuously*. Aalto University Executive Education Professional Development. https://www.aaltoee.fi/en/training-programs

Hathaway, M., Demchak, C., Kerben, J., McArdle, J., & Spidalieri, F. (2016, October). *Germany cyber readiness at a glance*. Potomac Institute for Policy Studies. https://potomacinstitute.org/images/CRI/CRI_Germany_Profile_PIPS.pdf

Inoue, Y. (2023, July 13). No longer a 'catastrophe,' Japan's cybersecurity could still improve. The Japan Times. https://www.japantimes.co.jp/news/2023/07/13/national/japan-cybersecurity-improvements-ransomware/

IT World Canada Staff. (2023, September 28). *Unveiling the hidden challenges of cybersecurity culture*. IT World Canada. https://www.itworldcanada.com/article/unveiling-the-hidden-challenges-of-cybersecurity-culture/547897

Japanese Law Tradition. (2014, November 12). The Basic Act on cybersecurity. https://www.japaneselawtranslation.go.jp/en/laws/view/3677/en

Lyttle, R. J. (2016). Is Canadian cyber culture secure?. Canadian Forces College – Collège des Forces Canadiennes, JCSP 40 – PCEMI 40. https://www.cfc.forces.gc.ca/259/290/301/305/lyttle.pdf

MixMode Threat Research. (2024, May 8). Global Cybercrime Report 2024: Which countries face the highest risk? MixMode. https://mixmode.ai/blog/global-cybercrime-report-2024-which-countries-face-the-highest-risk/

National Center of Incident Readiness and Strategy for Cybersecurity. (2018, July 27). Cybersecurity strategy. https://www.nisc.go.jp/eng/pdf/cs-senryaku2018-en.pdf

National Cyber Security Center. (n.d.). Cyber Aware Campaign. https://www.ncsc.gov.uk/cyberaware/home

NISC. (n.d.) Commitment to a free, fair and secure cyberspace. https://www.nisc.go.jp/eng/index.html

Novalnet. (n.d.). Alliance for cyber security: United against cyber threats. https://www.novalnet.com/alliance-for-cyber-security/

O'Toole, C. (2023, January 6). Culture of Cybersecurity. NYC design. https://medium.com/nyc-design/culture-of-cybersecurity-a8b65329af32

Public Safety Canada. (2018). National cyber security strategy: Canada's vision for security and prosperity in the digital age. https://www.publicsafety.gc.ca/cnt/rsrcs/pblctns/ntnl-cbr-scrt-strtg/index-en.aspx

Romaniuk, S. N., & Manjikian, M. (Eds.). (2021). *Routledge companion to global cyber-security strategy* (1st ed.). Routledge. https://doi.org/10.4324/9780429399718

Rupp, C., & Herpig, S. (2021, December). *Germany's cybersecurity architecture*. Translation of the 7th German Edition (October 2021). https://www.interface-eu.org/storage/files_for_publications/2023/231019_cyber_architecture/7thed_cybersecurityarchitecture.pdf

Schallbruch, M., & Skierka, I. (2018). Cybersecurity in Germany. In Sylvia Kierkegaard, John Mallery, Steven J. Murdoch, Kenneth Geers, & Michael Kasper (Eds.), *Cybersecurity in Germany* (pp. 31–47). Digital Society Institute. https://doi.org/10.1007/978-3-319-90014-8_4

Schumacher, D. (2022, April 12). Cyber security in Germany: Deceptive sense of security. IBsolutions. https://www.ibsolution.com/academy/blog_en/sap-cyber-security/cyber-security-in-germany-deceptive-sense-of-security

Sofio, D. G., Carter, W. A., Siedschlag, A., & Jerkovic, A. (2018). Putting US cybersecurity culture in perspective. In *Homeland security cultures: Enhancing values while fostering resilience* (pp. 103–126). Rowman & Littlefield Intl.

The Basic Act on Cybersecurity (Act No. 104 of 2014). https://www.japaneselawtranslation.go.jp/en/laws/view/3677/en

The National Cyber Security Centre. (n.d.). The National Cyber Security Centre. https://www.ncsc.gov.uk/

UK Government. (2022–2030). Government Cyber Security Strategy - Building a cyber resilient public sector. https://assets.publishing.service.gov.uk/media/61f0169de90e070375c230a8/government-cyber-security-strategy.pdf

Chapter 14

The future of cybersecurity culture

As the complexities of the digital age are navigated, the landscape of cybersecurity is continually evolving. Technological advancements, changing workforce dynamics, and an increasing number of cyber threats are reshaping the approach to cybersecurity. Understanding the future of cybersecurity culture is crucial for organizations to anticipate and prepare for these changes. This chapter aims to provide a comprehensive overview of these trends and challenges that will shape the future of cybersecurity.

The rapid development of technologies, such as Artificial Intelligence (AI), Machine Learning (ML), the Internet of Things (IoT), and Quantum Computing (QC), is transforming the cybersecurity field. These technologies offer both opportunities and challenges, requiring innovative approaches to protect digital assets and infrastructure. As these advancements continue to evolve, they will significantly impact how organizations manage and implement cybersecurity measures.

Workforce dynamics are also shifting, with remote work becoming more prevalent and the role of cybersecurity professionals expanding. Continuous education and learning new skills are essential to keep pace with the fast-changing threat landscape. For example, the role of the chief information security officer (CISO) is evolving to encompass strategic leadership and alignment with business objectives, highlighting the need for strong leadership knowledge and experience as well as cybersecurity training.

Ethical considerations in cybersecurity are becoming increasingly important as organizations strive to balance privacy and security. Issues such as ethical hacking, data protection, and human rights in the digital realm require careful navigation to ensure ethical practices in cybersecurity.

Emerging threats, including AI-powered attacks, IoT vulnerabilities, and quantum computing challenges, underscore the need for advanced defense strategies. Understanding these threats and developing mitigation techniques are critical for maintaining a secure digital environment.

This chapter will explore these future trends in detail, examining their implications for organizations and the broader cybersecurity landscape. Understanding these trends and preparing for the challenges ahead can help build a more secure and resilient digital future.

14.1 FUTURE TRENDS IN CYBERSECURITY CULTURE

Looking toward the future, one can see significant transformation in the field of cybersecurity. Emerging technologies, evolving workforce dynamics, and changing regulatory environments will all play critical roles in shaping the future of cybersecurity culture. Staying ahead of these trends is essential for organizations to safeguard their digital assets. This section explores key future trends, as shown in Figure 14.1, including technological

DOI: 10.1201/9781003368496-14

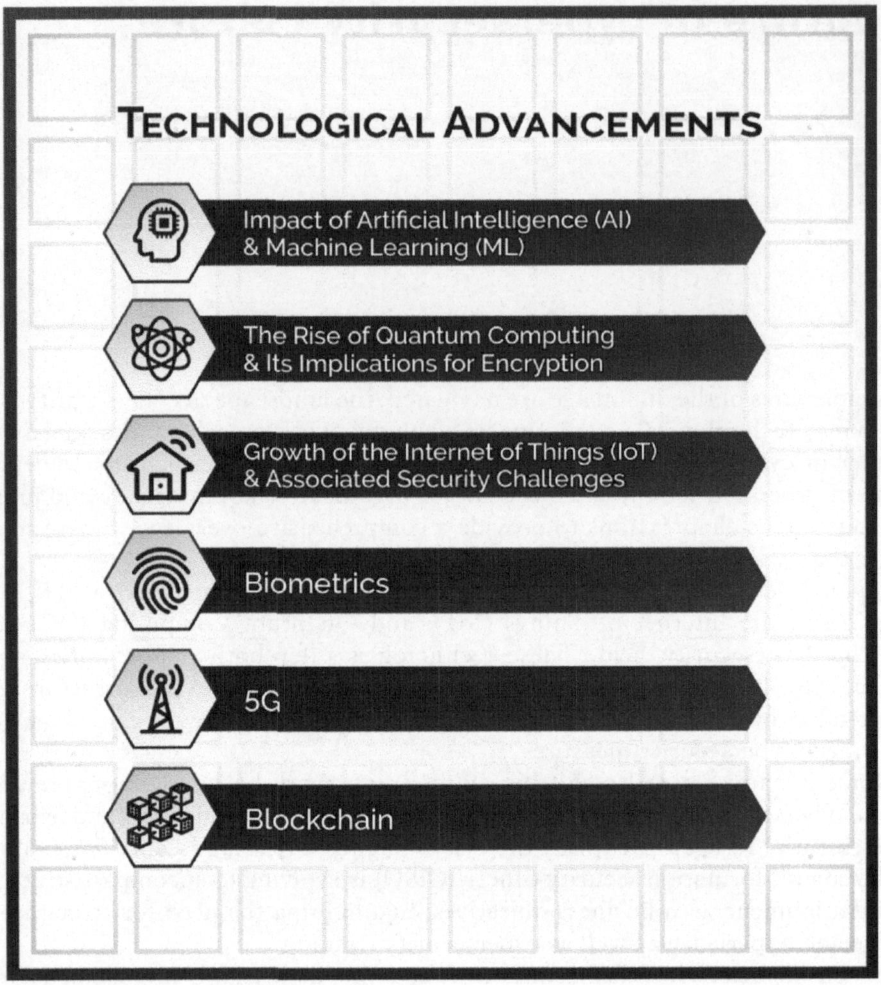

Figure 14.1 Technological advancements.

advancements like AI and quantum computing, the shift in workforce practices, the role of cybersecurity in sustainable development, and the evolution of education and training in the cybersecurity field. By understanding and preparing for these developments, organizations can navigate the complexities of the digital future with confidence.

14.1.1 Technological advancements

14.1.1.1 Impact of artificial intelligence (AI) and machine learning (ML) on cybersecurity

AI and ML are revolutionizing the field of cybersecurity. These technologies enable the automation of threat detection and response, allowing for faster and more accurate identification of potential cyber threats. AI can analyze vast amounts of data in real time, recognizing patterns and anomalies that might indicate a cyberattack. For example, AI-driven security systems can monitor network traffic and detect unusual activities that could signify a breach. Additionally, ML algorithms improve over time by learning from past incidents, making them more effective at predicting and preventing future attacks; however, the same technologies can also be used by cybercriminals to develop more sophisticated attacks, such as AI-generated phishing emails or automated vulnerability exploitation. This dual-use nature of AI and ML underscores the need for continuous innovation and vigilance in cybersecurity.

14.1.1.2 The rise of quantum computing and its implications for encryption

Quantum computing promises to revolutionize many fields, including cybersecurity. Unlike classical computers, quantum computers use the principles of quantum mechanics to process information at unprecedented speeds. This capability poses a significant threat to current encryption methods, which rely on the difficulty of solving complex mathematical problems. Quantum computers could potentially break these encryption algorithms in a fraction of the time it would take classical computers. To address this challenge, the development of quantum-resistant cryptographic algorithms is crucial. These new algorithms are designed to withstand the computational power of quantum computers, ensuring the continued protection of sensitive data. Organizations must stay informed about advancements in quantum computing and prepare to transition to quantum-resistant encryption methods as they become available.

14.1.1.3 Growth of the Internet of Things (IoT) and associated security challenges

The Internet of Things (IoT) is rapidly expanding, connecting billions of devices worldwide. While IoT offers numerous benefits, such as increased efficiency and convenience, it also introduces significant security challenges. Many IoT devices are designed with limited processing power and memory, making it difficult to implement security measures. Additionally, the sheer number of connected devices increases the attack surface, providing more entry points for cybercriminals. Ensuring the security of IoT ecosystems requires a multifaceted approach. Manufacturers must design devices with security in mind, incorporating features such as secure boot, encrypted communication, and regular firmware updates. Users must also be educated about the importance of securing their IoT devices, including changing default passwords and keeping software up-to-date. Regulatory frameworks may also play a role in establishing minimum security standards for IoT devices.

14.1.1.4 Biometrics

Biometric authentication, which uses unique biological traits such as fingerprints, facial recognition, or iris scans, is becoming increasingly popular as a method of securing systems and data. The appeal of biometrics lies in its ability to provide a high level of security that is difficult to replicate or steal; however, the use of biometrics also raises privacy concerns and introduces new security risks. For example, once biometric data is compromised, it cannot be changed like a password. To mitigate these risks, organizations must implement strong encryption and secure storage methods for biometric data, as well as consider multifactor authentication that combines biometrics with other forms of verification. As biometric technology advances, balancing security with privacy and ethical considerations will be crucial.

14.1.1.5 5G

The rollout of 5G technology marks a significant leap in telecommunications, offering faster speeds, lower latency, and the ability to connect a vast number of devices simultaneously.

That being said, with these advancements come new security challenges. The increased speed and connectivity provided by 5G can also facilitate faster and more complex cyberattacks. Additionally, the reliance on software-defined networks (SDNs) and virtualization in 5G networks introduces new vulnerabilities that cybercriminals could exploit. Ensuring the security of 5G networks requires effective measures, including secure network architecture, encryption of data in transit, and continuous monitoring for potential threats. As 5G becomes more widespread, organizations must be proactive in addressing these security concerns to protect their data and operations.

14.1.1.6 Blockchain

Blockchain technology, best known as the foundation of cryptocurrencies like Bitcoin, offers a decentralized and tamper-resistant method of recording transactions. Its potential applications in cybersecurity are vast, particularly in enhancing data integrity and transparency. By using blockchain, organizations can create immutable records that are resistant to tampering and fraud, making it an attractive option for securing sensitive data and transactions; however, blockchain is not without its challenges. The technology requires significant computational power and can be complex to implement and manage. Additionally, while blockchain itself is secure, the surrounding infrastructure, such as smart contracts and wallets, can be vulnerable to attacks. To fully leverage the benefits of blockchain in cybersecurity, organizations must carefully design and secure their blockchain implementations while remaining vigilant against emerging threats.

Understanding and addressing these technological advancements can better prepare organizations for the future of cybersecurity. Adapting to these changes will be essential in maintaining a secure digital environment in the face of evolving threats.

14.1.2 Changing workforce dynamics

14.1.2.1 Remote work and its impact on cybersecurity practices

The shift to remote work, accelerated by the COVID-19 pandemic, has fundamentally changed the cybersecurity landscape. With employees accessing corporate networks from various locations, securing remote work environments has become a priority. Remote work introduces several security challenges, such as securing home networks, managing personal devices used for work, and ensuring secure access to corporate resources. Organizations must adapt by implementing strong remote work policies, using virtual private networks (VPNs), multifactor authentication (MFA), and continuous monitoring to protect their digital assets. Additionally, employees must be trained in best practices for remote work security, such as recognizing phishing attempts, using secure passwords, and avoiding public Wi-Fi for work-related activities.

14.1.2.2 The evolving role of the chief information security officer (CISO)

The role of the chief information security officer (CISO) is evolving to meet the increasing complexity of the cybersecurity landscape. CISOs are now expected to be strategic leaders who not only manage cybersecurity risks but also align security initiatives with business objectives and organizational strategies. This expanded role requires CISOs to have a broad skill set, including technical expertise, strategic thinking, and leadership abilities. CISOs must collaborate with other departments, communicate effectively with executive leadership, and ensure compliance with regulatory requirements. They also play a critical role in fostering a culture of cybersecurity within the organization, ensuring that all employees understand their roles in protecting the organization's digital assets.

14.1.2.3 The importance of continuous education and professional development for cybersecurity professionals

The rapid pace of technological change and the evolving threat landscape make continuous education and professional development essential for cybersecurity professionals. Regular training and certification programs help professionals stay current with the latest tools, techniques, and best practices. Organizations should invest in the professional development of their cybersecurity teams, providing opportunities for training, certifications, and participation in industry conferences and workshops. Continuous education is not only about keeping up with technology but also about understanding new regulatory requirements and best practices. This ongoing education ensures that cybersecurity professionals are well-equipped to handle emerging threats and challenges, making the organization more resilient and prepared for the future.

Understanding and adapting to these changing workforce dynamics can help organizations build stronger cybersecurity postures. Embracing remote work security practices, empowering CISOs with strategic leadership roles, and investing in continuous education for cybersecurity professionals will be crucial in navigating the future of cybersecurity culture.

14.1.3 Regulatory and policy developments

14.1.3.1 Anticipating new regulations and compliance requirements

As cyber threats evolve, so do the regulations and compliance requirements aimed at protecting data and systems. Governments and regulatory bodies worldwide are continually updating their cybersecurity frameworks to address new threats and vulnerabilities. For instance, regulations like the General Data Protection Regulation (GDPR) in Europe have set high standards for data protection and privacy. Similar laws are being enacted globally, increasing the need for organizations to stay informed about these changes. Companies must ensure compliance with relevant regulations to avoid penalties and protect their reputations. This includes understanding the requirements of frameworks such as GDPR and HIPAA which both were covered in previous chapters, and new national cybersecurity laws as well as implementing the necessary measures to comply with them. Regular audits, updated policies, and compliance programs are essential components of a strong cybersecurity strategy.

14.1.3.2 The role of governments in shaping cybersecurity policies

Governments play a critical role in shaping cybersecurity policies and frameworks. They establish regulations, provide guidance, and enforce compliance to protect national security and economic interests. Governments also invest in cybersecurity research and development, support public awareness campaigns, and foster international collaboration to address global cyber threats. Governments can help organizations and individuals improve their cybersecurity posture by creating a supportive policy environment. For example, initiatives like the National Institute of Standards and Technology (NIST) Cybersecurity Framework in the United States provide guidelines for managing and reducing cybersecurity risk. Such frameworks offer a structured approach for organizations to follow, helping them build resilient cybersecurity programs.

14.1.3.3 Trends in international cybersecurity agreements and treaties

International collaboration is essential for addressing global cyber threats. Trends in international cybersecurity agreements and treaties reflect a growing recognition of the need for cooperative efforts. These agreements facilitate the sharing of threat intelligence, promote best practices, and establish norms for responsible behavior in cyberspace. Examples include the Budapest Convention on Cybercrime, which is one of the first international treaties seeking to address internet and computer crime by harmonizing national laws. This subsequently improved investigative techniques and increased cooperation among nations. Joint agreements between countries to combat cybercrime and enhance cybersecurity cooperation are also becoming more common. Such collaborations help create a unified global approach to cybersecurity, making it harder for cybercriminals to exploit jurisdictional gaps.

Organizations can better navigate the complexities of compliance and enhance their cybersecurity posture by understanding and anticipating regulatory and policy developments. Staying informed about new regulations, leveraging government frameworks, and participating in international agreements are crucial steps in building a strong cybersecurity culture.

14.1.4 Role of cybersecurity culture in sustainable development

Cybersecurity plays a vital role in achieving Sustainable Development Goals (SDGs). As digital technologies become integral to economic growth, social development, and environmental sustainability, protecting these technologies from cyber threats is crucial. Secure digital infrastructure ensures the reliable delivery of essential services such as healthcare, education, and financial services, which are foundational to sustainable development. For example, a secure health information system can protect patient data while ensuring that healthcare providers have timely access to accurate information, thereby improving health outcomes.

Cybersecurity also supports innovation and the digital economy, which are critical drivers of sustainable development. Protecting intellectual property and sensitive business information can foster secure environments where innovation can thrive. This, in turn, contributes to economic growth and job creation, aligning with SDG goals and economic growth. Cybersecurity also helps protect critical infrastructure from cyberattacks. It ensures the stability of services that underpin modern societies, such as energy, water, and transportation.

Integrating cybersecurity into national development plans is crucial for building sustainable digital ecosystems. Governments should incorporate cybersecurity strategies into their broader development agendas, ensuring that cybersecurity measures are aligned with economic and social objectives. This integration promotes a holistic approach to development, where cybersecurity is seen as an enabler of progress rather than a standalone issue. For instance, national policies can mandate the inclusion of cybersecurity in the design and implementation of new digital services and infrastructure projects. This ensures that security considerations are integrated from the outset rather than being an afterthought. Governments can invest in building cybersecurity capacity through education and training programs, fostering a skilled workforce capable of supporting the secure growth of the digital economy.

International cooperation is essential in integrating cybersecurity into sustainable development. Collaborative efforts can help share best practices, provide technical assistance, and develop global standards that enhance security across borders. Organizations such as the United Nations and the World Bank can play a pivotal role in facilitating these collaborations, ensuring that all countries, regardless of their level of development, can benefit from solid cybersecurity practices.

Building a culture of cybersecurity awareness is fundamental to achieving sustainable development. This involves educating the public about cyber threats and promoting responsible behavior online. Awareness campaigns, training programs, and public-private partnerships can help disseminate information about best practices for cybersecurity, empowering individuals and organizations to protect themselves and their data.

Integrating cybersecurity education into the curriculum in schools can prepare the next generation to navigate the digital world securely. For businesses, regular training and awareness programs can reduce the risk of human error, which is often a significant factor in security breaches.

In conclusion, the role of cybersecurity in sustainable development cannot be overstated. By supporting innovation, protecting critical services, and fostering a culture of awareness, cybersecurity enables the secure and sustainable growth of digital economies. Integrating cybersecurity into national development plans and international cooperation efforts further enhances this role, ensuring that all nations can benefit from secure digital progress.

14.1.5 Future of cybersecurity education and training

The future of cybersecurity education is evolving rapidly to meet the demands of this complex digital landscape. Educational institutions are incorporating cutting-edge technologies and innovative teaching methods to prepare the next generation of cybersecurity professionals. Virtual labs and simulation environments are becoming essential tools in cybersecurity education. These platforms allow students to gain hands-on experience by engaging in real-world scenarios, such as defending against cyberattacks, conducting penetration tests, and managing security incidents. For instance, students can participate in simulated cyber war games that test their skills in a controlled, risk-free environment.

14.1.5.1 Online learning platforms

These include massive open online courses (MOOCs) and offer flexible and accessible cybersecurity education to a global audience. These platforms provide high-quality content developed by leading experts in the field, enabling learners to acquire new skills and knowledge at their own pace. Partnerships between educational institutions and industry leaders are helping to bridge the gap between theoretical knowledge and practical application. Collaborative programs, internships, and mentorship opportunities give students valuable insights into the real-world challenges faced by cybersecurity professionals.

14.1.5.2 Gamification and simulation

These are transforming cybersecurity training by making learning more engaging and effective. Gamified training platforms use elements such as points, badges, leaderboards, and rewards to motivate learners and track their progress. These platforms create an interactive yet competitive environment that encourages continuous improvement and skill development. For example, cybersecurity professionals can participate in Capture-The-Flag (CTF) competitions, where they solve challenges and vulnerabilities to earn points and advance on the leaderboard.

14.1.5.3 Simulation-based training

It provides a realistic and immersive learning experience. Replicating real-world cyber threats and scenarios allows trainees to practice responding to incidents in a safe and controlled setting. This hands-on approach helps build practical skills and confidence, preparing individuals to handle actual cybersecurity incidents more effectively. Organizations can use simulation platforms to conduct regular drills and exercises, testing their incident response plans and identifying areas for improvement.

14.1.5.4 Continuous professional development

The rapidly changing nature of cyber threats and technologies makes **continuous professional development** essential for cybersecurity professionals. Organizations must invest in the ongoing education of their cybersecurity teams to stay ahead of emerging threats. This includes offering regular training sessions, certifications, and opportunities to attend industry conferences and workshops. For example, certifications such as Certified Information Systems Security Professional (CISSP), Certified Ethical Hacker (CEH), and Offensive Security Certified Professional (OSCP) provide specialized knowledge and skills that are highly valued in the cybersecurity field.

Organizations can also create internal development programs that encourage knowledge sharing and collaboration among employees. Mentorship programs and cross-departmental projects help build a culture of continuous learning and improvement. The growing demand for cybersecurity professionals has highlighted a significant skills gap in the industry. To address this challenge, it is crucial to attract and train a diverse pool of talent. Initiatives to promote cybersecurity careers among underrepresented groups, such as women and minorities, can help broaden the talent pool and bring fresh perspectives to the field. Outreach programs, scholarships, and partnerships with schools and community organizations can inspire and support the next generation of cybersecurity professionals.

Educational institutions and industry leaders must collaborate to align cybersecurity curricula with the needs of the job market. This involves regularly updating course content to reflect the latest threats, technologies, and best practices. Apprenticeship programs and on-the-job training opportunities provide practical experience and help bridge the gap between education and employment.

In conclusion, the future of cybersecurity education and training is characterized by innovation, flexibility, and a focus on practical skills. Embracing new technologies, gamification, and continuous professional development can better prepare individuals to meet the challenges of the cybersecurity landscape. Looking toward the future, it's clear that the landscape of cybersecurity will be shaped by rapid technological advancements, evolving workforce dynamics, and ever-changing regulatory frameworks. Embracing innovations such as AI, quantum computing, and IoT will be crucial for staying ahead of emerging threats while adapting to new work environments, and continuous education will ensure a well-prepared and resilient cybersecurity workforce. Furthermore, integrating cybersecurity into sustainable development plans highlights its critical role in supporting broader economic and social goals; however, with these advancements come new ethical challenges. The balance between privacy and security, the ethical implications of surveillance, and the responsible use of emerging technologies are just a few of the considerations that will become increasingly important. As these complexities are navigated, it is essential to maintain a strong ethical foundation in cybersecurity practices.

The following section will investigate the ethics of cybersecurity culture. It will explore how ethical considerations intersect with technological and strategic developments and discuss the principles that should guide your actions in this field. Understanding and addressing these ethical challenges will be crucial in building a secure, fair, and trustworthy digital future.

14.2 ETHICS IN CYBERSECURITY CULTURE

Ethical considerations are becoming increasingly important in the field of cybersecurity as advanced technologies are implemented and new strategies are developed to protect digital environments. It is imperative to consider the ethical implications of our actions. Balancing privacy and security, ensuring responsible use of data, and protecting individual rights are just a few of the ethical challenges that cybersecurity professionals face. This section, as summarized in Table 14.1, will explore the fundamental ethical principles that should guide cybersecurity practices, examine the ethical dilemmas that arise in the field, and discuss how organizations can foster a culture of ethical behavior in their cybersecurity efforts.

14.2.1 Balance between privacy and security

One of the most significant ethical challenges in cybersecurity is finding the **right balance between privacy and security.** On one hand, organizations need to implement strong security measures to protect sensitive data and prevent cyberattacks. On the other hand, these measures can sometimes infringe on individuals' privacy rights. For example, extensive

Table 14.1 Ethical challenges

ETHICAL CHALLENGES			
ETHICAL CHALLENGE	DESCRIPTION	POTENTIAL RISKS	BEST PRACTICES FOR ETHICAL MANAGEMENT
Balancing Privacy and Security	Finding a balance between implementing security measures and protecting individuals' privacy rights.	· Overstepping privacy boundaries · Leading to distrust · Potential legal challenges	· Implement transparent policies that clearly define the scope of data collection and use · Ensure compliance with privacy laws
Ethical Hacking and Penetration Testing	Ensuring that ethical hacking practices, such as penetration testing, are conducted with proper authorization and transparency.	· Unauthorized access · Data breaches · Misuse of discovered vulnerabilities	· Obtain explicit consent · Ensure actions align with legal and ethical guidelines
Responsible Vulnerability Disclosure	Determining when and how to disclose vulnerabilities responsibly without putting systems at greater risk.	· Delays in disclosure could leave systems vulnerable · Immediate disclosure could lead to exploitation	· Follow responsible disclosure guidelines, coordinate with affected parties · Allow time for patch development
Ethical Use of Data and User Consent	Using collected data ethically, with informed user consent and clear communication about how data will be used.	· Data breaches · Misuse · Loss of trust · Legal penalties for non-compliance	· Adopt transparent data policies · Secure data storage · Regularly review consent practices
Surveillance and Monitoring	Navigating the fine line between necessary surveillance for security and potential overreach or misuse.	· Creating a culture of surveillance · Eroding trust · Potentially violating privacy rights	Ensure surveillance measures are necessary, proportionate, and comply with legal standards
Human Rights Considerations	Protecting fundamental human rights, such as freedom of expression and privacy, while maintaining cybersecurity measures.	· Excessive control · Censorship · Surveillance that infringes on human rights	· Develop policies that protect both security and human rights · Advocate for balanced regulations

monitoring and data collection practices can help detect and prevent malicious activities but can also lead to concerns about surveillance and the misuse of personal information. Cybersecurity professionals must navigate this delicate balance, ensuring that security measures do not violate privacy rights, and that personal data is handled ethically and transparently.

14.2.2 Ethical hacking and penetration testing

These are essential practices in cybersecurity, helping organizations identify and fix vulnerabilities before malicious actors can exploit them; however, these activities raise ethical questions about the boundaries of acceptable behavior. For instance, ethical hackers must obtain explicit permission before testing systems, and they must handle any discovered data responsibly. There is the ethical issue of disclosure—how much information about vulnerabilities should be shared with the public or third parties, and when? Cybersecurity professionals must adhere to strict ethical guidelines to ensure that their actions are legal, authorized, and conducted with the highest integrity.

14.2.3 Ethical dilemma of how to disclose

When cybersecurity professionals discover vulnerabilities, they face the **ethical dilemma of how to disclose** this information responsibly. Immediate public disclosure can lead to widespread exploitation of the vulnerability before a fix is available while delaying disclosure can leave systems exposed for longer periods. The responsible disclosure process typically involves privately informing the affected organization and allowing them time to develop and implement a patch before making the information public. This approach balances the need to protect users and systems with the ethical obligation to inform and protect the broader community. Notwithstanding, this process can be complicated by various factors, including the responsiveness of the affected organization and the potential impact on users.

14.2.4 Use of data and ensuring user consent

The ethical **use of data and ensuring user consent** is a crucial aspect of cybersecurity. Organizations collect vast amounts of data to improve services, enhance security, and drive business decisions; however, ethical dilemmas arise when it comes to obtaining informed consent from users, protecting data from breaches, and ensuring that data is used for its intended purpose. Cybersecurity professionals must implement stringent data protection measures, be transparent about data collection practices, and ensure that users are fully informed about how their data will be used. They must also consider the ethical implications of data usage, such as avoiding discriminatory practices and respecting user autonomy.

14.2.5 Surveillance and monitoring

Surveillance and monitoring are common practices in cybersecurity to detect and prevent cyber threats; yet, these practices raise ethical concerns about privacy and the potential for abuse. For instance, extensive monitoring of employee activities can lead to a culture of mistrust and infringes on personal privacy. Similarly, government surveillance programs aimed at enhancing national security can sometimes overreach, leading to concerns about civil liberties. Cybersecurity professionals must carefully consider the ethical implications of surveillance and monitoring, ensuring that these practices are proportionate, transparent, and conducted with respect for individual rights.

14.2.6 Human rights

Cybersecurity practices can have significant implications for **human rights**, including freedom of expression, access to information, and the right to privacy. For example, measures to combat cybercrime and terrorism must be balanced with the need to protect human rights and avoid excessive censorship or surveillance. Cybersecurity professionals must navigate these complex issues, ensuring that their actions support and protect human rights rather than undermine them. This involves advocating for policies and practices that promote both security and human rights and being vigilant about the potential for abuse in the name of security.

Navigating ethical dilemmas in cybersecurity requires a strong commitment to ethical principles. Adhering to ethical guidelines and considering the broader implications of their actions can help cybersecurity professionals build a more secure, fair, and trustworthy digital world. As these challenges are navigated, it is clear that ethical considerations are not just an add-on but a fundamental component of a cybersecurity strategy. This draws attention to the emerging threats on the horizon—threats that not only test the limits of technological defenses but also challenge the very ethical principles most strive to uphold.

14.3 EMERGING THREATS

As the digital landscape continues to evolve, so too do the threats that organizations face. Emerging technologies and new attack vectors pose significant challenges for cybersecurity professionals. Understanding these emerging threats, as indicated in Figure 14.2, is essential for developing effective defense strategies and keeping them strong.

14.3.1 AI-Powered attacks

AI is a double-edged sword in cybersecurity. While it promises to revolutionize defenses, it also empowers a new generation of threats. AI-driven attacks leverage ML to automate, scale, and refine traditional cyberattacks, making them more sophisticated and elusive. For instance, AI can rapidly identify and exploit vulnerabilities in complex systems or create highly convincing deepfakes to deceive individuals and organizations; moreover, AI can be used to orchestrate large-scale, coördinated attacks that overwhelm traditional defenses. Beyond these, AI can power highly targeted cyber espionage campaigns, automate the spread of misinformation, and even develop autonomous malware capable of adapting to countermeasures in real time.

AI in cybersecurity faces several significant hurdles. First, the lack of AI autonomy means that AI systems still require human oversight and intervention, limiting their ability to operate independently in complex scenarios. Second, concerns about data privacy are paramount, as AI systems often require access to vast amounts of sensitive information to function effectively, raising risks of data breaches or misuse. Third, the absence of a sufficient legal framework leaves many AI applications in a regulatory gray area, complicating issues related to accountability and compliance. Finally, ethical concerns, such as bias in AI algorithms and the potential for AI to be used maliciously, pose additional risks that must be addressed.

These challenges highlight the need for cautious and responsible integration of AI into cybersecurity strategies, ensuring that its benefits are maximized while its risks are mitigated. As AI continues to evolve, addressing these challenges will be crucial in maintaining a secure and ethical digital environment.

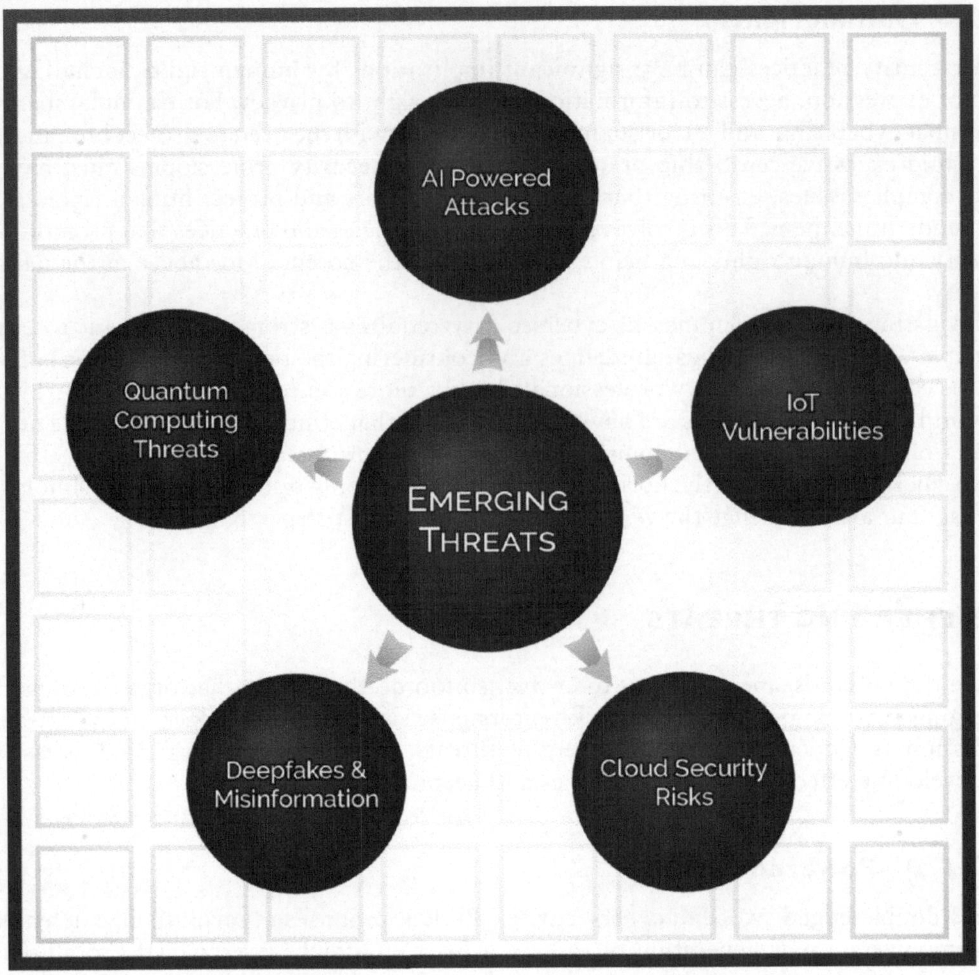

Figure 14.2 Emerging threats.

14.3.2 IoT vulnerabilities

The rise of IoT devices has introduced new security challenges. IoT devices often have limited processing power and memory, making it difficult to implement security measures. The sheer number of connected devices increases the attack surface, providing more entry points for cybercriminals. Common vulnerabilities in IoT devices include weak passwords, lack of encryption, and outdated firmware. To mitigate these risks, manufacturers must design devices with security in mind, incorporating features such as secure boot, encrypted communication, and regular firmware updates. Users also play a critical role in securing IoT devices by changing default passwords, keeping software up to date, and following best practices for network security.

14.3.3 Cloud security risks

As more organizations move their operations to the cloud, securing cloud environments has become a critical concern. Cloud security risks include data breaches, misconfigurations, insecure interfaces, and unauthorized access. The shared responsibility model of cloud security means that while cloud service providers (CSPs) are responsible for securing the infrastructure, customers must secure their data and applications. Best practices for ensuring cloud security include using strong authentication methods, encrypting data at rest and in transit, regularly auditing and monitoring cloud environments, and implementing access controls. Organizations should also ensure that their cloud providers comply with relevant security standards and certifications.

14.3.4 Deepfakes and misinformation

Deepfake technology uses AI to create realistic but fake audio and video content. This technology poses significant threats to cybersecurity and information integrity. Deepfakes can be used for malicious purposes, such as creating fake news, impersonating individuals, and conducting social engineering attacks. For example, a deepfake video of a company CEO making false statements could manipulate stock prices or damage the company's reputation. Combating deepfakes requires advanced detection technologies and public awareness. Educating the public about the existence and potential misuse of deepfakes can help mitigate their impact. Platforms and organizations should invest in technologies that can identify and flag deepfake content to protect themselves from possible implications.

14.3.5 Quantum computing threats

Quantum computing represents a significant leap in computational power, capable of solving complex problems much faster than classical computers. While this has positive implications for many fields, it also poses a threat to current encryption methods. The main concern lies in quantum computers' ability to break current encryption protocols, such as RSA and ECC, which are used to protect sensitive data and secure communications across the digital landscape. The quantum computing capability of breaking these encryptions threatens the security of encrypted financial transactions, personal data, state secrets, and public key infrastructures (PKI), which underpin much of the internet's secure communications. The challenge of transitioning to post-quantum cryptography, which is being developed to resist quantum attacks, adds complexity to the issue. The good news is that the National Institute of Standards and Technology (NIST) released three post-quantum encryption standards in August 2024. These encryptions have the power to resist the attack of quantum computers. While post-quantum algorithms offer promise, updating the vast array of systems reliant on today's encryption standards will require significant time and coordination.

Emerging threats in cybersecurity are continually evolving, driven by advancements in technology and the increasing sophistication of cybercriminals. Understanding these threats, from AI-powered attacks and IoT vulnerabilities to cloud security risks, deepfakes, and the impending impact of quantum computing, is crucial for developing defense strategies. Organizations can protect their digital assets and ensure resilience in the face of new and evolving challenges by staying informed and proactive.

14.4 CONCLUSION

When looking at the future of cybersecurity culture, rapid technological advancements, evolving workforce dynamics, and an ever-changing regulatory environment will shape the landscape. Embracing innovations, such as AI, quantum computing, and IoT, is essential for staying ahead of emerging threats. Additionally, adapting to new work environments and prioritizing continuous education will ensure that cybersecurity professionals are well prepared to tackle future challenges.

Ethical considerations will play a pivotal role in guiding cybersecurity practices. Balancing privacy and security, ensuring responsible data use, and protecting individual rights are critical to maintaining trust in digital systems. Organizations that address these ethical challenges can foster a culture of integrity and accountability.

From AI-powered attacks to quantum computing vulnerabilities, emerging threats underscore the need for defense strategies and proactive risk management. Understanding these threats and developing innovative mitigation techniques will be crucial for maintaining a secure digital environment.

As this exploration of cybersecurity culture concludes, it is clear that the journey does not end here. The digital landscape will continue to evolve, presenting new challenges and opportunities. Embracing innovation, upholding ethical principles, and fostering collaboration can help build a cybersecurity culture that is adaptable, resilient, and prepared for the future. This holistic approach will ensure the protection of digital assets while building a foundation of trust and security that supports the continued growth and development of our digital society.

In the end, the future of cybersecurity culture depends on everyone's collective efforts. As individuals, organizations, and nations, it is important to remain vigilant, adaptable, and committed to safeguarding the digital world. By working together and embracing the principles outlined in this book, you can create a safer, more secure, and more equitable digital future for all.

DISCUSSION QUESTIONS

1. How do technological advancements like AI, ML, and quantum computing present both opportunities and challenges for cybersecurity? What strategies can organizations adopt to balance these dual aspects?
2. In what ways do changing workforce dynamics, such as the rise of remote work, impact cybersecurity practices? How can organizations better secure remote environments?
3. What is the evolving role of the chief information security officer (CISO) in today's cybersecurity landscape, and how can CISOs align cybersecurity strategies with broader business objectives?
4. How do ethical considerations in cybersecurity, such as balancing privacy with security, shape organizational practices? What frameworks can guide ethical decision-making in this context?
5. What are the potential risks and benefits of incorporating biometrics, 5G, and blockchain technology into cybersecurity strategies? How can organizations address the associated challenges?
6. How can organizations prepare for emerging threats like AI-powered attacks, IoT vulnerabilities, and quantum computing risks? What defense strategies should be prioritized?
7. What role does cybersecurity play in sustainable development, and how can organizations integrate cybersecurity into broader national development plans?
8. What are the key components of future cybersecurity education and training? How can gamification, simulation, and continuous professional development enhance the preparedness of cybersecurity professionals?
9. How can international cooperation and treaties help address global cybersecurity threats? What are the potential challenges and opportunities associated with these agreements?

10. What steps can organizations take to foster a culture of continuous learning, ethical behavior, and proactive cybersecurity practices? How can leadership contribute to shaping this culture?

BIBLIOGRAPHY

Althobaiti, O. S., & Dohler, M. (2020). Cybersecurity challenges associated with the Internet of Things in a post-quantum world. *IEEE Access*, *8*, 157356–157381. https://doi.org/10.1109/ACCESS.2020.3019345

Apruzzese, G., Laskov, P., Montes de Oca, E., Mallouli, W., Rapa, L. B., Grammatopoulos, A. V., & Di Franco, F. (2024). The role of machine learning in cybersecurity. *Digital Threats: Research and Practice*, *4*(1), Article 8, 1–38. ACM Digital Library. https://doi.org/10.1145/354557

Aspen Digital. (2023, October). The evolving role of the CISO: More than just security. https://www.aspendigital.org/wp-content/uploads/2023/10/Aspen-Digital_The-Evolving-Role-of-the-CISO_October-2023.pdf

Atstāja, L., Rūtītis, D., Deruma, S., & Aksjoņenko, E. (2021). Cyber security risks and challenges in remote work under the COVID-19 pandemic. In M. Ozsahin (Ed.), *New strategic, social and economic challenges in the age of Society 5.0: Implications for sustainability* (Vol. 121, pp. 12–22). European Publisher. https://doi.org/10.15405/epsbs.2021.12.04.2

Brunner, T. (2021). Cybersecurity in beyond 5G: Use cases, current approaches, trends, and challenges. *Communication Systems*, *XIV*, 28. https://files.ifi.uzh.ch/CSG/teaching/FS21/IFI_2021_02.pdf#page=28

Cabaj, K., Domingos, D., Kotulski, Z., & Respício, A. (2018). Cybersecurity education: Evolution of the discipline and analysis of master programs. *Computers & Security*, *75*, 24–35. https://doi.org/10.1016/j.cose.2018.01.015

Christen, M., Gordijn, B., & Loi, M. (Eds.). (2020). *The ethics of cybersecurity*. Springer Open. https://doi.org/10.1007/978-3-030-29053-5

Debas, E. A., Alajlan, R. S., & Hafizur Rahman, M. M. (2023). Biometric in cybersecurity: A mini review. In *2023 International Conference on Artificial Intelligence in Information and Communication (ICAIIC)* (pp. 570–574). IEEE. https://doi.org/10.1109/ICAIIC57133.2023.10067017

Deloitte. (2023). *Global future of cyber survey*. Deloitte Global. https://www.deloitte.com/global/en/services/risk-advisory/content/future-of-cyber.html

Familoni, B. T. (2024, March 22). Cybersecurity challenges in the age of AI: Theoretical approaches and practical solutions. *Computer Science and IT Research Journals*, *5*(3). https://doi.org/10.51594/csitrj.v5i3.930

Gregory, J. (2024, April 2). *The evolution of a CISO: How the role has changed*. Security Intelligence. https://securityintelligence.com/articles/ciso-role-evolution/

Hossain Faruk, M. J., Tahora, S., Tasnim, M., Shahriar, H., & Sakib, N. (2022). A review of quantum cybersecurity: Threats, risks and opportunities. In *2022 1st International Conference on AI in Cybersecurity (ICAIC)* (pp. 1–8). IEEE. https://doi.org/10.1109/ICAIC53980.2022.9896970

Hussain, A., Mohamed, A., & Razali, S. (2020). A review on cybersecurity: Challenges & emerging threats. In *NISS '20: Proceedings of the 3rd International Conference on Networking, Information Systems & Security* (Article No. 28, pp. 1–7). ACM Digital Library. https://doi.org/10.1145/3386723.3387847

Kshetri, N. (2017). Blockchain's roles in strengthening cybersecurity and protecting privacy. *Telecommunications Policy*, *41*(10), 1027–1038. https://doi.org/10.1016/j.telpol.2017.09.003

Lone, A. N., Mustajab, S., & Alam, M. (2023). A comprehensive study on cybersecurity challenges and opportunities in the IoT world. *Security and Privacy*, *6*(3), e318. Wiley Online Library. https://doi.org/10.1002/spy2.318

Miller, A. (2023, September 19). Blockchain and cybersecurity: Exploring the promises and challenges. *AgileBlue*. https://agileblue.com/blockchain-and-cybersecurity-exploring-the-promises-and-challenges/

Mohan, J. P., Sugunaraj, N., & Ranganathan, P. (2022). Cyber security threats for 5G networks. In *2022 IEEE International Conference on Electro Information Technology (eIT)* (pp. 446–454). IEEE. https://doi.org/10.1109/eIT53891.2022.9813965

Monzelo, P., & Nunes, S. (2019). The role of the chief information security officer (CISO) in organizations. In *CAPSI 2019 Proceedings (Paper 36)*. https://aisel.aisnet.org/capsi2019/36

NIST. (2024, August 13). NIST releases first 3 finalized post-quantum encryption standards. https://www.nist.gov/news-events/news/2024/08/nist-releases-first-3-finalized-post-quantum-encryption-standards

Okoli, U. I., Obi, O. C., Adewusi, A. O., & Abrahams, T. O. (2024). Machine learning in cybersecurity: A review of threat detection and defense mechanisms. *World Journal of Advanced Research and Reviews*, *21*(1), 2286–2295. https://doi.org/10.30574/wjarr.2024.21.1.0315

Sabin, J. (2021). The future of security in a remote-work environment. *Network Security*, *2021*(10), 15–17. https://doi.org/10.1016/S1353-4858(21)00118-5

Shelke, Y. (2024). Rethinking cybersecurity through blockchain. *Infosys*. https://www.infosys.com/insights/cyber-security/cybersecurity-blockchain.html

Sodiya, E. O., Umoga, U. J., Amoo, O. O., & Atadoga, A. (2024). Quantum computing and its potential impact on U.S. cybersecurity: A review: Scrutinizing the challenges and opportunities presented by quantum technologies in safeguarding digital assets. *Global Journal of Engineering and Technology Advances*, *18*(02), 049–064. https://gjeta.com/sites/default/files/GJETA-2024-0026.pdf

Stavrou, E., & Piki, A. (2024). *Cultivating self-efficacy to empower professionals' re-up skilling in cybersecurity*. Information & Computer Security. Emerald Publishing Ltd. https://doi.org/10.1108/ICS-02-2024-0038

Stoica, I.-T. (2024). The future risk of biometric data theft in cybersecurity. *International Journal of Information Security and Cybercrime*, *13*(1), 49–58.

Wirkuttis, N., & Klein, H. (2017). Artificial intelligence in cybersecurity. *Cyber, Intelligence, and Security*, *1*(1), 113–119. https://www.academia.edu/36264684/Artificial_Intelligence_in_Cybersecurity

Index

Note: **Bold** page numbers refer to **tables** and *Italic* page numbers refer to *figures*.

C

L

M

N